# NJATC

A C    T H E O R Y

NJATC AC Theory, 3rd Edition is intended to be an educational resource for the user and contains procedures commonly practiced in industry and the trade. Specific procedures vary with each task and must be performed by a qualified person. For maximum safety, always refer to specific manufacturer recommendations, insurance regulations, specific job site and plant procedures, applicable federal, state, and local regulations, and any authority having jurisdiction. The electrical training ALLIANCE assumes no responsibility or liability in connection with this material or its use by any individual or organization.

M27304

# ACKNOWLEDGMENTS

## NJATC ACKNOWLEDGMENTS

### PRINCIPAL WRITER

Stan Klein, NJATC Staff

### CONTRIBUTING WRITER

John McCord, Instructor, Vineland, NJ

### TECHNICAL EDITORS

Ken Haden, NJATC Director
Jeff Keljik, Dunwoody College
    of Technology

## ADDITIONAL ACKNOWLEDGMENTS

This material is continually reviewed and evaluated by industry professionals who are members of NJATC Curriculum Workgroups. The invaluable input provided by these individuals allows for the development of instructional material that is of the absolute highest quality. At the time of this printing, the NJATC AC Theory Curriculum Workgroup, previously chaired by Chris Kelly and now under Dave McGraw, was composed of the following members: Richard Brooks, Robert Doustou, Carl Latona, Terry McKinch, Dan Sellers, and James Tosh. The NJATC would like to thank Fred Rossnagel and Jim Paladino for their invaluable contributions and expertise during the development of this title and its supplementary materials.

# CONTENTS

This text has been strengthened from top to bottom with many new features and enhancements to existing content. All-new chapter features provide structure and guidance for learners. Enhanced and concrete Chapter Objectives are complemented by solid and reinforcing Chapter Summaries, Review Questions, and Practice Problems. Chapter contents are introduced at the beginning of each chapter, and then bolstered before moving on to the next chapter. Throughout each chapter, concepts are explained from their theoretical roots to their application principles, with reminders about safety, technology, professionalism, and more.

*AC Theory, Third Edition,* has been expanded to more fully explore a number of concepts through a major reorganization of the chapters. Combining related topics and bolstering them with additional content makes the book even more reader-friendly. As the student progresses from basic electrical fundamentals learned in DC, the increased complexity of AC is added gradually to lead the student in a sequential process of adding components to create more complex circuits.

The fundamental theory of production of AC and identification of circuit parameters is used to build each additional chapter. The basic components of AC circuits are thoroughly explained; then each component is placed in a circuit to study the effects on the AC circuit. Calculations to verify circuit conditions are shown step-by-step to familiarize the students with the process and check results.

*See the following pages for examples of these new features.*

**Glossaries are included in each chapter along with a comprehensive glossary at the end of the book.**

**High-contrast images give a clear and colorful view that "pops" off the page.**

**High-interest content is given in FieldNote! and TechTip! sidebars to make real-world connections to lessons learned in the chapters.**

---

Chapter Glossary    **57**

## SUMMARY

This chapter took the AC waveform and applied it to a conductor that was coiled. The coil may be loosely coiled or tightly coiled on a metal core. The AC magnetic field caused the coil to create self-induction within the coil, causing a CEMF to be induced. The coil, or inductor, produces the back voltage, which acts like an opposition to the applied current. The opposition is measured in ohms of inductive reactance, or $X_L$. The inductive reactance is vectored in drawings of the vectors as a 90° opposition and the ohms of resistance as shown at a 0° vector. The resultant of the vector addition is the total opposition to the current and is referred to as the impedance of the inductor, which is measured in ohms. The formula symbol is the letter $Z$. The behavior of the CEMF is expressed in Lenz's law. This principle of $X_L$, $Z$, and the effects of induction are critical to understanding how electric equipment powered by AC works. The idea that an angle developed by the reactance and impedance of the coils is essential to understanding AC theory.

## CHAPTER GLOSSARY

**Arctangent** Abbreviated *arctan* and shown on most calculators by the symbol $tan^{-1}$. The inverse function of the tangent of an angle $\frac{1}{tangent}$. This calculates what arc has a tangent of the referenced decimal number.

**CEMF (counter EMF)** The voltage induced in an inductor by the changing magnetic field. The voltage induced is "counter to" the voltage, or in opposition to, the voltage that produced the original magnetic field.

**Cosine** Abbreviated *cos*. For a given angle other than the 90 degree angle in a right triangle, the trigonometric function that is the ratio between the leg adjacent to the given angle and the hypotenuse.

**Henry** Unit of measure for inductance. A coil has an inductance of 1 henry when a current change of 1 ampere per second causes an induced voltage of 1 volt. The henry is a value based on the physical characteristics of the inductor (coil). The unit of measure is the henry, abbreviated as H. The symbol used in formulas is L.

**Impedance** The vector sum of the op-

**Inductance** The property of an electric circuit displayed when a varying current induces an electromotive force in that circuit or in a neighboring circuit. A circuit has inductance when magnetic induction occurs.

**Inductor** The name given to an electrical circuit component that exhibits the properties of inductance. If a coil of wire creates self-induction, creating a counterelectromotive force (CEMF), then it is referred to as an inductor.

**Leakage flux** Flux lines that do not link properly in an inductor. Some flux lines are lost to the surrounding space and do not complete the magnetic path. Leakage flux reduces the overall magnetic field and the resulting inductance.

**Permeability** The degree to which a material focuses magnetic lines of flux, or the ease with which magnetic lines of force distribute themselves through a material. Permeability is a factor compared to air (permeability factor of 1). There is no unit of measure, just a factor compared to air. The symbol used for magnetic permeability in a formula is the lowercase Greek letter mu ($\mu$).

---

Lenz's Law    **47**

5. After having been at the maximum, the current flow begins to decrease (change), and the magnetic field begins to react by collapsing inward (changing the direction in which it is moving relative to the conductor). The field does not change polarity, just strength.

6. The current continues to decrease, and the field continues to decrease relative to the current flow.

7. The current changes direction and is increasing, but this time in a negative direction. Since the current is increasing in the opposite direction, the magnetic field expands outward but with reverse polarity (polarity opposite to what was found during the positive portion of the sine wave).

8. As the current flow continues to increase, the field also continues to expand.

**Out-of-Phase EMF and CEMF**

Figure 3–5 The EMF and smaller CEMF are 180° out of phase.

**Directions of Magnetic Flux**

Figure 3–6 The applied current waveform produces resultant magnetic flux directions.

---

**FieldNote!**

Many of the terms used in the electrical industry are synonymous. It just depends on where you learned the theory and what part of the country you are from. The term inductor is used to describe a coil or a particular piece of equipment that exhibits inductive characteristics. Variable inductors may have moveable cores. Inductors may be deliberately designed to choke off high current, as in the case of power supplies, in which case the same component is referred to as a choke. Inductors are important components in AC electrical systems.

**TechTip!**

One of the concepts to keep in mind is that a coil does not change its henry value with a change of frequency or a change in the current value. A 100 μH coil is still a 100 μH inductor whether you apply DC, 60 Hz AC, or 100 Hz AC. The way it reacts to the circuit will change, but the inductive value will not change unless you change the physical characteristics.

**New photos and illustrations are located near their text references and clarify explanations.**

*Figure 2–16* These slow hydroelectric generators are operating at 100 rpm.

*Figure 2–11* Variable frequency drives (VFDs) are electronic motor speed controllers.

**Step-by-step sample problems and solutions relate to the end-of-chapter exercises.**

**Example**

Find the henry value of an inductor with the following dimensions: The number of turns on the coil of wire is 100, the area of the core in the middle of the coil is 1 square inch, the permeability of the iron core is 150, and the length of the core is 2 inches.

**Solution:**
$$L = \frac{3.19 \times 100^2 \times 1 \times 150}{10^8 \times 2}$$
$$= 0.0239 \text{ H}$$

Use the same coil of wire but insert a different core material with twice as much permeability and note that the henry value increases.

Change the core material to air, or no metal material; the permeability goes to 1 and the inductance is $\frac{1}{150}$ of the original, or:
$$L = \frac{0.0239}{150} = 0.0001593 \text{ H}.$$

**PRACTICE PROBLEMS**

1. Draw and label an impedance (phasor diagram) triangle for a RC circuit.
2. In Figure PP6–1, if $E_C = 80$ V, what is the voltage across the resistor?
3. What is $X_C$ in problem 2?
4. What is $I_T$?
5. What is the value of the resistor in problem 2?
6. Find the impedance of the circuit of problem 2. Prove it.
7. Find the power factor in Figure PP6–1.
8. A circuit has $E_T = 15$ V at 2 kHz with a resistor (3 kΩ) and a capacitor in series. If there is a 4 mA current flow, what is the value of the capacitor?
9. Find the $C_1$ of a series circuit if $C_2$ is 50 μF, $C_3$ is 75 μF, and the total capacitance is 23 μF.
10. Calculate the $C$ of a capacitor if the voltage across the capacitor is 50 V, the circuit current is 2 A, and the circuit frequency is 60 Hz.
11. Find the volt-amps for a circuit with a power factor of 80% and a watt measurement of 200 W.

*Figure PP6–1*

**End-of-chapter problems reinforce critical concepts and relate to the worked-out examples in the chapter.**

## INTRODUCTION

Welcome to the third edition of *AC Theory*, which has been redesigned and updated to provide knowledge of the fundamentals to electrical technologists in apprenticeship programs, vocational-technical schools and colleges, and community colleges. The text emphasizes a solid foundation of classroom theory supported by on-the-job hands-on practice. Every project, every piece of knowledge, and every new task will be based on the experience and information acquired as each technician progresses through his or her career. This book, along with the others in this series, contains a significant portion of the material that will form the basis for success in an electrical career.

This text was developed by blending up-to-date practice with long-lived theories in an effort to help technicians learn how to better perform on the job. It is written at a level that invites further discussion beyond its pages while clearly and succinctly answering the questions of *how* and *why*. Improvements to this edition were made possible by the continued commitment by the National Joint Apprenticeship and Training Committee (NJATC) to deliver the very finest in training materials for the electrical profession.

For excellence in your electrical and telecommunications curriculum, look no further. The NJATC has been *the* source for superior electrical training for thousands of qualified men and women for over 65 years. Curriculum improvements are constant as the NJATC strives to continuously enhance the support it provides to its apprentices, journeymen, and instructors in over 285 training programs nationwide.

## SUPPLEMENTAL PACKAGE

The Instructor Resource Kit is geared to provide instructors with all the tools they need in one convenient package. Instructors will find that this resource provides them with a far-reaching teaching partner that includes the following:

- Electronic PowerPoint slides for each book chapter that reinforce key points and feature illustrations and photos from the book

- The Computerized Test Bank in ExamView format, which allows for test customization for evaluating student comprehension of noteworthy concepts
- An electronic version of the Instructor's Manual, with supplemental lesson plans and support

## ABOUT THE NJATC

Should you decide on a career in the electrical industry, training provided by the International Brotherhood of Electrical Workers and the National Electrical Contractors Association (IBEW-NECA) is the most comprehensive the industry has to offer. If you are accepted into one of their local apprenticeship programs, you'll be trained for one of four career specialties: journeyman lineman, residential wireman, journeyman wireman, or telecommunications installer/technician. Most importantly, you'll be paid while you learn. To learn more, visit *http://www. njatc.org.*

## ABOUT THIS BOOK

The efforts for continuous enhancement have produced the volume you see before you: this technically precise and academically superior edition of *AC Theory.* Using a distinctive blend of theory-based explanation partnered with hands-on accounts of what to do in the field and peppered with Technical Tips and Field Notes, this book will lead you through the study of AC Theory, from DC fundamentals, to production of AC and identification of circuit parameters, to applications of AC in generators and transformers.

# 1

# INTRODUCTION TO ALTERNATING CURRENT

# TOPICS

ELECTRON THEORY

CONDUCTORS, INSULATORS,
    AND SEMICONDUCTORS

OHM'S LAW

DC CIRCUIT ANALYSIS

VOLTAGE DROP IN WIRE

PERMANENT MAGNETS

MAGNETISM, CONDUCTORS, AND MOVEMENT

# OVERVIEW

Alternating current, usually abbreviated as AC, is used to provide over 90% of the world's electrical power requirements. In the early years of electrical power, direct current (DC) was the most widely used form of electricity. The beginnings of the transition from a DC world to an AC world were turbulent and full of technical and political disagreements and intrigue. Thomas Edison and George Westinghouse, outspoken competitors in those early years, staked their reputations and their businesses on their particular systems.

Eventually, for a variety of technical and business reasons, Westinghouse won the dispute. His AC transformers and motors, developed by the brilliant technical genius Nikola Tesla, provided an edge over Edison's DC systems. Even so, in spite of this fairly early victory for AC, a few large American cities continued to use DC distribution in their downtown areas until the 1970s.

This brief history begins your study of AC theory. Your success in understanding the material presented in the chapters of this book is dependent on how well you understand the basic principles of DC theory. Many of the principles that applied to DC circuitry also apply to AC circuits. However, the effects of AC create many variations on the same rules, and the degree of understanding becomes more complex. The skills of a professional electrician rely on the thorough understanding of how and why AC circuits operate.

This chapter is designed to lead you from a review of DC and the theories and practices used to solve those circuit problems into the application used in AC.

# OBJECTIVES

After completing this chapter you will be able to:

· Describe the difference between electron flow theory and conventional current flow theory
· Explain how materials that are classified as good conductors, good insulators, or semiconductors differ from one another
· Describe various sources of electricity
· Use Ohm's law and Watt's law to explain simple circuit behavior
· Describe the effects of current flow, both DC and AC, on straight conductors
· Calculate circuit quantities on DC circuits in series, in parallel, and in combinations
· Describe the electromagnetic effects that occur around straight and coiled conductors

**Diagram of an Atom**

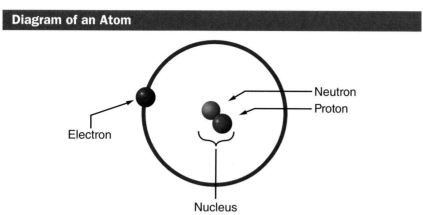

**Figure 1–1** An isotope of hydrogen called deuterium has one electron and one proton.

## ELECTRON THEORY

Electricity is an invisible force that can produce heat, motion, light, and any number of other physical effects. This invisible "driving force" provides power for lighting, radios, motors, the heating and cooling of buildings, and many other applications. The common link among all of these applications is the electrical charge. All the materials we know of—gases, liquids, and solids—contain two basic particles of electrical charge: the electron and the proton. The electron has an electrical charge with a negative polarity. The proton has an electrical charge with a positive polarity.

Atoms have three main parts: electron, proton, and neutron. The proton and neutron combine to form the atom's nucleus. Hydrogen, the simplest of all elements, has a single proton and a single electron. Figure 1–1 is a diagram of an isotope of hydrogen called deuterium. Deuterium has one electron, one proton, and one neutron. Recall that the electron has a negative (−) charge and the proton a positive (+) charge. The neutron, as the name suggests, has no electrical charge. In other words, the neutron is electrically neutral and has no effect on the electrical characteristics of the material.

You can tell the type of an element by the number of protons in the atom's nucleus. For example, silver has 47 protons in its nucleus, iron 26, and oxygen 8. The number of protons also equals the element's atomic number in the **periodic table of elements** (Figure 1–2). Although there are many possible ways in which electrons and protons might be grouped, they come together in specific combinations that produce stable arrangements (atoms). Again, the simplest element is hydrogen and its isotopes.

Figure 1–3 shows a copper atom with a number of rings filled with electrons in orbit around the atom's nucleus.

**Periodic Table of Elements**

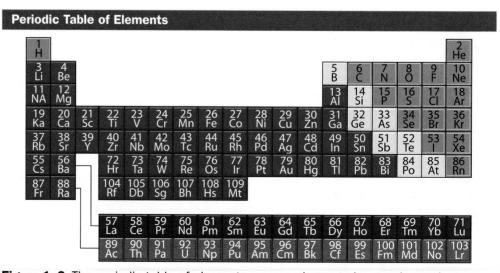

**Figure 1–2** The periodic table of elements groups elements by atomic number.

Infinite orbital rings (shells) around a nucleus can hold electrons, although, so far, scientists have not discovered any elements that use more than five shells. More information about the rings is described in the section "Conductors, Insulators, and Semiconductors."

## ELECTRON FLOW THEORY

As you studied **direct current** systems, you found that electricity is a form of energy. Movement of electrons can be generated at one location, transported to another location, and then converted to another form of energy such as heat, light, sound, or mechanical motion. With DC, the electrons move through the wires in one direction. That direction is from a point of excess electrons to a point of a deficiency of electrons, in other words, from a point that has too many negatively charged electrons to a point that has a deficit of electron charges or a positive charge. This book follows the **electron flow theory,** which states that electricity (electrons) flows from negative to positive. This process is still true in AC circuitry. The major change is that the supply of electrons, or the source, continually changes electrical polarity from negative to positive and back to negative over time. This introduction of another variable (time) is a major influence on the effects of AC.

## SOURCES OF ELECTRICAL ENERGY

Six methods are known to force electrons from the valence ring of an atom to become a potential electrical current participant:

1. Friction: You receive a shock, for example, as you shuffle your feet across a wool carpet
2. Chemical: A battery produces electrical output
3. Heat: Thermocouples are used to detect flame in a furnace and control the electric gas valve
4. Pressure: Sensors are used to detect weight and produce an electrical signal

**Copper Atom**

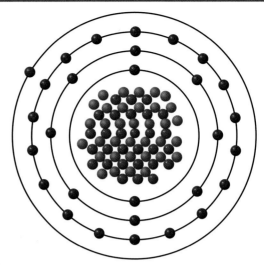

**Figure 1–3** The copper atom has 29 electrons and 29 protons.

5. Light: Photoelectric cells produce electrical output based on light input
6. Magnetism: Generators use a magnetic field to create electrical power

Except for friction, electrical energy can produce the same effects as those used to create it. That is, if the proper load is connected across an electrical source, any one (or more) of the following effects occurs:

1. Chemical action: Recharging of a battery
2. Heat: Electric heat from a toaster
3. Pressure: In the ear, sound reproduction such as hearing aids
4. Light: Incandescent or fluorescent lamps
5. Magnetic fields: Motors and transformers, which work by electromagnetism

The chemical source of electricity is best represented in our everyday lives by the battery. The battery is a primary source of DC. Batteries are usually divided into two categories: primary cells and secondary cells. Primary cells, like the batteries used in portable radios and flashlights, cannot be recharged. Once they have depleted their chemical action, they must be thrown away.

## FieldNote!

As you know, the movement of electrons from negative potential to positive potential is still called the electron flow theory. However, there is another way of looking at electrical flow. This original thinking, referred to as the conventional current flow theory, says that because a current flows from a positive or surplus source of current toward a point that has a negative supply of electrons, the current therefore flows from positive toward negative. Many of the devices for determining current flow and magnetic field direction are exactly opposite between the two theories. When discussing circuit behavior with other people with an electrical background, be sure you are using the same theories. The end results of the effects are the same, but they can be quite confusing when halfway through an analysis. Electricians tend to subscribe to the electron flow theory.

electrons. Usually, the effect of heating a wire is undesirable. For certain applications, heat can be a desirable outcome. A transfer of electrons can also take place when two dissimilar metals are joined together at a junction and then heated. This is known as the thermoelectricity process. Increases in the temperature (heat) cause a greater transfer of electrons. This type of device is called a thermocouple (Figure 1–4).

Figure 1–5 illustrates a piezoelectric device. Certain crystalline substances, when placed under pressure, generate minute electromotive forces. These forces cause the electrons to be driven out of orbit in the direction of the force. The electrons leave one side of the material and collect on the other side. Electricity derived from pressure is known as the **piezoelectric** effect. It is possible to reverse the piezoelectric process and produce pressure with an electrical current.

**Thermocouple**

Secondary cells, like those used in automobiles, can be recharged several times.

Heat is generated whenever a current flows through a wire. This happens because energy is used to move

**Figure 1–4** A thermocouple produces electricity when heated.

**Piezoelectric Strain Gauge and Microphone**

**Figure 1–5** A piezoelectric strain gauge and microphone derive electricity from pressure.

This principle is used in some applications, such as in very small earphones that use a piezoelectric crystal to produce the sound vibrations from an electrical signal.

Light energy can produce electricity, and electricity can produce light. It works both ways. Light is made up of small particles of energy called photons. When photons strike certain types of photosensitive material, they release energy into the material. There are three types of photoelectric effects of interest in the study of electricity: photoemission, photovoltaic (Figure 1–6), and photoconduction.

Electrical current produces light if enough current is passed through a poor conductor. In this example, not only is heat generated but many materials also begin to glow red or even white hot, as in an incandescent lamp (Figure 1–7). Three other methods of producing light with electricity do not result in as much heat loss: electroluminescence, phosphorescence, and fluorescence.

Magnetism is the primary source of electrical power. Heat and a magnetic field are generated whenever a current flows through a conductor. When a conductor (a material in which the valence electrons can be easily removed from their orbit) moves through a magnetic field, electrons move from one end of the conductor to the opposite end, creating a potential source between the two ends of the conductor. This process of producing electrical energy is known as magnetoelectricity, and it makes electrical devices such as electrical magnets, motors, and transformers possible. Magnetoelectricity is the basis for commercial generators. Most electrical power is generated by this method (Figure 1–8).

# CONDUCTORS, INSULATORS, AND SEMICONDUCTORS

The transfer of electrons from atom to atom is the actual transfer of energy along a conductive path. As you stud-

**Photovoltaic Cells**

**Direct-Coupled Systems**

Array — DC Load —

**Figure 1–6** Photovoltaic cells produce a voltage when light strikes the device.

**Incandescent Lamp**

**Figure 1–7** A lamp incandesces as it is heated to produce light.

ied the atomic structure of atoms, you found that some elements have many electron shells and some have fewer. If the shells are farther from the nucleus, there is less physical attraction to the nucleus and the electron can be moved to another neighboring atom with added energy. As you saw in Figure 1–3, an atom of copper has 29 electrons.

**Magnetoelectric Generator**

**Figure 1–8** A magnetoelectric generator uses magnetism to create electricity.

Each orbital ring has a maximum number of electrons needed to fill that ring—or shell. The innermost ring holds $2 \times 1^2$ or 2 electrons. The second ring may hold $2 \times 2^2$ or 8 electrons. The third ring may hold $2 \times 3^2$ or 18 electrons, and the fourth ring could hold $2 \times 4^2$ or 32 electrons. If the rings are full of electrons, the next ring begins to fill. Therefore, the first three rings hold $2 + 8 + 18 = 28$ electrons. The 29th electron in the copper atom begins a new shell. If there is only one electron in the furthest ring, the **valence ring,** then the valence electron can move more easily as energy is added to the mix. Therefore, the best **conductors** are made of elements that have one valence electron in the valence shell. For instance, copper is a good conductor, as are silver and gold. Aluminum is also a conductor, but not as good as copper or silver because aluminum has two valence electrons. As more electrons are in the valence shell, there is more cohesion to the nucleus and much more energy is needed to move the electrons out of their orbits. Elements with a large number of valence electrons, eight or more, are good **insulators** of electrical flow. Glass, rubber, and most plastics are considered insulators. If enough energy is added, electrons can be made to flow through the material and the electrical insulation is said to be broken down. Materials that are between a conductor and an insulator are known as semiconductors. **Semiconductors,** such as silicon and germanium, usually have four valence electrons and are neither good conductors nor good insulators. With the right voltage applied to the material they can conduct electricity, or with absence of voltage applied they can insulate against the flow of electrons.

## OHM'S LAW

You learned Ohm's law in DC theory. The same rules apply to **alternating current** circuits when applying Ohm's law. Several variations of the law can be applied to AC circuits under various circumstances. For instance, the voltage dropped across a coil of wire with AC current flowing is only partially calculated by using a strict interpretation of Ohm's law. As we apply the rules to series and parallel circuits the same principles apply, but they can become a little more involved when we consider how frequency, or the AC waveform, plays a part in the oppositions encountered in an AC circuit.

The original Ohm's law is a law of electrical proportionality. It states that one volt will push 1 ampere (A) through 1 ohm ($\Omega$) of resistance. Another way to look at this relationship is that the current ($I$) in amperes is directly proportional to the voltage ($E$) in volts and inversely proportional to the resistance ($R$) in ohms. Ohm's law can be expressed mathematically as:

$$E = I \times R \text{ or } I = \frac{E}{R} \text{ or } R = \frac{E}{I}$$

You are already familiar with these units of measure. The **volt** is the unit of electrical pressure expressed in the formula as $E$ for **electromotive force.** The unit for current flow is expressed as **amperes** and is represented as the letter $I$ in the formula because it was understood to represent intensity of flow. The opposition to electron flow is measured in **ohms** of resistance and is represented in the formula as $R$ for resistance.

---

### Example

A circuit has a voltage of 24 V and has a current of 2 A. What is the resistance of the circuit?

**Solution:**

Using Ohm's law, $R$ becomes:
Given: $E = 24$ V, $I = 2$ A

$$R = \frac{E}{I} \text{ or } R = \frac{24}{2} = 12 \ \Omega$$

## CROSS-SECTIONAL AREA AND RESISTANCE

The cross-sectional area of a material has a great effect on the resistive characteristics of any conductor using that material. As conductors are made larger in diameter, the number of atoms contributing free electrons increases and tends to reduce the resistance for that conductor.

For example, a #6-AWG copper wire (Figure 1–9) has a diameter of 0.162 inch; therefore, the cross-sectional area is:

$$A = \pi r^2 \text{ or } \pi \left(\frac{d}{2}\right)^2 = 3.14 \times \left(\frac{0.162}{2}\right)^2$$

$$= 3.14 \times 0.00651 \text{ in.}^2 = 0.0206 \text{ in.}^2$$

However, because of the inconvenience of working with such small numbers, most calculations are done using the circular-mil area of a conductor. A mil is defined as 1/1,000th of an inch, or 1,000 mils equal 1 inch. To convert from wire diameters that are expressed in inches to wire diameters in mils, simply multiply the number by 1,000. The #6 wire mentioned earlier would have a diameter of 0.162 × 1,000, or 162 mils.

The circular-mil area of a conductor is defined as the diameter of the conductor in mils squared. The circular-mil (abbreviated as cmil) area can be found by simply taking the diameter of the wire in mils multiplied by itself. The #6 wire would have a circular-mil area of:

$$A = 162 \times 162 = 26,244 \text{ cmils}$$

Figure 1–10 shows two examples of cross-sectional areas and diameters for wires. Circular mils designated for various size wires can also be found in the *National Electrical Code®* book.

**Cross-Sections of Conductors**

Diameter = 5 mils
Circular – Mil Area = $d^2$ = 25 cmils

Diameter = 10 mils
Circular – Mil Area = $d^2$ = 100 cmils

**Figure 1–10** The cross-sectional conducting area of round conductors is measured in circular mils.

**Different Sizes of American Wire Gauge**

#10          #8          #6

**Figure 1–9** American wire gauge (AWG) shown in sizes #6, #8, and #10.

## TechTip!

We use this concept of wire resistance and the voltage drop and watt losses in a conductor later in this study of AC and AC systems.

### EDDY CURRENTS

When AC flows through a conductor, it causes certain voltages to develop within the conductor. These voltages create small internal currents to flow (Figure 1–11). The name given to this current flow is eddy current as it resembles the small current that circulates in flowing water. While these internally induced currents are not flowing from one end of the conductor to the other, they are nevertheless flowing or moving internally within the conductor. Since any current flow is the result of the flow of free electrons, eddy currents are also using the free electrons to move within the conductor. Because some of the free electrons are used, fewer free electrons are available for use by the current flowing through the conductor from one end to the other. The net effect of the eddy current is power loss within the conductor. This movement of electrons within the conductor uses energy and increases the overall resistance of the conductor.

### SKIN EFFECT

In a DC circuit, the electrons travel evenly through the entire cross-section of the conductor. However, in an AC circuit conductor, besides setting up eddy currents, the voltage that creates the eddy current also causes the current flow in the conductor to be repelled away from the center of the conductor toward the outside of the conductor. The current is then forced to travel near the surface of the conductor (Figure 1–12). This effect, known as the skin effect, creates the same consequence as reducing the cross-sectional area of the conductor because the electrons are forced to flow in a smaller area concentrated near the surface of the conductor. The skin effect also causes an increase in the conductor resistance in the circuit due to power losses.

**Eddy Currents in Conductors**

**Figure 1–11** Eddy currents circulate inside the conductors and restrict current flow.

**Skin Effect in AC Conductors**

**Figure 1–12** The skin effect in AC conductors causes the current to flow near the surface and not in the center of the conductor.

Both eddy currents and the skin effect are directly related to the frequency of the circuit. Therefore, as the frequency increases, the magnitude of the eddy currents increases, causing the skin effect to also increase.

Generally, the effects of eddy currents and the skin effect do not have a critical negative impact on circuits except at higher frequencies. The use of stranded cables, which provide more surface area than a solid conductor of an equal size, also helps reduce the overall negative effect of these two elements within the AC circuit.

## DC CIRCUIT ANALYSIS

There are three basic types of DC circuits: series, parallel, and combination (for a combination of series and parallel).

### SERIES CIRCUITS

The total resistance in a series circuit is the sum of the individual resistors and can be calculated by the following equation:

$$R_T = R_1 + R_2 + R_3 + \ldots R_N$$

Where:
$R_T$ = the total resistance and
$R_N$ = the total number of resistors in the circuit

Since all the series circuit current flows through every component in the circuit, each component represents a

### FieldNote!

If a series circuit had two 100 W lamps connected in series and each had the proper rated voltage applied, the total wattage of the circuit would be 200 W. In Figure 1–14, a 60/W–rated lamp is in series with a 100/W–rated lamp, and each is designed for 120 V operation. If this series circuit has 120 V total applied, you will notice that the 60 W lamp appears brighter than the 100 W lamp. Try to explain why before reading the answer under the diagram. The "Parallel Circuits" section explains how the voltage is equal for each load in a parallel circuit (the currents are not). Therefore, if both bulbs were connected in parallel in Figure 1–14, they would both operate to their expected brightness.

load (resistive element) in determining the total current (Figure 1–13). Ohm's law defines this relationship for voltage, resistance, and current as:

$$I_1 = I_2 = I_3 = I_T \text{ and } I_T = \frac{E_T}{R_T}$$

Where:
$I_T$ = total circuit current
$E_T$ = total circuit voltage
$R_T$ = total circuit resistance

The total voltage source in a series circuit is the algebraic sum of the individual voltage drops:

$$E_T = E_1 + E_2 + E_3 + \ldots E_N$$

Where:
$E_N$ = total number of voltage drops in the circuit

Remember to keep track of the polarity of each voltage source. Voltages with opposite polarities will subtract from each other.

### Series Circuit

**Figure 1–13** A series circuit with three resistive elements.

### Lamps in a Series

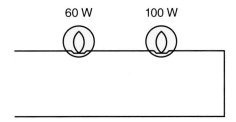

**Figure 1–14** Two incandescent lamps of different rated watts can be connected in series.

Like $E_T$ and $R_T$ in a DC circuit, the power consumed by the entire circuit is the sum of the power used by each component:

$$P_T = P_1 + P_2 + P_3 + P_4 + \ldots P_N$$

Where:
$P_T$ = total power
$P_N$ = the total number of components in the circuit

---

### E x a m p l e

In the circuit in Figure 1–13, the actual dissipated watts of each resistor are added together to determine total watts (or power) used in the circuit. If $R_1$ dissipates 50 W, $R_2$ dissipates 25 W, and $R_3$ dissipates 15 W, the total power dissipated is 90 W:

$$P_T = P_1 + P_2 + P_3$$

---

Each lamp is rated for use with 120 V, but the 60 W lamp has more resistance than the 100 W lamp. To find the resistance of the lamps when operating, use the formula: $R = \dfrac{E^2}{P}$.
So that:

$$\frac{120 \text{ V}^2}{60 \text{ W}} = 240 \ \Omega$$

AND

$$\frac{120 \text{ V}^2}{100 \text{ W}} = 144 \ \Omega$$

The 60 W lamp has more resistance at 120 V (240 Ω) than does the 100 W lamp (144 Ω). Therefore, it takes a bigger percentage of the 120 series voltage and appears closer to its expected brightness than does the 100 W lamp.

## PARALLEL CIRCUITS

Parallel circuits are circuits that have more than one path for current to flow (Figure 1–15). These different paths are called parallel branches. The voltage applied to each of the parallel branches is equal to the voltage across the branch. The sum of the branch currents is equal to the total current.
Mathematically,

$$E_T = E_1 = E_2 = E_3 = \ldots E_N$$

AND

$$I_T + I_1 + I_2 + I_3 + \ldots I_N$$

Where:
$N$ = the number of branches in the parallel circuit

The total resistance of a parallel circuit is always less than the smallest resistance of any one branch. To calculate the total resistance in a parallel circuit, the so-called reciprocal formula is used. The reciprocal equation was developed in the *DC Theory* text and can take either of two equivalent forms, either:

$$\frac{1}{R_T} = \frac{1}{R_1} + \frac{1}{R_2} + \frac{1}{R_3} + \frac{1}{R_N}$$

or, by rearranging the equation algebraically,

$$R_T = \frac{1}{\left( \dfrac{1}{R_1} + \dfrac{1}{R_2} + \dfrac{1}{R_3} + \dfrac{1}{R_N} \right)}$$

Where:
$N$ = the number of branches in the parallel circuit

---

**Parallel Circuit with Resistive Branches**

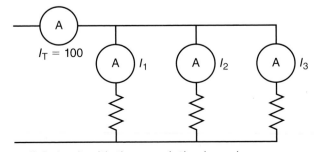

**Figure 1–15** A parallel circuit with three resistive branches.

What is the total resistance of a parallel circuit with three branches:

$R_1 = 50\ \Omega$, $R_2 = 25\ \Omega$, and $R_3 = 15\ \Omega$?

**Solution:**

To calculate the total resistance, use the reciprocal equation:

$$R_T = \frac{1}{\left(\dfrac{1}{50} + \dfrac{1}{25} + \dfrac{1}{15}\right)} = 7.89\ \Omega$$

$$= \frac{1}{0.02 + 0.04 + 0.67}$$

$$= \frac{1}{0.1267} = 7.89\ \Omega$$

Notice that the total resistance ($R_T$) is less than the smallest branch resistance (15 $\Omega$).

Power calculations for parallel circuits are the same as power calculations for series circuits. The total power in a parallel circuit is the sum of the power in the individual components of that circuit, just as the total power in a series circuit is equal to the sum of the power in the individual components of that circuit:

$$P_T = P_1 + P_2 + P_3 + \dots P_N$$

Power calculations for these two types of circuits are also the same in that, in both circuits, the total power is the product of the source voltage and the total circuit current:

$$P_T = E_T \times I_T$$

## COMBINATION CIRCUITS

The first step in analyzing a combination circuit is to reduce (simplify) the circuit as much as possible. Each section to be reduced should be a group of two or more resistors with the equivalent resistance results taking the place of the group. The series resistors should be reduced first. In the example circuit shown in Figure 1–16, only one series combination exists, and it must be reduced first. Subsequently, the parallel combinations are reduced.

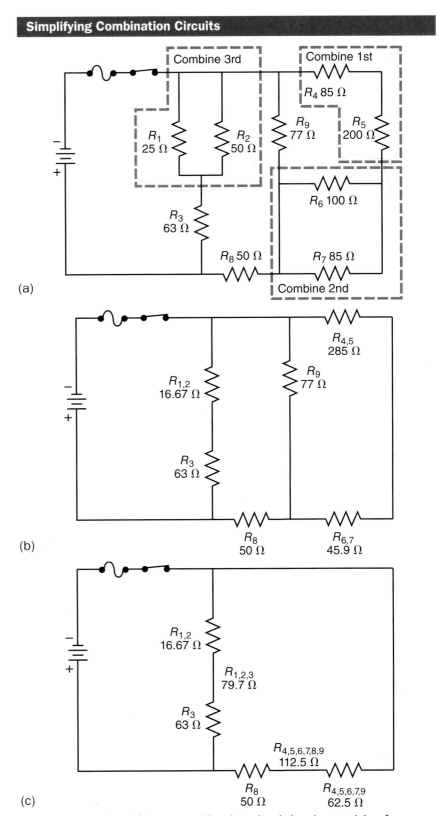

**Simplifying Combination Circuits**

(a)

(b)

(c)

**Figure 1–16** Simplifying a combination circuit involves solving for series and parallel resistance.

Reducing a more complex circuit to its equivalent series resistor is performed much the same as previously discussed. The general approach is as follows:

1.  Identify the series and parallel current paths
2.  Reduce only one part at a time
3.  Ensure that all series resistors have been combined before a parallel portion is reduced
4.  Combine parallel portions to a single resistor
5.  Repeat combining equivalent resistors until all portions are reduced to one equivalent resistance

Once you know the total resistance in a combination circuit and the total source voltage, you can use Ohm's law to calculate the total current. However, the value of current through each respective resistor must be calculated in reverse order. Work backward from the total equivalent resistance calculated for Figure 1–16. As each equivalent branch resistance is found, apply the voltage to that branch and calculate the total branch current. Repeat the steps until all resistances, their voltage drops, and calculated currents are known.

Combine series section 1:

$$R_{4,5} = (R_4)\ 85 + (R_5)\ 200 = 285\ \Omega$$

Combine parallel section 2:

$$R_{6,7} = \frac{(R_6)\ 100 \times (R_7)\ 85}{(R_6)\ 100 + (R_7)\ 85} = \frac{8,500}{185}$$

$$= 45.9\ \Omega$$

Combine parallel section 3:

$$R_{1,2} = \frac{(R_1)\ 25 \times (R_2)\ 50}{(R_1)\ 25 + (R_2)\ 50} = \frac{1,250}{75}$$

$$= 16.67\ \Omega$$

This gives you the simplified circuit seen in Figure 1–16b.

Combine series section $R_{4,5}$ and $R_{6,7}$:

$$R_{4,5,6,7} = (R_{4,5})\ 285 + (R_{6,7})\ 45.9$$

$$= 330.9\ \Omega$$

Combine parallel section $R_{4,5,6,7}$ and $R_9$:

$$R_{4,5,6,7,9} = \frac{(R_{4,5,6,7})\ 330.9 \times (R_9)\ 77}{(R_{4,5,6,7})\ 330.9 + (R_9)\ 77}$$

$$= \frac{25,479.3}{407.9} = 62.5\ \Omega$$

This gives you the further simplified circuit seen in Figure 1–16c.

Combine series section $R_{4,5,6,7,9}$ and $R_8$:

$$R_{4,5,6,7,8,9} = (R_{4,5,6,7,9})\ 62.5 + (R_8)\ 50$$

$$= 112.5\ \Omega$$

Combine series section $R_{1,2}$ and $R_3$:

$$R_{1,2,3} = (R_{1,2})\ 16.7 + (R_3)\ 63 = 79.7\ \Omega$$

Combine parallel section $R_{1,2,3}$ and $R_{4,5,6,7,8,9}$:

$$R_{1,2,3,4,5,6,7,8,9} =$$

$$\frac{(R_{1,2,3})\ 79.7 \times (R_{4,5,6,7,8,9})\ 112.9}{(R_{1,2,3})\ 79.7 + (R_{4,5,6,7,8,9})\ 112.9}$$

$$= \frac{8,998}{192.6} = 46.7\ \Omega$$

Ignoring rounding errors, this yields an approximate total resistance ($R_T$) value of 47 $\Omega$.

If you have an applied total voltage, you can then calculate all of the component currents, the component voltages, and the watts dissipated by each component.

As with other types of circuits we have studied, the total power used in a combination circuit is the sum of the power dissipated in individual components in that circuit. It is also equal to the power used by the "equivalent resistance" of the circuit. If two of the three parameters of each component are known (voltage, current, resistance), power can be calculated for each. Total power is then derived by adding all the individual powers:

$$P_T = P_1 + P_2 + P_3 + \ldots P_N$$

Where:

$N$ = the number of components in the combination circuit

## OHM'S LAW AND POWER

The unit of electrical power is the watt. Power in a circuit is the amount of work being done per unit of time. The load in a circuit uses the energy at a certain rate called power. Power, in equation form, looks like this:

$$\text{Power} = \frac{\text{Work}}{\text{Time}}$$

The work in this equation is the force applied to the circuit times the distance that the force moves something. In an electrical circuit, the power is the volts (joules/coulomb) times the amps (coulombs/second) and equals watts (joules/second). Another way to look at power is the amount of energy used per second. Mathematically, the heat or power produced can be shown as:

$$P = E \times I$$

Since $E = (I \times R)$, then substitution allows:

$$P = (I \times R) \times I \text{ or } P = I^2 \times R$$

The heat produced by the current through the resistance in the circuit is called "$I^2R$" losses because it is heat lost in the system.

Also, since $I = \dfrac{E}{R}$, then substitution allows:

$$P = E \times \frac{E}{R} \quad \text{or} \quad P = \frac{E^2}{R}$$

### Example

What is the power dissipated due to heat in a motor that draws 20 A of current and has a resistance of 5 Ω?

**Solution:**

Since we know current and resistance, the formula to use is $P = I^2R$:

$$P = I^2R = 20^2 \times 5 = 2,000 \text{ W}$$

### Example

A room heater has a rating of 2,000 W and uses 120 V. What is the resistance of the heater?

**Solution:**

Since we know the power and the voltage, the formula to use is:

$$P = \frac{E^2}{R}$$

or, transposing the formula:

$$R = \frac{E^2}{P}$$
$$= \frac{120^2}{2,000} = 7.2 \ \Omega$$

## VOLTAGE DROP IN WIRE

In the *DC Theory* text, you learned that the voltage drop $E_{\text{VD}}$ across a load is equal to $I \times R$ and that the resistance of wire is found by using the formula:

$$R = \frac{K \times L}{A_{\text{cmil}}}$$

Where:
  $R$ = the resistance of the wire in ohms
  K = the resistivity of the wire in ohms per mil-foot (Figure 1–17)
  $L$ = the length of the wire in feet
  $A_{\text{cmil}}$ = the area of the wire in circular mils

**Resistivity of Wire Per Mil-Foot**

1 foot

.001 inch diameter

**Figure 1–17** A mil-foot of wire that is 1 foot long and 1 mil in diameter has a resistance expressed as ohms per mil-foot.

This formula shows that wire resistance is fixed and does not exist as a condition or result of voltage or current. Another variation of the formula is used to calculate the voltage drop in a single-phase circuit. This variation is:

$$E_{VD} = \frac{K \times I \times 2 \times L}{A_{cmil}}$$

Note that the multiplier of 2 takes into account that the wire makes a round-trip from the source to the load. Later you will learn to calculate the voltage drop of a three-phase circuit using a similar formula.

---

## Example

Figure 1–18 illustrates this example. The total distance to the load is 300 feet. The wire is #12 AWG with a circular-mil area of 6,530 cmils and is copper with a $K$ of 11. The load current is 14 A. How much voltage is dropped due to wire resistance? If we started with 208 V, how much is left at the load?

**Solution:**

$$E_{VD} = \frac{(11 \times 14 \text{ A} \times 2 \times 300 \text{ feet})}{6,530 \text{ cmils}} = 14.15 \text{ V dropped in the wire}$$

(this is 7.075 V to the load and 7.075 V returning from the load)

If we started with 208 V at the breaker panel, then:

$$208 \text{ V} - 14.15 \text{ V} = 193.85 \text{ V at the load}$$

This translates to:

$$\frac{14.15 \text{ V}}{208 \text{ V}} = 6.8\% \text{ drop}$$

(This percent drop would be excessive and would not meet most specifications.)

---

**Distance from Source to Load**

**Figure 1–18** The distance to the load is 300 feet, but the total length of the conductor is 600 feet.

---

## Example

Apply the calculation to Figure 1–18 using an aluminum conductor:

$$E_{VD} = \frac{K \times I \times 2 \times L}{A_{cmil}}$$

The factors stay the same except that the $K$ of aluminum is higher than that of copper. Because aluminum does not conduct as well as copper, the resistivity is higher. For this example, use a $K$ of 18 $\Omega$ per mil-foot.

The formula then looks like:

$$\frac{18 \times 14 \times 2 \times 300}{6,530} = 23.15 \text{ V}$$

dropped on the conductors of Figure 1–18.

## PERMANENT MAGNETS

Because electricity and magnetism are so closely intertwined, a thorough understanding of magnetism is essential. You have previously studied magnetism in *DC Theory,* but a quick review can be helpful. There are three basic classifications of magnetic materials: ferromagnetic, paramagnetic, and diamagnetic. Both ferromagnetic and paramagnetic materials are metals (Figure 1–19). The magnetic properties of ferromagnetic materials allow the lines of magnetic flux to easily pass through. In ferromagnetic materials, such as iron and nickel, the lines of flux concentrate, or focus. The ability to easily concentrate these lines of flux makes the ferromagnetic materials the most easily magnetized. Paramagnetic materials, such as titanium, tend to somewhat block the passing through and concentration of the lines of flux and are therefore not magnetized as easily or as strongly. The resistance to the magnetic lines of flux is called **reluctance.** The best permanent magnets are made of steel, which is an alloy of iron and other metals. A magnet made with only soft iron does not hold its magnetism long.

## Ferromagnetic Materials versus Paramagnetic Materials

Flux Lines

Ferromagnetic

Paramagnetic

Fewer
Flux Lines

**Figure 1–19** Ferromagnetic materials have a high magnetic ability. Paramagnetic materials have a lower magnetic ability with the same magnetizing force.

The third type of material, diamagnetic material, can be made of metallic or nonmetallic materials. These materials do not allow any magnetic flux lines to pass through them but cause the magnetic lines of flux to pass around the diamagnetic material. A diamagnetic material that has a large value of reluctance is a good shield for magnetism. One example of a diamagnetic material is brass.

## ELECTROMAGNETISM

Whenever current flows through a material, the electron flow produces a magnetic field around the material. If the material is an electrical conductor, the magnetic lines of force called flux lines emanate from the conductor in concentric circles. The flux lines have a direction of force that is perpendicular to the conductor and do have a magnetic direction. The effect can be determined by using the left-hand rule for a conductor (Figure 1–20).

Whenever current "flows," a magnetic field is produced that is proportional to the amount of flow. The larger the current, the larger and more intense the magnetic field becomes.

## TechTip!

Voltage drop is nothing more than using Ohm's law and applying it to the resistance in the wire and the current carried by the wire. In other words, how much voltage does it take to get the current to the load and back to the source? Take the resistance of the wire as resistance equals ohms per mil-foot (the $K$ of the particular type of wire) times the length of the wire to and from the load measured in feet, and divide by the circular mils of the wire. This number is the total resistance of the circuit due to the wire. Multiply the total resistance by the total current to get the total voltage drop due to wire resistance. The formula $VD = \dfrac{2 \times K \times I \times L}{cmils}$ takes all these factors into account.

## Left-Hand Rule for Conductors

**Figure 1–20** The left-hand rule for a conductor places the thumb in the direction of electron flow and the fingers will indicate the direction of the magnetic field.

**Electron Current Flow and Magnetic Field**

**Figure 1–21** As the electron current flow reverses, the magnetic field changes direction.

**Current Flow Direction**

**Figure 1–22** The X or tail feathers of the arrow indicate that current is flowing into the page in a two-dimensional drawing.

**Left-Hand Rule for Coils**

**Figure 1–23** The left-hand rule for a coil states that the fingers are in the direction of magnetic flux and the thumb points to the north magnetic pole.

If the current stops, the magnetic field diminishes to zero. If the current flows in the opposite direction, then the magnetic field again builds around the conductor but with the opposite magnetic polarity (Figure 1–21).

As you notice the cross-section of the conductors and the current direction notations in Figure 1–22, the conductor on the left has current flowing out of the page so that what you see is the "head of the arrow" coming toward you. Using your left hand to grasp the conductor with the thumb in the direction of the current, the fingers indicate the direction of the magnetic field; the direction of subsequent magnetic flux is clockwise around the conductor. Conversely, the conductor on the right of Figure 1–22 has current flowing into the page so that the notation is the "tail feathers of the arrow" moving away from you. The left hand again indicates the concentric lines of force, and the flux wraps counterclockwise around the conductor.

The left-hand rule for coils states that if you grasp a coil of wire as shown in Figure 1–23 with your fingers in the direction of the electron flow, your thumb will point to the north pole of the electromagnetic field that is created. This understanding of electromagnetic coils, with magnetic fields producing a known direction of magnetic flux when a known direction of current flows, will now enable you to determine the way that generators work, as explained in Chapter 2.

## MAGNETIC COILS

If a wire is wound into a coil, as shown in Figure 1–24, and current is passed through it, the individual loops behave like small side-by-side wires with current moving in the same direction. This aiding magnetism creates one large magnetic field with a north pole and a south pole like a permanent magnet. Such coils are called electromagnets.

The intensity of the field depends on two factors:
1. Number of coils: A greater number of coils creates a larger magnetic field
2. Current magnitude: A higher current creates a larger field around the wire and thus a larger overall field

## Magnetic Field Expansion

**Figure 1–24** The magnetic field expands around each conductor affecting the neighboring coiled wire.

Magnetism is used in many ways in everyday life. One method of recording data was the magnetic tape used in cassettes or the floppy disks of computers. The tape or disk was a magnetic material that was magnetized by the recording head. When this worked properly, the magnetic material stayed aligned as the tape was stored. Then the tape was played or the magnetic field was read by the playback head. As you may know, the magnetic media were susceptible to other magnetic fields and to heat. Heat would allow the stored magnetic fields to move, and the stored magnetic data would be ruined. Likewise, if a large magnetic field was brought close to the magnetic media, the stored magnetism would also be remagnetized and the data lost. New storage media is in the form of laser disk storage and other electronic storage that is not as susceptible to magnetic effects.

Multiplying these two factors results in ampere-turns, which represent the total number of magnetic lines created by the electromagnet.

The effect that an electromagnet has is only partially determined by its intensity. The density of the magnetism (usually expressed as number of lines per area) is a direct measure of how "strong" the electromagnet will be. In a coil, at least two factors are important:

1. Wrapping the coils closer together or reducing the coil radius decreases the leakage flux and increases the density of the magnetic field. Figure 1–25 shows this effect.

2. If the coil were wrapped around a core of ferromagnetic material, the number of flux lines passing through the center of the coil would increase, and so would the strength of the electromagnet. This happens because the individual molecules in the core material become polarized (aligned) in relation to the magnetic field produced by the coil.

The type of core material is also a major consideration of the strength of the electromagnet. If the material has high permeability, the core allows magnetic lines of force to pass easily through the material. The area of the core material, measured as the cross-sectional area of the core face at the ends, also affects the amount of magnetic flux density at the poles. As the core area increases, the magnetic flux increases. As the length of the core increases without changing the number of windings, the magnetic effect decreases. Therefore, changing the shape of the core affects the total magnetic influence of the electromagnetic core.

## Coil Density and Magnetic Field Strength

Original coil with an electromagnet strength of 10 ampere-turns.

Closer (more dense) coil (same amount of turns) with electromagnet strength of 30 ampere-turns.

Closer (more dense) coil + more turns with electromagnet strength of 300 ampere-turns.

**Figure 1–25** Changing the dimensions of the coil changes the magnetic field strength.

# MAGNETISM, CONDUCTORS, AND MOVEMENT

Conductors have magnetic fields produced as current moves through them. As a conductor moves through a magnetic field, the magnetic induction process causes a difference of electrical potential between opposite ends of the conductor, and current flows if there is a complete circuit (Figure 1–26).

**Direction of Current Flow from EMF**

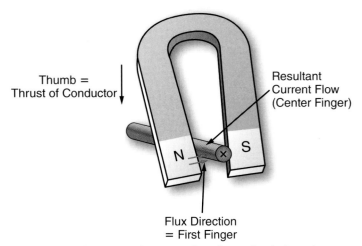

Thumb = Thrust of Conductor

Resultant Current Flow (Center Finger)

Flux Direction = First Finger

**Figure 1–26** The direction of current flow from the induced electromotive force (EMF) as the conductor is moved through a magnetic field is shown.

Just as more current causes a larger magnetic field in a conductor, a stronger magnetic field would cause a greater current flow in a conductor. The rate at which a conductor passes through or "cuts" a magnetic field also determines the amount of voltage difference that is induced. Figure 1–27 is another view of the direction of current flow when a conductor cuts through a magnetic field.

The left-hand rule for generators can easily predict the direction that current would flow if the direction of the magnetic field and the direction of motion are known (Figure 1–28).

The thumb points in the direction of movement, the first finger indicates the direction of magnetic flux (from north to south), and the direction of current is shown by the center finger.

## AC AND DC GENERATORS

Take a look at Figure 1–29. This simple AC generator is constructed of a permanent magnet, slip rings, brushes, and a single loop (armature). The armature is the rotating part of the machine in which the voltage is induced. The magnets set up the required magnetic field.

**Measuring Current Flow**

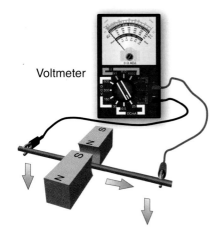

Voltmeter

**Figure 1–27** Current flows when a meter is connected. Note that the left end of the conductor will be the negative terminal of the generated voltage.

**Left-Hand Rule for Generators**

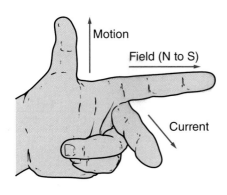

Motion

Field (N to S)

Current

**Figure 1–28** The left-hand rule for generators uses the electron flow theory.

As the loop rotates, each side of the loop cuts lines of flux at the same time. As the lines of flux are cut, a voltage is produced at the ends of the loop. The voltage is connected to the voltmeter by a set of sliding contacts (the slip rings). A slip ring is attached to each end of the loop.

DC generators work basically the same as AC generators, except the voltage is removed from the armature by a commutator instead of slip rings (refer to Figure 1–30; see *DC Theory* for further explanation). Each commutator segment is connected to the end of one side of each loop in the generator. As the commutator segment aligns with each brush, the current flow is always in the same direction. The left brush in Figure 1–30 passes the current from the left side of the loop, and the right brush passes the current from the right side of the loop. This means that the left brush is always negative and the right brush is always positive, even though the loops change polarity as they rotate.

## AC Generator Connected by Slip Rings

**Figure 1–29** An AC generator with armature connections through slip rings.

## DC Generator Connected by Commutator

**Figure 1–30** A DC generator has the same generator principles as those of an AC generator, but the armature is connected to the load through a commutator.

## SUMMARY

The operating principles and calculations required for AC circuits require a thorough understanding of DC fundamentals. This chapter reacquainted you with the concepts we build on in this book. Electron theory reviewed how we can get electrons to move in their orbits, and electron flow theory defined direction of movement. The energy or force needed to move the electrons was described in the "Sources of Electrical Energy" section. The differences among insulators, conductors, and semiconductors were defined to allow you to analyze the differences and help you understand that many materials can conduct if enough electrical pressure is applied.

Conductors do have resistance to the flow of electrons, and the opposition can take many forms. Wire resistance was discussed, as well as skin effect and eddy current losses. A review of DC circuit analysis was designed to remind you of all the rules for DC; most also apply to AC, and some need to be modified. Permanent magnets and electromagnets were also reviewed as a critical part of AC circuit theory and operations. The basic theory of generation was presented to link the DC generator to the AC generator and as an introduction to subsequent chapters.

## CHAPTER GLOSSARY

**Alternating current** A current that varies, or "alternates," from one polarity to another. The current still flows from negative to positive, but the power source changes polarity in relation to time.

**Ampere** The unit of electrical current flow, often abbreviated as amp or just A. It is a measure of the movement of electrons as 1 coulomb per second past a fixed point.

**Conductor** A material that easily passes electrical current. Examples include silver, copper, and aluminum.

**Direct current** A current that flows in one direction only without relationship to time.

**Electromotive force** The electrical pressure generated between two areas with different amounts of electrical charge. The unit of measure is the volt and represented in formulas with "$E$" representing electromotive force.

**Electron flow theory** The theory in which current flows from a negative charge to a positive charge.

**Insulator** A material that does not allow electrical current to flow easily. Examples include rubber, plastic, and mica.

**Ohm** The unit of electrical resistance, often shown as the Greek letter omega ($\Omega$).

**Periodic table of elements** A tabular arrangement of the elements according to their atomic numbers so that elements with similar properties are in the same column.

**Piezoelectric** Electricity being created by stress or pressure in a material—especially a crystalline material.

**Reluctance** The opposition that materials present to the flow of magnetic lines of flux (similar to electrical resistance). Permanent magnets have a high reluctance and temporary magnets have a low reluctance. The symbol is the Greek letter rel ($R$) and the force is measured in ampere-turns per weber.

**Semiconductor** A material that falls between conductors and insulators in terms of electrical conductivity.

**Valence ring or shell** The outermost shell of electrons in an atom.

**Volt** The electromotive force that pushes electrons through the conductors, wires, or components of a circuit. It is similar to the pressure exerted on a system of fluid using pipes. The higher the pressure, the more flow. Specifically, the volt is the amount of work done per coulomb of charge (volts = joules per coulomb) and is represented by the letter "V." In calculations, voltage is represented by the letter "E." Remember that voltage is the force required in creating flow but that volts do not flow through the circuit.

# REVIEW QUESTIONS

1. Describe how good electrical conductors are different from insulators and semiconductors.
2. How is the resistance of a conductor related to its diameter, its cross-sectional area, and its resistivity?
3. List four forms of electricity production.
4. Describe Ohm's law.
5. What is the effect of "skin effect" in electrical circuits?
6. What is the left-hand rule for generators? How can it be used to determine the polarity of a generator voltage output?
7. Explain what is meant by circular mils.
8. What is the effect of eddy currents on the current flow in a conductor?
9. By adding more resistors in parallel to a circuit, the line current goes _____.
10. If current is flowing toward you while you look at the end of a conductor, the magnetic field will move in the (clockwise or counterclockwise) direction.
11. Write two different formulas for finding power in a circuit using current, voltage, and resistance.
12. As the American Wire gauge number gets larger, the cross-sectional area of the wire gets _____.

## PRACTICE PROBLEMS

**Figure PP1–1**

1. Look at Figure PP1–1 and assume that the power supply is a 120 V battery. Calculate the following:
   a. Total circuit current
   b. Total circuit power
   c. Voltage drop, current flow, and power dissipation for each of the five resistors
2. Refer to Figure PP1–2. What is the magnetic polarity of the right end of the magnetic coil with the circuit polarity as shown?

*NORTH*

**Figure PP1–2**

3. Using the information in Figure PP1–3, calculate the voltage drop between the source and the load.

4. Use the reciprocal formula to find the resistance of three resistors; 10 Ω, 20 Ω, and 30 Ω connected in parallel.

5. Write the formula to find the resistance of 1,000 feet of 3,000 cmil copper wire, that has a K factor of 10.5.

6. Find the actual operating resistance of a 100 W, 120 V lamp.

7. In an AC circuit that contains only resistance, find the total current if the total voltage is 120 V and three 20 Ω resistors are in series.

8. If three 100 W, 120 V lamps were connected in parallel across a 120 V supply, find the total watts dissipated by the circuit.

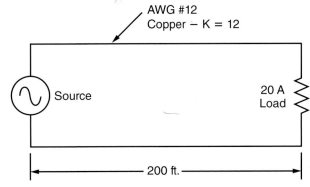

**Figure PP1–3**

9. If three 100 W, 120 V lamps were connected in series across a 120 V supply, find the total watts dissipated by the circuit.

10. In Figure PP1–1, if another resistor were added to the two 30 Ω resistors in parallel, the total resistance of the circuit would go _____.

# 2

# PRODUCTION OF THE AC SINE WAVE

# O V E R V I E W

The production of AC is a relatively simple concept, but to understand the process and the results of the AC generation is a more complex study. In the production of electricity, the need for motion is usually accomplished by a mechanically driven system (prime mover). Some sort of energy is needed to create the voltage. This is accomplished in large systems by steam turbines. The steam is developed by burning coal, or other fossil fuels, or by creating steam by nuclear fission. On smaller-scale generators, the mechanical motion (or prime mover) is provided by gasoline or diesel engines. There are other methods too, but these are the most common. Electricians are usually concerned not with the mechanical input power but with the electricity that is generated. AC has many new terms and conditions that are not studied in DC theory.

# O B J E C T I V E S

After completing this chapter you will be able to:
· Describe the factors needed to generate a voltage
· Name the components of the AC sine wave
· Calculate the instantaneous values, root mean square (RMS), peak amplitude, peak-to-peak values, period, frequency, and average values of AC
· Determine the synchronous speed of a generator to produce a desired frequency
· Calculate the number of poles of a generator given the speed and the frequency
· Explain the relationship of mechanical degrees, electrical degrees, and number of poles

## AC GENERATORS

Generation of AC is the most widely used form of production of electricity. The concept of electromagnetic mechanical generation of power is a simple one. The items needed to generate voltage are a conductor, a magnetic field, and relative motion between the conductor and the magnetic field. AC generators, or alternators, are energy converters. They change mechanical energy from the prime mover to electrical energy. The opposite conversion may take place at the other end of the circuit where a motor converts electrical energy back to mechanical energy.

A simple AC generator is shown in Figure 2–1. This figure illustrates the three components needed for generation. The magnetic flux is composed of invisible magnetic lines of force traveling between the north magnetic pole face and the south magnetic pole face of the magnets. A second component of generation is a conductor, which is illustrated as the windings in the illustration. The third needed component is the relative motion of the conductor (winding) as it spins through the magnetic field.

Figure 2–2 demonstrates the left-hand rule for generation in electron flow theory analysis. The first finger of the left hand represents the direction of the magnetic flux, pointing toward the south magnetic pole. As the conductor moves across the face of the south pole, the conductor thrust upward is represented by the thumb of the left hand. The result of the movement (cutting magnetic flux) causes a displacement of the electrons in the conductor, creating a surplus at one end and a deficiency at the other end.

In other words, a difference in potential or a voltage difference is created. If there is a circuit for current to flow such as shown by the meter, electron current will flow from the negative to the positive terminal in the connected circuit as would be indicated by the center finger. Be aware that this is the external circuit and that internally to the generator it looks like the current is flowing to the negative terminal. You need this information later when you analyze other circuits. By following the same conductor to the opposite side of the generator, you notice that the direction for the thrust is now downward. By positioning your left hand correctly, you notice the direction of the current flow is reversed. Sometimes this is easier to see in a two-dimensional drawing, as in Figure 2–3. Because the external circuit is still connected to the same end of the same conductor through the slip ring, the current flow in the external circuit also reverses.

**AC Generator**

**Figure 2–1** This simple rotating armature AC generator has slip rings.

**Left-Hand Rule for Generators**

**Figure 2–2** The left-hand rule for generators is used with electron flow theory.

In Figure 2–3, the symbol ✕ represents current going into the coil conductor and the • symbol indicates current coming out of the coil conductor. You can see that every time one side of the coil passes under one pole it has one electrical polarity and that it creates an opposite polarity when it crosses the opposite magnetic pole. This two-pole generator has voltage induced into the spinning conductor (known as the **armature**) whenever it cuts a magnetic field. When the conductor cuts through 10 million lines of magnetic flux in 1 second, it produces 1 V, as shown in the following formula: $10^7$ magnetic lines per second = 1 V.

The number of lines cut depends on the strength of the electromagnetic flux. As you notice, the speed of the cutting is also a factor in the amount of voltage induced in one conductor.

Figure 2–4 shows a conductor spinning in a circular motion. If we just refer to one end of the spinning conductor at 0° of rotation, there is no cutting action and no voltage induced. The graph of this is shown at the right. As the conductor spins clockwise, we begin to cut flux lines and the voltage graph increases with time. As the conductor is directly under the north pole, it is cutting the maximum lines of flux and it is 90° through its rotation. Continuing through the rotation to 180° of rotation, we again are traveling parallel to the lines of flux and no cutting action takes place; so again, we have no voltage, as indicated at 180° on the corresponding graph. At 270° of rotation, we are cutting the maximum amount of flux but the current in the conductor is reversed, as indicated by the graphical representation. As the conductor travels parallel to the magnetic field, which it does at the left and right of the arc, it induces no voltage and the output voltage goes to zero. Thus, a waveform with a maximum and a zero point is achieved as the conductor spins in a circle.

A sine wave is the result of a spinning conductor within a magnetic field.

**Direction of Electron Flow**

**Figure 2–3** The direction of electron flow can be expressed in two-dimensional representation.

FieldNote!

The oscilloscope is a tool that provides visual representation of a waveform. Through the amplitude controls, we can measure the various components of the waveform, such as peak or peak-to-peak values. The scope allows us to adjust the time to see small fractions of a second so that we can actually view 60 cycles per second or more with relative ease. The oscilloscope can be thought of as a voltmeter, but we can actually see the waveform displayed on the screen.

**Sine Wave Production**

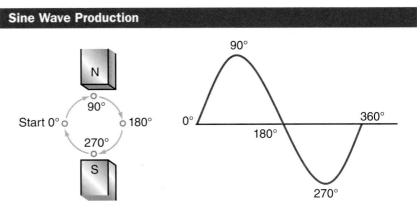

**Figure 2–4** A circular motion produces mechanical generation of a sine wave and the resultant waveform.

If you use the sine of the angle of movement and multiply it by the expected maximum voltage, then the resultant is plotted on a graph. For each of the 360° of rotation, you see a figure known as an AC sine wave. As indicated by Figure 2–5, the sine wave for the generated voltage is constantly changing from zero to maximum and back to zero. It then reverses direction of voltage and increases to maximum negative peak before again returning to zero.

This full rotation took 360° of mechanical rotation, and because it is the sine of those mechanical degrees, the electrical wave follows the same degrees but is expressed as electrical degrees. One cycle of voltage from zero to positive, zero to negative, and back to zero voltage is one cycle of AC voltage. If we can spin the conductor one revolution in one second, we record one cycle per second (Figure 2–6). The measure of how frequently we can produce a sine wave is called the **frequency** of the waveform. If we can get 60 cycles in a second, then we record 60 cycles per second (CPS). *CPS* is an older term, and you may see it on old equipment. Hertz is the newer term for the cycles per second unit of measure

(60 CPS = 60 hertz, or Hz). In some instances, we refer to the real time it takes for a waveform to complete a full cycle—360°—as a period. The period is calculated by taking the inverse of the frequency in hertz. The period of a 60 Hz waveform is $\frac{1}{60}$, or 0.0167 second. This tells us exactly how much time elapses as the AC oscillates completely through its two half cycles.

There are different ways to measure AC and designations given to various parts of the waveform. Most times we are concerned not with the actual waveform but rather with its effects in the electrical circuits. As you study motor controls and electronic systems, you need to be aware of the specific waveforms and how we use them to provide different functions.

## INSTANTANEOUS VALUE OF A SINE WAVE

As you learned earlier, the AC waveforms used in electrical power applications are in the form of sine waves. This means that any instantaneous value on the wave can be determined by using the formula:

**Oscilloscope View**

**Figure 2–5** An oscilloscope gives a view of a 60 Hz sine wave.

**Instantaneous Value Graph**

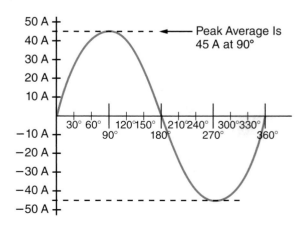

**Figure 2–6** A plot of all instantaneous values creates a sine wave.

$$I_{inst} = I_{peak} \times \sin(\theta)$$

$$E_{inst} = E_{peak} \times \sin(\theta)$$

Where:

$E_{inst}$ = value of the voltage at any part of the sine waveform determined by the angular position of the conductor in the generation process

$E_{peak}$ = value of the voltage that occurs at 90° and 270° of the voltage waveform; this is the maximum value that can be generated by a particular generator with set parameters

$I_{inst}$ = instantaneous value of the current at any point during the waveform

$I_{peak}$ = maximum value of current obtained during any point of the waveform

$\sin(\theta)$ = sine function of any angle theta (the lowercase Greek letter) represented by the degrees of waveform

Refer to Figure 2–6. You can find the instantaneous value by multiplying the peak voltage, or current, by the sine of the angle at this specific point (a specific point on the sine wave at a specific point in time) at which you want the measurement. The formula for this calculation is given next.

---

### Example

What is the instantaneous current value of a 45 A (peak) AC circuit at 30°, 45°, and 60°?

**Solution:**

$I_{inst} = I_{peak} \times \sin(\theta)$

$I_{inst} = 45 \times \sin(30°) = 45 \times 0.5$

$\quad = 22.5$ A

$I_{inst} = 45 \times \sin(45°) = 45 \times 0.707$

$\quad = 31.8$ A

$I_{inst} = 45 \times \sin(60°) = 45 \times 0.866$

$\quad = 38.97$ A

---

# AC SINE WAVE MEASUREMENTS

Four designations are used to measure current and voltage associated with AC sine waves: peak, peak-to-peak, root mean square (RMS), and average. These values are used at various points in your study of AC.

## PEAK AND PEAK-TO-PEAK (P-TO-P) VALUES

The peak value is measured from zero to the highest value obtained in either the positive or the negative direction. Therefore, the peak-to-peak value is twice that of the peak value because it is measured from one peak value to the other. Particularly in the study of electronic control of AC power, the **peak-to-peak** (or P-to-P) values become important. The electronics actually have to be sized to handle the full peak value in one direction and have to be able to block the full peak value in the opposite direction. The peak-to-peak value is the real waveform available at the typical receptacle outlet.

The sine wave creates a shape that is not a semicircle, so the typical circle or half circle calculations do not provide a true equation of the effect of the sine wave. The shape of the wave creates a condition where the peak value of the voltage waveform can be calculated by using the effective value of the voltage times the square root of two ($\sqrt{2} = 1.414$). If we measure the RMS value of 120 V AC at the receptacle, we know the actual sine wave peak is 120 V $\times$ 1.414, or 169.7 V. This takes into account the sine wave shape and allows us to calculate the actual values if we were to plot all the individual voltage points along the waveform. The reciprocal of 1.414 is 0.707. This allows us to multiply the peak value by 0.707 to determine the RMS value.

To determine the full sine wave value from peak to peak, we multiply the peak value by 2.

## FieldNote!

Measuring 120 V with the standard meter really means the peak is nearly 170 V and the peak-to-peak (P-to-P) value is nearly 340 V (Figure 2–7).

### ROOT MEAN SQUARE (RMS) VALUE

The **root mean square (RMS)** value is also called the effective value, or $E_{eff}$. It is so called because the AC waveform has peaks and valleys but the effective value of the waveform has the same heating effect as a DC voltage of the same value. Consider Figure 2–8. The straight red trace is a DC voltage equal to 120 V. If the effective voltage of 120 V was applied to a 100 Ω resistor, the power dissipated could be calculated using the familiar power formula:

$$P = \frac{E^2}{R} = \frac{120^2}{100} = \frac{14,400}{100} = 144 \text{ W}$$

What is the peak voltage value of an AC sine wave that will dissipate the same amount of power as 120 V DC? Imagine connecting an AC voltage source and a wattmeter to the 100 Ω resistor. Now, gradually increase the AC voltage until the same 144 W are being dissipated. For a sine wave, this occurs when the peak voltage is at 120 × $\sqrt{2}$ = 169.71 V. Put another way, 120 V is the effective value of an AC voltage with a peak of 169.71 V.

This value can be calculated mathematically by squaring each instantaneous point on the AC waveform and then taking the mean (average) of all the squared values and finding the square root of the average, which is the root of the mean of the squares or RMS of the AC waveform. This is where the term RMS originates. In a standard AC-generated waveform, the voltage and the current each create a sine wave pattern. For either the voltage, current, or power waveform, the RMS value is calculated by using the peak of the waveform divided by 1.414 (the square root of 2). This calculation is true for the voltage, current, or power of an AC sine wave. You can also calculate the RMS value by multiplying the peak waveform value by 0.707, which is the reciprocal of 1.414.

**Figure 2–7** The 120 V RMS on the meter is actually approximately 340 V peak-to-peak.

## Example

A circuit has a peak value of 423 volts. Find the RMS value.

**Solution:**

$$E_{RMS} = \frac{E_{peak}}{\sqrt{2}}$$

$$= \frac{423 \text{ V}}{1.414} = 299 \text{ V}$$

OR

$$E_{RMS} = 423 \text{ V} \times 0.707 = 299 \text{ V}$$

A circuit has an RMS value of 115 volts. Find the peak value.

**Solution:**

$$E_{peak} = E_{RMS} \times \sqrt{2} = 115 \text{ V} \times 1.414 = 162.6 \text{ V}$$

### AVERAGE VALUE

The average value does not apply to a pure AC sine wave. It is used primarily when an AC sine wave is changed to a rippling DC waveform by a full-wave rectifier. Recall that the effective value causes the same amount of heat throughout both the positive and the negative half cycles as the same value of DC. The average value is the actual

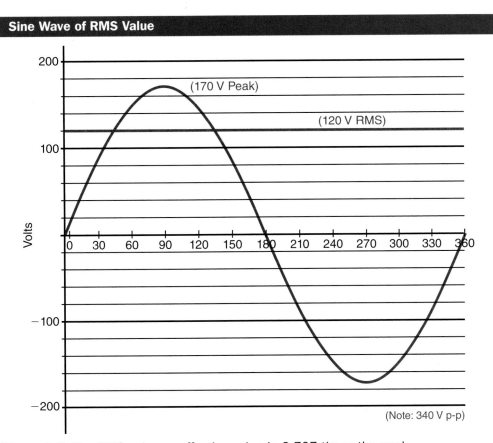

**Sine Wave of RMS Value**

**Figure 2–8** The RMS value or effective value is 0.707 times the peak.

## FieldNote!

Another way to do this same calculation is instead of dividing the peak value by 1.414 to get to the RMS value, to multiply the peak times the inverse of 1.414. This value is 0.707. The peak of 169.7 × 0.707 = 120 (approximately). Because 1.414 and 0.707 are inverses of each other, it might be easier to multiply instead of divide. You must make sure you use the proper multiplier. Remember the peak value will always be larger than the RMS value. Most meters used in the field to measure voltage are RMS meters. Older meters were actually designed to read average value even though they claimed to be reading RMS. Now meters must state if they read true RMS.

average of all the instantaneous voltage or current values across a full cycle. This is the reason that a pure sine wave has no DC value; it is above the zero exactly as much as it is below. Therefore, a pure AC sine wave's average is zero.

A rectified sine wave, on the other hand, has most or all of its waveform above zero. The actual DC value depends on whether it is a full-wave rectifier (Figure 2–9) or a half-wave rectifier (Figure 2–10). As you note

in the figures, the electron flow flows against the arrow symbols of the diode rectifiers. This is a result of the differences between electron flow theory and conventional flow theory. As you look at the two figures of Figure 2–9, the arrows indicate the two directions of the AC applied voltage, looking at them as one voltage polarity at a time. The input to the full-wave rectifier is an AC waveform, but the output to the load is a pulsating DC waveform.

We have covered formulas relating to the sine wave here. The calculations for half-wave and full-wave rectifiers are covered in more detail in the *Semiconductors* text.

To go from RMS back to peak, the RMS value is multiplied by the square root of 2, or 1.414. For a full-wave rectified circuit, the average DC value is found by multiplying the peak value of the sine wave by $\frac{2}{\pi}$.

The formula for calculating the average value of a full-wave rectified circuit then becomes:

$$E_{avg} = \frac{2 \times E_{peak}}{\pi} = \frac{2 \times E_{RMS} \times \sqrt{2}}{\pi}$$

**Figure 2–9** Calculating the average voltage value for a full-wave rectified DC waveform.

## Example

An AC voltage of 30 V is connected to a full-wave rectifier. Find the rectified average value.

**Solution:**

$$E_{avg} = \frac{2 \times E_{RMS} \times \sqrt{2}}{\pi}$$

$$= \frac{2 \times 30 \times 1.414}{3.1416}$$

$$= \frac{84.84}{3.1416} = 27 \text{ V}$$

# FieldNote!

Note that a shortcut can be used for this formula based on the fact that $\frac{(2 \times \sqrt{2})}{\pi} = 0.9$. Thus, multiplying the RMS value of the full-wave rectified sine wave by 0.9 gives the average value.

If you were to surmise that the average value of a half-wave rectified sine wave would be equal to half the value of a full-wave rectified sine wave, you would be right. The formula for calculating the average value of a half-wave rectified sine wave is:

$$E_{avg} = \frac{E_{peak}}{\pi} = E_{peak} \times 0.381$$

OR

$$E_{avg} = \frac{E_{RMS} \times \sqrt{2}}{\pi}$$

OR

$$E_{avg} = E_{RMS} \times 0.450$$

### Half-Wave DC Waveform

Half-wave rectifier average value is 0.318 x peak for the complete cycle.

**Figure 2–10** Calculating the average voltage value for a half-wave rectified DC waveform.

# CONSTRUCTION OF AC GENERATORS

AC generators are designed in two styles. One style, the revolving armature, is the easiest to visualize and the easiest to explain. As was seen in the previous section, the conductor loop spinning in the magnetic field has a voltage induced into it. This loop is referred to as the armature. The amount of voltage induced in one wire is small, cutting 10 million lines of flux per second. The amount of voltage generated can be increased if we add the effects of many conductors together. In effect, we place them all in series and the voltage induced in each conductor is added to the circuit. To do this, the conductor is wrapped in a coil so that many conductors are traveling through the magnetic field together. The more "turns" of the coil, the larger the voltage. This is a design feature of the generator and is not easily altered as the generator is in use. As was previously explained, if the magnetic field is more dense, more lines of flux are cut and the voltage induced is increased. There is a limit to how strong the magnetic field can be.

Another factor previously discussed is the speed of the cutting action. The more flux lines cut per second, the higher the voltage. Assuming the flux density stays the same, speed can affect the voltage. This factor of speed creates a problem for AC generation. The speed of the rotating armature is also directly related to how many complete sine waves are produced in one second.

## FieldNote!

Electricians need to understand basic electronics. The circuits used in many pieces of equipment use the fundamentals of rectification, changing AC into DC and inverting, changing DC back to AC. One piece of equipment that you will no doubt encounter is the variable frequency drive (VFD) (Figure 2–11). This drive is the electronic control of motor speed. Various schemes are used to control the frequency that is supplied to an AC motor, but all methods use a rectification process and then an inversion process to create AC at various frequencies.

**Variable Frequency Drives**

**Figure 2–11** Variable frequency drives (VFDs) are electronic motor speed controllers.

The hertz of the output voltage is affected. Remember one revolution per second for a two-pole generator creates 1 Hz. A speed of 3,600 revolutions per minute (rpm) for a two-pole generator is the same as 60 revolutions per second;

60 revolutions per second for a two-pole generator produces the standard U.S. frequency of 60 Hz.

The formula for determining the exact speed that a generator must spin to create a desired frequency is the **synchronous speed** formula:

$$\text{Synchronous speed} = \frac{(120 \times \text{Frequency})}{\text{Number of poles}}$$

Where:

synchronous speed = exact speed a generator must spin to develop the desired frequency output

120 = a constant that results from converting cycles per second to revolutions per minute, a factor of 60, and converting number of poles from actual pole faces to pairs of poles, a factor of 2, yielding a constant conversion of 120

frequency = measured in hertz

number of poles = an even number

## REVOLVING ARMATURE AC GENERATORS

The **revolving armature AC generator** is not as common as the revolving field generator. It is similar in construction to the DC generator in that both types use some form of mechanical device to connect the external circuit to the armature circuit. The AC generator uses slip rings instead of a commutator. The purpose of the slip rings is to directly connect the armature windings to the load. Since no commutator is used, the output is an alternating voltage instead of a direct voltage.

The slip ring, unlike the segmented DC generator commutator, is constructed as a continuous ring and is not broken into isolated segments. Each end of the rotating loop of the armature is connected to a separate **slip ring** (Figure 2–12).

Although the revolving armature AC generator can produce an alternating output voltage, the slip rings and brushes limit the size of load it can carry.

The higher currents require large slip rings, large brushes, and highly increased maintenance. The high voltages required by some loads mean that much heavier insulation must be used. Taken together, these features limit the kilovolt-ampere (kVA) capacity of the revolving armature generator.

## ALTERNATOR CONSTRUCTION

Another more practical alternator is the **revolving field generator.** This approach allows the magnetic field to spin and the coils of wire where voltage is induced—still in the armature—to remain firmly attached to the stationary part of the generator known as the stator. This means that the slip rings used to connect to the circuit in the revolving armature-type generator are no longer needed to collect the induced voltage. These sliding contacts on the slip rings are a point of concern. If we can avoid the use of a slip ring to connect to the load circuit, we can eliminate many problems.

The same three factors are needed for the generator. The conductor is coiled and is now placed in the stator. The magnetic field is placed on the rotating component (the rotor), and there is still relative motion between the two.

## REVOLVING FIELD AC GENERATORS

The same synchronous speed formula holds true whether the magnetic field rotates or the armature rotates. The same sine wave is produced as the sine of the angle of mechanical rotor movement is used to plot the AC waveform from zero, to peak, to zero, to negative peak, and back to zero. Figure 2–13 shows a two-pole rotating field alternator.

In small-scale generators, the magnetic fields we have discussed that may be mounted on the stator or the rotor could be a permanent magnet.

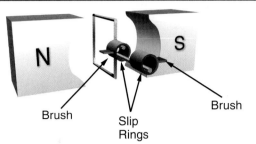

**Brushes and Slip Rings of Generator**

Brush    Slip Rings    Brush

**Figure 2–12** A revolving armature generator has brushes and slip rings.

These generators are referred to as **permanent magnet generators (PMGs).** For most large commercial and electric utility generators, the magnetic field is an electromagnet. As you know, the strength of the electromagnet can be changed by adjusting the amount of amperage that flows through the coil. The electromagnet is powered by DC so that the magnetic polarity of the magnetic field does not change. If the generator is a revolving armature, then the DC is directly connected to the stator windings to form a stationary magnetic field, as you previously saw. If the magnetic field is on the rotor, as in the revolving field generator, then DC must be supplied to the rotating member. This may be done with slip rings or other means that are discussed later. It may be difficult at first to determine whether an alternator is a revolving field or a revolving armature.

**Revolving Field AC Generator**

Coils

N · S  ← Rotating Magnetic Field

Coils

**Figure 2–13** A revolving field AC generator has a stationary armature and permanent armature connections.

## GENERATOR EXCITATION

We have now generated a sine wave, with a specific frequency based on the synchronous speed and the number of poles. We can change the voltage by changing the quantity of flux lines cut by the armature. To do this, we need to control the DC current to the DC electromagnet. This DC electromagnet, whether spinning or stationary, is referred to as the **exciter.** The amount of current, called the **excitation current,** and voltage supplied to the exciter are the excitation power. The excitation power is the DC input to a generator that causes the AC RMS voltage generated to increase or decrease; the number of conductors cannot change and the speed cannot change because of the need to maintain a desired frequency. The excitation power input of the electromagnet exciter affects the peak-to-peak voltage but not the frequency. Figure 2–14 shows a two-pole rotating field alternator with slip ring input.

## MULTIPLE-POLE GENERATORS

The synchronous speed required of a two-pole generator to maintain 60 Hz output is 3,600 rpm. If we add another set of magnetic poles—north and south—and space them around the stator at the one-quarter rotation point and then spin a conductor past them, we can get a conductor to pass north and south poles with only 180° of mechanical rotation (Figure 2–15). This means the voltage creates a complete sine wave in 180° or two sine waves in 360° of mechanical rotation. The formula for electrical degrees relating to mechanical degrees is:

Elect. deg. = mech. deg. × pairs of poles

In this case, with four magnetic poles, we generate 360 electrical degrees = 180 mechanical degrees × 2 pairs of poles.

**Rotating Field Power**

Slip Rings

**Figure 2–14** DC power is supplied to the rotating field by slip rings.

**Four-Pole AC Generator**

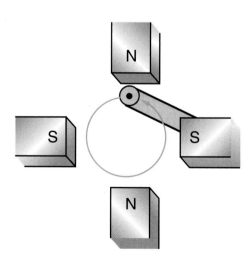

**Figure 2–15** A four-pole AC generator produces two full sine waves for 360° of rotation.

In other words, we only need to spin the armature half as fast to get the same number of cycles per second. This is confirmed in the synchronous speed formula:

Synchronous speed =

$$\frac{120 \times 60 \text{ Hz}}{4 \text{ poles}} = \frac{7{,}200}{4} = 1{,}800 \text{ rpm}$$

We must always have an even number of poles—a matched set of north and south. If we add two more poles for a total of six, we see that we need to move even fewer mechanical degrees to get a 360° sine wave: 360 electrical degrees = $X$ mechanical degrees × 3 pairs of poles.

Transposing the formula:

$$\frac{360 \text{ elect. deg.}}{3 \text{ pairs of poles}} = 120 \text{ mech. deg.}$$

For synchronous speed of a six-pole generator producing 60 Hz:

$$\frac{120 \times 60 \text{ Hz}}{6 \text{ poles}} = 1{,}200 \text{ rpm}$$

Thus, 1,200 rpm is one-third as fast as the two-pole generator to get the same frequency.

We have now discussed the generation of single-phase AC and the resulting AC waveform. We discuss other forms of generation and the methods to control the generator output other than frequency in later chapters.

## FieldNote!

An example of a multiple-pole generator is pictured in Figure 2–16. This generator is operating in a hydroelectric generating station and is producing 60 Hz. It has 72 poles. What is the synchronous speed? 100 rpm.

**Multiple-Pole Generator**

**Figure 2–16** These slow hydroelectric generators are operating at 100 rpm.

## SUMMARY

For the production of electricity or the force to move electrons, we need three factors. We need a conductor with the electrons able to move, a magnetic field, and motion between the conductor and the magnetic field. The left-hand rule for generation allows us to predict which way the electrons will move as the conductor cuts through magnetic flux lines. As the conductor is coiled and placed on a rotor, the output of the generator can be taken directly off the armature with a slip ring and the resultant voltage oscillates between two electrical polarities. Not only does the polarity change, but the amount, or amplitude, of the voltage changes, producing a sine wave. By adjusting the speed of the rotor, we can produce more or fewer sine waves per second, thereby changing the frequency of the waveform.

Each feature of the sine wave can be identified by the instantaneous value at any point along the waveform by using the sine of the angle. Likewise we can identify the peaks, the peak-to-peak am-plitude, and the frequency and period of the waveform. The measurement we use daily is the RMS value of the AC sine wave. The average value of the AC was introduced in this chapter as a feature used with electronic conversion of the sine wave.

Finally, in this chapter we analyzed how to produce voltage by several styles of generators. The basic concept using a rotating armature was expanded to a stationary armature-rotating field generator where the magnetic field spins and the electricity comes off solid connections to the armature on the stator. The concept of multi-poled generators was explained as a way to get the same frequency of the waveform, although it needs a slower synchronous speed. This changes the relationship between the mechanical degrees of rotation and the number of electrical degrees on the waveform. The waveform stays at 360°, but the mechanical generator no longer needs to spin 360 mechanical degrees.

## CHAPTER GLOSSARY

**Armature** The winding in a generator where an induced voltage is created.

**Excitation current** The current supplied to the field of an AC generator. The excitation current creates the magnetic field that the armature cuts through.

**Exciter** DC magnetic field for a generator, whether spinning or stationary.

**Frequency** The number of complete waveforms completed in 1 second. Frequency is a measure of how often the waveform is completed in relation to time, expressed in cycles per second. The unit of measure is the hertz (Hz), named after Heinrich Hertz.

**Peak-to-peak value** The full value of the AC sine wave measured from the positive peak to the negative peak, also referred to as the P-to-P value.

**Permanent magnet generator (PMG)** In this type of generator, the field is provided by a very strong permanent magnet.

**Revolving armature AC generator** A generator that has the field windings on the stator and the armature windings on the rotor.

**Revolving field generator** A generator that has the field windings on the rotor and the armature windings on the stator.

**Root mean square** The root mean square (RMS) of an AC waveform is the square root of the mean, or average, of all the instantaneous values squared. The RMS gives the effective value of the AC. This RMS value has the same heating effect as DC of the same value.

**Slip rings** Continuous bands of metal installed around a shaft. Slip rings are connected to the rotating windings and provide a path for the current to reach the brushes.

**Synchronous speed** The exact speed of a rotating member to produce a desired frequency for a generator. This same term is used to describe the speed that is produced by a specific frequency to make an induction motor run.

# REVIEW QUESTIONS

1. Describe how to determine direction of electron flow when a conductor is moved through a magnetic field.
2. What is an advantage of a revolving field generator?
3. What factor do you use to multiply the peak voltage to get RMS voltage?
4. Describe the RMS value of voltage.
5. Write the formula that shows the relationship between the number of poles of a generator, the mechanical degrees of rotation, and the electrical degrees of generation produced in the generator output waveform.
6. With a two-pole AC generator, a complete sine wave will be produced with _____ degrees of rotation.
7. Explain what is meant by the "instantaneous value" of a sine wave.
8. After rectification by a full-wave bridge rectifier, how do you determine the average DC value before filtering?
9. Describe why slip rings would be used to collect an AC voltage from a revolving conductor in an alternator.
10. Explain what is meant by the "frequency" of a waveform.

## PRACTICE PROBLEMS

1. To produce 60 Hz from a four-pole generator, what is the synchronous speed?
2. What is the actual time that elapses for one cycle of a 50 Hz waveform?
3. Calculate the instantaneous value of current at 30° if the peak current is 100 A on an AC sine wave.
4. What is the peak value of a sine wave that measures 120 V AC RMS?

Use Figure PP2–1 to answer the following questions.

5. If the peak of the sine wave is 141.4 V, find the RMS voltage value.
6. If the effective value of the AC sine wave is 50 V, find the peak value.
7. Find the peak-to-peak voltage of the AC sine wave if the RMS value is 230 V.
8. If the second half of the waveform is inverted and appears above the zero reference line, the waveform is called a(n) _____ voltage waveform.
9. If the peak-to-peak value of the AC waveform is approximately 340 V, find the AC RMS voltage.
10. If the waveform takes $\frac{1}{60}$th of a second to complete a full sine wave, what is the frequency?
11. What is the relationship between the numbers 1.414 and 0.707?
12. Explain why the DC average is lower for a half-wave rectifier circuit when compared to a full-wave rectifier circuit.
13. Assume the waveform is a current waveform. If the effective AC current is 15 A, what is the peak-to-peak current?
14. At what degree points on the waveform do peak values occur?

**Figure PP2–1**

# 3

# INDUCTORS, SELF-INDUCTION, INDUCTIVE REACTANCE, AND IMPEDANCE

# O V E R V I E W

The previous chapter introduced you to the AC sine wave and how it was produced. The benefit of AC is that it can be easily transformed from one voltage level to another. This chapter introduces you to the effects AC has on a circuit that are not experienced with DC systems. Specifically, the effect that induction has on a wire that is coiled up creates a significant difference. As you have already learned and reviewed, the three factors needed to induce a voltage into a conductor are a conductor, a magnetic field, and relative motion. All three of these factors affect every coil of wire when AC is applied but not when there is a steady current such as with DC. This means the same wire reacts differently to AC than it does to DC. The effects of self-induction are explained.

# O B J E C T I V E S

After completing this chapter, you will be able to:
- Define inductance
- Determine when self-inductance is used and its effects
- Calculate inductive reactance under various conditions
- Determine the angle between resistance and inductive reactance
- Determine the impedance of a coil
- Apply Ohm's law equations to determine circuit quantities

## INDUCTANCE

**Inductance** is the ability of a current-carrying conductor, coil, or circuit to induce a voltage into itself or adjacent circuits. Self-inductance is the ability to induce a voltage into itself. Some self-inductance is present in all AC circuits because of the continuously changing magnetic fields.

**Inductor Symbols**

Air Core Inductors          Variable Inductor

Iron Core Inductors         Powdered Iron Core Inductor

**Figure 3–1** Inductor symbols with different core types.

## FieldNote!

Many of the terms used in the electrical industry are synonymous. It just depends on where you learned the theory and what part of the country you are from. The term inductor is used to describe a coil or a particular piece of equipment that exhibits inductive characteristics. Variable inductors may have moveable cores. Inductors may be deliberately designed to choke off high current, as in the case of power supplies, in which case the same component is referred to as a choke. Inductors are important components in AC electrical systems.

**Single Conductor Coil**

**Figure 3–2** A single conductor can be coiled to make an inductor.

## INDUCTORS

A coil of wire wrapped around a core is called an inductor. Its name **inductor** comes from the fact that a voltage can be induced into it by moving it through a magnetic field or by moving a magnetic field around it. This induced voltage produces a current. You also learned that passing current through a wire produces a magnetic field around it. Inductors have many characteristics that are present with AC current connected and are not present with DC current connected. The same inductor with 100 V DC may have 10 A DC total current. The same coil connected to 100 V AC may only have 1 A of total current at 60 Hz and even less if the 100 V AC is at 100 Hz. The AC effects on inductors and the way inductors affect the AC circuits are discussed next. The schematic symbol for the inductor is shown in Figure 3–1.

## THEORY OF SELF-INDUCTION

As you know, whenever there is a current flow in a conductor, a magnetic field is produced. When AC is used, the current, and therefore the magnetic field, is constantly increasing, decreasing, or reversing. The effect is that the magnetic field is always moving. As you recall, the factors needed for generation of an induced voltage are (1) a magnetic field, (2) a conductor, and (3) relative motion between the conductor and the magnetic field. The effects of generation are apparent as we make a single conductor into a coil so that the conductors are on top of one another in close proximity (Figure 3–2). The result of this close physical location is that the magnetic field developed in the wire as it is expanding and contracting following the current sine wave actually expands or "cuts through" the neighboring conductor.

## Magnetic Lines of Force

**Figure 3–3** Cutaways of a coil show representative magnetic lines of force interacting.

Likewise, as the expanded magnetic field contracts, it cuts through the neighboring conductor again. As it magnetically moves through the conductor, it generates a voltage in the conductor. Just as in a generator, the small voltages in each segment add up to a larger voltage total in the length of the wire that is coiled up. This effect in a coil of wire with AC current flowing is called **self-inductance.**

Consider the coil shown in Figure 3–3. The magnetic field created by the changing current through the conductor expands and collapses with the current. This changing magnetic field cuts through the turns of the coil, inducing a voltage in the coil that opposes the change in current. Electrical loads, such as motors and transformers, contain these coils.

The total effect of all this can be summarized in three statements:

1. As the current increases, the magnetic field that it produced builds (increases).

2. As the current decreases, the magnetic field that it produced collapses (decreases).

3. When the current changes direction, the magnetic field it produced changes magnetic polarity.

Table 3–1 illustrates the entire process and introduces some important considerations. This table shows that as the magnetic field collapses it creates a voltage that opposes the original change in voltage. If the current in the coil decreases, the collapsing magnetic field cuts through the coil conductors and induces a voltage that tries to prevent the decrease. If the current in the coil increases, the expanding magnetic field cuts through the coil conductors and induces a voltage that tries to prevent the increase. The magnitude of the opposing voltage created is determined by how fast the current is changing. Remember that the voltage induced is a function of how many lines of flux are being cut each second. Thus, this overall effect is one in which the increasing or collapsing magnetic field induces a voltage that is 180° out of phase with the applied voltage.

| Table 3–1 | | | |
|---|---|---|---|
| **Applied Voltage** | **Current Flow** | **Magnetic Field Created by Current** | **Voltage Induced by Magnetic Field Change** |
| Constant (DC) | Constant | Constant | Zero |
| Decreases | Starts to decrease | Decreases | Opposes change |
| Increases | Starts to increase | Increases | Opposes change |
| Magnetic Field Action in an Inductor and Induced Electromotive Force | | | |

For example, assume an inductor with no resistance is connected to a 120 V AC supply. Further assume a point in time when the collapsing (or increasing) magnetic field is inducing 108 V into the coil. Since an equal amount of applied voltage must be used to overcome the induced voltage, there will only be 12 V to push the current through the conductor. Figure 3–4 shows the 180° phase relationship between the applied voltage and the induced voltage, as well as the vector calculations for the resultant voltage.

Since the induced electromotive force (EMF) appears only during a change in the current flow, the magnitude of the self-induced EMF depends on the rate of change of the current and the amount of the inductance. The induced EMF is also called the counter EMF and is abbreviated **CEMF.** As indicated in the formula in Figure 3–4, the 120 V of applied voltage is the reference point at an angle ($\angle$) of 0°. Add to it a CEMF of 108 V at 180°, and the opposing vectors cancel except for the remaining 12 V resultant at 0°.

**Figure 3–4** Vector representation of electromotive force (EMF) opposing CEMF with the resultant voltage.

## LENZ'S LAW

Heinrich Lenz, a German physicist, discovered that a magnetic field that induces voltage and a magnetic field that is produced by the induced current oppose each other. This is the basic principle used to determine the direction of an induced voltage. Lenz's law states that an induced voltage or current opposes the motion that created the induced voltage or current. The induced voltage and related current are 180° out of phase from the applied voltage and resulting current.

When the current through an inductor changes, the magnetic field around the inductor will change. This change in magnitude causes the field to move (expand or collapse) relative to the coil. The relative motion induces a voltage that opposes the change in current that produced the change in the field. Figure 3–5 shows the phase relationship between the applied voltage and the induced voltage. The basic rule is that inductors always oppose a change in AC current.

It is important to understand the concept of applied voltage (EMF) and induced voltage (EMF) and their respective currents as they relate to the magnetic field surrounding a conductor. Figure 3–6 may help explain that relationship. The following explanations reference the sine wave shown in Figure 3–6 and the numbered points along that waveform.

1. With no current flowing, there is no field.
2. As the current flow begins to increase, the field begins to expand, cutting the conductor in the direction shown (moving outward).
3. As the current flow continues to increase, the field continues to expand.
4. The current is at its maximum and is momentarily unchanging. The field is also not changing (not moving) because of the stable state of the current flow.

5. After having been at the maximum, the current flow begins to decrease (change), and the magnetic field begins to react by collapsing inward (changing the direction in which it is moving relative to the conductor). The field does not change polarity, just strength.

6. The current continues to decrease, and the field continues to decrease relative to the current flow.

7. The current changes direction and is increasing, but this time in a negative direction. Since the current is increasing in the opposite direction, the magnetic field expands outward but with reverse polarity (polarity opposite to what was found during the positive portion of the sine wave).

8. As the current flow continues to increase, the field also continues to expand.

**Out-of-Phase EMF and CEMF**

Applied Voltage    Induced Voltage

0°  45°  90°  135°  180°  225°  270°  315°  360°

**Figure 3–5** The EMF and smaller CEMF are 180° out of phase.

**Directions of Magnetic Flux**

Field Is NOT Moving

Current Sine Wave

No Current No Field

CEMF

EMF

Field Is NOT Moving
No CEMF
Current Is Maximum
and Unchanging

No Current
No Field

**Figure 3–6** The applied current waveform produces resultant magnetic flux directions.

9. The field is at its maximum as a result of the current being at its maximum negative value. The magnetic field is neither expanding nor decreasing at this point.
10. After having been at the maximum negative value, the current value begins to decrease (become less negative), and the field also continues to decrease (collapse inward, changing the direction in which it is moving relative to the conductor); however, the polarity does not change.
11. As the current continues to decrease, the field also continues to decrease.
12. With no current flow, there is no field.

## HENRY

The term inductance is used to describe the property of a coil to produce self-induction. Therefore, a coil has the property of inductance if it will react to an AC current in a specific way. We can predict how the coil will react to a current based on its physical properties. A formula allows us to produce a coil that has a certain amount of inductance, which is measured in **henries**. It is named after the American scientist Joseph Henry. Based on the coiled wire around a circular core, the formula for a henry, symbol $L$, is:

English units: $L = \dfrac{3.19\, N^2 \times A \times \mu}{10^8 l}$

OR

Metric units: $L = \dfrac{0.4 \times \pi \times N^2 \times A \times \mu}{l}$

Where:
$L$ = inductance in henries
$0.4\,\pi$ = metric constant for a circular core
$3.19$ = English constant for a circular core
$N$ = number of loops or "turns" of the conductor
$A$ = area of the core in square meters for metric units or square inches for English units

$\mu$ = (lowercase Greek letter mu, pronounced *mew*) the magnetic permeability of the core material
$l$ = length of the core in meters for metric units or inches for English units

*Note:* These formulas are for circular cores only. Other core shapes use similar but different equations.

### Example

Find the henry value of an inductor with the following dimensions: The number of turns on the coil of wire is 100, the area of the core in the middle of the coil is 1 square inch, the permeability of the iron core is 150, and the length of the core is 2 inches.

**Solution:**

$$L = \frac{3.19 \times 100^2 \times 1 \times 150}{10^8 \times 2}$$
$$= 0.0239 \text{ H}$$

Use the same coil of wire but insert a different core material with twice as much permeability and note that the henry value increases.

Change the core material to air, or no metal material; the permeability goes to 1 and the inductance is $\dfrac{1}{150}$ of the original, or:

$$L = \frac{0.0239}{150} = 0.0001593 \text{ H.}$$

## PHYSICAL FACTORS AFFECTING INDUCTANCE

A number of factors determines the amount of inductance in a coil. The following sections describe those factors.

### NUMBER OF TURNS OF WIRE

The self-inductance of a wire or arrangement of wires is directly related to the number of times the wire is coiled.

To understand why this is, start by looking at Figure 3–7. In the figure, a conductor has been looped into one coil. Using the left-hand rule for the magnetic field, you can see that the fields from each side of the coil add to the fields set up by their opposite sides. Therefore, by creating a single coil, the number of flux lines and hence the inductance have been increased.

Figure 3–8 shows what happens when more turns are added. The physical arrangement causes each coil's field to add to those of the other coils. Clearly, the total number of flux lines and the inductance are directly related to the number of turns of wire.

## SPACING BETWEEN THE TURNS

Notice in Figure 3–8 that not all of each coil's flux lines link all other coils. Some of the flux lines from one coil may link with only one other coil, two other coils, or perhaps no coils. The flux lines that do not link all other coils do not contribute to total inductance and are called **leakage flux.** One way to reduce the amount of leakage flux is to wind each coil closer to the others.

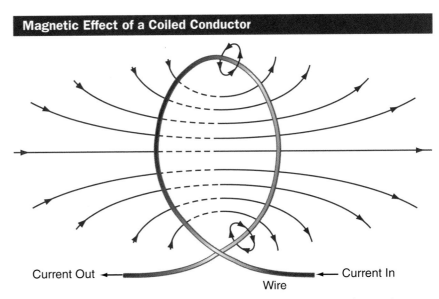

**Magnetic Effect of a Coiled Conductor**

Current Out ← Current In
Wire

**Figure 3–7** The magnetic flux around a single conductor shows the magnetic effect of a coiled conductor.

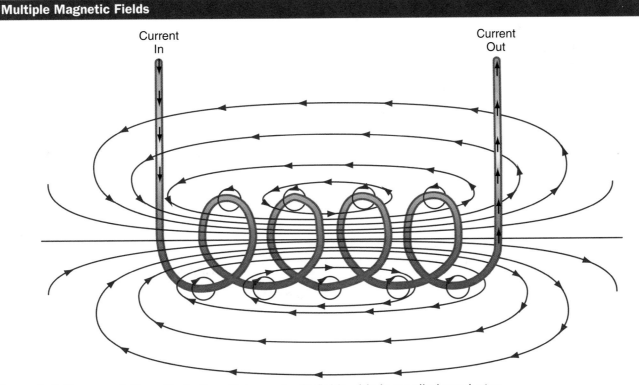

**Multiple Magnetic Fields**

Current In

Current Out

**Figure 3–8** The cumulative effect of multiple magnetic fields aids in a coiled conductor.

## CROSS-SECTIONAL AREA OF THE CORE

The inductance of a coil is also related to the density, or concentration, of the flux lines. To understand this, think of the magnetic field of the Earth. The intensity of the Earth's magnetic field is immense, yet it does not "snatch the watch right off of your wrist." The reason is that the Earth's lines of flux are spread across a vast area. The total strength of any magnetic field is a function of both the number of lines and the density of those lines.

## PERMEABILITY OF THE CORE MATERIAL

Magnetic **permeability** is the ability of a material to allow or conduct magnetic lines of flux. Iron has a permeability that is on the order of 1,000 times greater than air. This means that if an iron core is inserted into a coil, the lines will be concentrated, and the resulting magnetic field and inductance will be increased. Table 3–2 lists

| Table 3–2 | |
|---|---|
| **Material** | **Relative Permeability** |
| Iron, 99.8% pure | 150 |
| Iron, 99.95% pure | 10,000 |
| 78 Permalloy | 8,000 |
| Superpermalloy | 100,000 |
| Cobalt, 99% pure | 70 |
| Nickel, 99% pure | 110 |
| Steel, 0.9% C | 50 |
| Alnico 5 | 4 |

Magnetic Properties of Ferromagnetic Materials

the relative permeability of some ferromagnetic materials.

When all the effects of these various characteristics are evaluated and measured, the formula for henries can be used for a coil with a circular core:

- For other shaped cores (oval, square, or triangular), different equations apply.
- Inductance has no effect on a DC circuit as long as the current is constant. It does have an effect if the supply is turned off and on or when the DC current changes in value.

The amount of voltage induced into the neighboring conductor depends on the strength of the magnetic field and, as importantly, how fast the magnetic field moves. Also, the direction of the induced voltage or EMF is of utmost importance. As shown in the formula for CEMF below, the coil value in henries is multiplied by the change in current ($\Delta I$—uppercase Greek letter delta, $I$—indicates change in current) divided by the change in time ($\Delta t$—uppercase Greek letter delta, $t$—indicates change in time). The negative sign in front of $L$ indicates that the voltage is a negative, or counter, voltage. The more the current changes in amplitude, the more CEMF is generated. The faster the current changes, the more CEMF is produced.

 TechTip!

When the lights go down in a theater the voltage to the lighting is reduced through a dimmer. This used to be accomplished with an inductor. By changing the amount of iron in the core, by pushing the core in or retracting it so that the core became more air and less iron, the inductance of the coil would change. If the core was removed, the inductance changed because more flux lines leaked out and did not cut neighboring conductors.

Therefore, the self-induction would change because of the core position, and the amount of CEMF and the resultant current flow would be affected. As electronics became more prevalent, the old theater dimmers were mostly replaced. The concept of changing the henry value by adjusting the core is still used in various applications.

**Note:** During the performance, theater lights are not completely powered off; even when the lights are called to be off, the dimmer system keeps a small amount of voltage and current running through them. This is so small that no light is produced. This is known as "pre-heat" and is done to keep the bulbs from cooling down before being turned on and off repeatedly. This saves lamp life.

Lenz's law paraphrased states: The direction of the induced EMF is always opposite to the voltage that created the original current in the coil. The opposite induced voltage is referred to as the CEMF. This is sometimes referred to as the "back" EMF, which has the same meaning.

The formula for determining how much CEMF is produced is:

$$CEMF = \frac{-L \times \Delta I}{\Delta t}$$

Where:
$CEMF$ = amount of voltage produced
$L$ = the henries of the coil
$\Delta I$ = the change in the current
$\Delta t$ = the change in time

The amount of voltage is directly proportional to the changing amount of AC current in the conductor and inversely proportional to the change in the time that occurs. The rate of change of amps per second of the changing current determines the amount of CEMF. The faster the frequency of the current waveform, the more CEMF is produced.

 TechTip!

One of the concepts to keep in mind is that a coil does not change its henry value with a change of frequency or a change in the current value. A 100 μH coil is still a 100 μH inductor whether you apply DC, 60 Hz AC, or 100 Hz AC. The way it reacts to the circuit will change, but the inductive value will not change unless you change the physical characteristics.

## INDUCTIVE REACTANCE

Because this CEMF is in opposition to the original (applied) voltage, it tends to oppose the current that is flowing in the coil, making it harder to get current to flow in the original desired direction. Because there is an opposition to current flow, it was originally characterized as a resistance and was measured in ohms. *Be aware* that even though this is still measured in ohms it is not really a resistance but rather a reaction to the effects of the CEMF. This reaction due to induction in an inductor is known as inductive reactance. The inductive reactance is measured in ohms as expressed in the formula:

$$X_L = 2 \times \pi \times f \times L$$

Where:
$X_L$ = inductive reactance measured in ohms
$2 \times \pi$ = constant for sine wave fluctuations
$f$ = the frequency of the AC measured in hertz
$L$ = the inductance of the coil measured in henries

---

### E x a m p l e

If a 1 H coil has a changing current of 1 A in 1 second, the CEMF is a −1 V as proven by the formula:

$$CEMF = \frac{-L \times \Delta I}{\Delta t}$$

$$= \left(\frac{-1 \times 1A}{1 \text{ sec}}\right) = -1 \text{ V}$$

If the same henry coil has a changing current of 2 A in 1 second, then the CEMF is −2 V as proven by the formula:

$$CEMF = \left(\frac{-1 \times 2A}{1 \text{ sec}}\right) = -2 \text{ V}$$

If the same coil has a 1 A change in 2 seconds, the CEMF is −½ V as proven by the formula:

$$CEMF = \left(\frac{-1 \times 1A}{2 \text{ sec}}\right) = -½ \text{ V}$$

 TechTip!

To make it easier to use your calculator, you might take a shortcut. Whenever you are using the quantity (2πf) and the standard frequency is 60 Hz, as it is in the United States, a rounded figure of 377 will usually suffice. Unless you are looking for precise values, the factor of 377 instead of 2πf will get you close to the correct values.

## Example

**Examples of $X_L = 2 \times \pi \times f \times L$**

Find the inductive reactance of a coil if the 0.5 H coil is connected to 120 V AC at 60 Hz:

$$X_L = 2 \times 3.1416 \times 60 \text{ Hz} \times 0.5 \text{ H} = 188.5 \text{ } \Omega$$

Or, using the Tech Tip:

$$X_L = 377 \times 0.5 \text{ H} = 188.5 \text{ } \Omega$$

Connect the exact same coil to a 120 V, 120 Hz power supply:

$$X_L = 2 \times 3.1416 \times 120 \text{ Hz} \times 0.5 \text{ H} = 377 \text{ } \Omega$$

Find the frequency of a 1 H coil connected to AC with an inductive reactance of 150 $\Omega$:

$$X_L = 2 \times \pi \times f \times L$$

OR

$$f = \frac{X_L}{2 \times \pi \times L}$$

$$= \frac{150 \text{ } \Omega}{2 \times 3.1416 \times 1} = 23.87 \text{ Hz}$$

Suppose you calculate the inductive reactance of a coil as 0.5K $\Omega$. The frequency is 60 Hz, as observed on an oscilloscope. Calculate the inductance of the inductor:

$$X_L = 2 \times \pi \times f \times L$$

OR

$$L = \frac{X_L}{2 \times \pi \times f}$$

$$= \frac{500 \text{ } \Omega}{2 \times 3.1416 \times 60} = 1.32 \text{ H}$$

### Current and Voltage in a Perfect Inductor

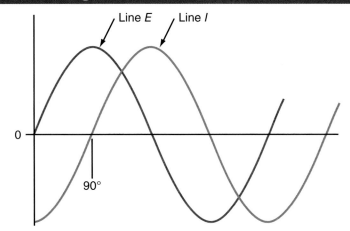

**Figure 3–9** A current "lags" the voltage in a perfect inductor.

## LAGGING CURRENT

The reaction of the CEMF on the circuit is apparent. For example, if you measure the actual resistance of a coil of wire with an ohmmeter, you might measure 6 $\Omega$. If you supply 120 V AC to that coil, you might assume there would be 20 A, according to Ohm's law $\left(\frac{120 \text{ V}}{6 \text{ } \Omega} = 20 \text{ A}\right)$. However, the actual current reading is much less than that, only 12 A. There is more opposition to the AC current than you can measure with an ohmmeter. The "other" opposition is the inductive reactance. You have seen how to calculate this value but you cannot measure it directly. The inductive reactance actually creates a condition that causes the current to lag behind the voltage by 90 electrical degrees. The explanation for this is as follows.

As the current in the circuit is constantly varying from zero to maximum and back to zero, the magnetic flux around the conductor is also varying from zero to maximum and back to zero. As the flux lines reach their maximum value, corresponding to the line current, the magnetic lines are strongest and create the greatest CEMF in the same conductor. The greatest CEMF creates the most opposition and in a perfect circuit would stop the flow of current. Since the voltage and the original flux are moving in unison in the conductor, the maximum flux will produce the maximum opposition, therefore causing the least amount of current. There is more applied voltage than there is CEMF, so the applied current continues to flow. Sometimes this difference is referred to as the differential value. See Figure 3–6 to review.

By referring to Figure 3–9, you can see that the actual current lags the line voltage by 90°. In a perfect inductor, the current lags the applied voltage by the 90 electrical degrees indicated.

Since this lagging effect is the result of the CEMF, caused by inductive reactance, the inductive reactance is shown as lagging the actual wire resistance of the circuit by the same 90° in a vector diagram and an opposition triangle. We now have a total opposition right triangle known as the impedance triangle (Figure 3–10).

The impedance triangle is developed by using vector representation of the opposition forces developed in the coil as a reaction to the AC fluctuations. The resistance of the coil, measured in ohms, is drawn as a vector starting at the 0° axis of a grid, and is on the horizontal axis. The inductive reactance of the coil, measured in ohms, is drawn at a 90° angle to the horizontal, vertically upward. To find the resultant effect that these two oppositions have on the circuit, we need to add them vectorially. To do this we can create a box of the horizontals and vertical components as shown in Figure 3–10. This process is called "using rectangular components," as described in Appendix A, and is used to visually represent the two vectors to create a composite of the two forces in a new direction. The result is the **vector sum** represented by the length of the vector and a new angle to the horizontal between 0° and 90°. Normally, the impedance vector is drawn in the first quadrant on the grid, with the resultant right triangle shown at the bottom right. This typical representation is shown in Figure 3–11.

## IMPEDANCE

To understand the calculations needed to predict the behavior of inductors in an AC circuit, you must understand the mathematics of right triangles and associated elementary understanding of trigonometry. As mentioned before, the $X_L$ of a coil is measured in ohms. The resistance of the wire in the coil is also measured in ohms. The

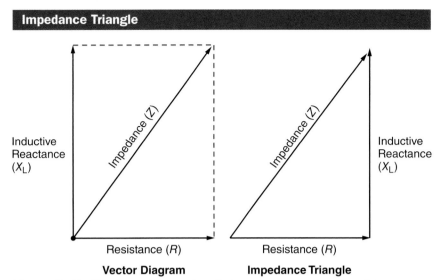

**Figure 3–10** The impedance triangle has components of resistance and inductive reactance, and the resultant hypotenuse is impedance. All are measured in ohms.

total opposition is measured in ohms as well. The total opposition to the AC current is called the **impedance** and is noted in calculations as $Z$. The impedance is not just an arithmetic sum of the two oppositions. Instead, it is the vector sum of resistance ($R$) and inductive reactance ($X_L$) (Figure 3–11).

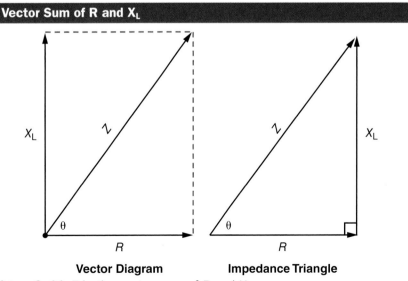

**Figure 3–11** $Z$ is the vector sum of $R$ and $X_L$.

## Inductive Effect

**Figure 3–12** The result of inductance would be to cause the current sine wave to lag the voltage sine wave by 90°.

As mentioned earlier, the inductive reactance $X_L$, or CEMF, is 180° out of phase with the applied voltage and causes the current to lag the applied line voltage by 90° (Figure 3–12). As you know, the actual wire resistance opposes current in the circuit; it is considered "in phase" or is drawn on the 0° reference line as $R$. The CEMF, which is a result of $X_L$, would cause the current to lag the voltage by 90°. This opposition is drawn at 90° to the horizontal and

labeled as $X_L$, as shown in Figure 3–13. Using trigonometry and the right triangle, we can calculate the actual angle of lagging current. It is between 0° and 90°, as represented by the angle theta. The opposition to current that the total circuit exhibits is calculated by how it impedes the current. The total opposition is referred to as impedance.

From the original example of the coil that really only had 12 A of AC current instead of the 20 A expected, you can see that the hypotenuse of the triangle is 10 Ω of $Z$ when the resistance is 6 Ω and the $X_L$ is 8 Ω. The additional information that we can determine is that the current is no longer "in phase" with the voltage, nor is it "90° out of phase" with the voltage. Instead, it is somewhere between the two extremes. The actual value that the current lags the voltage in the circuit is found by using trigonometry to find angle theta in the impedance triangle in Figure 3–14. The number of degrees the current follows the sine wave voltage is the same as the angle between the $R$ and the $Z$ in the impedance triangle. The use of right triangles and trigonometry is needed to calculate the values that occur in AC circuits. Pythagoras developed a theorem that establishes the sides of a right triangle in proportion to each other.

## AC Oppositions Triangle

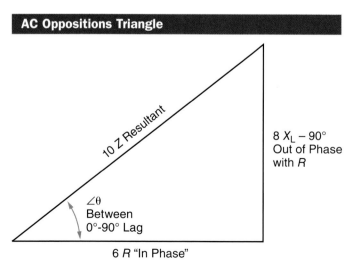

**Figure 3–13** The AC oppositions form a right triangle with $R$, $X_L$, and $Z$ and angle theta ($\theta$).

## Angle Theta and Current Lag

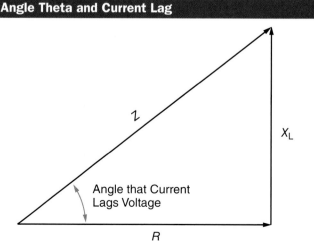

**Figure 3–14** The angle theta ($\theta$) is the angle of lag between the voltage and the current in the sine wave.

His theorem is called the Pythagorean Theorem. The triangle in Figure 3–14 has one 90° angle in the lower right corner, thus establishing the triangle as a right triangle. The horizontal side is marked R in this case, and the vertical side is marked $X_L$. These two sides are identified as either side a or side b by Pythagoras. The third and longest side is the hypotenuse and is always designated as side c in the theorem. No matter what the unit of measure is, the proportions of the right triangle always equate to the following: the square root of the sum of the squared value of the units for the sides, will equal the units value for the hypotenuse. In mathematical form, the theorem appears as the following formula:

$$\text{side c}^2 = \text{side a}^2 + \text{side b}^2$$

OR

$$\text{side c} = \sqrt{\text{side a}^2 + \text{side b}^2}$$

$$\left(c = \sqrt{a^2 + b^2}\right)$$

In Figure 3–14 this would be:

$$Z = \sqrt{R^2 + X_L{}^2}$$

Trigonometry can also be used to find the degrees of the angle formed by the horizontal side and the hypotenuse or to find the angle formed by the vertical side and the hypotenuse. This trigonometric function is explained later in the text. See Appendix A for sections on vectors, scalars, trigonometry, and vector addition.

To help place all the preceding information in context, the resistance causes part of the opposition and the resultant vector at 0° and can be measured with an ohmmeter. Likewise, the $X_L$ causes part of the opposition. The vector is drawn at 90° (matching the $X_L$) and is calculated by the formula for inductive reactance. The total current of the circuit is calculated by: $I_T = \dfrac{E_T}{Z_T}$ (Figure 3–15).

The $I_T$ can be measured as the current of the circuit with an ammeter and is really the current due to the Z of the circuit.

### AC Circuit with Inductor

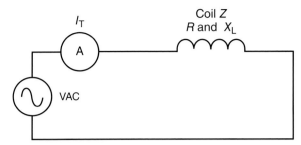

**Figure 3–15** An AC circuit with an inductor has current calculated by using the voltage and the circuit impedance.

### Example

Example of Z in other applications:
A coil has a calculated value of 120 Ω of $X_L$. The same coil has a measured resistance of 50 Ω. Find the impedance of the coil.

**Solution:**

$$Z = \sqrt{R^2 + X_L{}^2} \text{ (Pythagorean Theorem)}$$

$$= \sqrt{50^2 + 120^2}$$

$$= \sqrt{2{,}500 + 14{,}400} = 130 \text{ } \Omega$$

Connecting 120 V AC to the coil in the above example would result in an ammeter reading of 0.92 A:

$$\left(\frac{120 \text{ V applied}}{130 \text{ } \Omega} = 0.92 \text{ A}\right)$$

Measuring across the coil with a voltmeter would result in a reading of 120 V. You can verify the impedance by restructuring the calculation:

$$\left(\frac{120 \text{ V applied}}{0.92 \text{ A}} = 130 \text{ } \Omega\right)$$

However, if you measured the resistance of the coil with a standard ohmmeter, you would not read 130 Ω. We investigate phase angles in more detail later, but for now it is sufficient to know that the actual angle of lagging current is not 90° as you saw vectored between the inductive reactance and the resistance. Instead, the angle that the current lags the voltage through the coil is the same angle as the one formed between the impedance vector and the resistance vector. In the example, you can find the angle theta by using trigonometry.

**Impedance Triangle**

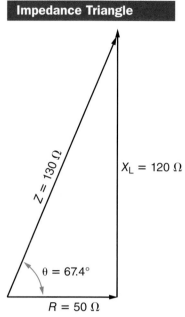

$X_L = 120 \ \Omega$

$Z = 130 \ \Omega$

$\theta = 67.4°$

$R = 50 \ \Omega$

**Figure 3–16** This impedance triangle has the current lagging the voltage by the angle $\theta$ of 67.4°.

Since all sides of the impedance triangle are known (Figure 3–16), you can use any trigonometric function (**sine, cosine, tangent**) to obtain the angle theta. For now, however, use the tangent function to find the tangent of angle theta:

$$\tan = \theta \ \frac{\text{opposite side}}{\text{adjacent side}} = \frac{120 \ \Omega}{50 \ \Omega} = 2.4$$

Use the inverse tangent, or **arctangent** (tan⁻¹), function on your calculator, then, to find the angle theta:

$$2.4 \ (\tan^{-1}) = 67.38°$$

This means that the current that flows through the coil is 67.4 electrical degrees behind (lagging) the applied voltage.

Do you think the current would double if the frequency were to be reduced to 30 Hz? Even though the inductive reactance would go to half of the original value, the value does not change at the same rate because it is the hypotenuse of the triangle, or the vector sum of $R$ and $X_L$.

# SUMMARY

This chapter took the AC waveform and applied it to a conductor that was coiled. The coil may be loosely coiled or tightly coiled on a metal core. The AC magnetic field caused the coil to create self-induction within the coil, causing a CEMF to be induced. The coil, or inductor, produces the back voltage, which acts like an opposition to the applied current. The opposition is measured in ohms of inductive reactance, or $X_L$. The inductive reactance is vectored in drawings of the vectors as a 90° opposition and the ohms of resistance as shown at a 0° vector. The resultant of the vector addition is the total opposition to the current and is referred to as the impedance of the inductor, which is measured in ohms. The formula symbol is the letter $Z$. The behavior of the CEMF is expressed in Lenz's law. This principle of $X_L$, $Z$, and the effects of induction are critical to understanding how electric equipment powered by AC works. The idea that an angle developed by the reactance and impedance of the coils is essential to understanding AC theory.

# CHAPTER GLOSSARY

**Arctangent** Abbreviated *arctan* and shown on most calculators by the symbol $tan^{-1}$. The inverse function of the tangent of an angle $\frac{1}{tangent}$. This calculates what arc has a tangent of the referenced decimal number.

**CEMF (counter EMF)** The voltage induced in an inductor by the changing magnetic field. The voltage induced is "counter to" the voltage, or in opposition to, the voltage that produced the original magnetic field.

**Cosine** Abbreviated *cos*. For a given angle other than the 90 degree angle in a right triangle, the trigonometric function that is the ratio between the leg adjacent to the given angle and the hypotenuse.

**Henry** Unit of measure for inductance. A coil has an inductance of 1 henry when a current change of 1 ampere per second causes an induced voltage of 1 volt. The henry is a value based on the physical characteristics of the inductor (coil). The unit of measure is the henry, abbreviated as H. The symbol used in formulas is L.

**Impedance** The vector sum of the oppositions found in some AC circuits. The vectors may include inductive reactance, capacitive reactance, and resistance. The vector addition of these components results in the total opposition to the AC current flow. Impedance is measured in ohms and is represented by the letter $Z$ in formulas.

**Inductance** The property of an electric circuit displayed when a varying current induces an electromotive force in that circuit or in a neighboring circuit. A circuit has inductance when magnetic induction occurs.

**Inductor** The name given to an electrical circuit component that exhibits the properties of inductance. If a coil of wire creates self-induction, creating a counterelectromotive force (CEMF), then it is referred to as an inductor.

**Leakage flux** Flux lines that do not link properly in an inductor. Some flux lines are lost to the surrounding space and do not complete the magnetic path. Leakage flux reduces the overall magnetic field and the resulting inductance.

**Permeability** The degree to which a material focuses magnetic lines of flux, or the ease with which magnetic lines of force distribute themselves through a material. Permeability is a factor compared to air (permeability factor of 1). There is no unit of measure, just a factor compared to air. The symbol used for magnetic permeability in a formula is the lowercase Greek letter mu ($\mu$).

**Self-inductance** The property of an electrical component (such as a coil of wire) to induce a voltage into itself as the current through the component changes.

**Sine** Abbreviated *sin*. For a given angle other than the 90 degree angle in a right triangle, the trigonometric function that is the ratio between the leg opposite the given angle and the hypotenuse.

**Tangent** Abbreviated tan. For a given angle other than the 90 degree angle in a right triangle, the trigonometric function that is the ratio between the leg opposite the given angle and the leg adjacent to the given angle. Also equal to the sine of the given angle divided by the cosine of the given angle.

**Vector sum** The binary vector operation that yields a vector of which the length and direction are represented by the diagonal of a parallelogram of which the sides represent the given vectors being added.

## REVIEW QUESTIONS

1. The unit of measure for inductance is the _____. It is determined by the formula _____.
2. Explain what is meant by inductance.
3. If AC is applied to an inductor, then DC is applied to an inductor. Will the inductance increase, decrease, or stay the same?
4. Why is CEMF produced in a coil of wire with AC applied?
5. CEMF is a(n) _____ to applied current and is measured in _____.
6. If you increase the frequency of the voltage on a coil, will the inductive reactance increase, decrease, or stay the same?

7. Basically, Lenz's law states: _____ _____.
8. What does impedance mean?
9. If you were to install a second coil with the same physical dimension as another coil but the permeability of the second core was higher, would the impedance increase, decrease, or stay the same?
10. What type of instrument is used to measure $X_L$?
11. Why will the current in an inductor always lag the voltage?

## PRACTICE PROBLEMS

1. Determine the CEMF produced in a 2 H coil if the current is changing at a rate of 0.5 A every 2 seconds.

2. Find the inductance in henries of a coil that has 450 $\Omega$ of $X_L$ when 120 V AC 60 Hz is applied.

3. An inductor has 500 turns of copper wire wound on a soft iron core 10 inches long and 3 inches in diameter. The permeability of the iron is 100. Suppose 100 V, 60 Hz is applied. Find the inductance.

4. If a coil has a resistance of 30 $\Omega$ and a Z of 50 $\Omega$, what is the reactance at 60 Hz?

5. Calculate the inductive reactance of a 0.5 henry coil when it is operating at 30 Hz.

6. If a coil has 10 $\Omega$ of inductive reactance and 10 $\Omega$ of resistance, calculate the impedance of the coil.

7. Find the $X_L$ of a coil if the Z is 100 $\Omega$ and the R is 50 $\Omega$.

8. If a coil connected to 120 V, 60 Hz supply voltage produces 2 A of AC current through the coil, as measured by an ammeter, calculate the impedance.

9. If an inductor has an L of 2.5 H at 60 Hz, calculate the inductance at 120 Hz.

10. Find the angle theta of an impedance right triangle that has a Z of 100 $\Omega$ and an R of 70.7 $\Omega$.

# 4

# RESISTORS AND INDUCTORS IN SERIES

# O V E R V I E W

Inductors play an integral part in the performance of AC circuits. Usually the inductors are placed in a circuit to provide required functions. Occasionally, the placement of an inductor is unintended and the results are unintentional. Either way, an understanding of the interaction of inductors and their circuit characteristics is necessary to gain an understanding of AC fundamentals.

This chapter covers the way in which inductors react in a circuit when they are connected in series. Most of the formulas in this chapter depend on each inductor acting independently of the others in the circuit. The inductors are usually connected in the circuit so that the magnetic field from each one does not induce voltage and current into the others. If the inductors are close to one another, the effects of aiding and opposing fields are discussed. The voltage that a coil induces into itself is caused by the characteristic of self-inductance. The effects of this self-induction require us to calculate many of the circuit characteristics since we cannot measure the self induction directly. The inductance affects the opposition to current, the way the voltage is distributed, and even the way power is calculated and measured.

It takes the added variable of time for voltage and current to change in an AC circuit. The time it takes for current to build up to its maximum value in a coil is based on an exponential curve called the LR time constant curve. It has been established that the number of time constants for a particular inductor and resistor combination is always five time constants. The actual elapsed time in seconds is determined by the inductance (L) and the resistance (R) of the circuit.

# O B J E C T I V E S

After completing this chapter, you will be able to:
- Solve for total inductance in a series circuit containing more than one inductor
- Find total inductive reactance in a series circuit containing more than one inductor
- Solve for unknowns in circuits containing more than one inductor in series when the values of other variables are specified
- Solve for the total inductance of series inductors when the magnetic fields are aiding or opposing
- Determine all the calculated values for oppositions, voltages, and currents in a series RL circuit
- Determine the dissipated power, the apparent power, and the reactive power of a series RL circuit
- Compute the power factor, the phase angle, and the components of the power triangle
- Determine the time required for one time constant and the time for a complete inductive current charge or discharge

## INDUCTORS CONNECTED IN SERIES

When inductors are connected in series, the total inductance is the sum of the inductances of all the inductors. If the magnetic field of one inductor does not affect the other coil's magnetic field, then the effect on the circuit is similar to resistors connected in series. Because coils offer opposition to the current due to their wire resistance and their inductive reactance, the effect is equivalent to adding resistors in series. The opposition offered to an AC current is expressed as the impedance ($Z$) of the coil. Before you can see the total effects, you need to determine how the physical coil determines the total inductance of the circuit. The total henry value is calculated by the formula:

$$L_T = L_1 + L_2 + L_3 + \ldots L_N$$

where $N$ is the total number of inductors in the circuit.

---

### Example

The circuit in Figure 4–1 shows three inductors connected in series. $L_1$ has an inductance of 0.3 H, $L_2$ has an inductance of 0.5 H, and $L_3$ has an inductance 0.6 H. What is the total inductance of the circuit?

**Solution:**

$L_T = L_1 + L_2 + L_3$

$\quad = 0.3\text{ H} + 0.5\text{ H} + 0.6\text{ H}$

$\quad = 1.4\text{ H}$

---

**Three Inductors in Series**

$L_T = L_1 + L_2 + L_3$

**Figure 4–1** Three inductors are connected in series to a 70 Hz AC source.

---

We now know that inductive reactance is represented as a vector drawn at 90° to the horizontal. This reactive opposition depends on the inductance of the coil and the frequency of the circuit. Each coil in a series circuit has the same frequency applied. We can add all the inductive reactances ($X_L$) because they are all at the same angle (90°). See the section "Vector Addition" in Appendix A.

It is easy to show that the total inductive reactance in a series inductive circuit is equal to the sum of the individual reactances. Start by remembering the formula for calculating the inductive reactance if the inductance and frequency are known:

$$X_L = 2\pi fL$$

THEN

$$L = \frac{X_L}{2\pi f}$$

Substituting into the preceding equation yields:

$$\frac{X_{LT}}{2\pi f} = \frac{X_{L1}}{2\pi f} + \frac{X_{L2}}{2\pi f} + \frac{X_{L3}}{2\pi f} + \ldots \frac{X_{LN}}{2\pi f}$$

Multiplying the previous equation by $2\pi f$ gives:

$$X_{LT} = X_{L1} + X_{L2} + X_{L3} + \ldots X_{LN}$$

---

### Example

The inductors in Figure 4–1, $L_1$, $L_2$, and $L_3$, have inductive reactance of 132 Ω, 220 Ω, and 264 Ω, respectively. What is the total inductive reactance of the circuit?

**Solution:**

$X_L = 2\pi fL$

Use the henry values from the example at the left and 70 Hz frequency.

$X_{L1} = 2 \times 3.1416 \times 70 \times 0.3\text{ H} \approx 132\ \Omega$

$X_{L2} = 2 \times 3.1416 \times 70 \times 0.5\text{ H} \approx 220\ \Omega$

$X_{L3} = 2 \times 3.1416 \times 70 \times 0.6\text{ H} \approx 264\ \Omega$

$X_{LT} = X_{L1} + X_{L2} + X_{L3}$

$\quad = 132\ \Omega + 220\ \Omega + 264\ \Omega = 616\ \Omega$

Adding inductors in series with a circuit that already contains inductors increases the total inductive reactance of the circuit. Also, remember from Chapter 3 that inductive reactance is measured in ohms (like resistance) and can be calculated when using Ohm's law as substituted for opposition.

## FieldNote!

When doing quick approximations for the impedance of a coil, the ratio of the inductive reactance to the resistance is considered. If the resistance is less than $\frac{1}{10}$th of the $X_L$, then we disregard the $R$ and claim that the total opposition of the coil is made up of reactance. This helps speed the process of determining the oppositions in the circuit and helps us approximate the degrees that the current lags the voltage in inductive circuits. Remember, this process is for approximations only.

## E x a m p l e

Prove that the listed frequency of 70 Hz in Figure 4–1 is true based on the example on page 60.

**Solution:**

The inductive reactance and the inductance are related by frequency:

$$X_{LT} = 2\pi f L_T$$

Solving this equation for $f$ and inserting the total inductance and inductive reactance from the previous examples yields:

$$f = \frac{X_{LT}}{2\pi(L_T)}$$

$$= \frac{616}{2\pi(1.4)} = 70 \text{ Hz}$$

**Note:** $f$ can also be proven by using one inductor (e.g., $L_1 = 0.3$ H)

$$X_{L1} = 2\pi f L_1 \quad \therefore \quad f = \frac{X_{L1}}{2\pi L_1}$$

$$f = \frac{132 \ \Omega}{2 \times 3.1416 \times 0.3 \text{ H}} = 70 \text{ H}$$

## E x a m p l e

Assume the series circuit in Figure 4–1 has a 48 V power supply with a 400 Hz signal. Assuming no $R$ in the coils, only $X_L$, what is the current?

**Solution:**

$$X_L = 2\pi f L$$

$$= 2\pi \times 400 \text{ Hz} \times 1.4 \text{ H}$$

$$= 3,518.6 \ \Omega$$

Substituting $X_L$ for $R$ in Ohm's law gives:

$$I = \frac{E}{X_L}$$

$$= \frac{48 \text{ V}}{3,518.6 \ \Omega} = 13.6 \text{ mA}$$

**Mutual Induction**

(a)

(b)

(c)

**Figure 4–3** Mutual induction and the coefficient of coupling shows (a) coils with fields aiding, (b) coils with fields opposing, and (c) coils at 90° to each other—neither aiding nor opposing fields.

# INDUCTORS WITH AIDING OR OPPOSING FIELDS

When coils are placed close to one another, the magnetic fields generated by one coil with power applied may affect other coils nearby. The mutual induction is the characteristic that allows us to use transformers. Look at Figure 4–2 to see how coils may be placed on a common iron core to increase the flux linkage. This is just an example to show how the magnetic fields may interact if the magnetic field of coil 1 is linked to coil 2. If the two coils are connected in series you would expect the total $L_T$ to be the sum of $L_1$ and $L_2$. However, if you use the calculation $L_T = L_1 + L_2$ to verify this fact, the answers won't match. You will find the total $L_T$ is either more than or less than the expected $L_T$. If the two coils are aiding each other, the magnetic field becomes stronger and the total $L_T$ increases. If the fields are opposing each other, the magnetic field becomes weaker and the total $L_T$ decreases (see Figure 4–3). This is shown in the formula:

$$L_T = L_1 + L_2 + 2M$$

if the fields are aiding and:

$$L_T = L_1 + L_2 - 2M$$

if the fields are opposing. $M$ is the amount of mutual induction added or subtracted from the total sum of $L_1$ and $L_2$. The amount of mutual inductance ($M$) is calculated by the formula:

$$M = k\sqrt{L_1 \times L_2}$$

The $k$ in this formula is the decimal equivalent of the percentage of coefficient of coupling. In other words, what percentage of the magnetic fields of the coils are affecting each other? If the coils are on the same core and the fields interact 100%, then the $k = 1$. If there is no interaction because the coils are far apart, then the percentage of interaction is 0, the coefficient of coupling is 0, and there is no effect on $L_T$.

For example: If the henry value of $L_1$ is 3 H and the henry value of $L_2$ is 3 H, then we might assume the $L_T$ of these two coils connected in series is 6 H.

**Two Interactive Coils**

Coil 2

Coil 1

**Figure 4–2** Two coils are placed so that the magnetic fields interact with each other.

If the two coils are placed close to each other, have 50% coupling of the magnetic fields, and aid each other, then:

$$L_T = L_1 + L_2 + 2M \text{ (in henries)}$$

First, you must solve for mutual induction ($M$):

$$M = k\sqrt{L_1 \times L_2} \text{ (in henries)}$$

$$= 0.5 \sqrt{3 \times 3} = 0.5\sqrt{9}$$

$$= 0.5 \times 3 = 1.5 \text{ H}$$

THEN

$$L_T = 3 + 3 + 2(1.5) = 9 \text{ H}$$

Now consider keeping the physical spacing of the coils the same and reconnecting the $L_2$ coil connections so that the magnetic field is opposite to what it was originally. Now the magnetic fields oppose each other. The formula becomes:

## TechTip!

The two coils need to be parallel to each other for their fields to create a coefficient of coupling and affect the mutual inductance. By placing the coils perpendicular to each other, the magnetic fields do not interact and the coefficient of coupling or $K$ is zero. Whether you want the coils to interact or not may determine the physical placement of the coils.

$$L_T = L_1 + L_2 - 2M \text{ (in henries)}$$

$$M = k\sqrt{L_1 \times L_2} \text{ (in henries)}$$

$$= 0.5 \sqrt{3 \times 3} = 0.5\sqrt{9}$$

$$= 0.5 \times 3 = 1.5 \text{ H}$$

$$L_T = 3 + 3 - 2(1.5) = 3 \text{ H}$$

## Example

Find the coefficient of coupling if the two coils connected in series are 5 H each. Assuming negligible resistance due to the wire in the coils, we find that the total $X_{LT}$ is 4,524 $\Omega$ at 60 Hz.

**Solution:**

Given two 5 H coils connected in series, the $L_T$ should be 10 H. The $X_{LT}$ should be $X_{LT} = 2\pi fL$ or $(377 \times 10) = 3,770 \ \Omega$. Since the actual $X_L$ is 4,524 $\Omega$, we conclude there is an additive field causing more inductive reactance. We must use the formulas:

$$X_{LT} = 2\pi f L_T$$

$$L_T = \frac{X_{LT}}{2\pi f}$$

$$= \frac{4,524 \ \Omega}{377} = 12 \text{ H}$$

$$L_T = L_1 + L_2 + 2M \quad (\textbf{Note:} \text{ “+2M” is used because } X_L \text{ is larger than expected.})$$

$$12 \text{ H} = 5 \text{ H} + 5 \text{ H} + 2M$$

$$(12 \text{ H} - 10 \text{ H}) = 2M$$

$$2 \text{ H} = 2M$$

Therefore, 1 H = $M$, or the mutual induction amounts to 1 H.
The coefficient of coupling is:

$$M = k\sqrt{L_1 \times L_2} \text{ (in henries)}$$

$$k = \frac{M}{\sqrt{L_1 \times L_2}}$$

$$= \frac{1}{\sqrt{5 \times 5}} = \frac{1}{5} = 0.2$$

Therefore, the coefficient of coupling is 20%.

## IMPEDANCE OF AN INDUCTOR

A quick review is provided here of the impedance calculation of a coil using the $R$ of the wire resistance and the $X_L$ of the inductive reactance to produce impedance. As pointed out in the Field Note on page 63, sometimes we neglect the $R$ of the coil if it is so small compared to the reactance that the total opposition of the coil, or $Z$ of the coil, is essentially the $X_L$. However, if the $R$ is comparatively large or the $X_L$ is relatively small, then they must be included in the calculation.

---

### Example

Assume that the coil in Figure 4–4 has an inductive reactance of 100 Ω and a resistance of 150 Ω. What is the total impedance?

**Solution:**

$$Z = \sqrt{R^2 + X_L{}^2}$$
$$= \sqrt{150^2 + 100^2}$$
$$= \sqrt{22,500 + 10,000}$$
$$= \sqrt{32,500}$$
$$\approx 180 \ \Omega$$

---

**Figure 4–4** A coil with an inductive reactance value and resistance value can be represented by a series circuit of an $X_L$ and $R$ in series.

## Q OF A COIL

The quality factor of a coil is referred to as the $Q$ of the coil. The $Q$ refers to the ratio of inductive reactance to resistance. A formula to find the $Q$ is:

$$Q = \frac{X_L}{R}$$

The larger the ratio, or the more $X_L$ there is compared to the $R$ of the wire, the higher the quality of the coil. In practice, for coils with a $Q$ of 10 or greater, the $R$ is ignored as being insignificant. If the $Q$ is under 10, you should consider the $R$ in your calculations.

---

### Example

What is the $Q$ of a 0.058 H coil at 400 Hz and a resistance of 15 Ω?

$$X_L = 2\pi f L$$
$$= 6.28 \times 400 \times 0.058$$
$$= 145.7 \ \Omega$$

AND

$$Q = \frac{X_L}{R}$$
$$= \frac{145.7}{15}$$
$$= 9.7$$

---

## RESISTORS AND COILS IN SERIES

### ONE RESISTOR AND COIL

When adding resistive elements to a circuit that already has a coil, the oppositions to the current increase. A purely resistive element such as represented by an incandescent lamp adds $R$ to the calculation. This $R$ is drawn vectorially at a 0° angle to the horizontal as seen in Figure 4–5.

**Figure 4–5** An incandescent lamp is a resistive element and is represented by a vector at 0°.

This $R$ is added to the $R$ of the coil caused by the resistance of the wire in the coil. Remember you can actually measure this resistance with an ohmmeter. The $X_L$ of the coil is also part of the opposition of the coil and is drawn at 90°. Now using vector addition, the "$R$ of the lamp" plus the "$R$ of the coil" add together arithmetically because they are at the same angle (0°). Vectorially, add this to the $X_L$ to get the triangle shown in Figure 4–6. The hypotenuse of this new triangle is the impedance of the series circuit. The angle theta ($\theta$), 79.8° in this particular case, is now the angle of the hypotenuse to the horizontal. In any typical impedance triangle, this angle represents the actual angle that the current lags the voltage in the circuit (Figure 4–7).

## RESISTORS AND A COIL

By adding another 100 ohm resistor (Figure 4–8), the circuit again changes. It is represented vectorially (Figure 4–9) with three resistive components and one $X_L$ component. Notice that the triangle becomes flatter and the angle $\theta$ becomes smaller. This means that the current is not lagging by as big an angle as before and the circuit behaves more like a resistive circuit.

## TWO COILS IN SERIES

Now examine two coils in series and see what happens as the total oppositions of each coil are added to the circuit. Coil 1 has 20 $\Omega$ of resistance and 30 $\Omega$ of inductive reactance. Coil 2 has 10 $\Omega$ of resistance and 40 $\Omega$ of inductive reactance.

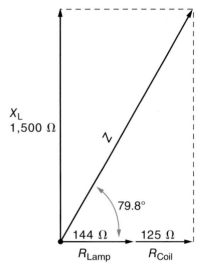

**Figure 4–6** The $R$ vector of the lamp is added to the $R$ of the coil and vectorially to the $X_L$.

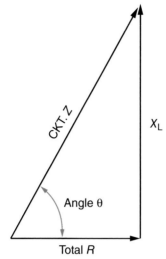

**Figure 4–7** The impedance right triangle contains the three components and the resultant total opposition at the circuit angle $\theta$.

**Figure 4–8** The circuit diagram shows a resistor a lamp and a coil in series.

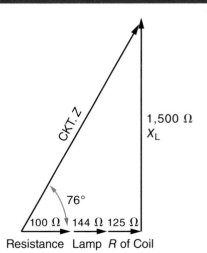

**Figure 4–9** This vector diagram shows the circuit represented in Figure 4–8.

## FieldNote!

Electric circuits are made of various combinations of three basic components: resistance, inductance, and capacitance. Two of these components are in many of the items we use everyday. The components are in series such as in electric motors or in other household and commercial equipment. Where the inductive reactance and resistance are both factors, we need to consider how this affects the circuit. If the circuit is mostly resistive, as in a waffle iron or a toaster, the impedance is the same as the resistance and the impedance triangle appears flat or 0° of lagging current. If the load is a refrigeration motor, the impedance is made up of reactance and the impedance triangle has a larger angle θ; thus, the angle of lagging current moves more toward 90° lag. Normally the lagging angle is not measured in the residential application, but that same angle is measured and may be charged for if it is too large in commercial accounts.

Each coil has $R$ and $X_L$, as shown in Figure 4–10. Adding vectors together allows us to add $R_{coil1}$ and $R_{coil2}$ together and then add $X_{coil1}$ and $X_{coil2}$ together to get a triangle, as shown in Figure 4–11. You cannot add the original $Z$s of the two separate triangles together because they are at different angles. The new large triangle

**Impedance Triangle of Two Coils**

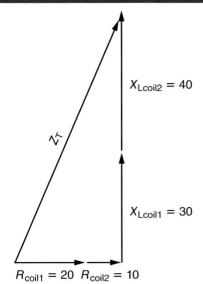

$X_{Lcoil2} = 40$

$X_{Lcoil1} = 30$

$R_{coil1} = 20$  $R_{coil2} = 10$

**Figure 4–11** This impedance triangle represents $R$ and $X_L$ components of two coils.

now has a new $Z_T$, which represents the new circuit total. This new circuit $Z$ allows us to determine the actual current in the circuit by the formula:

$$I_T = \frac{E_T}{Z_T}$$

We can also calculate the angle that the current lags the voltage in the circuit by the angle θ for the total circuit triangle. In this case, the hypotenuse can be calculated using the Pythagorean Theorem. The angle theta can be calculated using the inverse tangent or arctangent ($\tan^{-1}$) trigonometric function:

$$\tan \theta = \frac{\text{opposite side}}{\text{adjacent side}} = \frac{70\ \Omega}{30\ \Omega} = 2.33$$

$$\text{arctan } (\tan^{-1})\ 2.33 = 66.8°$$

## TOTAL *Z*, *E*, AND *I* AND COMPONENT *Z*, *E*, AND *I* IN A SERIES CIRCUIT

As you studied earlier, the impedance triangle changes as each new component is added. More resistance causes the triangle to become flatter (smaller phase angle), and more $X_L$ causes the triangle to become taller (larger phase angle).

**Two Different Impedance Triangles**

$X_L = 30\ \Omega$

$X_L = 40\ \Omega$

$R = 20\ \Omega$
Coil 1

$R = 10\ \Omega$
Coil 2

**Figure 4–10** Two coils having different characteristics connected in series.

The phase angle changes as the right triangle shape changes. When the angle is small, the current is closer to a 0° angle and the current is more in phase with the voltage. As the angle becomes larger, the degree of lag between the applied voltage and the resulting current becomes larger and the current moves toward the 90° lag situation. The total *Z* is always calculated by adding the vectors or by using the Pythagorean Theorem. The $Z_T$ is used to calculate the total current, and the angle θ determines the degrees that the current lags. This current is the same in every component of the series circuit. The circuit in Figure 4–12 has a 1 H coil and a 200 Ω resistor in series. This coil has a very small ohms of resistance compared to the $X_L$ of the coil so that the Q of the coil is larger than 10. In this case, the resistance of the coil wire will be ignored. With 60 HZ applied to the 1 H coil, the $X_L$ is approximately 377 Ω. The circuit looks like the circuit in Figure 4–12. The applied line voltage is 120 V 60 Hz. With 200 Ω of resistance, the impedance triangle looks like Figure 4–12, and the impedance is the hypotenuse of the triangle, or 426.8 Ω.

The angle of lag is the arc that has a tangent ratio of:

$$\tan\theta = \frac{377}{200} = 1.89$$

$$\text{arctan } (\tan^{-1}) \ 1.89 = 62°$$

To calculate the voltage drop across just the 200 Ω resistor, you must first know the circuit current. To find the current, use:

$$I_T = \frac{E_T}{Z_T}$$

$$= \frac{120 \text{ V}}{426.8 \text{ Ω}} = 0.28 \text{ A}$$

Then, to find the voltage drop across the resistor, use:

$$E_R = I_T \times R$$

$$= 0.28 \text{ A} \times 200 \text{ Ω} = 56 \text{ V}$$

To calculate the voltage drop across the coil use:

$$E_{coil} = I_T \times X_L$$

$$= 0.28 \text{ A} \times 377 \text{ Ω} \approx 105.6 \text{ V}$$

If you add the two voltage drops by simple arithmetic, they do not equal the source voltage of 120 VAC. Instead, you need to add the voltages vectorially, as in Figure 4–13. Now the voltage triangle resembles the impedance triangle, and the resultant vector, or the hypotenuse, is the circuit total of approximately 120 V. The answer may not be exact because we have rounded some values for ease in calculating.

**Z Total Impedance Triangle**

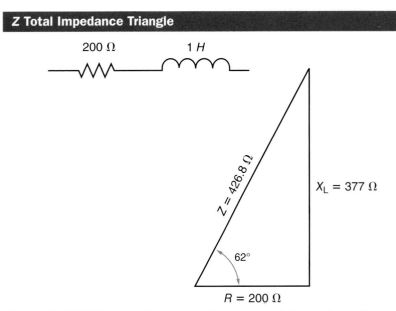

**Figure 4–12** This impedance triangle has a resistor and a coil, as well as the *Z* total.

**Total Circuit Values**

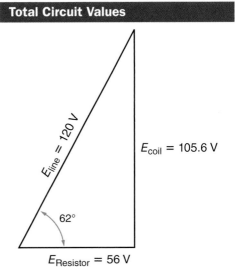

**Figure 4–13** By adding component voltage vectors, you get total circuit values.

**Highly Resistive Circuit Impedance Triangle**

$$X_L = 1\ \Omega$$
$$R = 10\ \Omega$$
$$Z = 10.04\ \Omega$$

**Figure 4–14** An impedance triangle of large circuit resistance and small inductive reactance yields a Z made up of mostly R.

When a circuit containing both resistance and inductance is connected to alternating current, the total current will lag the applied voltage at an angle between 0° and 90°. The exact amount of the phase angle difference is determined by the ratio of inductive reactance as compared to resistance. This is the opposite side of the impedance triangle compared to the adjacent side or $\dfrac{X_L}{R}$. The tangent of the angle θ is this decimal equivalent.

If a circuit contains a large amount of resistance and a small amount of inductance, the resistance and therefore the impedance will be nearly the same (Figure 4–14).

**Power Triangle**

**Figure 4–15** A power triangle is congruent to the voltage vector. The different components of power can be visualized.

# POWER FACTOR, PHASE ANGLE, AND WATTS IN A SERIES CIRCUIT

We now have an impedance triangle and a voltage triangle that have identical (congruent) shapes. To determine the power dissipated by each component as shown in Figure 4–12, refer to Figure 4–15. The power triangle will, again, resemble the impedance or the voltage triangle.

The watts dissipated by the resistor will be the current through the resistor times the voltage drop across the resistor. Using our previous current and voltage calculations, we can determine the watts, or **true power,** dissipated through the resistor as follows:

$$P_{\text{true}} = 0.28\ \text{A} \times 56\ \text{V} = 15.68\ \text{W}$$

The **reactive power** used by the coil is in volts-amperes reactive (VARs) and is not consumed power but rather stored power that is returned as the magnetic fields dissipate. This reactive power is calculated by:

$$P_{\text{reactive}} = I_T \times E_{XL}$$
$$= 0.28\ \text{A} \times 105.6\ \text{V}$$
$$= 29.57\ \text{VARs}$$

You CANNOT use the circuit totals of $E_T \times I_T$ as we did in DC circuits to get the total watts in an AC circuit with reactive values. In this case, if we were to multiply the $E_T$ by $I_T$, we would get a value of the hypotenuse of the power triangle and it would be the total **apparent power** of the circuit measured in the units called volt-amperes.

In this case, the apparent power is:

$$120\ \text{V} \times 0.28\ \text{A} = 33.6\ \text{VA}$$

If you actually calculated the hypotenuse of the power triangle using trigonometry or the Pythagorean Theorem, you would notice a slight discrepancy due to rounding in our previous calculations.

The power triangle looks like Figure 4–15 with watts on the horizontal, volt-amperes reactive on the vertical, and volt-amperes on the hypotenuse.

The actual true power value dissipated or consumed by the circuit is in watts. Apparently the power going to the circuit is the volt-amperes or the apparent power. The power that creates the magnetic fields is the reactive power measured in VARs. Comparing the power triangle with the impedance triangle and the voltage triangle, they will be congruent, or have the same proportions on each side, and the angle theta will be the same (or approximately the same) if we allow for rounding of values in our calculations.

The measurement of volt-amperes (VA) is greater than the amount of watts in a reactive circuit. There is a factor that compares the true power to the apparent power of an AC circuit. This ratio is referred to as the **power factor**. It is a ratio comparison, or a factor, applied to the apparent power in VA to yield the true power in watts. The calculation is:

$$\text{Power factor} = \frac{\text{Watts}}{\text{Volt-Amps}}$$

or another version of the same comparison is:

Percent Power factor =

$$\frac{\text{Watts}}{\text{Volt-Amps}} \times 100$$

The power factor of the circuit could also be found by taking the cosine of the angle theta multiplied by 100. This works because the cosine is the ratio given by dividing the adjacent side of the power triangle (watts) by the hypotenuse of the power triangle (volt-amperes).

Using Figure 4–15 and preceding calculations, the power factor of this circuit is:

$$\% \text{ PF} = \frac{15.68 \text{ W}}{33.6 \text{ VA}} \times 100 = 46.67$$

OR

$$\cos 62° \times 100 = 46.9\%$$

Again, notice the slight difference because of rounding.

## FieldNote!

In geometry you can evaluate equivalent shapes of figures as the same shape with different actual dimensions. This concept is as if you were creating a scale model of one shape by changing the dimensions without changing the look of the original figure. In geometric shapes we say that the shapes are "congruent," meaning they have the same proportional sides, angular measurement, and shape but may have different actual side dimensions.

## TYPES OF POWER

### TRUE POWER

When an AC voltage is applied to a resistor, the current wave shape is a copy of the voltage; that is, it rises and falls at the same rate and in the same direction as the voltage and reverses in polarity at the same time that the voltage reverses polarity. In this condition, the current is said to be in phase with the voltage (Figure 4–16).

This in-phase power component can be calculated by the formula:

$$P = E \times I$$

and is known as true power. It is also resistive power, or power dissipated as heat. True power is expressed in units of watts (W).

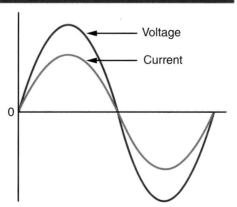

**Voltage and Current In Phase**

**Figure 4–16** AC voltage and current are "in phase" if they hit peaks and zero points simultaneously.

## REACTIVE POWER

In an inductive component such as a coil, when an alternating current is applied, the current through the coil lags behind the coil voltage. By referring to Chapter 3, we know that in an ideal inductor the coil current lags behind the coil voltage by 90°, as indicated in Figure 4–17. This lagging effect is caused by the magnetic field of the coil. Because the voltage and the current are not synchronized with each other, the formula $E \times I$ does not give us true power. Instead, the power is only true, or dissipated power, when both current and voltage sine waves are both positive or both negative. Figure 4–18 shows a 90° lagging current and the power that results from this displacement. Note that there is just as much power above the 0 axis as there is below the 0 axis. The total true power of this example is the sum of the positive and negative power values or zero true power. When the angle of lag is a full 90°, there is no true power in the circuit. This is a theoretical "perfect inductor" circuit.

In a realistic circuit, the angle of lag is between 0 and 90 degrees be-cause there is circuit resistance with which to contend. To find the watts of a circuit with reactive power we need to look at a power triangle such as Figure 4–19. If we know the angle of lag (angle theta), we can find the watts of true power. The cosine of the angle will indicate the power factor. The power factor of the triangle times the VA will yield the true power. Likewise, the sine of angle theta times the VA will yield the VARs. For example, if the current lags the voltage by 45°, as in Figure 4–19, then the power would be developed as per the power curves in Figure 4–20. You can see that at the times when both the current and voltage are both positive or both negative, a positive power wave above zero is developed. The time when either the voltage or the current are not both on the same side of zero reference is a relatively smaller portion of the power shown as a negative wave below zero reference, representing returned power. In this case the percent power factor is cos 45° $\times$ 100 = 70.7. This means that 70 percent of the apparent power is used as positive or true power. The remaining "negative power" is reactive power.

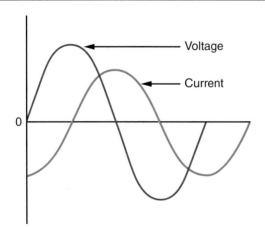

**Figure 4–17** In a pure inductive circuit, current lags voltage by 90 electrical degrees.

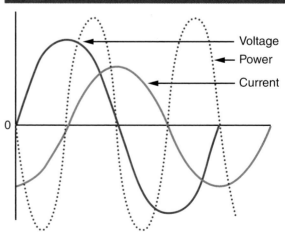

**Figure 4–18** The result of current that is 90° out of phase is indicated by true power that has equal positive and negative pulses that average zero over one full cycle.

## APPARENT POWER

Apparent power, expressed as volt-amps (VA), can be computed by multiplying the circuit voltage ($E_{applied}$) by the total current flow ($I_T$) with no regard for phase angle. Remember that total circuit current is determined by combining the reactive and the resistive components. The total current would be the measured current, as it is the amount of current that is apparently being used by the circuit and therefore is a measurable quantity. For instance, in a circuit with 220 V and total current of 14 A, the volt-amps (VA) are:

$$VA = E_{applied} \times I_T$$
$$= 220 \text{ V} \times 14 \text{ A}$$
$$= 3{,}080$$

## POWER FACTOR

The power factor is not an angular measure but a numerical ratio. This is the ratio of true power to apparent power. If the ratio is 1, or unity, it means that the circuit is a resistive circuit. The opposite is also true: if the circuit has no resistive component and is entirely reactive, the power factor is 0. The power factor of a circuit can be calculated by dividing the circuit's resistive value ($R$) by its total impedance value ($Z$), by dividing the voltage drop across the circuit's resistance ($E_{R\ total}$) by the total applied voltage ($E_{applied}$), or by dividing the circuit's true power (W) by its apparent power (VA):

$$PF = \frac{R}{Z}$$
$$PF = \frac{E_{R\ total}}{E_{applied}}$$
$$PF = \frac{W}{VA}$$

For example, given a circuit with a true power of 1,936 W and an apparent power of 3,080 VA, find the power factor ($PF$). To turn the decimal into a percentage, multiply the answer by 100:

$$\% \ PF = \left(\frac{W}{VA}\right) \times 100$$
$$= \frac{1{,}936}{3{,}080} \times 100 = 62.9\%$$

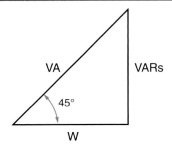

**Figure 4–19** A power triangle illustrates the 45° lagging-power factor and the relationship between watts and volt-amps in an RL circuit.

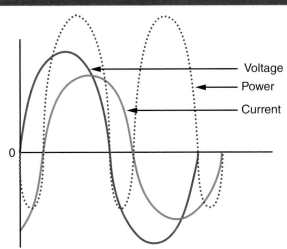

**Figure 4–20** The result of current that is 45° out of phase is indicated by true power that has a predominantly positive pulse over one full cycle.

### Power Triangles

To finish the circuit represented in Figure 4–12, we need to analyze the power triangle that represents the power values calculated. The true power is always represented on the horizontal line of the triangle. The VARs are represented on the vertical line of the right triangle, and the apparent power is the hypotenuse of the right triangle. The triangle is congruent to the impedance triangle and the voltage vector.

**Power Triangle**

**Impedance Triangle**

**Voltage Triangle**

The phase angle between the horizontal and the hypotenuse is calculated by the cosine of the angle, or adjacent side divided by the hypotenuse, using this formula:

$$\%PF = \left(\frac{\text{True power}}{\text{Apparent power}}\right) \times 100$$

Power factor could also be calculated from the impedance triangle because the congruent angles are the same as the angles in the power triangle, so the formula would be:

$$\%PF = \left(\frac{\text{Resistance}}{\text{Impedance}}\right) \times 100$$

The voltage triangle also has the same angles, so you could use the following formula as well:

$$\%PF = \left(\frac{\text{Resistive voltage drop}}{\text{Applied line voltage}}\right) \times 100$$

In all cases, the power factor is 62.9%.

## VARIATIONS IN CIRCUIT VALUES

The series RL circuit changes based on variables. By using Table 4–1, you can see that changing the frequency, the inductive value of the coil, or the resistance can change many circuit quantities and outcomes. Some of the quantities are not obvious as the shape of the triangles changes, and not all values change proportionally. Keep in mind that, in a series resistor and inductor circuit, if only the resistance increases, true power will increase. And, if only resistance decreases, true power will decrease.

## RISE TIME OF INDUCTOR CURRENT

When DC voltage is applied to a resistive load, as shown in Figure 4–21, the current instantly rises to its maximum value. For example, a resistor has a value of 6 Ω, and it is connected to a 12 V source. When the switch is closed, the current rises instantly to a value of 2 A:

$$I = \frac{E}{R} = \frac{12}{6} = 2 \text{ A}$$

If an inductor is added to the circuit, as shown in Figure 4–22, and the switch is closed, the current cannot change instantaneously because of the CEMF produced by the inductor. When the switch is first closed, the current tries to rise to its maximum value, just as it did in the circuit in Figure 4–21;

| Table 4–1 | | | | | | | | | |
|---|---|---|---|---|---|---|---|---|---|
| Variable | $X_L$ | $E_L$ | $E_R$ | $I_T$ | $Z_T$ | $P_A$ | P true | VARs | Phase Angle | PF |
| f inc | Inc | Inc | Dec | Dec | Inc | Dec | Dec | Inc | Inc | Dec |
| f dec | Dec | Dec | Inc | Inc | Dec | Inc | Inc | Dec | Dec | Inc |
| H inc | Inc | Inc | Dec | Dec | Inc | Dec | Dec | Inc | Inc | Dec |
| H dec | Dec | Dec | Inc | Inc | Dec | Inc | Inc | Dec | Dec | Inc |
| R inc | Same | Dec | Inc | Dec | Inc | Dec | Inc | Dec | Dec | Inc |
| R dec | Same | Inc | Dec | Inc | Dec | Inc | Dec | Inc | Inc | Dec |

*Inc = increase; Dec = decrease.*

Use this table to compare what will happen if you change one variable at a time in a series RL circuit. The top line identifies the calculated value, and the left column indicates which way the variable changes. Use the chart to predict the effects of different calculations as the variables are changed one at a time. Use the impedance, voltage, and power triangles to verify trends.

however, the sudden change in current (from zero) causes the inductor to induce a CEMF that opposes the current to rise immediately to the maximum value. Remember that:

$$\text{CEMF} = \frac{-L \times \Delta I}{\Delta t}$$

The CEMF opposes the rise in current and increases the amount of time required for it to reach maximum. As the current flow increases and approaches the maximum current flow value, the rate of change decreases, as does the amount of induced voltage. When the current reaches (or gets close to) its maximum, the inductor no longer creates any CEMF; consequently, the maximum current in both circuits (Figures 4-21 and 4-22) is the same.

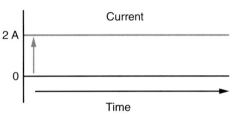

**Figure 4–21** Compare a DC resistive circuit and associated graph of time to current flow after the switch closes.

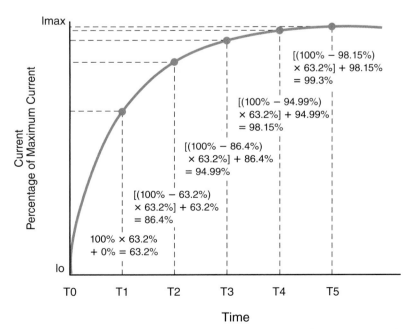

**Figure 4–22** A DC resistive-inductive circuit and associated time constant charge graph showing current flow after the switch closes.

## FieldNote!

Rise times and decay time of the coil current are consistent. The result of this five-time constant consistency allows us to use this effect for timing circuits. Another reason to use the effects of the $\frac{L}{R}$ time is to protect a circuit from the voltage spike caused by a collapsing inductor magnetic field. If we allow the magnetic field to collapse quickly, there is a large voltage produced in the coil and that voltage may ruin other circuit components. If we place a resistor with low ohms in the circuit with the coil, the time constant becomes longer than with no resistor (very large resistance). The effect is to allow the current to decay over a longer period and reduce the voltage "inductive kick."

The amount of time required for the current flow to reach the maximum value is expressed in time constants. In a circuit with inductance and reactance, the time constant is defined from the following formula:

$$T = \frac{L}{R}$$

Where:

$T$ = time constant in seconds
$L$ = circuit inductance in henries
$R$ = circuit resistance in ohms

As the switch is initially closed, the circuit experiences the greatest amount of change in current flow. The circuit reaches 63.2% of the maximum current flow in the first time constant.

As the current increases through the next time constant, it reaches 63.2% of the remaining maximum current. The next time constant sees another 63.2% increase of the remaining total current and so forth. After five time constants, the current has reached 99.2% of the maximum and the increase is considered complete. The amount of change in current for each time constant remains the same percentage from 0% to 100%, and the number of time constants (five) necessary to reach the maximum constant current is consistent, regardless of the size of the inductor and the source voltage. The total time in seconds varies depending on the circuit values because the time constant in seconds varies. This type of current change is called an exponential change. The inductance affects the circuit during charge and discharge. Just as the circuit takes five time constants to reach a value close to the maximum circuit current when the switch is closed, the same circuit also takes five time constants to reach a near-zero value once the switch is opened.

Take a look at Figure 4–23. Assume that switch S1 is closed and the current flow has reached its maximum value of 2 A. If S1 is suddenly opened and S2 is simultaneously closed, the inductor magnetic field will start to collapse.

**Decay Time**

**Figure 4–23** The decay time for current to return to zero is also 5 time constants.

As it does, the CEMF induced in the inductor will cause current to flow through the resistor and switch S2. Initially, the current will be 2 A since the current through an inductor will not change instantaneously. Gradually, however, the current will decay, and it will do so in the same amount of time it took to rise to the final value.

# EXPONENTIAL RATES AND TIME CONSTANTS

The exponential curve describes a rate of occurrences in nature. The curve is divided into five time constants or divisions. Each time constant has a change equal to 63.2% of the remaining difference or value. During the first time constant, the value rises from 0% to 63.2% of its total value, during the second time constant it rises to 63.2% of what is left to the maximum, and so on.

| Table 4–2 | | |
|-----------|----------------------------------|-------------------------|
| **Time** | **Rise** | **Final Current** |
| 1 | 63.2% × 10 A = 6.32 A | 6.32 A |
| 2 | 63.2% × (10 A − 6.32 A) = 2.33 A | 2.33 A + 6.32 A = 8.65 A |
| 3 | 63.2% × (10 A − 8.65 A) = 0.853 A | 0.853 A + 8.65 A = 9.5 A |
| 4 | 63.2% × (10 A − 9.5 A) = 0.316 A | 0.316 A + 9.5 A = 9.81 A |
| 5 | 63.2% × (10 A − 9.81 A) = 0.12 A | 0.12 A + 9.81 A = 9.93 A |

Five Time Constants

### Example

It takes 5 seconds for the current to rise to a maximum 10 A in a circuit. This means that the one time constant is 1 second. Table 4–2 shows the rise times and the total current for each time constant.

An important point needs to be made about this type of current change: Theoretically, the current will never reach the final value. You can see this by inspecting the values in Table 4–2, to see the changes described in the example. Notice that with each time constant the total current gets closer to the final value. Notice also, however, that with each time constant the change in current gets smaller. In this example, the current actually reaches only 99.3% of the maximum. Another time constant would make it closer but still not reach maximum.

## SUMMARY

In this chapter, you practiced solving for the total inductance in a series circuit containing more than one inductor. You also learned how to find total inductive reactance in a series circuit containing more than one inductor. Each inductor has to be physically independent from other inductors in the circuit for these formulas to work; that is, their magnetic fields must not interfere with one another. If the magnetic fields do interact, mutual induction formulas using the coefficient of coupling must be used. Like resistances in series, other circuit unknowns are calculated to make a complete circuit analysis. When inductors are connected in series, the total inductance is equal to the sum of all the inductors.

Once all the inductance and inductive reactance are determined, the circuit must be calculated with all additional series resistors. The total opposition is called the impedance of the circuit. The impedance can be calculated using the Pythagorean Theorem to determine the hypotenuse of the right triangle, or the same impedance can be calculated using trigonometry and finding the vector sum of the $R$s and $X_L$s.

The final impedance triangle is congruent with the final voltage vector. The voltage across each component in the circuit is calculated by the total current multiplied by the total opposition of the component. All the voltages must add up (vectorially) to the total voltage applied. Along with the voltage triangle, the power triangle will also be congruent. The true power is measured in watts, the reactive power is measured in VARs, and the hypotenuse of the power triangle is the apparent power and is measured in VAs.

Finally, the rise time and decay time of LR circuits were examined. It was determined that no matter what the henry value is or the resistance value of the circuit is, the current always takes five time constants to reach maximum or decay to zero in the circuit. The time constant measured in seconds depends on $\frac{L}{R}$.

## CHAPTER GLOSSARY

**Apparent power** The amount of power that is delivered to an AC circuit. It is calculated by multiplying line voltage and line current. It is the amount of power apparently consumed but is not the true power of a circuit with reactive components.

**Power factor** A factor applied to the apparent power to yield true power. The power factor decimal is expressed as a percentage. It is also the ratio of watts divided by volt-amperes expressed as a percentage of true watts compared to apparent volt-amperes.

**Reactive power** The form of power that is produced by the reactive components of a circuit, such as the inductive or capacitive reactance. It is energy stored in a magnetic field or an electrostatic field and is returned to the circuit as the fields diminish. Even though this is a form of energy for the circuit, it is not consumed. It is measured in volts-amperes reactive (VARs) because it is caused by the reactive current, 90° out of phase with the voltage.

**True power** The actual dissipated watts of a circuit. This is the form of energy expended by the conversion of electric energy into other forms of energy. It is the power measured in watts.

# REVIEW QUESTIONS

1. If three inductors are connected in series with no mutual induction, explain how to calculate the total inductance of the series circuit.

2. Explain two different ways to determine the total inductive reactance of a series circuit if you know the values of inductance and the frequency.

3. How is the impedance of a coil used in an AC circuit different from the inductive reactance?

4. Explain the effect of an opposing coefficient of coupling on the circuit inductance.

5. What is meant by the term "lagging current"?

6. Describe what is meant by "power factor."

7. Why is the total time for current increase or current decay considered to be five time constants?

8. Explain what is meant by VARs.

9. How is apparent power calculated for an AC circuit?

10. How is power factor calculated when the phase angle is known?

## PRACTICE PROBLEMS

1. Three coils are connected in series. Assuming no mutual induction and the value of the coils are 0.3 H, 0.7 H, and 1 H, respectively, what is the inductance of the total circuit?

2. Each of the coils in Problem 1 is connected to a 120 V AC circuit at 60 Hz. What is the total inductive reactance of the circuit?

3. If two 5 H coils are connected in series and they have an aiding 50% coefficient of coupling, what is the total inductance of the circuit?

4. Find the degree lag of the current in an AC circuit when a 100 $\Omega$ resistor is connected in series with a coil with 50 $\Omega$ of resistance and 150 $\Omega$ of reactance.

5. Find the circuit $Z$ of a series circuit with two resistors, each 75 $\Omega$, and a coil with 30 $\Omega$ of $R$ and 100 $\Omega$ of reactance.

6. If a coil creates a 30° lagging current and the total $Z$ is 50 $\Omega$, what is the $X_L$?

7. Determine the voltage dropped across the coil and the resistor in the circuit of Figure PP4–1.

8. Find the total $Z$ and the angle $\theta$ for the series circuit totals of Figure PP4–2.

9. Compute the power factor for the circuit in Figure PP4–2.

10. Refer to Figure PP4–2. Assume the voltage is 240 V AC. Calculate the true power, the apparent power, and the reactive power for the circuit totals.

11. How long does the current take to reach maximum after first energized, using a 2 H coil and a 1K $\Omega$ resistor?

**Figure PP4–1**

**Figure PP4–2**

# 5

# CAPACITORS, CAPACITANCE, AND CAPACITIVE REACTANCE

# T O P I C S

# O V E R V I E W

So far, you have learned a great deal about resistance and resistive circuits, and you have learned the fundamentals of inductance and inductive reactance in series circuits. In this chapter, you will learn about the third type of passive element: the capacitor.

Inductance, as you learned, opposes a change in the current flow. It does this by creating a counter electromotive force (CEMF) when the current tries to change. Capacitance is the complement of inductance. Capacitors store an electrical charge. If the applied voltage is greater than the stored charge, current flows into the capacitor. If the capacitor's stored charge is greater than applied voltage, capacitive current flows back toward the source. If the capacitor charge is equal to the applied voltage, no current flows. The capacitor appears to oppose a change of voltage. Capacitors do have an opposition to current flow known as capacitive reactance.

Capacitors are used in electrical circuits of all kinds. They are used to block DC and pass AC, to correct power factor problems in systems, and to set timing constants for various types of oscillators, as well as for a variety of other applications.

Generally, capacitor operation is not as intuitive as inductor operation. The formulas, concepts, and circuit analysis used when capacitors are involved are similar to those involving inductors.

# O B J E C T I V E S

After completing this chapter, you will be able to:

· Define capacitance
· Determine factors affecting capacitance based on physical characteristics
· Calculate capacitance based on formulas
· Identify types of capacitors and their uses
· Describe the causes of leading current in capacitive circuits
· Determine time constants and charge and discharge rates
· Determine capacitive reactance

## CAPACITANCE

**Capacitance** refers to the capacity of a circuit or circuit component to store an electrical charge. This charge is in the form of voltage and the storage medium is the electrostatic field between the conducting plates of the capacitive device. As you have learned, inductors have a characteristic to oppose a change in current as it slows or impedes the current waveform. Capacitors have the characteristic to oppose a change in voltage. Inductors store energy in a magnetic field. Capacitors store energy in an electrostatic field. The effect of capacitors in an AC circuit counteracts the effects of inductors. The effects oppose each other.

Capacitance appears in many forms with various conducting surfaces and various insulators between the conducting surfaces. The closest analogies to a capacitive storage device would be static electricity stored as you move across a carpet or the buildup of charges in the cloud-to-ground lightning storm. An electrical charge of electrostatic energy is built up with a normal insulating material between the two potentials. When the potential is too large or the insulation is too weak, the electrostatic field discharges. We can use this capacity to hold a charge, without breaking down the insulating layer to our advantage, as we use the storage medium to control the voltage needs of the circuit.

Capacitance is measured in **farads,** represented by the symbol F. One farad of capacitance is measured when 1 V applied to the capacitor's plates results in 1 coulomb of charge. Remember that 1 coulomb is a quantity of electrons. One coulomb is $6.28 \times 10^{18}$ electrons. In other words, when 1 coulomb of electrons collects on one plate compared to the other plate, there is a 1 V difference between the plates. As you will see, the electrons do not pass through the insulating dielectric but do exert electrical pressure. One farad of capacitance is a fairly large value, so submultiples of capacitance are often used. A common submultiple of the farad is the **microfarad,** represented as μF. The microfarad is 0.000001 farad, or $1 \times 10^{-6}$ farads. Another common submultiple is the **picofarad,** also known as the **micro-microfarad** or $10^{-12}$ farads. This can be represented by pF or μμF. A less common multiple is the **nanofarad,** or $1 \times 10^{-9}$ farad. This can be represented by nF.

### SCHEMATIC SYMBOLS AND MARKINGS

The symbol most used in schematics is a straight line opposed by an arc (Figure 5–1). Other variations are used at different times and in different circuit designs around the world.

## CAPACITANCE FORMULAS

The general formula for capacitance is:

$$C = \frac{Q}{E}$$

Where:
$C$ = capacitor value in farads
$Q$ = charge in coulombs
$E$ = voltage applied

This formula is used to compare the charge a capacitor can hold per volt that is applied to the capacitor. To illustrate this concept, the larger the plates of the capacitor, the more electrons (measured in coulombs) the capacitor can hold for every volt of potential applied; therefore, it has a larger capacity or capacitance.

---

**Capacitor Symbols**

Fixed Value Capacitor

Variable Value Capacitor

**Figure 5–1** Schematic symbols are used for capacitors, both fixed and variable.

---

| E x a m p l e |
|---|
| What is the capacitance of a capacitor if you have a charge of 0.1 coulomb when 100 V are applied? |

**Solution:**

$$C = \frac{Q}{E}$$

$$= \frac{0.1}{100}$$

$$= 0.001 \text{ F or } 1,000 \ \mu\text{F}$$

> ## Example
>
> What voltage would need to be applied to a 500 μF capacitor to get a 0.05 coulomb charge?
>
> **Solution:**
>
> $$C = \frac{Q}{E} \text{ transposed to } E = \frac{Q}{C}$$
>
> $$= \frac{0.05}{0.0005 \text{ F}}$$
>
> $$= 100 \text{ V}$$

# CAPACITOR CONSTRUCTION AND RATINGS

## PHYSICAL CHARACTERISTICS

A **capacitor** may perform a variety of jobs, such as storing an electrical charge to produce a large current pulse, providing voltage for timing circuits, or making a correction to power factor. Take a look at Figure 5–2. A capacitor consists of two conducting surfaces, usually referred to as plates, separated by some type of insulating material, called the **dielectric.** The plates are opposite electrical polarities (+, −). The insulating material can also use air as the dielectric.

Factors that affect the capacitance of the capacitor include the area of the plates, the distance between the plates, the type of dielectric used, and the number of capacitive actions. The formula for calculating the capacitance of a capacitor measured in farads is:

$$C = \frac{0.225 \, A\text{K}}{d \times 10^6} \text{ in English units}$$

Where:

$C$ = capacitance in microfarads

$A$ = the cross-sectional area of one plate in square inches

K = the dielectric constant of the material between the plates (for air, K = 1)

$d$ = the thickness of the dielectric (or the distance between the plates) measured in inches

OR

$$C = \frac{8.85 \, A\text{K}}{d \times 10^{12}} \text{ in metric units}$$

Where:

$C$ = farads

$A$ = the area of the plates in square meters

K = the dielectric constant

Because capacity of a capacitor is based on physical characteristics, like the inductance of an inductor, we can compute the capacity from the preceding formula without any circuit conditions needed.

These two formulas are derived from the physical characteristics of capacitors. The original formula was created by experimentation with conductive surfaces and air as the dielectric. The experimentation used metric units and the formula for capacitance in farads was found when using "free space" or air between the conducting services.

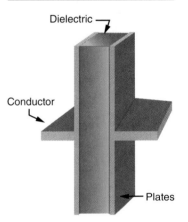

**Capacitor Construction**

Dielectric

Conductor

Plates

**Figure 5–2** The basic capacitor construction consists of plates and dielectric.

FieldNote!

The original capacitor was known as a Leyden jar. Around 1745, a group of professors at the University of Leyden in the Netherlands discovered that an electrical charge could be held on conducting surfaces if the surfaces were separated by an insulator (glass). Therefore, the first capacitors were called Leyden jars. Michael Faraday did extensive research into the effects of electrostatic and electromagnetic fields in the mid-1800s. The unit of measure for the capacity of a capacitor, the farad, was named in Faraday's honor.

The dielectric value, or permittivity—the ability to permit an electric field—in free space has a constant value of 8.85 $\times$ $10^{-12}$ farads per meter. The K is the dielectric constant compared to air. We know the area of the conductive plates (*A*) has a directly proportional effect on the total capacitance, and the distance between the plates has an inversely proportional effect on the capacitance.

Thus the formula:

$$C = \frac{8.85 \times 10^{-12} \, A\text{K}}{d}$$

OR

$$C = \frac{8.85 \, A\text{K}}{d \times 10^{12}} \text{ was derived.}$$

A second formula was derived as a corollary to the original using the English units of feet and inches. In this formula, conversions were made to measure the surface area of the conductive plates in square inches and the distance between the plates in inches. The same proportionality exists, but the constant changed to accommodate different units of measure. The constant for permittivity in free space in English units is $0.225 \times 10^{-12}$.

The formula for farads of capacitance using inches as a measure is:

$$C = \frac{0.225 \, A\text{K}}{d \times 10^{12}}$$

Because farads are cumbersome units to use and a 1 farad capacitor would be very large, we tend to use smaller units such as microfarads. Therefore, if we multiply the farad for-mula by $10^6$ we can change the equation to yield the capacitance in microfarads, as in the following formula:

$$C = \frac{0.225 \, A\text{K}}{d \times 10^6}$$

### Example

Find the capacitance in farads for a capacitor with the following information: A two-plate capacitor has a dielectric of glass with a K of 10. The plate area that interacts with the other plate is 0.02 square meters. The distance between the plates is 0.001 meter.

**Solution:**

$$
\begin{aligned}
C &= \frac{8.85 \, A\text{K}}{d \times 10^{12}} \\
&= \frac{8.85 \times 0.02 \times 10}{0.001 \times 10^{12}} \\
&= \frac{1.77}{10^9} \\
&= 0.00000000177 \text{ F or} \\
&\quad 1.77 \text{ nanofarads (nF)}
\end{aligned}
$$

### Example

Find the microfarad value of a capacitor with the following dimensions: There are two plates separated by an insulating oil dielectric with a K of 4. The plates are 3 square inches each, and the distance between the plates is 0.2 inch.

**Solution:**

$$
\begin{aligned}
C &= \frac{0.225 \, A\text{K}}{d \times 10^6} \\
&= \frac{0.225 \times 3 \times 4}{0.2 \times 10^6} \\
&= \frac{2.7}{2 \times 10^5} \\
&= \frac{2.7}{200,000} \\
&= 0.0000135 \, \mu\text{F or} \\
&\quad 13.5 \text{ picofarads } (\mu\mu\text{F or pF})
\end{aligned}
$$

## TechTip!

The capacitance formulas appear in many forms in many publications. The two versions shown here are for English units and for metric units. You may see the exponents in various mathematical variations such as multiplying by $10^{-12}$ or dividing by $10^{12}$. Some formulas keep the scientific notation intact, while others use the exponents to convert directly to farads or microfarads. Be sure you know which factors are in which units of measure for the correct formula.

# THEORY OF CAPACITIVE ACTION

To charge a capacitor, you connect it to a DC power source and electrons are removed from the side connected to the positive polarity and deposited on the side of the capacitor connected to the negative polarity (Figure 5–3). This accumulation of electrons continues until the voltage across the capacitor equals the voltage across the source. When these two voltages become equal, the current stops, and the capacitor is charged. A good rule to know about capacitors and current is that current movement can occur or change only during the time when the capacitor is charging or discharging. Since there is no "flow" of electrons through the capacitor because the plates are separated by a dielectric (insulator), the current just seems to move through the conductor. As an example, see Figure 5–4. The current flows into the terminal of the capacitor and begins to fill the top plate with electrons, giving that plate a negative charge. The current appears to flow out of the bottom plate that is connected to the positive electrical source, and it draws electrons away from the bottom plate, giving it a positive charge. From the circuit perspective, the current appears to flow through the capacitor, but it does not. The electrons collect on the top plate and leave the bottom plate, which creates a potential difference between the plates. As this charge builds, the poten-

## TechTip!

As you look at the capacitor symbol, you can imagine the top curved section like a tank for water in a water system. Although we know the plates of the capacitor are not curved, this analogy may be useful. Refer to Figure 5–5. When the valve is opened, the water rushes from the full tank on the left (the power supply) to fill the empty tank on the right (the capacitor). At first, the water flow is rapid. As the right tank fills, the water volume slows until the two tanks are at equal water level and the water flow ceases. This is similar to the action of a capacitor and a power source as the power supply charges the capacitor.

**Current Flow**

**Figure 5–4** Current flows to the capacitor but not through the dielectric.

tial developed by the capacitor builds to eventually be equal and opposite to the applied source voltage. At this point, the capacitor is fully charged and the circuit current ceases.

In theory, the capacitor should remain charged forever if the source voltage is removed. In actual practice, it will not. No dielectric is perfect.

**Charging Circuit**

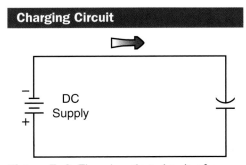

**Figure 5–3** The charging circuit of a capacitor has a capacitor charging voltage curve.

**Water System Analogy**

**Figure 5–5** An analogy compares a water system and a capacitor.

The electrons will eventually move from the negative plate to the positive plate or "leak through" the dielectric, causing the capacitor to discharge and become electrically neutral. This current flow is called leakage current and is inversely proportional to the resistance of the dielectric and directly proportional to the voltage across the plate. If the dielectric of a capacitor becomes weak, it will permit an unacceptable amount of current flow. Such a capacitor is called a leaky capacitor.

## ELECTROSTATIC CHARGE

Capacitance is the ability of a circuit component to store an electrical charge. In previous chapters, you learned that a coil has a constantly moving electromagnetic field. A capacitor, on the other hand, has a changing electrostatic field. The term electrostatic refers to the fact that it has an electrical charge that is stationary. This is the charge that is produced when the electrons are removed from one plate and deposited on the other. This storage of a potential difference, or voltage, causes tension and a pull on the electrons in the insulating material. Think of this as a slingshot being drawn back. When the two sides of the capacitor are shorted or have a circuit, the electrons are "fired" and the tension between the two sides of the capacitor is released, returning the dielectric material to neutral (Figure 5–6).

**Electrostatic Field**

Charged          Discharged

**Figure 5–6** The electrostatic field of a charged capacitor compared to an uncharged capacitor.

## VOLTAGE AND CURRENT RELATIONSHIP IN A CAPACITOR

You previously learned that the counter electromotive force induced within an inductor is given by the formula:

$$\text{CEMF} = \frac{-L \times \Delta I}{\Delta t}$$

Where:
CEMF = amount of voltage induced
   $L$ = the inductance in henries

This shows a relationship in voltage developed across the coil when the current changes per unit of time. You also learned that the term $\frac{\Delta I}{\Delta t}$ is the change in current with respect to the change in time. $\frac{\Delta I}{\Delta t}$ just represents a mathematical form that expresses a changing current with respect to time that creates a voltage drop. A capacitor has a similar formula that relates its voltage and current:

$$I_C = C \times \left(\frac{\Delta E_C}{\Delta t}\right)$$

Where:
$\Delta E_C$ = the change in voltage across the capacitor
   $I_C$ = the current through the capacitor
    $C$ = the capacitance in farads
   $\Delta t$ = the change in time

In the capacitor formula the capacitor current is the result when the voltage changes per unit of time. $I_C$, or resulting current flow, equals the capacitance times the change in voltage over change in time. If there is no longer a change in voltage across the capacitor, no more current flows.

Both of these formulas will be important as you learn about the phase shifts associated with capacitors and inductors.

We can now elaborate on the statement that is used throughout the electrical occupations: Inductors oppose a change in current, and capacitors appear to oppose a change in voltage.

Inductors create a CEMF to oppose current flow, and capacitors build a voltage to oppose the circuit-applied voltage.

## CAPACITORS AND CURRENT

Remember that a capacitor is made from two metal plates separated by an insulating material called a dielectric. The dielectric prevents the flow of electrons through the capacitor. When connected to an alternating voltage supply, current appears to flow through the capacitor. This appears so because, in an AC circuit, the polarity is continually changing and the current is changing direction. This causes the capacitor to continuously charge and discharge.

As a demonstration, look at Figure 5–7. The capacitor is represented by a hollow tube of metal. At one end of the tube is a stretchable membrane that flexes but does not allow material to flow through. As a golf ball is pushed into one end of the tube, the membrane stretches, forcing a golf ball to exit the other end. As more golf balls are added to the left side, more golf balls exit the right side. Since the golf balls all look the same, it appears that the balls are moving through the tube, but they are not. In fact, the membrane is stretching more and more until no more balls can enter the tube. The capacitor is full, but no balls have actually moved through the capacitor.

Before we analyze the capacitor voltage and current relationship in an AC circuit, we need to look at it from a DC vantage point. As the capacitor is charged—or filled—from the DC source, the voltage increases on the capacitor plates and eventually will oppose any further current flow. As we look at this process, we can see the voltage build across the capacitor. Initially, when the capacitor is empty of charge, it has 0 V across it, as represented in Figure 5–8. As the current begins to fill the capacitor, the capacitor

voltage increases; likewise, the current begins to decrease. As we watch the capacitor, the voltage increases as the current diminishes to zero as at point 1. When we compare the graphs of this occurrence in Figure 5–8, it appears as though the current "through" the capacitor is 90° ahead of the voltage

### Apparent Current Flow

**Figure 5–7** A representative capacitor has apparent current flow through the tube but no real current through the tube.

### Leading Current

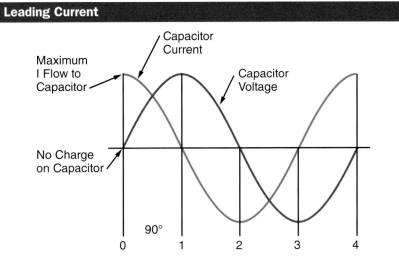

**Figure 5–8** Current leads voltage in a capacitor.

of the capacitor. Now, if we connect the voltage source to the capacitor in the opposite direction, we watch the current flow out of the capacitor in the opposite direction, filling the bottom plate with electrons while watching the voltage across the capacitor equalize to zero as at point 2. If we allow the capacitor to continue to charge, we again see the current going from peak toward zero as it flows to the capacitor in the opposite direction, and the voltage increases from zero to maximum at point 3 in Figure 5–8. This again makes it appear as if the current leads the voltage through the cycle. To complete the process, we reconnect the DC source back to the original polarities. The current goes from zero to maximum in the opposite direction until the voltage across the capacitor is again zero at point 4. This completes an alternation of applied voltage. The current in the capacitor circuit leads the voltage across the capacitor by 90 electrical degrees.

## VOLTAGE RATINGS

Voltage rating of a capacitor is the amount of voltage differential that the dielectric can withstand before puncturing or breaking down. The rating has to do with the dielectric strength or volts per mil multiplied by the mil-inches thickness of the dielectric. As the electric field intensity increases as voltage is applied, the orbits of the electrons stored on the plates actually distort and finally break through the dielectric. The electron flow punctures the insulator and creates an arc through, making the dielectric no longer useful. The overall voltage rating of the capacitor is based on the dielectric strength of the insulating material, measured in volts per mil-inch or volts per 0.001 inch multiplied by the thickness of the insulator in mils. Some example dielectric strengths are listed in Table 5–1.

| E x a m p l e |
| --- |

What is the voltage rating of a capacitor with an air dielectric that is 5 mils thick?

**Solution:**

$$\text{Volts per mil} \times \text{mils thickness} = \text{voltage rating}$$

$$\text{Rating} = \frac{\text{Volts}}{\text{Mil}} \times \text{Mils}$$

$$= \frac{80\ \text{V}}{\text{Mil}} \times 5\ \text{mils} = 400\ \text{V}$$

The voltage rating is extremely important for the life of the capacitor and should never be exceeded. The voltage rating indicates the maximum amount of voltage that the dielectric is intended to withstand without breaking down. If the voltage becomes too great, the dielectric will break down, allowing current to flow through the capacitor between the plates. In this condition, the capacitor is referred to as being shorted.

| Table 5–1 | |
| --- | --- |
| **Kind of Material for Dielectric** | **Approximate Dielectric Strength in Volts per Mil-inch (0.001")** |
| Air | ≈80 |
| Glass | ≈200–2,000 |
| Wax paper | ≈1,200 |
| Mica | ≈2,000 |
| Ceramic | ≈500–1,000 |
| The Approximate Values of Dielectric Strength in Volts per Mil-Inch | |

Since the AC voltage rating is an RMS value, the actual peak value of the applied voltage on the capacitor will be considerably higher. You can calculate this value by multiplying the AC voltage by an RMS conversion value of 1.414.

For example, a 28 V AC value applied to a capacitor would require the capacitor to have at least a peak voltage rating of 28 × 1.414 = 39.59 V.

Capacitors designed for use in AC circuits are considered nonpolarized capacitors, meaning they have no specific voltage polarity assigned to either plate. They operate the same way as in the previous discussion in that they store a charge of electrons on the plates for one half cycle at a time. The voltage applied to the capacitor is still determined by how much voltage can be applied in either direction before the dielectric breaks down. If the voltage rating on the capacitor is designated in AC volts, it is expressed as the RMS voltage that can be safely applied.

Some capacitors have their voltage rating expressed as Direct Current Working Volts, abbreviated DCWV. This tells you that the maximum voltage that the capacitor can withstand is listed in DC terms. If you want to know the maximum AC voltage that can be applied to this nonpolarized capacitor, you must multiply the AC RMS value of the connected circuit by 1.414 to calculate the peak of the voltage. The peak AC voltage cannot exceed the DCWV without destroying the capacitor. AC electrolytic capacitors are not polarity sensitive as they are nonpolarized.

Nonpolarized capacitors are for AC or DC. For nonpolarized capacitors, the voltage may be marked in AC RMS or DCWV. DCWV is the safe maximum DC voltage that can be applied. To use these capacitors on an AC circuit, use the 1.414 multiplier to find the peak of the AC waveform. This peak voltage must not exceed the DCWV rating.

Polarized capacitors are DC only and cannot be used for AC circuits. Polarized capacitors have lead markings to indicate the positive and negative leads. Polarized DC electrolytic capacitors are not to be used on AC circuits.

## EFFECTS OF DIELECTRIC THICKNESS

Dielectric thickness, or the spacing between the plates, affects the capacitor in two ways. As the spacing between the plates increases, the capacitance decreases as was verified previously in this chapter by the formula:

$$C = \frac{0.225\,AK}{d \times 10^6}$$

As $d$ increases, the $C$ value decreases. Imagine a capacitor plate separated by 10 feet of "air dielectric." There is virtually no capacity to that situation. As the conducting plates get closer, the electrostatic field between them increases and the capacity increases. We have found ways to create a very small distance between the plates yet maintain a high degree of electrical insulation to the dielectric by using different insulating materials. As discussed previously, the voltage rating of the capacitor also depends on the type of dielectric and the thickness of the insulating material, as you can tell by the formula for voltage rating. You will note that a larger dielectric thickness decreases the $C$ while increasing the voltage rating (Figure 5–9). The manufacturer of the capacitor determines the dielectric material. The material determines the dielectric constant and the subsequent thickness of the dielectric determines the dielectric strength.

**Figure 5–9** As the distance between the plates changes, it changes both capacitance and voltage rating.

# DIELECTRIC CHARACTERISTICS

## DIELECTRIC STRESS

When a capacitor is charged, a potential exists between its plates. The plate with the lack of electrons has a positive charge, and the plate with the excess has a negative charge. The molecules in the dielectric are like small electrical dipoles; that is, they are more positive on one side than they are on the other. The negatively charged plate attracts the positive side of the molecules, and the positively charged plate attracts the negative side of the molecules. This attraction causes the molecules in the dielectric to twist and stretch. They do not actually move to any great extent, but, like a strong spring or rubber band, they will store energy. This action stores energy in the dielectric of a charged capacitor. It has little effect on the capacitor during AC operations; however, it does have some ramifications during DC testing of insulation (Figure 5–10).

## DIELECTRIC CONSTANTS

The type of dielectric used is an important factor in determining the amount of capacitance a capacitor will have. Materials are assigned a number called the dielectric constant, usually abbreviated with an uppercase K or the Greek letter epsilon ($\epsilon$). Air is assigned the number 1 and is used as the reference point for comparison. Table 5–2

| Table 5–2 | |
|---|---|
| **Material** | **Dielectric Constant** |
| Air | 1 |
| Bakelite | 4–10 |
| Castor oil | 4.3–4.7 |
| Cellulose acetate | 7 |
| Ceramic (titanium dioxide) | 10–110 |
| Ceramic (barium-strontium titanate) | up to 7,500 |
| Dry paper | 3.5 |
| Hard rubber | 2.8 |
| Insulating oils | 2.2–4.6 |
| Lucite | 2.4–3.0 |
| Mica | 6.4–7.0 |
| Mycaflex | 8.0 |
| Paraffin | 1.9–2.2 |
| Porcelain | 5.5 |
| Pure water | 81 |
| Pyrex glass | 4.1–4.9 |
| Rubber components | 3.0–7.0 |
| Teflon | 2 |

Dielectric Constants for Typical Dielectric Materials

shows the dielectric constants for various materials. A change in the dielectric of the capacitor changes its rating. For instance, a capacitor with an air dielectric (1) and a capacitor rating of 5 $\mu$F would change its rating if the dielectric changed to Teflon (2):

5 $\mu$F $\times$ 2 (dielectric rating) = 10 $\mu$F

**Dieletric Stress**

**Figure 5–10** The effects of dielectric stress in a capacitor create an elliptical orbit.

**Commercial Capacitors**

**Figure 5–11** Oil-filled and electrolytic capacitors are among the commercial capacitor types available.

## Rolled Plate Capacitors

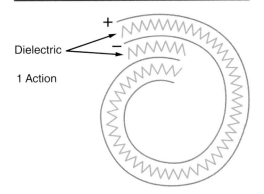

**Figure 5–12** Rolled plates of capacitors have large plates in small physical space.

Figure 5–11 shows some types of commercial capacitors that you may encounter during your career.

# NUMBER OF PLATE INTERACTIONS

Many capacitors are made up of long plates that are rolled into a cylinder, as shown in Figure 5–12. In the formula:

$$C = \frac{0.225\ AK}{d \times 10^6}$$

we assume there are only two plates. If there are more than two plates, as in Figures 5–13 and 5–14, the basic formula can be altered. For instance, look at Figure 5–13 and you see that there are three positive plates and three negative plates. The area of interaction is only where the plates overlap, so the actual area of the plates is only 2 square inches. However, the number of interactions increases to six locations where a negative plate reacts to a positive plate. Count the actual number of plates as seven. The number of interactions is one less than the number of plates, or number of plates minus one ($n - 1$), for flat plates. Rolled plates have an advantage in that the top positive plate reacts with the negative plate twice as it is rolled. The number of actions for an even number of rolled plates is the same as the number of plates. If the number of plates is odd, the number is again $n - 1$. There is no advantage to rolling an odd number of plates.

## Multiple Plate Capacitors

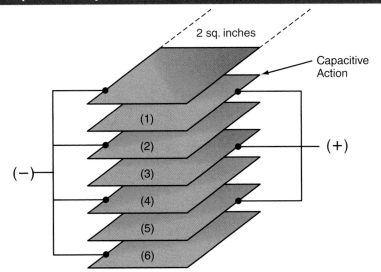

**Figure 5–13** A capacitor with multiple overlapping plates increases plate interactions.

## Rolled Multiple Plate Capacitors

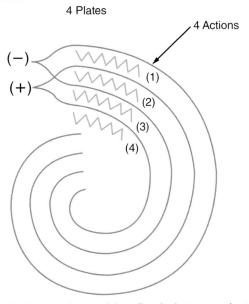

**Figure 5–14** Rolled capacitors with a fixed plate area but multiple dielectrics increase plate interaction.

Now we can modify the basic formula to:

$$C = \frac{0.225\ AK\ (n - 1)}{d \times 10^6}$$

for flat plates and odd number of rolled plates. This formula is universal when using English units, because we measure the actual overlap of plates as the area of plate and the $(n - 1)$ is the number of plates minus 1 to indicate how many times they interact.

## Capacitance and Plate Size

10 sq. inches

(−)

(+)

5 sq. inches

(−)

(+)

**Figure 5–15** Two large flat plates have the same capacitance as four plates that are half the size.

A two-flat-plate capacitor will still have only an interaction of one. From this example you can see that you can reduce the size of each plate but increase the number of plate interactions and still produce the same capacitance as in Figure 5–15.

### Example

Find the capacity and the voltage rating of a capacitor with the following construction: There are nine plates and each has 3 square inches of interactive surface. The dielectric is mica. The plates are separated by 0.001 inch.

**Solution:**

$$C = \frac{0.225 \, AK \, (n-1)}{d \times 10^6}$$

$$= \frac{(0.225 \times 3 \text{ in}^2 \times 7)(9-1)}{0.1 \times 10^6}$$

$$= \frac{37.8}{10^5}$$

$$= 0.000378 \ \mu F \text{ or } 378 \text{ pF}$$

The voltage rating is:

$$\text{Voltage rating} = \text{Volts per mil} \times \text{Mils thickness}$$

$$= \frac{2,000}{1 \text{ Mil}} \times 1$$

$$= 2,000 \text{ V}$$

## CAPACITOR TYPES

There are general classifications of capacitors. The variable capacitor, as seen in Figure 5–16, is sometimes thought of as the adjustable capacitor that is used to tune radio frequency circuits. The plates were set so the area that interacted with the opposite polarity plates could be adjusted to increase or decrease the effective plate area. As the plate area increased, the $C$ increased; similarly, when there was less plate interaction the $C$ decreased. In this example, the dielectric is air. The formula:

$$C = \frac{0.225 \, AK \, (n-1)}{d \times 10^6}$$

confirms that by keeping the distance between the plates the same but changing the effective area of plates ($A$) the capacity will change.

Another method of creating a variable capacitor is to adjust the distance between the plates. This method of adjusting the capacitance uses a small screw to physically move one plate closer to, or farther away from, a stationary plate. The capacitor style is referred to as a "trimmer" capacitor. As the screw is screwed in, the distance between the plates is reduced, decreasing $d$ in the formula and increasing the capacitance. Conversely, as the distance between plates is increased by turning the screw out, the capacitance decreases.

The second classification is the fixed capacitor. In this case, the capacitance is determined by the manufacturer using all the parameters previously discussed. Once the manufacturing is complete, the capacity is determined and the capacitor is marked.

## Variable Capacitor

**Figure 5–16** A variable capacitor with variable area of the plate interaction is used to tune circuits.

Other classifications of capacitors refer to the method of connection to the circuit. Polarized capacitors are capacitors that have definite positive and negative connection points for use in DC circuits. Nonpolarized capacitors can be used in DC and AC circuits without regard to the electrical polarity connected, which is imperative for AC circuits.

## ELECTROLYTIC

Electrolytic capacitors are used in many applications. They have a large capacity compared to their size. They are typically polarity sensitive, meaning they have a positive and a negative terminal but are also found in AC electrolytic values. A polarized electrolytic capacitor usually consists of two foil plates rolled into a metal can. As shown in Figure 5–17, the aluminum can housing forms one electrode and the other plate is aluminum foil rolled into the can. The dielectric is created when a current is passed through the capacitor when the foil is immersed in an electrolyte of a borax solution. As the current flows, it creates a very thin layer of aluminum oxide on the plates. This aluminum oxide is the dielectric and is extremely thin. Because it is so thin, the capacitance values can be very high compared to the space required. However, as you have learned, the voltage rating is decreased proportionally to the thickness of the dielectric. AC electrolytics again have high capacity for space required, but the dielectric is formed from two directions on the plates so that AC can be applied without damaging the dielectric. These are routinely used as starting capacitors on motors.

## OIL-FILLED CAPACITORS

As the name implies, oil-filled capacitors are filled with an insulating oil that works as the dielectric. The plates are typically rolled aluminum and are separated by a paper saturated in oil. They typically have lower capacity than electrolytics for the same physical size but have higher voltage ratings. This type of capacitor is used in motor duty, typically as a running capacitor.

## TechTip!

Ceramic, tantalum, and film capacitors (Figure 5–18) are most commonly used in electronic circuits. The theory of how they are used is exactly the same as the theory you have learned; however, the small size and specific applications will be best discussed in a text on electronic applications.

## TESTING CAPACITORS

Capacitors can be tested in a variety of ways. The basic theory of testing and knowledge of how a capacitor operates should guide you in the application of the test. Capacitators need to be tested for opens, shorts, or leaky conditions. As an example, we discuss how to test an AC electrolytic capacitor that may be the cause of motor starting problems. To do this, we use a meter set to ohms. *Note:* Be sure power is off, the capacitor is disconnected, and that the capacitor does not have a stored charge. Use an analog meter (easiest) and connect the ohmmeter to the capacitor. The meter should immediately go to very low ohms, indicating a large current flow from the battery in the meter to the capacitor. As you leave the meter connected, the meter will indicate more and more ohms as the capacitor charges and current flow decreases. Finally, when the capacitor is fully charged, the current flow ceases and the meter indicates infinite ohms.

**Polarized/Nonpolarized Capacitors**

**Figure 5–17** Polarized and nonpolarized capacitors look different.

**Capacitor Types**

**Figure 5–18** Tantalum, mica, and ceramic capacitors.

**Capacitance Check**

**Figure 5–19** Many newer digital multimeters have a built-in capacitance check feature.

**Fully Charged Capacitor**

**Figure 5–20** After five time constants, the capacitor will be fully charged to the supply voltage level.

If this happens, the capacitor is okay. A shorted capacitor will have a large current flow and will constantly indicate very low ohms. A leaky capacitor will charge slightly—indicated by a moderate ohm reading—but will never go to infinite. It is leaking some current through the dielectric.

Once these basic tests give a general indication of the capacitor's status, you can determine its capacity value by measuring the AC current and the voltage across the capacitor. The capacitive reactance is determined, and the capacitance can be calculated from

that reactance value. This is discussed later in this chapter. Another common method to test capacitance is done directly with a digital meter. Many digital meters such as that shown in Figure 5–19 have capacitance measurements built into the meter functions.

## CHARGE AND DISCHARGE RATES

Capacitors connected in series with resistors charge and discharge at an exponential rate, the curve of which is divided into five time constants. During each time constant, the voltage changes by 63.2% of the amount left to reach the fully charged state. During the first time constant, the voltage across the capacitor reaches 63.2% of the supply voltage connected across it. During the next time constant, the capacitor reaches a higher voltage equal to 63.2% of the voltage left between the first time constant voltage and the supply voltage, which is then added to the voltage reached in the first time constant, for a total of 86.4% of the supply voltage.

For example, assume that the capacitor in Figure 5–20 requires 10 seconds to reach the supply voltage of 20 V.

**FieldNote!**

Capacitors are often used for starting single-phase motors. The capacitor is used to create a shift in the phase angle of the current delivered to the starting winding of the capacitor start motor. These capacitors are susceptible to drying out and failing, creating a condition that prevents the motor from starting but not from running. The starting capacitors used are AC electrolytic and should be tested if a capacitor start motor fails to start. Even though these are AC electrolytic, the test with a meter will still determine if the capacitor is shorted, open, or leaky. If a replacement capacitor is needed, an AC motor reference will often have a chart to help determine the approximate microfarad rating.

**Table 5–3**

| Time Constant | Calculation | Final Voltage |
|---|---|---|
| 1 | 63.2% of 20 V = 12.64 | 12.64 V |
| 2 | (20 − 12.64) × 63.2% = 4.65 | 12.64 + 4.65 = 17.29 V |
| 3 | (20 − 17.29) × 63.2% = 1.71 | 17.29 + 1.71 = 19.00 V |
| 4 | (20 − 19.00) × 63.2% = 0.632 | 19.00 + 0.632 = 19.632 V |
| 5 | (20 − 19.632) × 63.2% = 0.232 | 19.632 + 0.232 = 19.864 V |

Table Showing the Calculation for an Exponential Charge of a Capacitor

The capacitor can charge only to the system supply voltage. Table 5–3 shows the voltages across the capacitor during the 10 seconds.

As you can see, by the end of the fifth time constant, the voltage across the capacitor has reached 99.3% of the total voltage. If this continues past the fifth time constant, the voltage will continue to get closer to the final value; however, it will never reach the maximum. Notice that the voltage charge on the capacitor behaves in exactly the same way as the current flow through an inductor. Figure 5–21 shows the entire curve.

The capacitor discharges in the same manner. At the end of the first time constant, the voltage decreases by 63.2% of its charged value.

**Figure 5–21** A voltage charge time curve is based on the time constants.

## Voltage Discharge Curve

**Figure 5–22** Voltage discharge curve based on the number of time constants.

Of equal importance is determining how long a time constant is in seconds. The length of one time constant is dependent on the size of the capacitor and the resistance in series with the capacitor; it is given by the formula:

$$\tau = R \times C$$

Where:

$\tau$ = one time constant in seconds
$R$ = circuit resistance in ohms
$C$ = circuit capacitance in farads

The lowercase Greek letter tau ($\tau$) is used to designate the time required for one time constant. The letter $T$ can also be used to indicate time.

### Example

In a circuit with a 10 kΩ resistor and a 20 μF capacitor, how long is one time constant? How long will it take for the capacitor to fully charge?

**Solution:**

$$\tau = R \times C$$
$$= 10 \text{ k}\Omega \times 20 \text{ μF} = 0.2 \text{ second}$$

To completely charge:

$$\tau \text{ total} = 5 \times \tau = 1 \text{ second}$$

The voltage continues to drop until it reaches approximately zero, when five time constants have elapsed (Figure 5–22).

Knowing that five time constants are required to reach the maximum charge is only half the picture.

### Example

If a 50 μF capacitor is fully charged to 100 V and a 10 kΩ resistor is connected to the discharge path, how long will it take to discharge to approximately 5 V?

**Solution:**

$$\tau = R \times C$$
$$= 10 \text{ k}\Omega \times 50 \text{ μF}$$
$$= 0.5 \text{ second}$$

Referring to Figure 5–22, 5 V remaining on the capacitor is about 5% of the initial voltage. This corresponds to three time constants of discharge. $3 \tau = 3 \times 0.5$ second, or 1.5 seconds to discharge to nearly 5 V.

## FieldNote!

When working on capacitive circuits, it is essential to your safety to always be sure capacitors are totally discharged before working to connect or disconnect them. If you know what resistor will be used to create the discharge path, you can approximate the time needed to discharge the capacitor. Some capacitor circuits have a discharge resistor available to automatically discharge the capacitor. An electrician may sometimes use a copper wire or even a screwdriver to provide the discharge path. This "shorting process" can create a large and sometimes dangerous arc and is not a recommended method of discharge.

**Capacitor Charge**

Maximum Current

0.00

Amps

100 VDC

$X_C = 0\ \Omega$

100.00

Amps

100 VDC

**Figure 5–23** As the capacitor charges, it opposes the line voltage and reacts to reduce line current.

# CAPACITIVE REACTANCE

To better explain the effects that a capacitor has on an AC circuit, we can look at a circuit with one-half of the AC sinewave applied. In Figure 5–23, we apply DC to illustrate the effect of charging the capacitor during a one-half cycle. This illustration shows that as the capacitor becomes fully charged, the current in the circuit goes to zero. The opposition increases from zero opposition at first, to maximum opposition when fully charged. This effective opposition of the charged capacitor to the current in the circuit is identified as an ohmic value. The opposition is caused by the reac-tion of the capacitor in the circuit. The opposition to the current is called **capacitive reactance.** Although there is no capacitive reactance in a DC circuit, it helps visualize what happens as the capacitor continually charges and discharges one-half cycle at a time.

You have learned that this is similar to the opposing voltage, or counter-voltage, in an inductive circuit caused by an inductor. In a perfect capacitor, the current leads the voltage by 90 electrical degrees. Capacitive reactance, like inductive reactance, is measured in ohms, but the symbol for reactance is $X_C$ and again is measured in ohms. The $X_C$ is added to other components by vector addition.

**Capacitive Reactance Vectors**

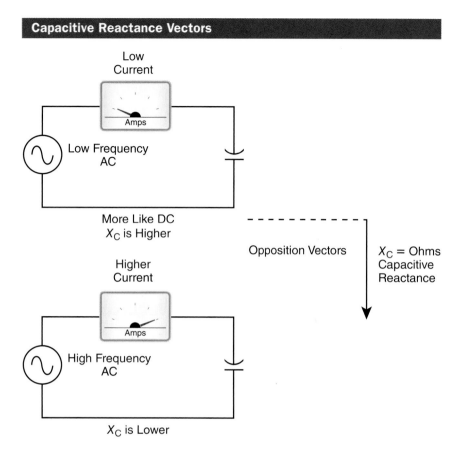

**Figure 5–24** The vector for ohms of capacitive reactance is vectored down from the horizontal reference.

**Capacitor Charge Cycle**

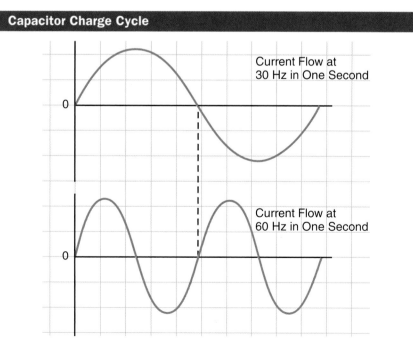

**Figure 5–25** Effects of increased frequency on the charge cycle of a capacitor can be seen graphically.

Because the current actually leads the voltage, the $X_C$ is vectored exactly opposite to the inductive reactance, or 90° down from the horizontal (Figure 5–24). The vector diagram in Figure 5–24 is used to compare with the vector diagram of a circuit with $X_L$. Although there is some internal resistance to the capacitor, it is typically disregarded because it is so small compared to the reactance.

## CAPACITIVE REACTANCE FORMULA

### Frequency Effects on Capacitive Reactance

The capacitive reactance in a circuit decreases as the frequency of the circuit increases. You will examine this based on the reaction of current flow in a capacitive circuit and how that current flow would be an indicator of the capacitive reactance. As you recall, current is the rate of flow of electrons. If you connect a capacitor and a resistor to an AC circuit and measure the current that flows with a 30 Hz source compared to a 60 Hz source for the same capacitor and resistor and the same voltage level, you find twice the current at 60 Hz compared to 30 Hz. This means the $X_C$ is inversely proportional to the frequency. Referring to Figure 5–25, you can see that, for a given time period, the capacitor would charge to maximum, discharge to zero, charge to maximum in the reverse direction, and then discharge back to zero in one cycle of the 30 Hz waveform. This would produce a specific amount of AC current flow. Now consider the 60 Hz waveform. You can verify that for the same time period the capacitor would go through two complete cycles of the same charge and discharge cycle. Therefore, for the same time period, twice as much current appears to flow in the circuit. If the current is twice as much with the same components and the same voltage level, the opposition to the current at 60 Hz must have gone to one-half the original opposition at 30 Hz.

The formula for verifying this effect is:

$$I = \frac{Q}{t}$$

Where:
 $I$ = current flow
 $Q$ = charge in coulombs
 $t$ = time in seconds

Using Ohm's law, you know that with the voltage the same in both situations the current and the opposition are inversely proportional.

A more common formula for calculating the $X_C$ in ohms is based on the size of the capacitor in farads, the frequency of charge and discharge, and the constant for a sine wave value expressed as:

$$X_C = \frac{1}{2\pi fC}$$

or, more simply,

$$X_C = \frac{159,000}{fC_{\text{microfarads}}}$$

Where:
 $X_C$ = capacitive reactance
 $\pi$ = 3.1416
 $f$ = frequency in hertz
 $C$ = capacitance in farads

---

## Example

A capacitor circuit has a 35 µF capacitor connected to a 48 V, 60 Hz line. How much current will flow through this line?

**Solution:**

First, find the capacitive reactance. The $C$ in the formula is in farads, so the conversion from µF to farads is multiplied by $10^{-6}$. Thus, the line has $35 \times 10^{-6}$ farads:

$$X_C = \frac{1}{2\pi fC}$$

$$= \frac{1}{[2 \times 3.1416 \times 60 \times (35 \times 10^{-6})]}$$

$$= \frac{1}{0.013195}$$

$$= 75.79 \ \Omega$$

If we use the equivalent formula mentioned in the Tech Tip on the next page, the equation solution is:

$$X_C = \frac{10^6}{2\pi fC_{\text{microfarads}}}$$

$$= \frac{10^6}{2 \times 3.1416 \times 60 \times 35}$$

Then, 377 can be substituted for $(2\pi f)$ when calculating at 60 Hz:

$$X_C = \frac{10^6}{377 \times 35}$$

$$= \frac{10^6}{13,195}$$

$$= 75.786 \ \Omega \text{ or } 75.79 \ \Omega, \text{ same as original formula}$$

Now use Ohm's law to calculate the current:

$$I = \frac{E}{X_C}$$

$$= \frac{48 \text{ V}}{75.79 \ \Omega}$$

$$= 0.63 \text{ A}$$

## TechTip!

Although this is the recognized formula for $X_C$, it assumes the unit of measure for capacitance is in farads. As discussed previously, the farad is a large unit of measure and we would rarely see a farad capacitor. The microfarad is a more common unit, especially for electricians, and we can more conveniently use an altered formula for ease in calculations. The formula:

$$X_C = \frac{10^6}{2\pi f C_{microfarads}}$$

is much easier to use when the capacitor is already in microfarads (µF). A simplified version would be:

$$X_C = \frac{159,000}{f C_{microfarads}}$$

## CALCULATING CAPACITANCE FROM CAPACITIVE REACTANCE

Now that you have calculated capacitive reactance, you can determine the capacitance of any capacitor if you already know the capacitive reactance. Note that capacitance is also dependent on frequency and $X_C$. The formula is:

$$C = \frac{1}{2\pi f X_C}$$

**Capacitor Circuit**

0.36 µF

12 V
200 Hz

**Figure 5–26** This capacitor circuit has a 0.36 µF capacitor and 200 Hz supply.

---

### Example

A capacitor is connected to a 220 V, 60 Hz line. The ammeter on the line indicates 3.2 A. What is the capacitance value of the capacitor?

**Solution:**

The first step is to calculate capacitive reactance using Ohm's law. Since:

$$X_C = \frac{E}{I}$$

THEN

$$X_C = \frac{220V}{3.2\ A}$$

$$= 68.75\ \Omega$$

$$C = \frac{1}{2\pi f X_C}$$

$$= \frac{1}{(2 \times 3.1416 \times 60 \times 68.75\ \Omega)}$$

$$= \frac{1}{25,918}$$

$$= 3.86 \times 10^{-5}\ or\ 38.6\ µF$$

---

### Example

Take a look at Figure 5–26. What is the reactance of a 0.36 µF capacitor connected to a source that delivers 12 V at 200 Hz?

**Solution:**

$$X_C = \frac{1}{2\pi f C}$$

$$= \frac{1}{(2 \times 3.1416 \times 200 \times 0.00000036}$$

$$= \frac{1}{0.00045239}$$

$$= 2,210.5\ \Omega$$

What is the current in this circuit?

$$I = \frac{E}{X_C}$$

$$= \frac{12\ V}{2,210.5\ \Omega}$$

$$= 0.00543\ A,\ or\ 5.4\ \ mA$$

# SUMMARY

Capacitors are devices used to store a charge, and that stored charge has the potential to create current flow. This potential is the voltage stored in the capacitor. The ability to store a charge and become a voltage source gives it the characteristic that appears to oppose a change in circuit voltage. Capacitors are manufactured in many ways, but all have the same physical characteristics. The capacitor is made up of conducting plates separated by an insulator known as a dielectric. In a capacitive circuit, the current appears to flow through the capacitor because of the continuous increase and decrease of voltage and the continuous change in polarity in an AC circuit. The current flows back and forth in the circuit but does not flow through the capacitor. Electrons build up on one side of the capacitor and then on the other side as current alternates. Figure 5–27 illustrates current flow for half this cycle.

Because of the relationship of the apparent flow of current through the capacitor, and the voltage that appears across the capacitor, the capacitive current leads the capacitive voltage by 90°. This is an important point, as the capacitive leading current is 180° out of phase—exactly opposite to the effects of an inductor, which causes current to lag behind the voltage by 90°.

Time constants play an important part in timing circuits and in the basic understanding of how and why capacitors operate in various AC or DC circuits. The rate at which a capacitor charges or discharges is dependent upon the series resistance and the actual capacity of the capacitor. $R \times C$ allows us to calculate the seconds for one time constant, and a full charge or discharge is considered to be five time constants.

The current flow in the capacitive circuit is limited by capacitive reactance. Capacitive reactance is inversely proportional to the capacitance of the capacitor and the frequency of the line voltage source. Capacitive reactance is similar to inductive reactance, as it is measured in ohms and can be substituted for resistance in the Ohm's law formula. In a pure capacitive circuit, the current leads the applied voltage by 90°.

If the frequency of a circuit is increased, the capacitive reactance is decreased. If the capacitance is decreased, the capacitive reactance is increased.

**One Half-Cycle Current**

**Figure 5–27** One-half cycle current flow moves "through" the capacitor.

## CHAPTER GLOSSARY

**Capacitance** 1. The property of a circuit element that permits it to store charge. The part of the circuit exhibiting capacitance. 2. The unit of measure is the farad and the formula variable is "C." The ratio of the electric charge transferred from one to the other of a pair of conductors to the resulting potential difference between them. (Excerpted from American Heritage Talking Dictionary. Copyright ©1997 The Learning Company, Inc. All Rights Reserved.)

**Capacitive reactance** The opposition to AC current flow caused by a capacitor. The symbol for capacitive reactance is XC. The formula to calculate capacitive reactance is $X_C = \dfrac{1}{2\pi fC}$

Where:

$X_C$ = ohms of reactance
$f$ = frequency of the applied voltage measured in hertz
$C$ = capacitance in farads

**Capacitor** An electric circuit element used to store charge temporarily. In general, it consists of two metallic plates separated and insulated from each other by a dielectric. A capacitor may also be referred to as a condenser. (Excerpted from American Heritage Talking Dictionary. Copyright ©1997 The Learning Company, Inc. All Rights Reserved.)

**Dielectric** A nonconductor of electricity, especially a substance with electrical conductivity less than a millionth (10 6) of a siemens. A dielectric has the ability to insulate against a current flow between conducting surfaces. (Excerpted from American Heritage Talking Dictionary. Copyright ©1997 The Learning Company, Inc. All Rights Reserved.)

**Farad** The unit of capacitance equal to the capacitance of a capacitor having an equal and opposite charge of 1 coulomb on each plate and a potential difference of 1 V between the plates. The larger the farad value, the more charge a capacitor can hold. (Excerpted from American Heritage Talking Dictionary. Copyright ©1997 The Learning Company, Inc. All Rights Reserved.)

**Microfarad** $1 \times 10^6$ farads. Abbreviated as μF.

**Micro-microfarad** See picofarad. Abbreviated as μμF.

**Nanofarad** $1 \times 10^9$ farads. Abbreviated as nF.

**Picofarad** $1 \times 10^{12}$ farads. Abbreviated as pF. Also called a micro-microfarad (abbreviated as μμF).

## REVIEW QUESTIONS

1. Explain what three physical factors must be present to have capacitance in a circuit.
2. What phenomenon causes a charge to be stored across the plates of a capacitor?
3. What are the units of measure for capacitance? Include the standard unit and three submultiples in your explanation.
4. What is the standard formula for farads when the physical characteristics of the capacitor are measured in the metric system?
5. Explain why no current flows through a capacitor but it appears that it does.
6. Provide a short explanation of the relationship of current and voltage in a capacitor.
7. Relate the current and voltage in an inductor to the voltage and current in a capacitor.
8. Explain the mnemonic "ELI the ICE man."
9. How are voltage ratings of a capacitor determined?
10. Explain the difference between dielectric strength and dielectric constant.
11. How many time constants does it take to charge a capacitor to 95% of its rated capacity?
12. Write two different formulas for determining $X_C$ of a circuit when you know the frequency and the $C$ rating of the capacitor.
13. Why does $X_C$ decrease as the $f$ increases?

**14.** In the capacitor formulas, the formula symbols have numerical measures. In what units are $X_c$, $C$, $f$, K, and $d$ measured?

**15.** Draw a directional vector representing 50 $\Omega$ $X_C$ on a diagram that uses resistance as the 0° reference.

**16.** If a capacitor is in good operating condition, what would a test with an analog ohmmeter read when first connected?

**17.** If you double the size of the plate interaction, what happens to the capacitance?

**18.** If you reduce the dielectric thickness of a capacitor by one-half, what happens to the voltage rating of the capacitor?

## PRACTICE PROBLEMS

**1.** A 20 $\mu$F capacitor operating in a circuit produces a voltage drop of 5 V at 1 kHz. What is the current?

**2.** What is the capacitance of a capacitor that has a reactance of 800 $\Omega$ at 10 kHz?

**3.** A 20 pF capacitor draws 10 mA at 95 V. What is the frequency?

**4.** An 80 $\mu$F capacitor is connected to a 240 V, 60 Hz supply. What is the current?

**5.** What is the charge in coulombs stored if a 50 $\mu$F capacitor is charged to 50 V?

**6.** Calculate the $C$ for a capacitor with the following characteristics: four plates each 0.025 m$^2$, a dielectric K of 10, and dielectric of 0.0002 meter thick.

**7.** Determine the voltage rating of the capacitor in question 6 if the $\frac{\text{volts}}{\text{cm}}$ is 50.

**8.** A 200 microfarad capacitor is connected in series with a 10 kilohm resistor to a 10 V supply. It charges for 6 seconds. What is the stored charge?

**9.** A certain capacitor and series resistor allow a capacitor to discharge to 13.6% of its original voltage. How many time constants have elapsed during discharge?

**10.** If a capacitor has a capacitive reactance of 100 $\Omega$ at 60 Hz, how many ohms of capacitive reactance will it have at 120 Hz?

# 6

# CAPACITORS AND RESISTORS IN SERIES

# OVERVIEW

Capacitors are used in many AC circuits to react to the other circuit components. The ability to counteract the effects of the coil, or to balance a circuit with inductors, is one of the major uses of the capacitor. The fundamentals of the capacitor were presented in Chapter 5. In this chapter, we address the application of capacitors in various series circuits.

As you will see, many principles used for the series equations for inductors also apply to the capacitor circuits. The connection of capacitors in a circuit in series has two major effects. The total capacitance of the circuit and the voltage rating of the circuit are both affected. Understanding the basic construction of the capacitor makes it easier to comprehend these variances from the inductor formulas.

The last section of the chapter includes a chart to help you decipher what happens in general when changes are introduced to a circuit with resistors and capacitors in series.

# OBJECTIVES

After completing this chapter, you will be able to:
· Solve for total capacitance in a series circuit containing more than one capacitor
· Find total capacitive reactance in a series circuit containing more than one capacitor
· Solve for unknowns in circuits containing more than one capacitor in series when the values of other variables are specified
· Determine all the calculated values for oppositions, voltages, and currents in a series resistance and capacitance (RC) circuit
· Determine the dissipated power, the apparent power, and the reactive power of a series RC circuit
· Compute the power factor, the phase angle, and the components of a power triangle
· Determine what happens to a series RC circuit as variables change

## CAPACITORS IN SERIES

Connecting capacitors in series has the same effect as increasing the distance between the capacitor plates (the physical distance between the plates does not actually increase), thereby reducing the total capacitance of the circuit. If you consider the circuit in Figure 6–1, with the same source voltage applied to each circuit, the circuit with two capacitors has twice as much dielectric thickness for the same applied circuit voltage. Using the formula:

$$C = \frac{0.225 \ AK}{d \times 10^6}$$

Where:

    $C$ = capacitance of a capacitor in microfarads

  0.225 = constant for English units

    $A$ = effective plate area of one plate in square inches

    K = dielectric constant of the dielectric material

    $d$ = distance between the plates measured in inches

you can verify that if $d$ increases, then $C$ decreases. Each capacitor of the two in a series has more dielectric or less volts per mil than does the single capacitor circuit. The electrostatic field has the ability to hold less charge when the volts per mil thickness is less. In other words, the plates are effectively separated by a larger distance and the fields of the electrons have less influence.

By using the formula:

$$C = \frac{Q}{E}$$

**Circuit Comparison**

**Figure 6–1** A circuit with one capacitor can be compared to a circuit with two capacitors that is otherwise identical to the single-capacitor circuit.

you can confirm the effects of adding capacitors in series. Take the capacitance of one capacitor and determine the $Q$ (quantity of electrons) charge that can be accumulated on the plates. Manipulate the formula to:

$$C \times E = Q$$

With one-half the original voltage applied to the single series capacitor, the $Q$ is one-half the amount of a single capacitor in the same circuit. That one-half charge can be equated to current flow to the capacitor. Since the two capacitors are in series, that same amount of current will flow to the second capacitor. The electrons move off the bottom plate of $C_1$ and move to $C_2$. This capacitor will only hold the same charge, namely, the same half charge, compared to the original single capacitor. By looking at the current flow, you can determine that only half the normal current will flow, thereby confirming that the, total capacity of the circuit is only half the original capacitance.

Still another way to analyze the process is to use the formula for capacitive reactance:

$$X_C = \frac{1}{2\pi fC}$$

where $C$ is in farads. If the circuit with one capacitor has an $X_C$ of 10 Ω and the circuit with two capacitors has an $X_C$ of 10 Ω each, the total opposition for the two-capacitor circuit is twice as much as the one-capacitor circuit. This is much like adding resistors in series. As you learned in the last chapter, you can determine the $C$ of the capacitor if you know the $X_C$. Using the formula:

$$C = \frac{1}{2\pi fX_C}$$

and inserting $X_C$ into the denominator, you can deduce that $C$ is smaller when $X_C$ is larger.

This leads to the formula for adding capacitors in series. As you add more capacitors in series, the total capacitance of the circuit decreases, similar to what happens as you add resistors in parallel.

When resistors are connected in parallel, there are several ways to calculate total resistance:

- When all the resistors are of equal value, the total resistance is equal to the resistance of one of the resistors or branches divided by the number of resistors or branches:

$$R_T = \frac{R}{N}$$

- If two resistors of unequal resistance are in parallel, the formula for the total is:

$$R_T = \frac{R_1 \times R_2}{R_1 + R_2}$$

- If more than two unequal resistors are in parallel, the formula is:

$$\frac{1}{R_T} = \frac{1}{R_1} + \frac{1}{R_2} + \frac{1}{R_3} + \dots \frac{1}{R_N}$$

OR

$$R_T = \frac{1}{\left(\frac{1}{R_1}\right) + \left(\frac{1}{R_2}\right) + \left(\frac{1}{R_3}\right) + \dots \left(\frac{1}{R_N}\right)}$$

## SERIES CAPACITOR FORMULAS

The formulas for capacitance in a series circuit are as follows:

- When all the capacitors are of equal value, the total capacitance is equal to the capacitance of one of the capacitors or branches divided by the number of capacitors or branches:

$$C_T = \frac{C}{N}$$

- If two capacitors of unequal capacitance are in series, the formula for the total is:

$$C_T = \frac{C_1 \times C_2}{C_1 + C_2}$$

- If more than two unequal capacitors are in series, the formula is:

$$\frac{1}{C_T} = \frac{1}{C_1} + \frac{1}{C_2} + \frac{1}{C_3} + \dots \frac{1}{C_N}$$

OR

$$C_T = \frac{1}{\left(\frac{1}{C_1}\right) + \left(\frac{1}{C_2}\right) + \left(\frac{1}{C_3}\right) + \dots \left(\frac{1}{C_N}\right)}$$

Where:

$C$ = capacitance of one capacitor
$N$ = number of equal capacitors connected in series (all individual series capacitors are equal)

---

### Example

What is the total capacitance of three capacitors connected in series with the values of $C_1 = 20\ \mu F$, $C_2 = 25\ \mu F$, and $C_3 = 45\ \mu F$?

**Solution:**

All the $C$ values are in microfarads, so $C_T$ is also in microfarads:

$$\frac{1}{C_T} = \frac{1}{C_1} + \frac{1}{C_2} + \frac{1}{C_3} \dots$$

$$C_T = \frac{1}{\dfrac{1}{20} + \dfrac{1}{25} + \dfrac{1}{45}}$$

$$= \frac{1}{0.05 + 0.04 + 0.022}$$

$$= \frac{1}{0.112}$$

$$= 8.91\ \mu F$$

---

### Example

Two 50 $\mu F$ capacitors are connected in series. Each capacitor is rated for 50 V.

1. Find the total circuit capacitance.
2. Find the total voltage that can be applied to the circuit.

**Solution:**

1. All the $C$ values are in microfarads, so $C_T$ is also in microfarads:

$$C_T = \frac{C_1 \times C_2}{C_1 + C_2}$$

$$= \frac{50 \times 50}{50 + 50}$$

$$= \frac{2,500}{100}$$

$$= 25\ \mu F$$

OR

$$C_T = \frac{C_T}{N}$$

$$= \frac{50}{2}$$

$$= 25\ \mu F$$

2. Because the dielectrics are each rated for 50 V (and the capacitors are in series), the total voltage of the circuit can be 100 V.

## FieldNote!

When in the field, it is not always convenient to find the exact replacement for a given capacitor. If the circuit needs to be repaired quickly, you may be able to find the right combination of capacitors to connect into the circuit. For instance, if you need 20 μF and you have two 40 μF capacitors, you may connect them in series to yield 20 μF. Be sure to observe the voltage rating. If you have two 50 V capacitors, they may be connected in series to yield 100 V rating but at a lower total capacity with two in series. You may install capacitors with a higher voltage rating than is required by the circuit but never those with a lower total voltage rating for your combination of capacitors than is required by the circuit voltage.

## CAPACITIVE REACTANCE IN SERIES

As capacitors are added in series, the total $C$ decreases. However, the total $X_C$ increases as it does with series resistors. Because each capacitor adds opposition to the circuit, the effect is cumulative. The formula for capacitive reactance in series is:

$$X_{CT} = X_{C1} + X_{C2} + X_{C3} + \ldots X_{CN}$$

The total reactance can also be calculated by using the total values and applying the generic $X_C$ formula:

$$X_{CT} = \frac{1}{2\pi f C_T}$$

Notice that as we added capacitors to a series circuit, the total $C$ decreased. Using this lower total $C$, the effect on $X_{CT}$ in the formula is to cause it to increase, thereby verifying that total reactance increases as capacitors are added in series.

## RESISTIVE CAPACITIVE SERIES CIRCUITS

All series circuits have two principles in common:

1. The current in all elements of the series circuit is equal to the total current.

2. The sum of the voltage drops across all circuit elements (including the sources) is equal to zero. Refer to Kirchoff's laws in your study of *DC Theory*.

A circuit that contains resistance and capacitance is called an RC circuit. The series RC circuit is similar to the RL circuit in that it uses the circuit current as the reference. The main difference is that the voltage drop across the capacitor lags the current by 90° (Figure 6–2).

If a pure capacitive load (no resistance) is connected in an AC circuit, the voltage and the current are 90° out of phase with each other. In a capacitive circuit, the current leads the voltage by 90° (Figure 6–3). Notice when evaluating series circuits that the current is always drawn as the reference at 0° on the horizontal.

When a circuit that contains both resistance and capacitance is connected to an AC power supply, the voltage and current will be out of phase by some amount between 0° and 90°. The size of the phase angle will be determined by the ratio between resistance and capacitive reactance. To determine what the circuit current will be, construct the total opposition due to the resistance and the capacitive reactance.

**Figure 6–2** Phase relationships of "perfect" RC and RL circuits have a 90° shifted current.

**Current and Voltage Vectors**

**Figure 6–3** Vectors are drawn to indicate value and relative direction representing voltage across a capacitor and current through a capacitor.

**Series RC Circuit**

**Figure 6–4** This series RC circuit has a 20 Ω resistor and a 30 Ω $X_C$ capacitor.

**Impedance Vector**

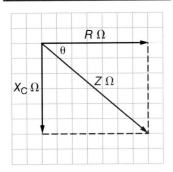

**Figure 6–5** $X_C$ is drawn down from the horizontal, representing that $C$ causes a leading effect.

Series RC circuits are similar to the series RL series circuits covered in Chapter 4. The formulas are basically the same with only minor modifications. Figure 6–4 shows a 20 Ω resistor in series with a capacitor that has 30 Ω of capacitive reactance. The voltage supply is 220 V at 60 Hz. This circuit is used for several of the examples in this chapter.

When we add the two voltage drops across the oppositions, we need to remember that the ohmic values are both ohms but are two types of opposition. Ohms of resistance are not necessarily in phase with the applied voltage, but are in phase with the voltage drop across the resistor, and are drawn as a vector at the 0° reference. The $X_C$ causes an ohmic value at a 90° angle leading to the voltage as shown in Figure 6–5. The combination is *not* added arithmetically but is instead added vectorially to get a resultant vector as the hypotenuse of the triangle. This resultant vector is called the impedance, as it was in the RL circuit.

# IMPEDANCE

Remember that the total impedance $(Z_T)$ is equal to the total opposition to current flow in the circuit. It is a combination of both resistance and capacitive reactance. Since this is a series circuit, the elements are vectorially added. Resistance and capacitive reactance are 90° out of phase with each other, and these form a right triangle, with the impedance forming the hypotenuse (Figure 6–5). The formula for $Z_T$ is:

$$Z_T = \sqrt{R^2 + X_C{}^2}$$

Solving for the impedance in the circuit in Figure 6–4:

$$Z_T = \sqrt{20^2 + 30^2} = \sqrt{400 + 900}$$

$$= 36 \ \Omega$$

TechTip!

The term flux capacitor may be familiar to many younger electricians. It was a term used in the movie *Back to the Future* to refer to the power production device on the vehicle that transported the main character back in time. The term is interesting as it combines the capacitor ideas of energy storage with the inductor ideas that use magnetic flux. As you know, energy is stored in an electrostatic field in a capacitor and in an electromagnetic field in the inductors. Current discussion about electric cars is focused on how to store energy for use in the electric motor of these vehicles. This storage is now done with batteries, but extensive research is being done to find better storage systems. One such new idea is to use capacitive storage. We must find a way to charge a capacitor with enough charge and then allow the charge to drive an electric motor. This discharge circuit resembles the RC discharge circuit described in Chapter 5.

### ADDING SERIES COMPONENTS

As we add series components, we still must follow the rules for series circuits. Opposition vectors that are at the same angle and direction can be added together. Therefore, as we add resistors and capacitors, as depicted in Figure 6–6, we can create a circuit impedance triangle with all the oppositions in the circuit, as in Figure 6–7.

**Multiple Resistors and Capacitors in Series**

**Figure 6–6** Series circuits can have multiple resistors and multiple capacitors.

**Added Resistors and Capacitors in Vector Drawings**

**Figure 6–7** Vectors represent added resistors and added capacitors.

Construct an impedance triangle using two resistors, each valued at 50 $\Omega$, and a 26.5 $\mu$F capacitor at 60 Hz, as shown in Figure 6–8.

**Solution:**

Total resistance is 100 $\Omega$ at a 0° angle and $X_C$ is 100 $\Omega$ at a 90° angle (Figure 6–9):

$$X_C = \frac{1}{2\pi fC}$$

$$= \frac{1}{2 \times 3.1416 \times 60 \times 0.0000265}$$

$$= 100\ \Omega$$

$$Z_T = \sqrt{R^2 + X_C{}^2}$$

$$= \sqrt{100^2 + 100^2}$$

$$= \sqrt{10,000 + 10,000}$$

$$= 141.4\ \Omega$$

**Series RC Circuit**

**Figure 6–8** A series circuit with two 50 $\Omega$ resistors and one 26.5 $\mu$F capacitor.

**Impedance Triangle**

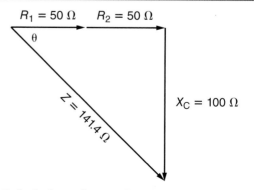

**Figure 6–9** An impedance triangle shows the calculation of total impedance.

# Example

Use the same components as in the previous example, but add a second 26.5 μF capacitor (Figure 6–10). Solve for the circuit impedance and for the circuit current if 200 V AC is applied.

**Solution:**

The impedance triangle appears as shown in Figure 6–11:

$$Z_T = \sqrt{R^2 + X_C^2} \text{ using total } R \text{ and total } X_C$$

$$= \sqrt{100^2 + 200^2}$$

$$= \sqrt{10{,}000 + 40{,}000}$$

$$= 223.6 \ \Omega$$

Using $Z_T$ and 200 V AC applied:

$$I_T = \frac{E_T}{Z_T}$$

$$= \frac{200 \text{ V}}{223.6 \ \Omega}$$

$$= 0.894 \text{ A or } 894 \text{ mA}$$

## Series RC Circuit

**Figure 6–10** This series circuit has the added component of a 26.5 μF capacitor.

## Four Component Impedance Triangle

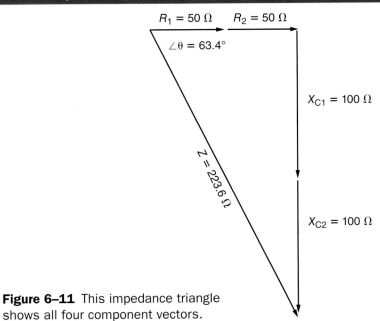

**Figure 6–11** This impedance triangle shows all four component vectors.

## CALCULATING VOLTAGE DROPS FOR SERIES RC COMPONENTS

Since the current is the same value at any point in a series circuit, the voltage drop across each capacitor can be computed using the capacitive reactance of each capacitor and the current flow of the circuit. Unlike the calculations for inductors that needed a $Z$ triangle for each coil, capacitors have so little resistance compared to the $X_C$ that the $R$ is ignored. Therefore, we just use the circuit current that appears to flow through the capacitor multiplied by the component opposition ($X_C$) to find the voltage drop across the capacitor.

---

### Example

Calculate the voltage drops for each of the capacitors in Figure 6–12.

**Solution:**

**1.** Find the capacitive reactance of each capacitor:

$$X_{C1} = \frac{1}{2\pi fC}$$

$$= \frac{1}{2 \times 3.1416 \times 60 \times 0.00002}$$

$$= 132.6 \ \Omega$$

$$X_{C2} = \frac{1}{2\pi fC}$$

$$= \frac{1}{2 \times 3.1416 \times 60 \times 0.000025}$$

$$= 106.1 \ \Omega$$

$$X_{C3} = \frac{1}{2\pi fC}$$

$$= \frac{1}{2 \times 3.1416 \times 60 \times 0.000045}$$

$$= 58.9 \ \Omega$$

**2.** Find the total capacitive reactance:

$$X_{CT} = X_{C1} + X_{C2} + X_{C3}$$

$$= 132.6 + 106.1 + 58.9$$

$$= 297.6 \ \Omega$$

**3.** Find the current in the circuit:

$$I_T = \frac{E_T}{X_{CT}}$$

$$= \frac{480 \ \text{V}}{297.6 \ \Omega}$$

$$= 1.61 \ \text{A}$$

## E x a m p l e

**4.** Find the voltage drop across each capacitor:

$$E_C = I_C \times X_C \text{ (for any one capacitor)}$$

$$E_{C1} = 1.61 \text{ A} \times 132.6 \text{ }\Omega$$

$$= 213.5 \text{ V}$$

$$E_{C2} = 1.61 \text{ A} \times 106.1 \text{ }\Omega$$

$$= 170.8 \text{ V}$$

$$E_{C3} = 1.61 \text{ A} \times 58.9 \text{ }\Omega$$

$$= 94.8 \text{ V}$$

Remember that to check this you can add the voltage drops together. The sum of the individual voltage drops should be equal to the total voltage from the supply, because they are all voltages at 90° lagging the current reference:

$$E_T = E_{C1} + E_{C2} + E_{C3}$$

$$= 213.5 \text{ V} + 170.8 \text{ V} + 94.8 \text{ V}$$

$$= 479.1 \text{ V}$$

The 0.9 V difference between the applied voltage (480) and the calculated voltage (479.1), is caused by math round-off errors throughout the calculations.

**Three Capacitor Series Circuit**

**Figure 6–12** A three-capacitor series circuit is used to calculate voltage drop on each component.

## IMPEDANCE AND VOLTAGE TRIANGLES FOR RC CIRCUITS

Refer back to Figure 6–10, with two resistors and two capacitors in series. As we calculated earlier, the impedance was at 223.6 $\Omega$ and the circuit current was at 0.894 A when 200 V AC was applied. This created the $Z$ triangle that appears in Figure 6–11. The angle to the horizontal current reference was a 63.4° leading current or can also be called lagging voltage. The impedance triangle shown in Figure 6–11 would be congruent to a voltage triangle for the same circuit. We can calculate the voltage drop across each component by using the total current of the series circuit as a constant.

This current is multiplied by the opposition of each component, and the voltage appears as the vector with the same characteristics as the opposition. The resistive components are drawn at 0° angles, and the voltage across the capacitors is drawn at 90° lagging to the horizontal. Now we can vectorially add all the vectors to verify the circuit total voltage.

---

**E x a m p l e**

**Solution:**

$$E_{R1} = I_{R1} \times R_1$$

$$= 0.894 \times 50 \ \Omega$$

$$= 44.7 \ \text{V}$$

$$E_{R2} = 0.894 \times 50 \ \Omega$$

$$= 44.7 \ \text{V}$$

$$E_{XC1} = 0.894 \times 100 \ \Omega \text{ of } X_C$$

$$= 89.4 \ \text{V}$$

$$E_{XC2} = 0.894 \ \text{A} \times 100 \ \Omega \text{ of } X_C$$

$$= 89.4 \ \text{V}$$

---

Total resistive voltage drop is approximately 89.4 V, and total capacitive voltage drop is approximately

178.8 V. Adding the vectors together and using the Pythagorean Theorem as shown in the example, the resultant hypotenuse is found to be 199.9 V, or nearly 200 V, thus confirming that we started with 200 V AC. We do not calculate exactly 200 V, as we rounded some calculations.

---

**E x a m p l e**

The total, or resultant, voltage may be calculated using the Pythagorean Theorem:

$$E_T = \sqrt{E_{RT}^2 + E_{XCT}^2}$$

$$= \sqrt{89.4^2 + 178.8^2}$$

$$= 199.9 \ \text{V}$$

---

We now have matching (similar or congruent) impedance (Z) triangle and voltage (E) triangle vectors (see Figure 6–13). We can again calculate the angle between the reference line current on the horizontal and the angle of the resultant voltage, or the circuit total applied voltage. We use the vectors at 90° angles, 178.4 V capacitive and 89.4 V resistive. Through trigonometry, we use 178.7 V (the opposite side) divided by 89.4 V (the adjacent side) and, using the arc that has a tangent of 2, we calculate the angle of leading current at 63.4°, the same as the Z triangle.

---

**E x a m p l e**

Angle theta may be calculated using the resistive voltage drop and capacitive voltage drop values:

$$\tan \theta = \frac{\text{Opposite side}}{\text{Adjacent side}}$$

$$= \frac{178.8 \ \text{V}}{89.4 \ \text{V}}$$

$$= 2$$

$$\text{arctan } (\tan^{-1}) \ 2 = 63.4°$$

---

**TechTip!**

By adding the individual voltages arithmetically, you get 89.4 + 178.8 V = 268.2 V, more than the 200 V with which you started. This practice of adding voltages together arithmetically to total more than originally applied often confuses even experienced electricians who have forgotten the effects of capacitor and resistor individual voltages. We become so focused on determining what is to happen in the circuit that we mistakenly apply DC rules to AC circuits.

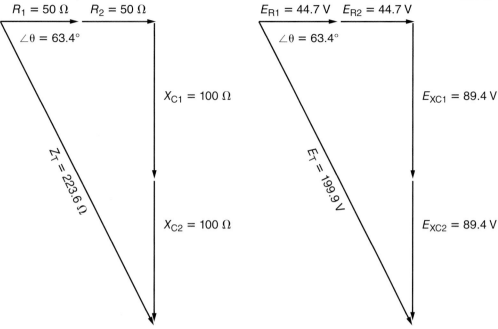

**Figure 6–13** Congruent impedance ($Z$) and voltage ($E$) triangles.

# POWER

As with the inductive circuits, the power is categorized by the relationship of the circuit current to the circuit voltage. The zero axis reference is the in-phase current and voltage. Again, there are three components to the RC power triangle. True power (watts) is still calculated by the line current and the resistance of a resistor using:

$$P_{\text{True}} = I^2 R$$

OR

$$P_{\text{True}} = I_T \times E_R$$

The reactive powers (VARs) are calculated by using:

$$P_{\text{Reactive}} = I^2 \times X_C$$

OR

$$P_{\text{Reactive}} = I_T \times E_C$$

With these two components, we can build another right triangle that is again congruent to the $Z$ and the $E$ triangles (Figure 6–14). The resultant side, the hypotenuse, is the apparent power of the circuit. When we multiply line current by line voltage, we apparently get power.

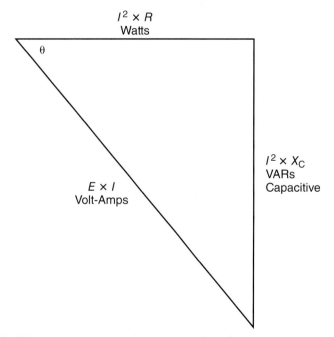

**Figure 6–14** A power triangle has appropriate formulas on each side.

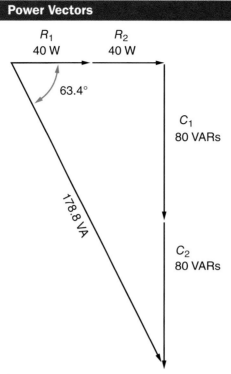

**Figure 6–15** These power vectors relate to the circuit depicted in Figure 6–10.

Again, this is apparent power, which is not the same as true or dissipated power. Using the same circuit as Figure 6–10 with two 50 Ω resistors and two 26.5 μF capacitors at 200 V AC and 60 Hz, we assume the power is:

$$P_{\text{Apparent}} = 0.894 \text{ A} \times 200 \text{ V}$$

$$= 178.8 \text{ VA}$$

True power is the power that is dissipated where current and voltage are in phase, namely, the horizontal portion of the power triangle. In this case, the true power is:

$$P_{\text{True}} = 0.894 \text{ A} \times (44.7 + 44.7) \text{ V}$$

$$\approx 80 \text{ W}$$

The reactive power is:

$$P_{\text{Reactive}} = 0.894 \text{ A} \times (89.4 + 89.4) \text{ V}$$

$$\approx 160 \text{ VAR}$$

The power triangle appears in Figure 6–15 with the same angle of 63.4° to the horizontal proven by trigonometry.

The power factor of this circuit can also be calculated the same as the RL circuits. The cosine of the phase angle multiplied by 100 equals the percent power factor, or by using the hypotenuse and the adjacent side to the phase angle, we find:

$$\% \; PF = \left( \frac{\text{watts}}{\text{volt-amps}} \right) \times 100$$

For the circuit in Figure 6–14, the watts are 80 and the volt-amps are approximately 179. Therefore:

$$\left( \frac{80 \text{ W}}{179 \text{ VA}} \right) \times 100 = 44.7\% \; PF$$

To corroborate with trigonometry:

$$\% \; PF = \cos \theta \times 100$$

$$= \cos 63.4° \times 100$$

$$= 0.448 \times 100 = 44.8\%$$

This means that 44.7% of the power delivered to the circuit in the form of volts and amps is actually used or consumed as watts. The remaining energy is stored in the form of electrostatic fields in the capacitor. In this case, the stored power is caused by a leading current (ICE) and the power factor is referred to as a leading power factor. This is an important point because the inductors caused a lagging power factor due to a lagging current.

## ANGLE THETA

The power factor of the circuit is the cosine of the phase angle. Since the power factor turned out to be 0.447, or 44.7%, angle theta (θ) can be calculated:

$$\cos \theta = PF$$

$$= 0.447$$

$$\text{arccos } (\cos^{-1}) \; 0.447 = \theta$$

$$\theta = 63.4°$$

Therefore, if we know the power factor for either the leading power factor or the lagging power factor, we can find the actual angle that the current leads or lags the voltage. Likewise, if we know the angle, we can use the cosine function to find the power factor.

### Example

Find the power factor of the following circuit. A single 120 Ω resistor is in series with two 40 μF capacitors, and the circuit is operating at 50 Hz and 200 V AC (Figure 6–16).

**Solution:**

Find the impedance triangle by determining the $X_C$ of the capacitors. Knowing that two 40 μF capacitors in series are the same as one 20 μF, capacitor, use the formula:

$$X_C = \frac{1}{2\pi f C} = \frac{1}{2 \times 3.1416 \times 50 \times 0.00002}$$

$$= 159.2\ \Omega$$

$$R = 120\ \Omega$$

$$Z = \sqrt{R^2 + X_C^2}$$

$$= \sqrt{120^2 + 159.2^2}\ \text{(Figure 6–17)}$$

$$= 199.4\ \Omega$$

The power factor is the cosine of the angle between the hypotenuse and the resistance. That angle is ≈ 53°:

$$\cos 53° = 0.60$$

$$PF = 0.60 \times 100 = 60\%$$

*(Continued)*

### Series RC Circuit

200 V
50 Hz

120 Ω    40 μF    40 μF

**Figure 6–16** This circuit has two capacitors and a resistor operating at 50 Hz.

### Impedance Triangle

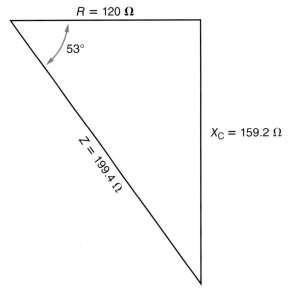

$R = 120\ \Omega$

53°

$Z = 199.4\ \Omega$

$X_C = 159.2\ \Omega$

**Figure 6–17** This impedance triangle relates to circuit in Figure 6–16.

### E x a m p l e (continued)

We can go directly to the power triangle to confirm this figure by first finding the line current:

$$I_T = \frac{E_T}{Z_T}$$

$$= \frac{200 \text{ V}}{199.4 \text{ }\Omega}$$

$$\approx 1 \text{ A}$$

Then the power triangle looks like Figure 6–18:

$$\text{Apparent power is } VA = V \times I_T$$

$$P_{\text{Apparent}} = 200 \text{ V} \times 1 \text{ A}$$

$$= 200 \text{ VA}$$

$$P_{\text{True}} = I^2 \times R$$

$$= 1^2 \times 120 \text{ }\Omega$$

$$= 120 \text{ W}$$

Then the power factor is $\frac{W}{VA}$:

$$\% \, PF = \frac{W}{VA} \times 100$$

$$= \frac{120}{200} \times 100$$

$$= 60$$

The angle of lead is arccos 0.60 = 53.1°. This is approximately the same as the angle found in the $Z$ triangle. It should be identical but is not because we rounded figures to make calculation procedures more clear.

---

**Power Triangle**

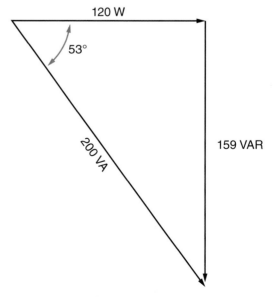

**Figure 6–18** This power triangle is for the circuit in Figure 6–16.

# THE EFFECTS OF CHANGING VARIABLES ON RC CIRCUITS

The effects of frequency on a series RC circuit can be analyzed by determining what happens to the $X_C$ of a capacitor. This effect can then be used to determine what happens to the impedance triangle. The $Z$ triangle affects the circuit current and the voltage dropped on each of the series components. This in turn affects the total power triangle. Assume a 100 μF capacitor that has 60 Hz applied. The circuit has a 25 Ω resistor in series (Figure 6–19).

If we decrease the applied frequency to 30 Hz, $X_C$ goes from 26.5 Ω to 53 Ω. The shape of the impedance triangle changes as well (Figure 6–20). The circuit impedance goes up, and the line current goes down. The voltage triangles change to be consistent with the $Z$ triangles, as in Figure 6–20. The voltage across the capacitor increases because $X_C$ increases at a higher proportion than the current decreased. The power triangle also changes to reflect the $Z$ and $E$ triangles. The power factor changes to become a lower percent power factor to coincide with the larger leading current angle as the circuit appears more capacitive. The watts decrease because the line current decreased, and the resistance does not change.

Refer to Table 6–1 for effects of frequency, capacitance, or resistance on RC series circuits when changing one variable at a time.

The top line identifies the calculated value, and the left column indicates which was the variable changes. Use the table to predict the effects of different calculations as the variables are changed one at a time. Use the impedance, voltage, and power triangles to verify trends.

As you can see from Table 6–1, many of the circuit conditions that may change affect the entire circuit. The results of a change in the circuit parameters may take some effort to determine because of the right triangle vector additions. A linear change in one variable does not always create a linear change in the results.

**Figure 6–20** The shape of the impedance triangle changes as the frequency drops to 30 Hz.

**Figure 6–19** This circuit contains a simple resistor and capacitor in series.

## Table 6–1

| Variable | $X_C$ | Impedance | Line Current | Capacitor Voltage | Phase Angle | Power Factor | Watts |
|---|---|---|---|---|---|---|---|
| Freq Inc | Dec | Dec | Inc | Dec | Dec | Inc | Inc |
| Freq Dec | Inc | Inc | Dec | Inc | Inc | Dec | Dec |
| Cap Inc | Dec | Dec | Inc | Dec | Dec | Inc | Inc |
| Cap Dec | Inc | Inc | Dec | Inc | Inc | Dec | Dec |
| Resis Inc | Same | Inc | Dec | Dec | Dec | Inc | Dec |
| Resis Dec | Same | Dec | Inc | Inc | Inc | Dec | Inc |

Freq = frequency; Cap = capacitance; Resis = resistance; Inc = increase; Dec = decrease

Results of One Variable at a Time in a Series RC Circuit.

## SUMMARY

In a pure capacitive circuit, the voltage and current are 90° out of phase with each other. In a pure resistive circuit, the voltage and current are in phase with each other. In a circuit containing both resistance and capacitance, the voltage and current are out of phase with each other by some angle between 0° and 90°. The amount of phase angle difference between voltage and current in a series RC circuit is equal to the angle whose tangent is the ratio of resistance to capacitive reactance.

To find the total capacitance of a series of capacitors, the formulas look like the formulas for parallel resistors, with the total C decreasing as more capacitors are added in series. This effect is the result of adding more dielectric thickness to the overall circuit voltage. Another effect of adding more dielectric material is that the overall voltage rating of the series of capacitors is equal to the arithmetic sum of the individual capacitor's voltage rating.

When we add a resistor in series with the capacitor, we must construct an impedance triangle to determine the total opposition in the circuit. The capacitor's $X_C$ is always drawn at 90° to the horizontal, and resistance is always drawn at 0°. The resultant side (the hypotenuse) is the total $Z$ at an angle $\theta$ to the horizontal. This is the angle at which the current leads the voltage of the circuit. This same angle determines the power factor of the circuit by taking the cosine of angle $\theta$. The same angle ($\theta$) is replicated in the voltage triangle vector for the circuit and for the power triangle for the circuit. These two triangles are congruent to the $Z$ triangle. The $E$ triangle vector uses the circuit current and $R$ and $X_C$ to determine the volt drops across each component. The hypotenuse should again equal the applied line voltage. The power triangle is made of vectors for watts, volt-amps, and VARs of capacitive power.

Once the circuit components and triangles are calculated, it makes it easier to determine what will happen to the circuit parameters as various variables change.

## REVIEW QUESTIONS

1. What is one of the major uses of capacitors?
2. Why does the total capacitance of a circuit decrease as more capacitors are added in series?
3. Write a formula for finding $C_T$ if you have two capacitors of the same value in series.
4. Explain what happens to the $X_C$ of a capacitor as the frequency of a circuit increases.
5. As multiple resistors are added to multiple capacitors in series, how do you calculate the effects on the circuit current?
6. Current _____ voltage in an RC circuit.
7. Explain what happens to the power factor by adding resistors to a series RC circuit.
8. Explain how the angle of leading current changes as capacitors are added in series.
9. The reference vector in a series circuit is generally the _____ vector on the horizontal axis.
10. Write the formula for calculating the total capacitive reactance of a circuit as capacitors are added in series.

## PRACTICE PROBLEMS

1. Draw and label an impedance (phasor diagram) triangle for a RC circuit.
2. In Figure PP6–1, if $E_C = 80$ V, what is the voltage across the resistor?
3. What is $X_C$ in problem 2?
4. What is $I_T$?
5. What is the value of the resistor in problem 2?
6. Find the impedance of the circuit of problem 2. Prove it.
7. Find the power factor in Figure PP6–1.
8. A circuit has $E_T = 15$ V at 2 kHz with a resistor (3 kΩ) and a capacitor in series. If there is a 4 mA current flow, what is the value of the capacitor?
9. Find the $C_1$ of a series circuit if $C_2$ is 50 µF, $C_3$ is 75 µF, and the total capacitance is 23 µF.
10. Calculate the $C$ of a capacitor if the voltage across the capacitor is 50 V, the circuit current is 2 A, and the circuit frequency is 60 Hz.
11. Find the volt-amps for a circuit with a power factor of 80% and a watt measurement of 200 W.

**Figure PP6–1**

# 7

# SERIES RLC CIRCUITS

# O V E R V I E W

You now know that inductance causes current in the circuit to lag behind the applied voltage and that capacitance causes the current to lead the applied voltage. The voltage across an inductor leads the current by 90°, and the voltage across the capacitor lags the current by 90°. Remember that current in a series circuit is the same at all points and therefore can be used as a reference to analyze the circuit. As stated before, using current for the reference is for learning purposes. Most technical proofs use vector diagrams with voltage as the reference. We need to determine the effects on the series circuits when both inductance and capacitance are connected. Although the steps to solve the circuit calculations are the same as the steps for either RL or RC, the combination creates new procedures. With the real world of inductors that actually have $R$ and $X_L$, the process for finding circuit quantities is a little more complicated. The need to keep accurate account of drawings and assigned values becomes more apparent. With the added dimension of changing line frequency of the circuit, the dynamics of changing $X_L$ and $X_C$ become more important.

# O B J E C T I V E S

After completing this chapter, you will be able to:
- Determine expected circuit values based on calculations
- Draw and describe vector diagrams representing circuit impedance
- Determine voltage drops across all components and verify these against circuit totals
- Describe the behavior of an RLC circuit regarding current and voltage relationships
- Calculate expected power values for each component and for circuit totals in a series RLC circuit
- Describe and analyze what happens in a series RLC circuit at, or near, resonance
- Find all values in a series circuit with $R$, $C$, and coil $Z$

# SERIES RLC CIRCUIT ANALYSIS

### CIRCUIT CALCULATIONS

The methods used to calculate what will occur as you build series circuits with resistive, inductive, and capacitive components are combinations of the last few chapters where we treated the circuits separately. When an AC circuit contains the elements of resistance, capacitance, and inductance connected in series, the current is the same through all parts but the voltage drops across the components are out of phase with one another. This is a characteristic of a series circuit.

The sequence of finding the total circuit effects is the same as previously described. The total impedance of the circuit is determined by the resistance at 0° to the horizontal, the $X_L$ at 90° lagging vectors, and the $X_C$ at 90° leading vectors. From these principles, you can conclude that in a series inductive-capacitive (LC) circuit, $X_L$ and $X_C$ are 180° out of phase with each other. Therefore, the value of one subtracts from the other (vectors in opposite directions) and the remainder determines whether the circuit is either inductive or capacitive. To find the effects on the total impedance of the circuit with reactive components of opposition, use the following formula:

$$Z_T = \sqrt{R^2 + (X_L - X_C)^2}$$

The value of the difference between $X_L$ and $X_C$ is simply a matter of subtracting vectors exactly opposite of each other. Just keep track of which reactive component is larger as you square the difference. You are creating a total effect–impedance triangle and you need to know which opposition has a greater effect (Figures 7–1 and 7–2).

**Series Circuit with Resistance, Inductance, and Capacitance**

**Figure 7–1** A series circuit that contains resistance, inductance, and capacitance.

**Impedance Vectors**

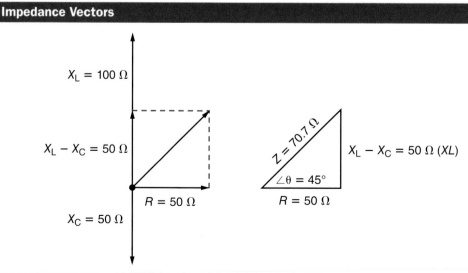

**Figure 7–2** Impedance vectors give resultant values.

## Example

Using the series circuit in Figure 7–1, find the oppositions and the current based on formulas learned in previous chapters.

Given:

Resistor $(R_1)$ = 50 $\Omega$

Inductor $(L_1)$ = 0.266 H (no resistance to this example coil)

$$X_L = 2\pi fL$$

$$= (6.28f)\ 0.266$$

$$= 100\ \Omega$$

Capacitor $(C_1)$ = 53 $\mu$F

$$X_C = \frac{1}{2\pi fC}$$

$$= \frac{1}{(6.28f) \times 0.000053}$$

$$= 50\ \Omega$$

$$Z_T = \sqrt{R^2 + (X_L - X_C)^2}$$

$$Z_T = \sqrt{50^2 + (100 - 50)^2}$$

$$= 70.7\ \Omega$$

$$I_T = \frac{E_T}{Z_T}$$

$$I_T = \frac{100\ V}{70.7\ \Omega}$$

$$= 1.414\ A$$

See Figure 7–2 for total impedance resultant of 70.7 $\Omega$.

As you note in Figure 7–2, the angle theta ($\theta$) is 45° and the effect of the circuit as it appears in the vector diagram is more inductive because of the effects of the inductive reactance. Therefore, the circuit current will react like the current in an inductive circuit and lag the voltage by 45°. This same angle will be replicated in the voltage vector and the power triangle, as it was in the previous chapters. The ratio of total reactance to resistance determines how much the applied voltage will lag or lead the circuit current. If the circuit is more inductive than capacitive, the current will lag the applied voltage and the power factor will be a **lagging power factor.** If the circuit is more capacitive than inductive, the current will lead the voltage and the power factor will be a **leading power factor.**

Since inductive reactance and capacitive reactance are 180° out of phase with each other, they subtract from each other in an AC circuit. This subtraction may mean a total reactance that could be 0 $\Omega$. This means that the current may be very high, depending on the value of $R$. Remember that

$$I_T = \frac{E_T}{Z_T}.$$

## FieldNote!

When referring to the power of a circuit, the terminology for leading and lagging power factor refers to the relationship of the circuit current to the circuit voltage. If the total circuit current leads the voltage, then the circuit is said to have a leading power factor. If the total circuit current lags the circuit voltage, then the circuit would have a lagging power factor.

## Voltage and Current Relationships

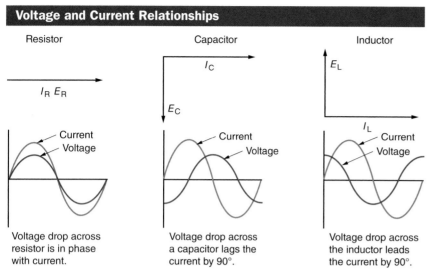

**Figure 7–3** Voltage and current relationships are different depending on resistance, pure inductors, and pure capacitors.

## Series RLC Circuit Voltage Relationships

**Figure 7–4** Voltage relationships that occur in a series RLC circuit, shown with circuit current.

## VOLTAGE DROP

The voltage drop across the resistor is in phase with the current. The voltage drop across the inductor leads the current by 90°, and the voltage drop across the capacitor lags the current by 90°. The three sinewave diagrams in Figure 7–3 show this.

Look at Figure 7–4. The sinewaves, shown at the top, represent total current and the voltage across each element. Notice that $E_R$ is in phase with the current, while $E_C$ and $E_L$ are 90° lagging and leading, respectively. This means that the inductive voltage and the capacitive voltage are 180° out of phase with each other.

The vectors representing those component values are also 180° out of phase, as seen in the vector diagram (Figure 7–5). These relationships are critical to understanding how the series RLC circuit components interact and perform.

Also, when Ohm's law is used on the circuit values, the sum of the voltage drops developed across these components can exceed the applied voltage. Using the same components as in the previous example from Figures 7–1 and 7–2, we can construct the congruent voltage triangle vector diagram to see how much voltage will appear across each component. We must use the original values of oppositions to determine what the actual value of voltage is, even though the net effect in the circuit will again be the vector addition of different direction vectors (Figure 7–6).

## Voltage Vectors

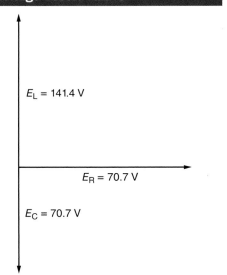

**Figure 7–5** Vector diagrams match voltage relationships.

## Voltage Vector Values

$E_L = 141.4$ V

$E_R = 70.7$ V

$E_C = 70.7$ V

**Figure 7–6** Vector diagrams illustrate circuit component values.

### Example

Using the circuit in Figure 7–1 and the values from the previous example, calculate the values of voltage across each component and the total circuit voltage.

Given:

$$R_1 = 50 \ \Omega$$

$$X_{L1} = 100 \ \Omega$$

$$X_{C1} = 50 \ \Omega$$

$$I_T = 1.414 \ \text{A}$$

$$E_{R1} = I_T \times R_1$$

$$= 1.414 \ \text{A} \times 50 \ \Omega$$

$$= 70.7 \ \text{V}$$

$$E_{L1} = I_T \times X_{L1}$$

$$= 1.414 \ \text{A} \times 100 \ \Omega$$

$$= 141.4 \ \text{V}$$

$$E_{C1} = I_T \times X_{C1}$$

$$= 1.414 \ \text{A} \times 50 \ \Omega$$

$$= 70.7 \ \text{V}$$

Angle 45° lagging current

$$E_T = \sqrt{(E_R + E_L - E_C)^2}$$

$$= \sqrt{70.7^2 + (141.4 - 70.7)^2}$$

$$\approx 100 \ \text{V (rounded)}$$

## FieldNote!

When referring to VARs in the circuit, several terms are used for indicating that the volt-amps reactive are capacitive. Sometimes they are called CVARs; they can also be written as –VARs or shown as VAR_C. These notations are used by different electrical personnel, but all denote that the reactive power is capacitive.

### Voltage Triangle

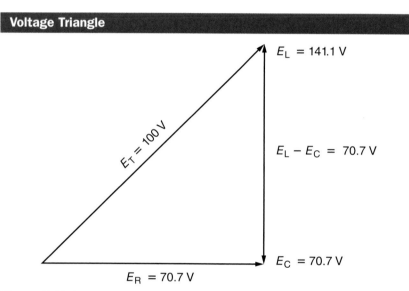

**Figure 7–7** A voltage triangle represents actual voltage measurements and total voltage.

### Series RLC Power Triangle

**Figure 7–8** A power triangle can be created for a series RLC circuit.

The current flow is the same throughout the series circuit, so 1.414 A will flow through all the components. With this current flowing in each component in the circuit, it would appear that the voltages all add up to more than the applied. As you now know, the voltage vectors have the same rules as the opposition vectors. As such, the effect on the circuit of the two reactive voltage vectors is to subtract, and the new total voltage triangle appears as shown in Figure 7–7. We now prove that the final triangle voltage vector can be constructed, and we can use either trigonometry or the Pythagorean Theorem to prove the resultant hypotenuse is the original line voltage of 100 V.

## POWER IN SERIES RLC CIRCUITS

Just as you have seen in series RL or series RC circuits, the power triangle follows the same patterns as the $Z$ triangle and the $E$ triangle vectors. (See Figure 7–8 for a power triangle.) The watts, or true power, are found on the horizontal line of the power triangle and can be calculated by current times voltage across the resistive components or by current squared times resistance. The VARs are found by circuit current times voltage across the capacitive components or circuit current times voltage across the inductive components.

These values can also be found by current squared times capacitive reactance or times inductive reactance. Finally, after subtracting the VARs capacitive and the VARs inductive, a final VARs component remains either more capacitive or more inductive. The two VARs can cancel each other to yield no reactive power in the final circuit; thus, only watts remain. In that case, the horizontal line is all that remains as watts and the power factor is 100%.

## E x a m p l e

Using the circuit in Figure 7–1 and the previous examples, determine the power calculations for the circuit.

Given:

$$R_1 = 50 \ \Omega$$

$$X_{L1} = 100 \ \Omega$$

$$X_{C1} = 50 \ \Omega$$

$$I_T = 1.414 \ A$$

Watts (W)

Dissipated by $R_1 = I_T \times E_R$

$$W_{R1} = 1.414 \ A \times 70.7 \ V$$

$$\approx 100 \ W \ (rounded)$$

Volt-Amps Reactive ($VAR_L$)

Reactive power for $L_1 = I_T \times E_L$

$$VAR_{L1} = 1.414 \ A \times 141.4 \ V$$

$$\approx 200 \ VARs \ inductive \ (rounded)$$

Volt-Amps Reactive ($VAR_C$)

Reactive power for $C_1 = I_T \times E_C$

$$VAR_{C1} = 1.414 \ A \times 70.7 \ V$$

$$\approx 100 \ VARs \ capacitive \ (rounded)$$

Volt-Amps (VA)

Resultant apparent power $= \sqrt{W^2 + (VAR_{L1} - VAR_{C1})^2}$

$$VA = \sqrt{100^2 + (200 - 100)^2}$$

$$= 141.4 \ VA$$

OR

$$VA = I_T \times E_T$$

$$= 1.414 \times 100$$

$$= 141.4 \ VA \ (reactive \ power)$$

Phase Angle ($\angle \theta$)

$$\cos \theta = \frac{\text{Adjacent Side}}{\text{Hypotenuse}}$$

$$= \frac{100 \ W}{141.4 \ VA}$$

$$= 0.707$$

$$\angle \theta = \arccos \ (\cos^{-1}) \ 0.707 = 45°$$

Percent Power Factor (% PF)

$$\% \ PF = \cos \theta \times 100$$

$$= \frac{100 \ W}{141.4 \ VA} \times 100$$

$$= 70.7\%$$

## FieldNote!

Power factor meters, watt meters, and VAR meters are available to measure these components of a power system. Power factor meters are used to measure the percent power factor whether the factor is for a leading power factor or a lagging power factor. Watt meters use current sensors and voltage sensors to determine the "in phase" power. VARs can also be measured by VAR meters. These meters shift the voltage to match the out-of-phase current and then directly measure VARs. See Figure 7–9 for an example of a power quality meter.

## POWER FACTOR

The power factor is calculated by dividing the true power (W) of the circuit by the apparent power (VA). The answer is multiplied by 100 to turn the decimal into a percentage; the percent power factor is also the cosine of the phase angle times 100. Cosine is calculated by dividing the adjacent side by the hypotenuse or, watts divided by volt-amps. In this case, we expect the power factor to be 70.7%, because the angle is the same in all the triangles.

**Power Quality Analyzer**

METER

**121.7** Volt

**Figure 7–9** A power quality meter can measure watts, VARs, and power factor with voltage probes and current sensors.

## FREQUENCY EFFECTS AND SERIES RESONANCE

When an inductor and a capacitor are connected in series, there is a frequency at which the inductive reactance and the capacitive reactance become equal. This is because, as frequency increases, inductive reactance increases and capacitive reactance decreases.

The point at which two reactance values become equal is called **resonance.** At resonance, all reactive components are canceled and only the resistance of the circuit remains. This reduces the impedance of the circuit, which in turn raises the circuit current. The phase angle goes to $0°$, and the power factor goes to 100%. The origin of the resonant frequency formula is to equate the $X_C$ equal to the $X_L$. Resonant circuits can be used to provide increases of current and voltage at the resonant frequency.

Since $X_L = 2\pi fL$ and $X_C = \dfrac{1}{2\pi fC}$, we know that when $2\pi fL = \dfrac{1}{2\pi fC}$ the two reactance values are equal. For any series circuit that has inductance and capacitance, we can insert the values of total $L$ and total $C$ to find which frequency will cause resonance. The formula used to determine the resonant frequency when the values of $L$ and $C$ are known is as follows:

$$X_L = X_C$$

$$2\pi f_r L = \frac{1}{2\pi f_r C}$$

$$f_r^2 = \frac{1}{(2\pi C)(2\pi L)}$$

$$\sqrt{f_r^2} = \sqrt{\frac{1}{(2\pi C)(2\pi L)}}$$

$$f_r = \frac{1}{2\pi\sqrt{LC}}$$

Where:
$f_r$ = frequency at resonance
$L$ = inductance in henries
$C$ = capacitance in farads

### Example

Find the resonant frequency for a series circuit with an inductance of 0.0154 H and a capacitance of 1.61 μF.

**Solution:**

$$f_r = \frac{1}{2\pi\sqrt{LC}}$$

$$= \frac{1}{2 \times 3.1416 \times \sqrt{(0.0154 \times 0.00000161)}}$$

$$= \frac{1}{6.28 \times (0.00016)}$$

$$= 995 \text{ Hz}$$

This circuit reaches resonance at 995 Hz when both the inductor and the capacitor produce equal reactances. At this frequency, the two reactances are moving in opposite directions, and since they are equal, they cancel each other out.

When a circuit is not at resonance, current flow is limited by the combination of inductive reactance and capacitive reactance. When frequency is lowered, the inductive reactance decreases; however, since the capacitive reactance increases, the total impedance increases. If the frequency is increased above the resonant frequency,

the inductive reactance increases, the capacitive reactance decreases, and the total impedance increases. In either case, more impedance exists than when both reactances cancel each other.

Take a look at Figure 7–10 to see the effects on current at resonance and at either higher-than-resonant or lower-than-resonant frequency. When the circuit reaches resonance (the frequency at which both $L$ and $C$ reactances are equal), the current suddenly increases because the only current-limiting factor is wire resistance. The effects on the circuit voltages can be predicted.

**Resonant Frequency**

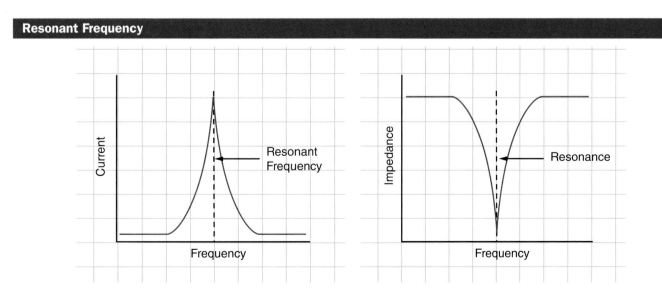

**Figure 7–10** Circuit current is maximum and impedance is minimum at resonant frequency for a series RLC circuit.

At resonance, the circuit current is at maximum. That current flows through each component, and the voltage across each component rises. The true power of the circuit goes up because the current peaks at resonant frequency, and the resistance values stay constant. At either side of resonance, the $X_C$ and $X_L$ are changing. With a lower-than-resonant frequency, the circuit appears more capacitive; at a higher-than-resonant frequency, the circuit appears more inductive. The phase angle and the power factor change rapidly around the resonant frequency point.

## SERIES CIRCUIT WITH COIL RESISTANCE

Two resistors, two capacitors, and a coil with a resistive component and reactive component all in series are shown in Figure 7–11. With this example, the coil has wire resistance as part of its opposition. Actually, the "wire resistance" is usually a very small part of the effective AC opposition in a coil. The coil has its own impedance, and the $Z$ triangle for the coil is added to the circuit oppositions. Remember from Chapter 4 the methods for calculating the current, voltage, and power of a coil with both inductive reactance and resistance.

The same process is used here with the addition of capacitors and resistors. We use common values of components to help keep the mathematics easy while keeping track of circuit conditions. As we construct the impedance triangle for the circuit, we need to pay attention to the vector directions and values for each component.

> ### Example
>
> The following representative values are assigned to the components for the circuit in Figure 7–11.
> Given:
> $$E_T = 150 \text{ V}$$
> $$R_1 = 50 \ \Omega$$
> $$R_2 = 50 \ \Omega$$
> $$X_{C1} = 50 \ \Omega$$
> $$X_{C2} = 50 \ \Omega$$
>
> Coil 1 has $X_L = 50 \ \Omega$, $R$ of coil $= 25 \ \Omega$

**Schematic of Series Circuit**

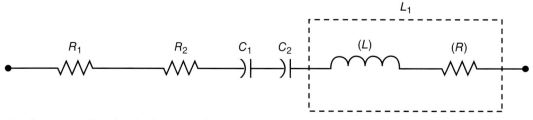

**Figure 7–11** A schematic of a circuit shows resistance, capacitance, and coil with impedance and resistance.

## Opposition Vector Diagrams

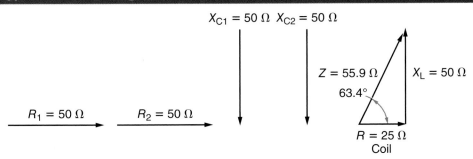

Figure 7–12 Individual opposition vector diagrams come from the circuit in Figure 7–11.

## RLC Opposition Vectors

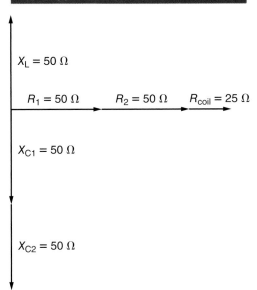

**Figure 7–13** Opposition vectors are all added in a series RLC circuit.

## Total Impedance Triangle

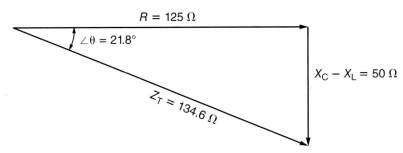

**Figure 7–14** A total impedance triangle shows values for individual components.

The individual opposition vectors appear as shown in Figure 7–12 and can be redrawn into a total impedance triangle, as shown in Figure 7–13. As the vectors are added, the final $Z$ triangle appears as in Figure 7–14. Note that each vector still represents an individual component, with the impedance of the coil shown as 55.9 $\Omega$ of $Z$. The impedance of the circuit ($Z_T$) is 134.6 $\Omega$. The triangle shows that the resultant of all components creates a more capacitive circuit and the current leads the line voltage by 21.8°. The line current is:

### FieldNote!

To find the total impedance of a coil, a right triangle is constructed using $X_L$ as the vertical component and using the resistance of the wire as the horizontal component. Refer to Figure 7–12. The hypotenuse of the triangle is the impedance $Z$ of the coil. Refer to Chapter 4 for more details.

$$I_T = \frac{E_T}{Z_T}$$

$$= \frac{150}{134.6} = 1.11 \text{ A}$$

To find the volt drop across each component, use the line current multiplied by the individual opposition.

$$E_{R1} = I_T \times R_1$$

$$= 1.11 \times 50$$

$$= 55.5 \text{ V}$$

$$E_{R2} = I_T \times R_2$$
$$= 1.11 \text{ A} \times 50 \text{ }\Omega$$
$$= 55.5 \text{ V}$$

$$E_{XC1} = I_T \times X_{C1}$$
$$= 1.11 \text{ A} \times 50 \text{ }\Omega$$
$$= 55.5 \text{ V}$$

$$E_{XC2} = I_T \times X_{C2}$$
$$= 1.11 \text{ A} \times 50 \text{ }\Omega$$
$$= 55.5 \text{ V}$$

$$E_{CoilR} = I_T \times R_{Coil}$$
$$= 1.11 \text{ A} \times 25 \text{ }\Omega$$
$$= 27.75 \text{ V}$$

$$E_{XL} = I_T \times X_L$$
$$= 1.11 \text{ A} \times 50 \text{ }\Omega$$
$$= 55.5 \text{ V}$$

$$E_{CoilZ} = I_T \times Z_{Coil}$$
$$= 1.11 \text{ A} \times 55.9 \text{ }\Omega$$
$$= 62 \text{ V}$$

As you have already discovered, if you add all voltages arithmetically your sum of 284 V is greater than the supply voltage, which is not possible. You must build a voltage triangle to prove that the figures in the preced-

ing example are accurate. See Figure 7–15 for the voltage vectors and the final voltage triangle. Even though each component can be measured with a voltmeter, each measurement, including the 62 V across the coil, can be added in the vector diagram. The total resultant of all vectors is approximately 150 V, which is the supply voltage. Our figures do not match exactly because of rounding off answers.

We can now construct the power triangle to verify calculated values. There are different methods to calculate the quantities desired. For instance, watts can be calculated by using $I^2 \times R$ or $I \times E$, as applied in the first two calculations. Likewise, VARs or volt-amps can be calculated by $I^2 \times$ opposition or $I \times E$ of the component. The methods are varied to show that different methods can be used.

$$W_{R1} = I^2 \times R_1$$
$$= 1.11^2 \times 50$$
$$= 1.23 \times 50$$
$$\approx 61.5 \text{ W}$$

***Note:*** $W_{R1}$ and $W_{R2}$ are found using two different methods. Either method could have been used for both.

**Voltage Vector Triangles**

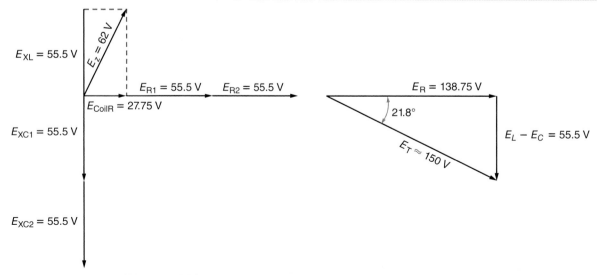

$E_{XL} = 55.5$ V

$E_Z = 62$ V

$E_{R1} = 55.5$ V    $E_{R2} = 55.5$ V

$E_{CoilR} = 27.75$ V

$E_{XC1} = 55.5$ V

$E_{XC2} = 55.5$ V

$E_R = 138.75$ V

21.8°

$E_T \approx 150$ V

$E_L - E_C = 55.5$ V

**Figure 7–15** A voltage triangle is created by individual component voltage vectors.

$$W_{R2} = I_T \times E_{R2}$$
$$= 1.11 \times 55.5$$
$$\approx 61.6 \text{ W}$$

$$VAR_{C1} = I_T \times E_{C1}$$
$$= 1.11 \times 55.5$$
$$= 61.6 \text{ VARs (capacitive)}$$

$$VAR_{C2} = I_T \times E_{C2}$$
$$= 1.11 \times 55.5$$
$$= 61.6 \text{ VARs (capacitive)}$$

$$VA_{L1} = I_T \times E_{\text{coil}}$$
$$= 1.11 \times 62$$
$$= 68.8 \text{ VA}$$

$$W_{L2} = I^2 \times R_{\text{coil}}$$
$$= 1.11^2 \times 25$$
$$= 1.23 \times 25$$
$$= 30.75 \text{ W}$$

$$VAR_{L1} = I^2 \times X_L$$
$$= 1.11^2 \times 50$$
$$= 1.23 \times 50$$
$$= 61.5 \text{ VARs}$$

**Note:** $VAR_{L1}$ could also be solved using the same formula for $VAR_{C1.}$

As you can see from the preceding calculations, the vectors for the power triangle are congruent with those of the other triangles. Adding all the watts together on the horizontal line yields 153.85 W, which is what a circuit watt meter would read. The coil has volt-amps developed across the coil, as well as VARs. The capacitors have only reactive power. See Figure 7–16 for the complete power triangle.

As you can see, the volt-amps of the circuit should be 1.11 A times the 150 V supply, or 166.5 VA. The power triangle resultant vector is approximately 166 VA. The circuit phase angle is the same throughout all the triangles at 21.8° leading current. The power factor is the cosine of that angle, or 92.8%. The power factor can be confirmed by using the formula:

$$\% \, PF = \frac{W}{VA} \times 100$$

In this case:

$$\frac{154 \text{ W}}{166 \text{ VA}} \times 100 = 92.8\%$$

these figures are rounded off to ease use of the calculation.

## Power Component Triangle

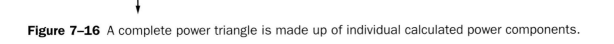

**Figure 7–16** A complete power triangle is made up of individual calculated power components.

## SUMMARY

The voltage drop across the resistor in a series RLC circuit is in phase with the current. The voltage drop across the inductor in a series RLC circuit leads the current by 90°, and the voltage drop across the capacitor in a series RLC circuit lags the current by 90°. The current is the same amperage value at all points in a series circuit.

Vector addition can be used in a series RLC circuit to find values of total voltage, impedance, and apparent power. In an RLC circuit, inductive and capacitive values are 180° out of phase with each other. The smaller value is subtracted from the larger value, resulting in a reduced larger value. Even though you can measure the component values independently, the total effects of the circuit must be added vectorially. All total vector diagrams that create right triangles for oppositions, voltage, and power are congruent.

Series resonant circuits are used for various circuit needs, such as material detection circuits in automated manufacturing processes that are frequency sensitive. The circuits can be used in band-pass filters, as discussed in Chapter 12, to detect the presence of a desired frequency. In series resonance, the combination of $X_L$ and $X_C$ are equal at a specific frequency. At this exact point, the $Z$ of the circuit is at a minimum and the circuit current is at a maximum.

Finally, we analyzed a circuit that introduced a more practical type circuit with a coil that had resistance rather than "theoretically" no wire resistance, which we used for some previous examples to build the process. This $Z$ of the coil can be added into the series circuit, and the results can be calculated.

## CHAPTER GLOSSARY

**Lagging power factor** Indicates that the circuit current waveform is behind or "lagging" the circuit voltage waveform. If the current lags the voltage, the power factor will be less than 1 or less than 100%. A lagging power factor indicates that the circuit has a net inductive effect on the current.

**Leading power factor** Indicates that the circuit current waveform is ahead of or "leading" the circuit voltage waveform. If the current leads the voltage, the power factor will be less than 1 or less than 100%. A leading power factor indicates that the circuit has a net capacitive effect on the current.

**Resonance** The value in hertz at which inductive reactance and capacitive reactance are equal (in resonance) in a circuit. At series *resonant frequency,* the circuit impedance is at a minimum and the circuit current is at a maximum.

# REVIEW QUESTIONS

1. What are the voltage relationships across each of the components in a series RLC circuit?
2. What are the current relationships in a series RLC circuit?
3. When solving a series RLC circuit, describe how you would calculate the following:
   a. Total impedance
   b. Total current flow
   c. Resistive voltage
   d. Inductive voltage
   e. Capacitive voltage
   f. Power factor
4. Explain what happens to $Z_T$ and $I_T$ in a series RLC circuit as the circuit frequency approaches resonance.
5. In a series RLC circuit operating at resonant frequency, what is the effect on circuit current?
6. Determine what the circuit power factor would be for a series RLC or LC circuit at resonant frequency.
7. How can you determine whether a series RLC circuit has a leading or lagging power factor by reviewing the impedance triangle from a mathematical standpoint?
8. What can you conclude about the frequency of a circuit when, no matter how you change the frequency, the wattmeter reads less than the original wattmeter reading?
9. In a series circuit containing a coil that has both a resistive and a reactive component, explain which component of the voltage triangle you will read with a voltmeter across the coil.
10. Write the formula used to calculate series resonant frequency.

# PRACTICE PROBLEMS

Problems 1 to 6 refer to Figure PP7–1.
1. Find the impedance.
2. Draw and label an impedance triangle for the series circuit as shown in Figure PP7–1.
3. Find $E_T$.
4. Find $E_R$, $E_C$, and $E_L$.
5. What is the true power of the circuit?
6. What is the phase angle and power factor?

Problems 7 to 13 refer to Figure PP7–2.

7. Draw and label an impedance triangle for the series circuit in Figure PP7–2.
8. Find $Z$.
9. Find $I$.
10. Find $E_R$, $E_L$, and $E_C$.
11. What power is used in this circuit? Prove it.
12. Find the total voltage and phase angle for the circuit in Figure PP7–2.
13. Draw and label a vector diagram of the circuit values for $E_C$, $E_L$, $E_R$, $I_T$, and $E_T$ and angle theta for the circuit in Figure PP7–2.

**Figure PP7–1**

**Figure PP7–2**

# 8

# PARALLEL RL CIRCUITS

# O V E R V I E W

We have connected coils in series with resistors. Now we move to AC parallel circuits. The process becomes more complicated than it was with parallel circuits in DC. The reason is that the currents and oppositions react differently to AC voltage. The current theoretically lags behind the voltage by 90° or somewhere between 0° and 90°. We develop several ways to solve the AC circuits with resistors and coils in parallel. After a quick review of parallel operation of resistors, coils are added to the circuits. This chapter adds "pure coils" or coils with no wire resistance, at first. Second, explanations involve coils that have both inductive reactance and resistance. We proceed through current triangles to vectors, find impedance, calculate power with a power triangle, and compute the power factor of the circuit.

# O B J E C T I V E S

After completing this chapter, you will be able to:

· Calculate total resistance when you know the branch resistances
· Determine the total inductance of coils in parallel
· Calculate the total inductive reactance of coils in parallel
· Explain the process of determining total current and impedance of coils and resistors in parallel
· Calculate circuit quantities of coils in parallel with resistors to find the $Z$ of the circuit
· Calculate branch and total current, impedance, voltage, and power for any parallel RL circuit
· Determine the power factor of a parallel RL circuit

## REVIEW OF PARALLEL CIRCUIT LAWS

A good review of the rules for parallel resistors and the methods of solving circuit calculations is appropriate. Remember that as resistors are added in parallel we are actually adding more paths for current to flow and therefore are actually decreasing the total opposition of the circuit. If we were to vector this type of circuit, the process would be to add together all current vectors at the same angle to find the total circuit current. From that current and the line voltage applied, we could compute the circuit opposition.

The formula is the standard Ohm's law to find the circuit totals: $R_T = \dfrac{E_T}{I_T}$. We use this same concept of adding current paths and adding currents together to yield the total current. The formula for $R_T$ with known resistors is:

$$\frac{1}{R_T} = \frac{1}{R_1} + \frac{1}{R_2} + \frac{1}{R_3} + \ldots \frac{1}{R_N}$$

OR

$$R_T = \frac{1}{\dfrac{1}{R_1} + \dfrac{1}{R_2} + \dfrac{1}{R_3} + \ldots \dfrac{1}{R_N}}$$

Many variations of the formula to calculate $R_T$ are possible; using product over sum, assuming a voltage, etc. A complete review of total resistance formulas can be found in the *DC Theory* textbook.

## INDUCTORS CONNECTED IN PARALLEL

When inductors are connected in parallel, the total inductance can be found using a formula that is similar to the one used for finding total resistance in a parallel circuit. The reciprocal of the total inductance is equal to the sum of the reciprocals of all the inductors (Figure 8–1). Calculations for Figure 8–1 are as follows:

**Three Coils in Parallel**

**Figure 8–1** Three coils in a parallel AC circuit can be combined for a total *L*.

$$\frac{1}{L_T} = \frac{1}{L_1} + \frac{1}{L_2} + \frac{1}{L_3} + \ldots \frac{1}{L_N}$$

OR

$$L_T = \frac{1}{\dfrac{1}{L_1} + \dfrac{1}{L_2} + \dfrac{1}{L_3} + \ldots \dfrac{1}{L_N}}$$

$$= \frac{1}{\dfrac{1}{L_1} + \dfrac{1}{L_2} + \dfrac{1}{L_3}} = \frac{1}{\dfrac{1}{5} + \dfrac{1}{10} + \dfrac{1}{20}}$$

$$= \frac{1}{0.2 + 0.1 + 0.05} = \frac{1}{0.35} = 2.86 \text{ H}$$

The same rules apply that we see for parallel resistors: that the total inductance of the circuit is smaller than the smallest branch inductance. The total inductance formula for two inductors in parallel is formatted the same way as the one for two resistors in parallel:

$$L_T = \frac{L_1 \times L_2}{L_1 + L_2}$$

### Example

Two coils are connected in a circuit in parallel. They have an inductance of 10 and 5 H. What is the total inductance of the two in parallel? Use the product-over-sum method.

**Solution:**

$$L_T = \frac{5 \text{ H} \times 10 \text{ H}}{5 \text{ H} + 10 \text{ H}}$$

$$= 3.33 \text{ H}$$

If all inductors are the same value, use the concept that the total inductance is the inductance of one coil divided by the number of coils, as follows:

$$L_T = \frac{L_C}{N}$$

Where:

$L_T$ = circuit total inductance
$L_C$ = common inductance
$N$ = number of like inductors

# INDUCTIVE REACTANCE IN PARALLEL

Because inductance and inductive reactance are directly proportional, the same rules that apply for inductors in parallel are used to determine inductive reactance in parallel. In other words, if the total inductance goes up, then the reactance increases. If the total inductance decreases, the total reactance decreases.

Adding additional inductors in parallel with a circuit that already contains inductors decreases the total inductive reactance of the circuit. This follows the same principle that adding additional resistor paths in parallel reduces the total resistance. Just as with resistors, the total opposition to current flow in the circuit containing parallel inductors is always less than the opposition caused by the lowest-value coil or inductor because each time another element is added in parallel the current has another path. Therefore, the same rules apply for inductive reactance as for resistors:

$$X_{LT} = \frac{1}{\dfrac{1}{X_{L1}} + \dfrac{1}{X_{L2}} + \dfrac{1}{X_{L3}} + \cdots \dfrac{1}{X_{LN}}}$$

For two reactive components:

$$X_{LT} = \frac{X_{L1} \times X_{L2}}{X_{L1} + X_{L2}}$$

**Two Coils in Parallel**

**Figure 8–2** Two identical coils in parallel can be reduced to an equivalent several ways.

## Field Note!

You can also use the formula for identical oppositions, as in:

$$X_{LT} = \frac{X_{L\ common}}{N} = \frac{50}{2} = 25\ \Omega$$

Where:

$X_{L\ common}$ = value of the common coil
$N$ = number of common coils

## Example

Find the total inductive reactance of the circuit in Figure 8–2 with two coils that are each 0.133 H and are operating at 60 Hz.

**Solution:**

$$X_{L1} = 2\pi fL$$
$$= 2\pi (60)(0.133)$$
$$= 50\ \Omega$$

$$X_{L2} = 2\pi fL$$
$$= 2\pi (60)(0.133)$$
$$\approx 50\ \Omega$$

$$X_{LT} = \frac{X_{L1} \times X_{L2}}{X_{L1} + X_{L2}}$$
$$= \frac{50 \times 50}{50 + 50}$$
$$= 25\ \Omega$$

Or use the total inductance as:

$$L_T = \frac{L_C}{N}$$
$$= \frac{0.133}{2}$$
$$= 0.0665\ H$$

$$X_{LT} = 2\pi f_{LT}$$
$$= 2\pi(60)(0.0665)$$
$$= 25\ \Omega$$

## PURE INDUCTORS AND RESISTORS IN PARALLEL

For circuits that contain resistors and inductors in parallel, the concept is the same as resistors in parallel but the mechanics of calculating the totals are more involved. We begin with a coil and a resistor in parallel. The coil shown in Figure 8–3 is a "perfect coil," having no resistance and only inductive reactance. We begin the process with this scenario to build understanding. Unlike two resistors in parallel, to find the total opposition we calculate the total current that will flow. As you know, the current in a perfect coil lags the voltage of the coil by 90 electrical degrees. As you also know about parallel circuits, the voltage is the same across all branches. Voltage is our constant and the reference is drawn on the 0° axis. All currents that are "in phase" with the line voltage are also referenced to the 0° axis. Therefore, the current that flows through the resistive branch is in phase with the applied voltage.

The current flow through the 100 Ω resistor of 1 A $\left(I = \dfrac{E}{R}\right)$ is represented by $I_R$ in Figure 8–4. The current through the 100 Ω of inductive reactance ($X_L$) is 1 A $\left(I = \dfrac{E}{X_L}\right)$ and is drawn 90° behind the voltage reference or drawn downward and labeled $I_L$. Be sure to label these vectors; they can become confusing depending on whether we are drawing $I_L$ or $X_L$ in series or in parallel.

Now that we have two vectors at 90° to each other, we can add them vectorially to obtain the resultant, or hypotenuse of 1.414 A at a 45° angle to the horizontal reference.

The total current of this circuit is 1.414 A, and it lags the line voltage by 45°. To find the impedance of this circuit, use $Z_T = \dfrac{E_T}{I_T}$. In this circuit, the total $Z$ is $\dfrac{100 \text{ V}}{1.414 \text{ A}} = 70.7$ Ω of impedance. We now have solved for the values for the current triangle for the circuit in Figure 8–4.

Another method to accomplish the same result involves the product-over-sum method used in parallel resistors for two components at a time. This process works well for two components but is more cumbersome for multiple branches. The result is to know the same quantities but not the phase angle. Although we can use product-over-sum for two resistors in parallel, the currents are both at a 0° angle to the voltage and we simply use:

$$R_T = \frac{R_1 \times R_2}{R_1 + R_2}$$

However, if the currents that are produced are not at the same angle, as in reactive current and resistive current, then the process becomes more

**Figure 8–3** A resistor and an inductor appear in parallel.

## Parallel RL Current Vectors

**Figure 8–4** Current vectors represent the magnitude and direction of the current in a parallel RL circuit.

difficult, but the following hybrid formula can be used to solve for impedance in situations like this:

$$Z_T = \frac{R \times X_L}{\sqrt{R^2 + X_L^2}}$$

By use of an example, we can verify that the formula works.

Using 10 V, 10 Ω of $R$, and 10 Ω of $X_L$, construct a current triangle of the calculated currents of 1 A $I_R$ horizontal and 1 A $I_L$. The resultant hypotenuse is $I_T = 1.414$ A. The impedance of the circuit ($Z$) is:

$$\frac{10 \text{ V}}{1.414 \text{ A}} = 7.07 \ \Omega$$

This hybrid formula uses just the opposition values, as was the case for two resistors in parallel. As mentioned, this formula takes the impedance of each opposition and calculates the magnitude of the resultant without assigning an angle. Not knowing the voltage but using the same value of 10 Ω $X_L$ and 10 Ω $R$, as in the calculation above, the impedance is:

$$Z_T = \frac{10 \times 10}{\sqrt{100 + 100}} = \frac{100}{14.14} = 7.07 \ \Omega$$

This formula applied to the values in Figure 8–3 is as follows:

$$Z_T = \frac{R \times X_L}{\sqrt{R^2 + X_L^2}}$$

$$= \frac{100 \times 100}{\sqrt{(10{,}000 + 10{,}000)}}$$

$$= \frac{10{,}000}{141.4}$$

$$= 70.7 \ \Omega$$

$$I_T = \frac{E_T}{Z_T}$$

$$= \frac{100 \text{ V}}{70.7 \ \Omega}$$

$$= 1.414 \text{ A}$$

## TechTip!

As you can see, there is more than one way to provide calculations. One method is more mathematical, using just algebra, while the other uses the visual aid of drawing vectors. Using the vectors seems less confusing as you add more components to a typical circuit and create circuits with R, $X_L$, and $X_C$, then finally with all three components in combinations of series and parallel. Although you need to use the system that is most comfortable for you, the vector addition methods you have already used are presented first.

## TechTip!

.........................................................................................

When using trigonometry to solve AC calculations and add vectors, be aware of formulas for sine, cosine, and tangent. In Figure 8–6, you need to know the angle created by the hypotenuse (Z) and the R of 75 Ωs. Calculate this angle with the tangent function, which is the ratio of opposite side to adjacent side, or $\frac{O}{A}$. Therefore, $\tan = \frac{O}{A}$.

This produces a decimal dividend that can be entered into a calculator to find the arc (angle) that has a tangent of $\frac{100}{75} = 1.3333$; the angle with a tangent of 1.3333 is 53.1°. You can use trigonometry to find the hypotenuse too, by using the angle of 53.1° and one of the sides. Use either $\sin = \frac{O}{H}$ or $\cos = \frac{A}{H}$ to solve for the hypotenuse (H). The hypotenuse can also be solved by using the two sides and the Pythagorean Theorem. A complete review of these and other trigonometric functions can be found in the appendix.

## COILS WITH IMPEDANCE IN PARALLEL WITH RESISTORS

The process becomes more involved as we add a "real coil" that contains both $R$ and $X_L$ to a parallel resistor, as shown in Figure 8–5. With the addition of the resistance of the coil wire to the inductive reactance of the coil, we create a series circuit in parallel with the 100 Ω resistance. We use the same reactance value from the first example, namely 100 Ω of $X_L$, but add 75 Ω of $R$ to the coil circuit. This effective wire resistance value is exaggerated to help you follow the process.

### A Resistor in Parallel with a Coil

**Figure 8–5** A resistor appears in parallel with a coil containing $R$ and $X_L$.

### Coil Impedance

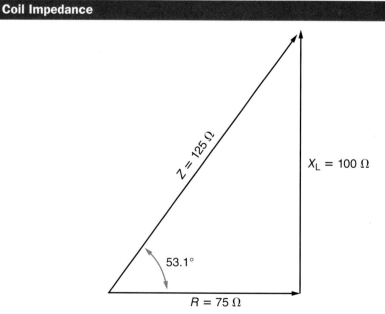

**Figure 8–6** A coil branch has $Z$ determined by opposition vectors' resistance and reactance.

We now rely on your skill in series circuit calculations to determine the current flow in the coil branch of Figure 8–5. Refer to Figure 8–6 to see the impedance created by the coil. The $Z$ of the coil is 125 Ω. The angle created by the total impedance vector is 53.1° lagging, or more inductive. Remember that this impedance has an effect on the current through that component, causing the current to lag the voltage by the same 53.1°. Now if we calculate the current through the coil, it is:

$$I_{coil} = \frac{E_{coil}}{Z_{coil}} \text{ or } I = \frac{100 \text{ V}}{125 \text{ Ω}} \text{ or } I = 0.8 \text{ A}.$$

Unlike the first example, the current through the coil is no longer theoretically 90° lagging but is really 53.1° behind the voltage. Referring back to the vector addition of currents in parallel, we must now add the current vectors together (Figure 8–7). When we add the vectors, one at 0° (the current through the resistor) and one at a 53.1° lag (the current through the coil), the resultant is the circuit current and the resultant angle, is the circuit voltage and current displacement. The resultant is 1.61 A at 23.4° lag. The line current (1.61 A) lags the line voltage (100 V) by 23.4°. The percent power factor for the circuit is the cosine of this angle theta (θ) × 100, or 0.918 × 100 = 91.8% power factor. We confirm this later in this chapter.

# CURRENT, IMPEDANCE, VOLTAGE, AND POWER

As you calculate the quantities involved, you need to track the angles, the vectors for the individual branches, and the power developed at each component. Be sure to verify that these individual values still add to the total and that the total makes sense with the applied source. For this verification example process, we again choose to ignore the resistance of the coil, meaning that it is a high Q, or quality factor, of 10, as referenced in Chapter 4—the reactance is at least 10 times the resis-

## TechTip!

When adding vectors at various angles, it is essential to construct vectors so that you can find the horizontal and the vertical components. In Figure 8–7, the current vector of 0.8 A is at an angle to the horizontal of 53.1°. To add this to the $I_R$ of 1 A, use the function of $\cos = \frac{A}{H}$, from trigonometry to find the adjacent side. The cosine of 53.1° is 0.6; $0.6 = \frac{A}{0.8}$, so the adjacent side is 0.48 A at 0° as shown. This triangle's vertical side is found with the sine function. The sin of 53.1° = 0.799, so $0.799 = \frac{Opposite}{0.8}$; therefore, the opposite, or vertical, component is 0.639. To get the resultant of the combination of the two original currents, add all horizontal components to get 1.48 A and create a right triangle with the 0.639 A of the vertical component. The hypotenuse can be calculated using trigonometry or the Pythagorean Theorem.

**Vector Addition**

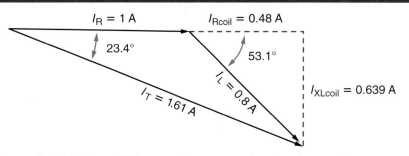

**Figure 8–7** Vector addition combines currents at various angles.

**Resistors and Coils in Parallel**

**Figure 8–8** Two resistors and two "perfect" high Q coils are shown in parallel.

tance. See Figure 8–8 for this example of two coils and two resistors. As you notice, the circuit values are designed to aid in understanding, not to be cumbersome in mathematical calculations.

**Current Triangle**

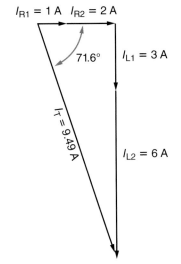

$I_{R1} = 1$ A    $I_{R2} = 2$ A

71.6°

$I_{L1} = 3$ A

$I_T = 9.49$ A

$I_{L2} = 6$ A

**Figure 8–9** This current triangle results from Figure 8–8.

Assuming we use 120 V AC, 60 Hz and the values of 120 and 60 Ω of resistance and 0.106 H, 40 Ω, $X_L$ and, 0.053 H, 20 Ω, $X_L$, respectively, we can easily calculate the total current flow from the source. Use the $X_L = 2\pi fL$ and 60 Hz to calculate the $X_L$ of each coil. See Figure 8–9 for the total current triangle based on the current flow through each branch. Even though the branches are 1, 2, 3, and 6 A, respectively, the total is *not* the arithmetic sum of 12 A. Instead, the resultant hypotenuse of the triangle is 9.49 A.

$$I_T = \sqrt{I_R^2 + I_L^2}$$
$$= \sqrt{(1 + 2)^2 + (3 + 6)^2}$$
$$= \sqrt{9 + 81} = \sqrt{90} = 9.49 \text{ A}$$

## FieldNote!

Power can only be dissipated or consumed by a resistive component; therefore, there is nothing to add up unless it involves resistance. The total power can be added mathematically by the power each resistor consumes; otherwise, it is VARs or volt-amps, which is very different. Theoretically, no power is consumed by either an inductor or a capacitor. The only other power we have in an AC circuit is *apparent power*, or $VA = E_{applied} \times I_T$.

Through trigonometry, we can calculate the circuit phase angle as 71.6°.

## IMPEDANCE OF THE CIRCUIT

The impedance of the circuit could be calculated using the product of the oppositions divided by the square root of the sum of the squares of the opposition, two components at a time, as shown below.

$$Z_T = \frac{R \times X_L}{\sqrt{R^2 + X_L^2}}$$

A more efficient manner is to use the vector sum of the branch current and divide by the source voltage, as follows:

$$Z_T = \frac{E_T}{I_T}$$
$$= \frac{120 \text{ V AC}}{9.49 \text{ A}}$$
$$= 12.64 \text{ }\Omega$$

For reference, this means that we have a total of 12.64 Ω of impedance at a 71.6° lagging angle to the purely resistive horizontal reference.

## VOLTAGE OF THE CIRCUIT

As is the rule for a parallel circuit in DC circuits as well as AC circuits, the voltage value is consistent for all branches of the circuit and it remains at 120 V. The current and the phase angle through each component are dictated by the opposition encountered in each branch. See Figure 8–8 for voltage verification.

## POWER IN THIS CIRCUIT

Power in the parallel circuit depends on the individual branches. Each branch acts as an independent load. Unlike the loads that are all in phase with one another, as in a parallel DC circuit, we are not allowed to add the power loads arithmetically unless they all have the same phase angle. The power measurements (watts, volt-amps, VARs) must be added based on their phase angle relationship with the voltage and current.

In this instance, the voltage across each opposition is the same and the current is based on the individual opposition. Therefore, to find the power we need to take the branch current times the branch voltage. Power for the resistive components is in the form of watts. Power for the reactive components is in VARs. Then each power component is vectorially added to yield the circuit totals. See the following calculations:

$$W_{R1} = E \times I_1$$
$$= 120 \text{ V} \times 1 \text{ A}$$
$$= 120 \text{ W}$$

$$W_{R2} = E \times I_2$$
$$= 120 \text{ V} \times 2 \text{ A}$$
$$= 240 \text{ W}$$

$$VAR_{L1} = E \times I_{L1}$$
$$= 120 \text{ V} \times 3 \text{ A}$$
$$= 360 \text{ VARs}$$

$$VAR_{L2} = E \times I_{L2}$$
$$= 120 \text{ V} \times 6 \text{ A}$$
$$= 720 \text{ VARs}$$

**Power Triangle**

**Figure 8–10** This power triangle results from Figure 8–8.

With these vectors, we can complete the power triangle seen in Figure 8–10. The resultant volt-amps, or hypotenuse of the triangle, is 1,138 VA.

$$VA = \sqrt{W^2 + VAR^2}$$
$$= \sqrt{(120 + 240)^2 + (360 + 720)^2}$$
$$= \sqrt{129,600 + 1,166,400}$$
$$= \sqrt{1,296,000} = 1,138.4$$

To confirm these calculations, we can take the line current times the line voltage to get circuit volt-amps of apparent power:

$$120 \text{ V} \times 9.48 \text{ A} = 1,138 \text{ VA}$$

The last step is to confirm the phase angle and the power factor. The power factor (PF) is still equal to $\left( \dfrac{\text{Watts}}{\text{Volt-amps}} \right)$ $\times$ 100. We can also use the cosine of the phase angle between circuit current and circuit voltage $\times$ 100 = % *PF*. See the following calculations:

$$\% \, PF = \frac{\text{True power}}{\text{Apparent power}} \times 100$$
$$= \left( \frac{W}{VA} \right) \times 100$$
$$= \left( \frac{360 \text{ W}}{1,138 \text{ VA}} \right) \times 100$$
$$= 0.316 \times 100$$
$$= 31.6\%$$

OR

$$\% \, PF = \cos 71.6° \times 100$$
$$= 0.3156 \times 100$$
$$= 31.6\%$$

**Parallel Impedance Formula**

Still another way to solve the last example is to add the resistors in parallel as you would with a DC circuit to get an equivalent circuit. Thus, 120 and 60 $\Omega$ in parallel create an equivalent value of 40 $\Omega$.

$$R_T = \frac{120 \times 60}{120 + 60}$$
$$= \frac{7,200}{180} = 40 \ \Omega$$

## FieldNote!

The most prevalent type of parallel circuit is the parallel circuit with multiple resistive values and some reactive values. A typical home may have a 20 A, 120 V kitchen circuit with multiple loads. In parallel could be a toaster, an electric can opener, a waffle iron, and an electric knife. Each of these loads can create its own branch of a parallel circuit with varying degrees of phase angle. The circuit can be calculated at the circuit breaker as the voltage source to determine how this AC circuit would react.

Then the reactance of the coils of 40 Ω and 20 Ω could be added together, using the product-over-sum method, to get a total $X_L$ of 13.3 Ω.

$$X_{LT} = \frac{40 \times 20}{40 + 20}$$

$$= \frac{800}{60} = 13.33 \ \Omega$$

See Figure 8–11 for an equivalent circuit. The final $Z$ is the same as calculated in earlier examples. You do not have the convenience of all the branch currents to quickly find power and it is harder to double check your results,

### Equivalent Circuit

**Figure 8–11** The equivalent circuit of two coils and two resistors is used to create the parallel impedance formula.

but the results are the same when you use high Q coils where you disregard the resistance in the coil circuits:

$$Z = \frac{R \times X_L}{\sqrt{R^2 + X_L^2}}$$

$$= \frac{40 \times 13.3}{\sqrt{40^2 + 13.3^2}}$$

$$= \frac{532}{\sqrt{1,600 + 176.9}}$$

$$= \frac{532}{\sqrt{1,776.9}}$$

$$= \frac{532}{42.2} = 12.6 \ \Omega$$

## MULTIPLE COILS WITH WIRE RESISTANCE AND RESISTORS IN PARALLEL

In this last example, we use two coils and two resistors, each with a different value. This might be similar to the kitchen circuit mentioned in the previous sidebar. Figure 8–12 provides an example. Again, the values may be exaggerated to show method and process rather than actual appliance values. A 60 Ω ($R_1$) resistor and a 120 Ω ($R_2$) resistor are in parallel with coil 1 ($L_1$), which has 16 Ω $X_L$ and 12 Ω $R$ and coil 2 ($L_2$), which has 48 Ω $X_L$ and 64 Ω $R$. The circuit voltage is 120 V. You can solve this problem using the following equations:

$$I = \frac{E}{R} \text{ (for restrictive branches)}$$

$$I = \frac{E}{Z} \text{ (for inductive branches)}$$

Find the current through the resistors:

$$I_{R1} = \frac{E_T}{R_1} = \frac{120 \text{ V}}{60 \ \Omega} = 2 \text{ A at } 0°$$

$$I_{R2} = \frac{E_T}{R_2} = \frac{120 \text{ V}}{120 \ \Omega} = 1 \text{ A at } 0°$$

Find the current through the coils:

$$Z_{L1} = \sqrt{R_{L1}^2 + X_{L1}^2}$$

$$= \sqrt{12^2 + 16^2} = 20 \ \Omega$$

$$Z_{L2} = \sqrt{R_{L2}^2 + X_{L2}^2}$$

$$= \sqrt{64^2 + 48^2} = 80 \ \Omega$$

$$I_{L1} = \frac{E_T}{Z_{L1}} = \frac{120 \text{ V}}{20 \text{ }\Omega} = 6 \text{ A at } 53.1°$$

$$I_{L2} = \frac{E_T}{Z_{L2}} = \frac{120 \text{ V}}{80 \text{ }\Omega} = 1.5 \text{ A at } 36.9°$$

Find the phase angle of the impedance for each branch using the trigonometric functions with $R$ and $X_L$ as the sides of the impedance triangle and $Z$ as the hypotenuse. Add the current vectors as shown in Figure 8-13 as follows:

$$I_T = \sqrt{I_R{}^2 + I_L{}^2}$$

The currents for each branch were found in equations for Figure 8–12. The two coil currents were at an angle to the horizontal, matching the impedance triangle for each coil that you would have calculated in Figure 8–12. The third branch had a coil with a phase angle of 53.1°, and the last branch had a coil with a phase angle of 36.9°. By using the branch currents at the appropriate phase angles, you can construct a vector addition problem using a head-to-tail method. By using trigonometry, the horizontal side of the 6 A vector at 53.1° is 3.6, and the vertical component of the same 6 A vector is 4.8. The fourth branch has a current of 1.5 A at an angle of 36.9°. The horizontal component is 1.2, and the vertical component is 0.9. You can now construct the large current triangle with all the horizontal and vertical components as shown. Using the Pythagorean Theorem, you find the hypotenuse as 9.66 A. The angle between the horizontal voltage reference and the hypotenuse is calculated by trigonometric function of sin, cos, or tan and the known sides. The circuit phase angle is 36.15°.

The vector sum is 9.66 A at 36.15° to the horizontal and is lagging because it is an inductive circuit. The voltage, since this is a parallel circuit, is a constant 120 V.

The power triangle is congruent to the current triangle, as in Figure 8–14.

**Different-Value Resistors and Coils in Parallel**

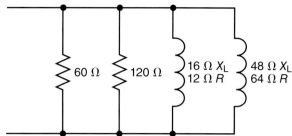

**Figure 8–12** Two different-value resistors and two different-value coils are shown in parallel.

**Vector Addition**

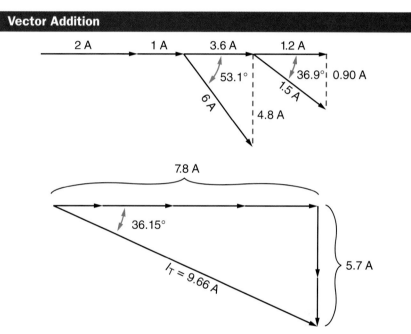

**Figure 8–13** Vector addition combines currents for the circuit in Figure 8–12.

**Power Triangle**

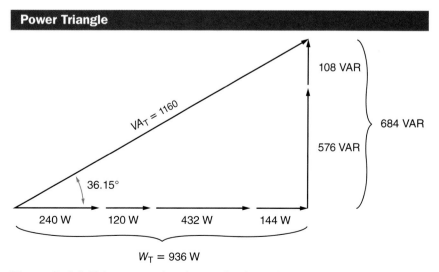

**Figure 8–14** This power triangle results from the circuit in Figure 8–12.

True power is measured in watts and is represented or shown along the horizontal axis because it has a 0° angle. The VARs are represented or shown along the vertical axis caused by and as a result of the reactive components. The volt-amps or apparent power is a product of the line current times the line voltage and forms the hypotenuse of the power triangle. The final figures are rounded off to ease the calculation process but maintain the theory:

$W = E \times I$ (branch voltage × branch current)

$W$ in $R_1 = 120 \text{ V} \times 2 \text{ A}$
$= 240 \text{ W}$

$W$ in $R_2 = 120 \text{ V} \times 1 \text{ A}$
$= 120 \text{ W}$

$W = I \times E$ (horizontal component of branch current triangle × branch voltage)

$W$ in $L_1 = 3.6 \text{ A}$ (resistive current)
$\times 120 \text{ V}$
$= 432 \text{ W}$

$W$ in $L_2 = 1.2 \text{ A}$ (resistive current)
$\times 120 \text{ V}$
$= 144 \text{ W}$

$VAR = I \times E$ (vertical component of branch current triangle × branch voltage)

$VAR$ in $L_1 = 4.8 \text{ A}$ (reactive) $\times 120 \text{ V}$
$= 576 \text{ VARs}$

$VAR$ in $L_2 = 0.9 \text{ A}$ (reactive) $\times 120 \text{ V}$
$= 108 \text{ VARs}$

$W_T = W_1 + W_2 + W_3 + W_4$
$= 240 + 120 + 432 + 144$
$= 936 \text{ W}$

$VAR_T = VAR_1 + VAR_2$
$= 576 + 108 = 684 \text{ VARs}$

$VA_T = $ line voltage × line current
$= 120 \text{ V} \times 9.66 \text{ A} = 1{,}160 \text{ VA}$

Power factor $= \left(\dfrac{936 \text{ W}}{1{,}160 \text{ VA}}\right) = 0.807$

OR

$\% PF = $ cosine $36.15° \times 100 = 80.7\%$

# SUMMARY

In this chapter, we created circuits with coils in parallel with resistors. Because the coils and resistors have different phase angles in an AC circuit, they cannot be inserted into an equation in the same way as with DC circuits.

One method of calculating $Z$ is to vectorially add the current vectors, find a total current, and then use total $E$ and total $I$ to get total $Z$. Other methods can be applied under special circumstances. The process of calculating all the circuit variables included the calculation of AC power, which was illustrated by the power triangle. This led to the power factor and the angle of lag, which was the same angle represented by a current triangle.

## REVIEW QUESTIONS

1. Explain why total resistance decreases as you add more resistors in parallel.
2. What is the relationship between total inductance and branch circuit inductance in parallel circuits?
3. Write a formula for finding the $X_{LT}$ of three different coils in a parallel AC circuit.
4. Explain a method of adding a branch resistor current to a separate branch inductor current to find the total circuit current.
5. Explain why the phase angle of a current triangle parallel current vector would be the same as a power triangle for the same circuit.
6. How would you calculate the voltage across a parallel circuit if you only knew the $X_L$ of one coil and the current through that coil?
7. What is meant by adding a "pure" inductance in parallel?
8. In a circuit with resistors and inductors in parallel, what happens to the phase angle as we add more inductors in parallel?
9. Explain how to find the percent power factor if you know the watts and the VAs of a circuit.
10. What is the process to find the total watts of a parallel R-L circuit?
11. A decrease in frequency in a parallel circuit causes the power factor to _____.

# PRACTICE PROBLEMS

1. What is the power factor of a circuit that has 30° lagging inductive current behind the resistive current?
2. If a circuit has 10 A line current and 200 V line voltage but only consumes 150 W with a watt meter, what is the reactive power (VARs)?
3. Find the percent power factor for the circuit in question 2.

Practice problems 4 through 10 refer to Figure PP8–1.

4. What is the current through the resistive branch?
5. What is the current through the inductive branch?
6. Find $I_T$.
7. Construct a current vector diagram.
8. What is the impedance of this circuit?
9. Show how to find the impedance in problem 8 using the parallel impedance formula.
10. Find the total circuit power factor of the RL circuit.

8 V
1 kHz

$R = 4.7\ \text{k}\Omega$

$X_L = 3.14\ \text{k}\Omega$

**Figure PP8–1**

# 9

# PARALLEL RC CIRCUITS

# T O P I C S

# O V E R V I E W

The calculations for solving parallel capacitor circuits are similar to those of parallel resistance and inductance circuits. The primary differences are that capacitors in series are calculated like resistors and inductors in parallel and that capacitors in parallel are calculated like resistors and inductors in series.

In Chapter 6, the series RC circuit was discussed. Remember that in series circuits the current is the same through all components and is the reference point. The voltages are in relation to the reference current.

In a parallel circuit, voltage is the same across all components. In parallel circuits that contain both resistance and reactance, the branch currents are out of phase and the voltage is the reference. Again, a parallel circuit that contains resistance and capacitance is called a parallel RC circuit. In this chapter, we analyze how the capacitive currents combine with the resistive currents and affect the circuit totals. We determine the impedance of the circuit based on the total current flow rather than on the vector additions of the oppositions provided by resistors and capacitors. Finally, we determine what the circuit trends are as we change variables in the parallel RC circuit.

# O B J E C T I V E S

After completing this chapter, you will be able to:
- Determine the effects of capacitors in parallel
- Calculate the total capacitance of a circuit with multiple capacitors in parallel
- Calculate the capacitive reactance of parallel capacitors
- Find all required circuit quantities such as current, impedance, voltage, and power
- Perform circuit calculations for all parallel RC circuits
- Describe the effects of changing parameters in a parallel RC circuit
- Determine mathematically unknown quantities in these circuits

## CAPACITORS IN PARALLEL

As first discussed in Chapter 6, we found the effects on the circuit when capacitors were connected in series. When the capacitors are connected in parallel, the areas of the individual plates are added together, increasing the capacitance. Connecting capacitors in parallel has the same effect as increasing the plate area of one capacitor. Look at Figure 9–1 to equate the plate size to parallel capacitors. The formula used to determine the capacitance when the dielectric constant ($K$), the area of the plates ($A$, in square inches), and the distance between the plates ($d$, in inches) also applies here. You can see that increasing the surface area of the plates increases the capacitance value ($C$). Capacitors in parallel are calculated similarly to inductors and resistors in series.

Previously, you learned that when inductors are connected in series, the total induction of the circuit equals the sum of the inductances of each of the inductors:

$$L_T = L_1 + L_2 + L_3 + \ldots L_N \quad \text{(series)}$$

The total resistance in a series circuit is found by adding the values of the resistors in the circuit:

$$R_T = R_1 + R_2 + R_3 + \ldots R_N \quad \text{(series)}$$

Connecting capacitors in parallel has the same effect as increasing the plate area of one capacitor. Capacitors in parallel are calculated similarly to inductors and resistors in series.

The total capacitance of a parallel capacitance circuit is given by:

$$C_T = C_1 + C_2 + C_3 + \ldots C_N \quad \text{(parallel)}$$

---

### Example

Calculate the total capacitance of the circuit shown in Figure 9–2.

**Solution:**

$$C_T = C_1 + C_2 + C_3$$

$$= 20 \ \mu\text{F} + 30 \ \mu\text{F} + 60 \ \mu\text{F}$$

$$= 110 \ \mu\text{F}$$

---

## CAPACITIVE REACTANCE IN PARALLEL

Capacitive reactance is an opposition to the flow of AC current, as discussed in Chapter 5. As such, we can treat the reactance of the capacitor as another ohmic value as we would ohms of resistance or ohms of inductive reactance. We can add the ohmic values of components that have the same reaction to the phase relationship in the AC circuit. As you know, the ohmic value is due to the voltage developed by the capacitor charge and creates a value that is 90° out of phase with the resistance. Therefore, when we add capacitive reactance in parallel, we just use the same rules as resistors or inductive reactance in parallel.

---

**Parallel Capacitors and Plate Area**

$$C = \frac{KA}{d}$$

(A) Gets Larger

**Figure 9–1** The effect of parallel capacitors equates to a larger plate area in the capacitance formula.

---

**Capacitors in Parallel AC Circuit**

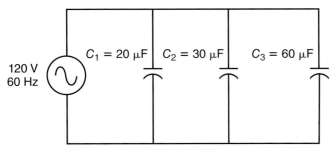

**Figure 9–2** Three separate capacitors appear in a parallel AC circuit.

By adding more parallel paths, we increase the number of current paths and reduce the total opposition of the circuit. We would use the following formulas for finding total $X_C$ when we know the individual capacitive reactance of the circuit:

$$\frac{1}{X_{CT}} = \frac{1}{X_{C1}} + \frac{1}{X_{C2}} + \frac{1}{X_{C3}} \cdots \frac{1}{X_{CN}}$$

OR

$$X_{CT} = \frac{1}{\dfrac{1}{X_{C1}} + \dfrac{1}{X_{C2}} + \dfrac{1}{X_{C3}} \cdots \dfrac{1}{X_{CN}}}$$

For product over sum for two branches at a time:

$$X_{CT} = \frac{X_{C1} \times X_{C2}}{X_{C1} + X_{C2}}$$

If all branches are alike and $N$ represents the number of like branches, then:

$$X_{CT} = \frac{X_C}{N}$$

If you know the $C_T$, then

$$X_{CT} = \frac{1}{2\pi f C_T} \text{ can be used.}$$

## Example

Calculate the total capacitive reactance of Figure 9–2 by using the individual capacitance values or the individual reactances at 60 Hz.

**Solution:**

Reactances in parallel behave the same as resistances in parallel. Therefore, the total reactance is:

$$C_T = C_1 + C_2 + C_3$$
$$= 20 \ \mu F + 30 \ \mu F + 60 \ \mu F$$
$$= 110 \ \mu F$$

$$X_{CT} = \frac{1}{2\pi f C_T} \quad \textbf{\textit{Note:}} \ C_T \text{ is in microfarads } (\mu F).$$
$$= \frac{1}{(377)(0.00011)}$$
$$= 24.1 \ \Omega$$

OR

$$X_{C1} = \frac{1}{2\pi f C_T} = \frac{1}{(377)(0.00002)}$$
$$= 132.6 \ \Omega$$

$$X_{C2} = \frac{1}{2\pi f C_T} = \frac{1}{(377)(0.00003)}$$
$$= 88.4 \ \Omega$$

$$X_{C3} = \frac{1}{2\pi f C_T} = \frac{1}{(377)(0.00006)}$$
$$= 44.2 \ \Omega$$

$$X_{CT} = \frac{1}{\dfrac{1}{X_{C1}} + \dfrac{1}{X_{C2}} + \dfrac{1}{X_{C3}} \cdots}$$
$$= \frac{1}{\dfrac{1}{132.6} + \dfrac{1}{88.4} + \dfrac{1}{44.2}}$$
$$= \frac{1}{0.00754 + 0.0113 + 0.0226}$$
$$= \frac{1}{0.0415}$$
$$= 24.1 \ \Omega$$

## PARALLEL RC CIRCUITS

When resistance and capacitance are connected in parallel, the voltage across all the devices is in phase and has the same value for each device. The current flow through the capacitor is 90° out of phase, or leading the capacitive voltage. The phase angle shift between the total current and the total voltage is determined by the ratio of the amount of resistance to the amount of capacitive reactance. Since the amount of capacitive reactance and amount of resistance independently determine the amount of current flowing through each branch, whether it is the resistive or the capacitive branch, the total cur-

rent flow can be determined only after those values are determined.

The capacitive branch of the circuit is directly affected by the capacitive reactance, which depends on the capacitance value and the frequency of the source.

## CIRCUIT VALUES

In Figure 9–3, the resistor (25 Ω) is connected in parallel with a capacitor that has a capacitive reactance of 20 Ω. The circuit power supply is 220 V at a frequency of 60 Hz. Remember that the resistive and capacitance branches have to be calculated separately and then combined for total circuit values.

### CIRCUIT CURRENTS

Refer to Figure 9–3 for the following calculations. The current flow through the resistor can be calculated using the following formula:

$$I_R = \frac{E}{R}$$
$$= \frac{220 \text{ V}}{25 \text{ Ω}}$$
$$= 8.8 \text{ A}$$

The current flow through the capacitor is calculated using the following formula:

$$I_C = \frac{E}{X_C}$$
$$= \frac{220 \text{ V}}{20 \text{ Ω}}$$
$$= 11 \text{ A}$$

In this simple circuit, we cannot determine the circuit current by adding the currents. Because the currents are not in phase with each other, they are not occurring at the same point in time. Therefore, we need to add them using the right triangle of the Pythagorean Theorem or vector addition. See Figure 9–4 for the triangle developed by adding the resistive current with the capacitive current that is 90° out of phase.

**Parallel RC Circuit**

**Figure 9–3** A parallel circuit shows resistance and capacitance.

**Current Triangle**

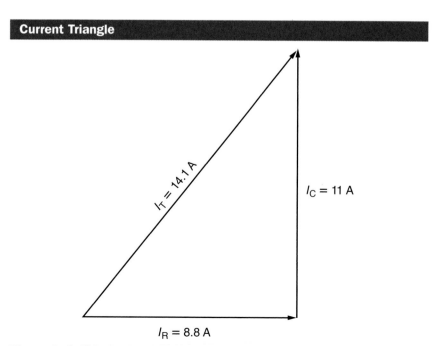

**Figure 9–4** This current triangle is for the circuit in Figure 9–3.

As you know, the vector addition of 8.8 A and 11 A does not equal 19.8 A but instead yields the resultant current of approximately 14.1 A. This resultant current is the current delivered by the circuit from the source of supply. We can also view the current triangle vector to find the angle of lead—the angle between the horizontal axis and the hypotenuse. We use trigonometry to calculate the arc, which has a tangent of ratio between the opposite and the adjacent sides to the angle. In this case, the formula for the current phase angle is as follows:

$$\tan \theta = \frac{\text{Opposite side magnitude}}{\text{Adjacent side magnitude}}$$
$$= \frac{I_C}{I_R}$$
$$= \frac{11 \text{ A}}{8.8 \text{ A}} = 1.25$$

Find the arc, which has a tangent of 1.25:

$$\arctan (\tan^{-1}) \ 1.25 = \theta \text{ of } 51.3°$$

We now can tell that the circuit current leads the circuit voltage by 51.3°. We can verify this fact as we work through the rest of the calculations.

Another way to get the total current with these two currents that are 90° out of phase with each other is to use the Pythagorean formula, as follows:

$$I_T = \sqrt{I_R^2 + I_C^2}$$
$$= \sqrt{8.8^2 + 11^2}$$
$$= \sqrt{77.44 + 121}$$
$$= 14.1 \text{ A}$$

### CIRCUIT IMPEDANCE

The total circuit impedance can be found using any of the total values and substituting $Z$ for opposition in the Ohm's law formula. Remember that circuit impedance is not found by vector addition of the individual oppositions. In parallel circuits, the current paths are the deciding criteria for the total opposition of the circuit. We need to find the total current and then determine what impedance caused that current

## FieldNote!

An ammeter placed in the individual branches of the circuit will actually read a resistive current of 8.8 A, a capacitive current of 11 A, and a total current of 14.1 A. To find actual circuit component values, you can use Ohm's law to determine the opposition based on the current and the voltage. If you do not know the capacitor value, you can calculate the value by measuring the current $I_C$ and using the formula $X_C = \dfrac{E}{I_C}$ to find the capacitive reactance. Then, working backward from that value, use the formula $C = \dfrac{1}{2\pi f X_C}$ to find the capacitor value in farads.

flow. The total impedance can be calculated using the following formula:

$$Z_T = \frac{E_T}{I_T}$$
$$= \frac{220 \text{ V}}{14.1 \text{ A}}$$
$$= 15.6 \ \Omega$$

## VOLTAGE

The circuit voltage in a parallel RC circuit stays the same throughout each branch of the circuit as it does in any parallel circuit. You need to remember that the current and the voltage in a resistive branch is in phase, or reaching peak and zero points of the respective sine wave at the same point in time. However, the current and the voltage for the capacitive branch are 90° out of phase. When we need to verify the voltage across the resistor, it is still:

$$E_R = I \times R$$

The voltage across the capacitor is:

$$E_C = I \times X_C$$

In the example in Figure 9–3, we could calculate the voltage across the capacitor as:

$$E_C = 11 \text{ A} \times 20 \ \Omega = 220 \text{ V}$$

When we consider the circuit values in total, we know that the circuit current is somewhere between 0° and 90° leading the circuit voltage. In the first example, the current is leading the voltage by 53.1° because it is a capacitive effect circuit.

# POWER IN PARALLEL RC CIRCUITS

Remember that true power is consumed in the resistive parts of a circuit where current flow is in phase with the voltage. The amount of true power in the circuit can be determined by using any of the values associated with the purely resistive part of the circuit. For Figure 9–3, true power can be found using the following formula:

$$P = E \times I_R$$

$$= 220 \text{ V} \times 8.8 \text{ A}$$

$$= 1{,}936 \text{ W}$$

### APPARENT POWER

The apparent power can be computed by multiplying the circuit voltage by the total current flow. This is the hypotenuse of the power triangle as shown in Figure 9–5:

$$VA = E \times I_T$$

$$= 220 \text{ V} \times 14.1 \text{ A}$$

$$= 3{,}102 \text{ VA}$$

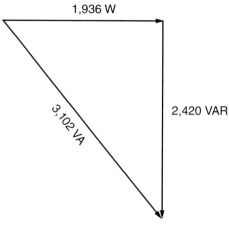

**Power Triangle**

1,936 W

2,420 VAR

3,102 VA

**Figure 9–5** This power triangle is for circuit in Figure 9–3.

### REACTIVE POWER

In this example of reactive power, energy is stored by the capacitor in the form of volts of pressure and coulombs of electric charge in the electrostatic field. The power that is delivered to the circuit is measured in VARs. We need to determine the amount of capacitive current and the amount of voltage across the capacitor circuit. These two values multiplied together yield the VARs of the RC circuit. In the example circuit, we calculated the current through the capacitor at 11 A and the capacitor voltage is 220 V. See Figure 9–5 for the total power triangle. The VARs formula is as follows:

$$VAR = E_{\text{line}} \times I_c$$

$$= 220 \text{ V} \times 11 \text{ A}$$

$$= 2{,}420 \text{ VARs}$$

Verify these values by using the power triangle as shown in Figure 9–5. If you verify the values for the power triangle using the Pythagorean Theorem, you will notice a slight discrepancy in the apparent power because of rounding errors in earlier calculations.

## FieldNote!

In parallel RC circuits, the voltage measured across each parallel component appears to be the same value. However, the voltages are out of phase with each other, which is not seen with a voltmeter. The vectors would look like this:

$$I \times X_C = E_C$$

$$I \times R = E_R$$

These vectors are not added together mathematically.

## POWER FACTOR

As is the case in all AC circuits, the power factor (*PF*) is a factor applied to the apparent power of the circuit. As we multiply the decimal equivalent of the percent power factor of the circuit times the apparent power of the circuit, the product yields the true power. The power factor is the ratio of true power to apparent power. One formula for determining the power factor is the following:

$$PF = \frac{\text{True power in watts}}{\text{Apparent power in volt-amps}}$$

$$\% \, PF = \left(\frac{W}{VA}\right) \times 100$$

$$= \left(\frac{1,936 \text{ W}}{3,102 \text{ VA}}\right) \times 100$$

$$= 62.4\%$$

## ANGLE THETA

Remember that the cosine of angle theta ($\theta$) is equal to the power factor. The angle $\theta$ is the angle that the current is out of phase with the voltage. In the power triangle, it is the angle determined by the ratio of watts to apparent power (*VA*). The formula is as follows:

$$\cos \angle\theta = \frac{\text{Adj}}{\text{Hyp}} = \frac{W}{VA}$$

$$= \frac{1,936}{3,102} = 0.624$$

$$\% \, PF = \cos \theta \times 100$$

$$= 62.4\%$$

$$\angle\theta = \cos^{-1} 0.624$$

$$= 51.3°$$

Remember that this angle is the same angle found in the current triangle of the 51.3° leading current. This sample problem has a leading power factor of 62.4%.

## TechTip!

As is the case in all AC circuits, the line current times the line voltage yields apparent power. Only in completely resistive circuits is the apparent power measured in volt-amps equal to the true power measured in watts. As you will see, you can always use the formula of $E \times I \times$ power factor to yield true power in an AC circuit. An example would be 120 V $\times$ 10 A = 1,200 VA in an AC circuit. True power in watts can be calculated by $P_{\text{True}} = E_{\text{Line}} \times I_{\text{Line}} \times \cos \theta$. If the circuit is totally resistive, the power factor is 100%, or a power factor of 1.0. Therefore $E \times I \times PF$ is 120 V $\times$ 10 A $\times$ 1.0 = 1,200 watts. The power factor can never be more than 100% and is only 100% for totally resistive circuits.

## MULTIPLE RESISTORS AND CAPACITORS IN PARALLEL

Multiple resistors and capacitors in parallel are not as difficult as true coils (high *Q*) and resistors in parallel. Because capacitors have so little resistance compared to their capacitive reactance, we do not need to include the *R* of the capacitor as we calculate the actual branch currents. Therefore, the addition of more resistors or capacitors is a relatively easy extension of the rules just presented. We need to vector current of the resistors at 0° and current of the capacitor at 90° leading. We find all parameters for the circuit as shown in Figure 9–6.

**Schematic Diagram**

**Figure 9–6** A schematic diagram shows an RC circuit with two capacitors and two resistors.

## Example

To keep the mathematics to a minimum, we use simple values. The steps are the same as those we previously used for parallel AC circuits: (1) find the branch currents; (2) add the appropriate values to create a circuit current triangle; (3) determine the circuit impedance if needed; (4) calculate the phase angle of the currents; (5) find the power components; (6) construct a circuit power triangle to determine each power component. In our simple circuit, we have two resistors rated as $R_1$, at 40 Ω and $R_2$ at 60 Ω and two capacitors with $X_{C1}$ at 20 Ω and $X_{C2}$ at 120 Ω. The supply voltage is 120 V AC at 60 Hz. Use the following formulas:

$$I_{R1} = \frac{E}{R_1}$$
$$= \frac{120}{40\ \Omega}$$
$$= 3\text{ A at }0°$$

$$I_{R2} = \frac{E}{R_2}$$
$$= \frac{120\text{ V}}{60\ \Omega}$$
$$= 2\text{ A at }0°$$

$$I_{C1} = \frac{E}{X_{C1}}$$
$$= \frac{120\text{ V}}{20\ \Omega}$$
$$= 6\text{ A at }90°$$

$$I_{C2} = \frac{E}{X_{C2}}$$
$$= \frac{120\text{ V}}{120\ \Omega}$$
$$= 1\text{ A at }90°$$

### Current Triangle

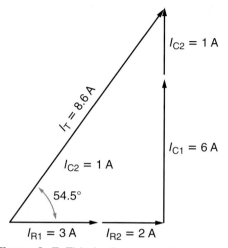

**Figure 9–7** This is the current triangle for the branch currents found in Figure 9–6.

The power components are as follows and as depicted in Figure 9–8:

$$W_{R1} = E \times I_{R1}$$
$$= 120\text{ V} \times 3\text{ A}$$
$$= 360\text{ W}$$
$$W_{R2} = E \times I_{R2}$$
$$= 120\text{ V} \times 2\text{ A}$$
$$= 240\text{ W}$$
$$VAR_{C1} = E \times I_{C1}$$
$$= 120\text{ V} \times 6\text{ A}$$
$$= 720\text{ VARs}$$
$$VAR_{C2} = E \times I_{C2}$$
$$= 120 \times 1\text{ A}$$
$$= 120\text{ VARs}$$

The final power triangle, as shown in Figure 9–8, verifies that the figures all coincide with the actual measured values if the circuit were constructed. The total volt-amps according to the Pythagorean Theorem is 1,032. This should be the same as the line current times the lines voltage, as follows:

$$VA = E_{\text{Line}} \times I_{\text{Line}}$$
$$= 120\text{ V} \times 8.6\text{ A} = 1,032\text{ VA}$$

Apparent power = 1,032 VA, the same as with the Pythagorean Theorem.

The angle θ is the arctangent of $\dfrac{VARs}{W}$

$$\text{angle }\theta = \text{arctangent }\frac{840\text{ VARs}}{600\text{ W}}$$

$$= 54.5°$$

Construct a circuit triangle with the currents as shown in Figure 9–7. Find the resultant vector by using the Pythagorean Theorem. The resultant current of 8.6 A is the current from the source, or $I_T$. The line current leads the line voltage by approximately 54.5°.

The impedance of the circuit is:

$$Z_T = \frac{E_T}{I_T}$$
$$= \frac{120\text{ V}}{8.6\text{ A}}$$
$$\approx 14\ \Omega$$

**Power Triangle**

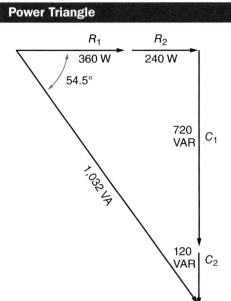

**Figure 9–8** This power triangle of vectors is for the circuit in Figure 9–6.

This angle matches the phase angle of the current triangle vector.

The percent power factor is the cosine of this angle θ × 100.

% $PF$ = cosine 54.5° × 100

= 0.58 × 100 = 58%

To verify this figure with another method:

% $PF$ = $\dfrac{W}{VA}$ × 100

Again, using circuit values of 600 W and 1,032 VA:

% $PF$ = $\dfrac{600}{1,032}$ × 100 ≈ 58%

## TechTip!

Oftentimes, you do not need to know the exact values of a circuit to troubleshoot the circuit. You can determine what is generally happening to the circuit by the readings you take and then change one parameter of the circuit to see whether it responds in a predicted manner. If you suspect that a capacitor is open, you can add another capacitor to the parallel circuit to see whether the circuit reacts as you suspect. Table 9–1 allows you to see the effects of changing one variable at a time.

The figures do not exactly match because we rounded many of the values.

## EFFECTS ON CHANGING CIRCUIT VARIABLES

As the circuit components or variables change, so do the circuit values. As shown in Table 9–1, changing the frequency changes the $X_C$ and a host of other dependent variables. This table indicates whether the values change or stay the same and what the trends are with the subsequent measurable quantities. Try to determine the effects on the circuit, and then verify the trend by checking the table.

Refer to Table 9–1 for effects of frequency, capacitance, or resistance on parallel RC circuits when changing one variable at a time.

**Table 9–1**

| Variable | $X_C$ | $I_C$ | $I_R$ | $I_T$ | $Z_T$ | VA | True Power (W) | VARs | Phase Angle | Power Factor |
|---|---|---|---|---|---|---|---|---|---|---|
| Freq Inc | Dec | Inc | Same | Inc | Dec | Inc | Same | Inc | Inc | Dec |
| Freq Dec | Inc | Dec | Same | Dec | Inc | Dec | Same | Dec | Dec | Inc |
| Cap Inc | Dec | Inc | Same | Inc | Dec | Inc | Same | Inc | Inc | Dec |
| Cap Dec | Inc | Dec | Same | Dec | Inc | Dec | Same | Dec | Dec | Inc |
| Resis Inc | Same | Same | Dec | Dec | Inc | Dec | Dec | Same | Inc | Dec |
| Resis Dec | Same | Same | Inc | Inc | Dec | Inc | Inc | Same | Dec | Inc |

*Inc = increase; Dec = decrease; Freq = frequency; Cap = capacitance; Resis = resistance.*

Trends in a Parallel RC Circuit When Changing One Variable at a Time

## SUMMARY

This chapter introduced you to the effects of capacitors in parallel and how to calculate the circuit quantities based on the capacitance or the capacitive reactance. A resistor and a capacitor in a parallel circuit created the effect of adding possible current paths for the circuit current, although the resistive current and the capacitive current were not in phase with each other. This led us to current vectors and current triangles. The phase angle for the circuit could be determined by the angle $\theta$ found in the current triangle and later

confirmed in the power triangle. The impedance of the circuit was determined based on the total current. The voltage stayed the same in all branches of the circuit as it does in all parallel circuits and thus is the circuit reference. Finally, the power triangle was constructed to determine all the power measurements, as well as to confirm the power factor.

Table 9–1 was used to determine how the circuit would change as we changed variables in the RC parallel circuit.

## REVIEW QUESTIONS

1. What is the effect of connecting capacitors in parallel?
   a. What does the size of the cross-sectional area of the plates affect?
   b. How does this affect the total capacitance?
2. Briefly describe how to calculate the total capacitance of capacitors in parallel and show the formula.
3. Briefly describe how to calculate the total capacitive reactance of capacitors in parallel and show the formula.
4. Describe how to find the following in a parallel RC circuit:
   a. Phase angle
   b. Power factor
   c. Voltage across the resistor
   d. Voltage across the reactance

5. Discuss impedance in a parallel RC circuit.
   a. How can it be calculated?
   b. How will it compare to resistance and capacitative reactance?
6. Draw a vector diagram for a parallel RC circuit and label all components.
7. By adding more capacitors in parallel, the total $X_C$ for the circuit will _____.
8. Increasing the frequency of the RC circuit would cause the VARs to _____.
9. The hypotenuse of the current triangle is a measurable current known as the _____ current.
10. Adding more resistors in parallel causes the circuit impedance to _____.

# PRACTICE PROBLEMS

1. What value of capacitor must be added in parallel with a 0.23 μF capacitor to get a total of 5,000 Ω of $X_C$ total in a 60 Hz, 1,000 V circuit?
2. What is the capacitive reactance of two 50 μF capacitors in parallel with 100 Hz applied?
3. A 5 V circuit at 100 kHz has a 1,000 pF capacitor in parallel with a 1,000 Ω resistor. Find $I_R$.

Using the circuit in Practice Problem 3, answer Problems 4–12.

4. Find $X_C$.
5. Find $I_C$.
6. Find $I_T$.
7. Find $Z$.
8. Find the phase angle.
9. Find the power factor.
10. What is the apparent power delivered?
11. What is the true power?
12. Will an increase in frequency to 200,000 Hz cause this circuit to be more or less capacitive? Prove your answer.
13. Find the total capacitance of three capacitors connected in series with values of 3, 5, and 10 μF.
14. What is the total capacitance of two capacitors connected in parallel having values of 310 and 50 μF?
15. What is the $X_{CT}$ of a circuit having two capacitors connected in parallel with values of 300 and 600 μF operating at 500 Hz?

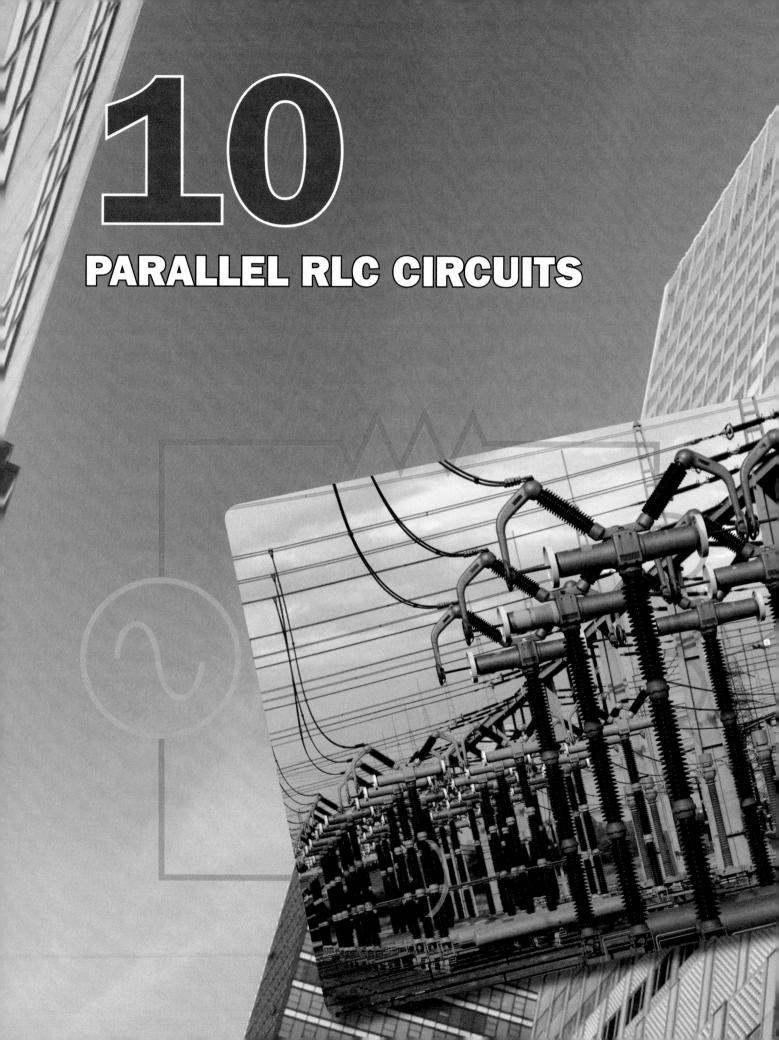

# 10

# PARALLEL RLC CIRCUITS

# TOPICS

# OVERVIEW

Most of the circuits you will work with in your professional career will contain some combination of resistance, inductance, and capacitance. Most AC loads tend to be resistive with inductance because of the heavy presence of inductive loads like motors and fluorescent light fixtures. Further, most of the circuits you will work with will be a combination of series and parallel circuits. The load circuits themselves are usually primarily either resistance (R) or resistance and inductance (RL) in series and are connected in parallel between the supply wires.

This chapter continues the work you did in the previous chapters. Remember that in a parallel circuit the voltage is the same across all branches and the current divides among the branches. In this chapter, we investigate how changing variables in the circuit affects the total circuit. These variations resemble the way the circuit changes each time you add or subtract an AC load to an existing circuit. We also explore resonance and how the resonant point of the circuit affects the power and the line current, and we explain what is meant by a "tank" circuit in parallel AC circuits with capacitance (C) and inductance (L).

Also in this chapter we use an "assumed voltage" to calculate the impedance of an AC parallel circuit. This is a way to determine the impedance of an RLC circuit without knowing what the voltage will actually be. We can use this method of calculation to temporarily calculate the total current of a circuit without knowing the exact voltage present. This concept can be useful to determine values in a complex circuit, where exact values are hard to decipher.

# OBJECTIVES

After completing this chapter, you will be able to:

· Determine the overall effects of parallel AC components
· Calculate for unknown quantities in an RLC circuit
· Calculate total current and total impedance in RLC circuits using alternate methods
· Find the power for RLC circuits with given variables
· Determine power factor and circuit phase angles
· Determine circuit impedance using an assumed voltage
· Explain the effect of an RLC circuit at resonance

## PARALLEL RLC CIRCUITS

When an AC circuit has the elements of resistance, inductance, and capacitance connected in parallel, the voltage across each branch is the same, as it is in any parallel circuit. The magnitude and phase angle of the currents flowing through each branch are out of phase with each other as determined by the resistance or reactance of the branch.

Referring to Figure 10–1, the phase relationship of each branch current in parallel is represented by the relationship of current to voltage in the individual branch. As you recall, the current in a pure resistive component would be in phase with the component voltage. In the pure capacitive circuit, the component current leads the component voltage by 90°, and the current in the pure inductive component is 90° behind the component voltage. In the total parallel circuit with all three branches, the line current and line voltage may be anywhere from a 90° leading current, to a 0° (or in phase) current, to a 90° current lagging the applied circuit voltage.

In a parallel RLC circuit, if the inductance is large, so is the $X_L$, causing a comparatively small amount of current to flow through the inductive branch. If the capacitive reactance is small, more of the circuit current flows through the capacitive branch. The circuit current would appear to have capacitive effects, and the line current would lead the line voltage. As we show, the effects of changing values in a parallel RLC circuit can depend on the frequency. The circuit may change from a leading to a lagging power factor depending on the changing values of inductive and capacitive reactance in the circuit.

## CALCULATING PARALLEL RLC CIRCUIT VALUES

To practice calculating parallel RLC circuit values, use Figure 10–2 as a reference. The following problems are solved using the circuit values shown in the drawing. You can analyze this circuit as you did the other parallel circuits. The most systematic way to solve parallel circuits is to determine the individual branch circuit characteristics and then add them into the total circuit equation.

**Figure 10–1** Current relationships shown in different branches of an RLC circuit.

Remember that the currents in the branches have amperage that you can read with a standard ammeter but that they also have a phase angle in relation to the branch voltage. Also recall that the voltage drop is the same across any component in a parallel circuit and is the main reference to the calculations.

First, calculate each current as follows.

## RESISTIVE CURRENT

The easiest value to calculate is the current flow through the resistor. This can be calculated using the Ohm's law formula:

$$I_R = \frac{E}{R}$$
$$= \frac{220 \text{ V}}{12 \text{ }\Omega}$$
$$= 18.3 \text{ A at } 0°$$

## INDUCTIVE CURRENT

The amount of current flow through the inductor is calculated using the adapted Ohm's law formula. Remember that in this "perfect" inductor there is no resistive component and the current lags the voltage by 90 electrical degrees:

$$I_L = \frac{E}{X_L}$$
$$= \frac{220 \text{ V}}{15 \text{ }\Omega}$$
$$= 14.67 \text{ A at } 90° \text{ lag}$$

## INDUCTANCE

You can calculate the amount of inductance in the circuit to verify the comparative values for henries versus farads as you equate the effects of this circuit later. The formula to use is the inductive reactance formula:

$$X_L = 2\pi f L$$
$$L = \frac{X_L}{2\pi f}$$

$2\pi f \approx 377$ at 60 Hz; therefore,

$$L = \frac{15}{(377)}$$
$$= 0.0398 \text{ H}$$

**Parallel RLC Circuit**

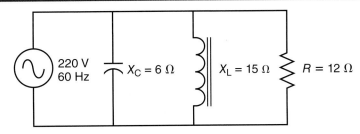

**Figure 10–2** This parallel RLC circuit is used for subsequent calculations.

## CAPACITIVE CURRENT

The remaining branch of the circuit is capacitive. Therefore, the current through this component can be measured with a standard ammeter, but you must realize that the current actually leads the branch voltage by 90 electrical degrees. The current flow through the capacitor can be found using the adapted Ohm's law formula:

$$I_C = \frac{E}{X_C}$$
$$= \frac{220 \text{ V}}{6 \text{ }\Omega}$$
$$= 36.67 \text{ A at } 90° \text{ lead}$$

## CAPACITANCE

For circuit comparison, you can find the actual capacitance of the capacitive branch for comparison to the inductive branch values. The value of circuit capacitance opposition can be calculated using the capacitive reactance formula, when the capacitance is in farads:

$$X_C = \frac{1}{2\pi f C}$$
$$C = \frac{1}{2\pi f X_c}$$
$$= \frac{1}{377 \times 6} = 0.000442 \text{ farad}$$
$$= 442 \text{ }\mu\text{F}$$

## IMPEDANCE

Impedance for this circuit can be calculated in two ways. The simplest way is to keep track of the currents, find the total current, and then calculate the opposition (impedance) that caused that circuit current.

The second way is to use the mathematical formula that adds the opposition of each branch. Remember from previous chapters that the impedance of the parallel circuit is the reciprocal of the sum of the reciprocals of the branches. Vector addition must be used because the values are out of phase. The formula that follows assumes that the reactance of two branches is combined into an equivalent reactance by using the product-over-sum method. Then the reactance and resistance can be used in a modified product-over-sum formula, where the denominator is the square root of the sum of the squares. This modification is needed because the resistance and reactance are 90° out of phase.

First, combine the two branch reactance values:

$$X_T = \frac{X_L \times X_C}{X_L + X_C}$$

Then, calculate circuit impedance using the following formula:

$$Z_T = \frac{R \times X_T}{\sqrt{R^2 + X_T{}^2}}$$

**Important:** When solving for $X_T$, $X_L$ is a positive number and $X_C$ is a negative number. It is vitally important that this concept be followed, as shown here for the circuit in Figure 10–2.

---

### Example

Calculate the total reactance for the circuit in Figure 10–2.

**Solution:**

Combine the branch reactance values:

$$X_T = \frac{15 \times (-6)}{15 + (-6)}$$
$$= \frac{-90}{9}$$
$$= -10$$

Then, calculate circuit impedance. The minus value shows that the net result is a capacitive reactance. Because the next part of the calculation uses the Pythagorean Theorem, the negative sign is not used:

$$Z_T = \frac{R \times X_T}{\sqrt{R^2 + X_T{}^2}}$$
$$= \frac{12 \times 10}{\sqrt{12^2 + 10^2}}$$
$$= \frac{120}{\sqrt{144 + 100}}$$
$$= \frac{120}{\sqrt{244}}$$
$$= \frac{120}{15.6}$$
$$= 7.68 \ \Omega$$

This final circuit impedance figure matches the figure found when vectoring currents, creating a current triangle vector diagram, and then using Ohm's law:

$$Z = \frac{E}{I}$$

# TOTAL CIRCUIT CALCULATIONS

## TOTAL CURRENT

The value for total current flow in the circuit can be calculated using vector addition of the current flow through each branch of the circuit. Refer to Figures 10–3a and b. As shown in Figure 10–3a, the inductive current is 180° out of phase with the capacitive current. These two currents tend to offset each other (subtract), the same way opposing reactances did in the series circuit. You subtract the smaller from the larger. The total circuit current is the hypotenuse of the resultant right triangle.

The following steps show how the total current in Figure 10–3b could be calculated using the Pythagorean Theorem:

$$I_T^2 = I_R^2 + (I_C - I_L)^2$$

$$I_T = \sqrt{I_R^2 + (I_C - I_L)^2}$$

$$= \sqrt{18.3^2 + (36.67 - 14.67)^2}$$

$$= \sqrt{18.3^2 + 22^2}$$

$$= \sqrt{334.89 + 484}$$

$$= \sqrt{818.89}$$

$$= 28.62$$

The same answer can be calculated using the same total current triangle and using trigonometric functions.

From this information, you know the total current of the circuit in Figure 10–4, as measured with an ammeter, is 28.6 A. As you know, the supply current is not in phase with the supply voltage. You can calculate the phase angle of lead by using the current triangle and finding angle theta (θ). By using trigonometry and the final circuit current triangle from Figure 10–3, you can determine the angle between the horizontal axis, representing the voltage reference, and the total circuit current of $I_T$, which is the hypotenuse of the right triangle.

## TechTip!

The reactive branch that has the largest current flow determines whether the line current leads or lags the applied voltages and determines the phase angle. The phase angle can be found by:

angle θ = arctan θ

$$= \text{arctan } (\tan^{-1}) \frac{X}{R}$$

**Branch Current Vectors**

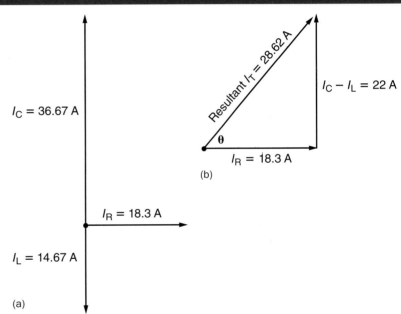

Figure 10–3 Vector diagrams show branch currents for the circuit in Figure 10–2.

**Ammeter Measuring Total Current**

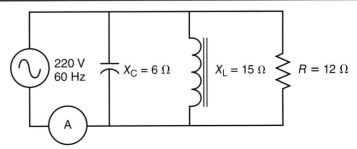

Figure 10–4 An ammeter can be used to measure the total current in the circuit in Figure 10–2.

## FieldNote!

A clamp-on-style ammeter is the typical way an electrician measures AC current in a circuit. By measuring the magnetic field around a conductor, the meter converts this measurement to amperes of current flow. You can measure the current at many different points, such as at the source of the current, at the resistive branch, or at the reactive branches. The meter only measures the amount of magnetic field and cannot determine whether the current is in phase with the voltage. If you simply add all of the AC currents together, as you did with DC parallel circuits, the sum total may exceed the supply current reading. Keep this in mind as you measure currents in parallel circuits for which you may not know for sure what type of load is connected for various branches.

The trigonometric function that is easiest to use in this case is the cosine function:

$$\cos \theta = \frac{\text{Adjacent side}}{\text{Hypotenuse}}$$

$$= \frac{18.3}{28.62}$$

$$= 0.6394$$

The angle is found by using the **arccosine** or the $\cos^{-1}$ function to find the angle that has a cosine of 0.6394, which is 50.2°. Thus, for this circuit, the angle is 50.2°.

### ALTERNATE WAY TO CALCULATE TOTAL CURRENT

A second way to calculate total current is to use the impedance value as shown:

$$I_\text{T} = \frac{E}{Z}$$

$$= \frac{220 \text{ V}}{7.68 \ \Omega}$$

$$= 28.65 \text{ A}$$

Note the slight difference in current values due to rounding.

## POWER CALCULATIONS

There are several ways to calculate the power of the original circuit with inductance, capacitance, and resistance all in parallel. One method is to construct a power triangle that is congruent to the current triangle using the current and voltage of each branch to build the power components.

### TRUE POWER

Remember that true power can be found only in the resistive leg of the circuit where current and voltage are in phase. The true power, or watts, can be calculated using the formula $P = E \times I_\text{R}$. Another way is to use $P = I^2 \times R$, where we must use only the branch current through the resistive branch. A third method of calculating the true power is to construct a power triangle. We verify the watts (horizontal vector) of that triangle as the true power.

$$P = E \times I_\text{R}$$

$$= 220 \text{ V} \times 18.33 \text{ A}$$

$$= 4{,}032.6 \text{ W}$$

OR

$$P = I^2 \times R$$

$$= 18.33 \text{ A}^2 \times 12 \ \Omega$$

$$= 4{,}031.8 \text{ W}$$

***Note:*** You can also use:

$$PF = \cos \theta = \frac{Z}{R}$$

$$= \frac{7.68 \ \Omega}{12 \ \Omega} = 0.64$$

$$P_\text{True} = E_\text{App} \times I_\text{T} \times \cos \theta$$

$$= 220 \text{ V} \times 28.62 \text{ A} \times 0.64$$

$$= 4{,}029.7 \text{ W}$$

A slight difference occurs when rounding repeating decimals.

### REACTIVE (VAR) POWER

The reactive (volt-ampere-reactive) power is made up of both volt-amps reactive (VARs) of inductive power and VARs of capacitive power. We use the inductive branch current and the circuit voltage (the applied voltage) to calculate the VARs. See Figure 10–5 as a representation of the VARs inductive vector from the following formula:

$$VAR_\text{L} = I_\text{L} \times E_\text{L}$$

$$= 14.7 \times 220 \text{ V}$$

$$= 3{,}234 \text{ VARs inductive}$$

**Vectored VARs**

**Figure 10–5** VARs are vectored as capacitive or inductive.

The next branch that creates reactive volt-amps is the capacitive branch, with $VAR_C$ calculated as follows:

$$VAR_C = I_C \times E_C$$
$$= 36.7 \times 220 \text{ V}$$
$$= 8,074 \text{ VARs capacitive}$$

As you will notice in Figure 10–5, the inductive and capacitive VARs subtract because they are in opposite directions. The net (difference) in VARs is:

$$8,074 \text{ VAR}_C - 3,234 \text{ VAR}_L = 4,840 \text{ VAR}_C$$

**APPARENT POWER**

Now that the total circuit current has been calculated, the apparent power or volt-amps (VAs) can be calculated using the total current in the following formula:

$$VA = E \times I_T$$
$$= 220 \times 28.62$$
$$= 6,296 \text{ VA}$$

The power factor can also be calculated using the following:

$$PF = \cos \theta = \frac{R}{Z}$$

We can also use the power triangle to verify the previous values. With watts at 4,032 and VARs at 4,840, we can simply use the Pythagorean Theorem to calculate the hypotenuse, also known as the apparent power (VA):

$$VA = \sqrt{W^2 + VAR^2}$$
$$= \sqrt{4,032^2 + 4,840^2}$$
$$= 6,299.4 \text{ VA}$$

The slight discrepancy in the final volt-amp numbers is due to rounding of numbers.

**POWER FACTOR**

Since the volt-amps and watts are known, the power factor (PF) can be determined using the following formula:

$$PF = \frac{\text{True power (W)}}{\text{Apparent power (VA)}}$$
$$\% \, PF = \left(\frac{W}{VA}\right) \times 100$$
$$= \left(\frac{4,032 \text{ W}}{6,299 \text{ VA}}\right) \times 100$$
$$= 0.64 \times 100$$
$$= 64\%$$

**ANGLE THETA**

Remember that the power factor is the cosine of angle theta ($\theta$). Therefore, angle $\theta$ is:

$$\cos \theta = 0.64$$
$$\arccos 0.64 = \theta$$
$$\theta = 50.2°$$

**Power Triangle**

(6,299.4 VA — 4,840 VAR — 4,032 W)

## TechTip!

Angle θ can also be calculated using the following:

angle θ = arctan θ

$$= \text{arctan} \ (\text{tan}^{-1}) \ \frac{X}{R}$$

This 50.2° angle is the exact same angle found when vectoring the circuit currents, thus confirming the congruency of the power triangle and current triangles and verifying that the calculations are correct.

## DETERMINING IMPEDANCE USING THE ASSUMED VOLTAGE METHOD

Consider the parallel circuit shown in Figure 10–6. Here is how the assumed voltage method works for determining the impedance of a parallel circuit.

1. When possible, assume a voltage that results in currents for all parallel legs that are whole numbers. "Assuming" means that you simply use a voltage value that easily divides by the resistive, inductive reactance, and capacitive reactance values. This assumed (fictitious) voltage is just a temporary value that makes the math easier. When you assume a fictitious voltage, the currents that result from this assumed voltage are assumed currents. Remember that these currents are not actual measurable currents in the branches.

2. An assumed voltage of 24 V is used for this circuit.

3. Using Ohm's law for AC circuits, the current through each leg is determined as shown in Table 10–1.

4. The total current for the circuit can now be determined for the assumed voltage of 24 by the formula $I_T = \sqrt{I_R^2 + (I_C - I_L)^2}$, where the absolute value of $I_C - I_L$ is used:

$$I_T = \sqrt{I_{RT}^2 + (I_C - I_{LT})^2}$$

$$= \sqrt{6 \ A^2 + (4 \ A - 2.5 \ A)^2}$$

$$= \sqrt{6 \ A^2 + (1.5 \ A)^2}$$

$$= \sqrt{36 \ A + 2.25 \ A}$$

$$= \sqrt{38.25 \ A}$$

$$= 6.18 \ A$$

### Multiple Branches

?V  $X_{L1}$ 24 Ω  $X_{L2}$ 16 Ω  $X_C$ 6 Ω  $R_1$ 6 Ω  $R_2$ 12 Ω

**Figure 10–6** This circuit has multiple branches.

| Table 10–1 | | | | |
|---|---|---|---|---|
| $I_{L1} = \dfrac{E}{X_{L1}}$ | $I_{L2} = \dfrac{E}{X_{L2}}$ | $I_C = \dfrac{E}{X_C}$ | $I_{R1} = \dfrac{E}{R_1}$ | $I_{R2} = \dfrac{E}{R_2}$ |
| $I_{L1} = \dfrac{24 \ V}{24 \ \Omega}$ | $I_{L2} = \dfrac{24 \ V}{16 \ \Omega}$ | $I_C = \dfrac{24 \ V}{6 \ \Omega}$ | $I_{R1} = \dfrac{24 \ V}{6 \ \Omega}$ | $I_{R2} = \dfrac{24 \ V}{12 \ \Omega}$ |
| $I_{L1} = 1 \ A$ | $I_{L2} = 1.5 \ A$ | $I_C = 4 \ A$ | $I_{R1} = 4 \ A$ | $I_{R2} = 2 \ A$ |
| Individual Branch Circuit Values for the Circuit in Figure 10–6 | | | | |

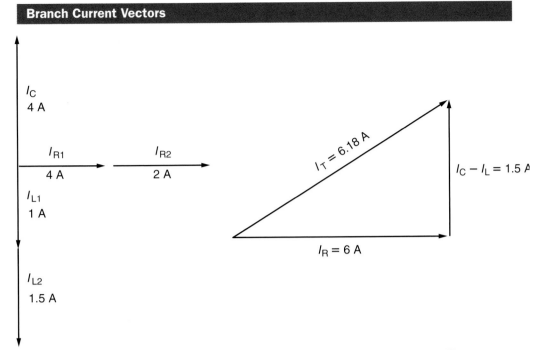

**Branch Current Vectors**

**Figure 10–7** These vector diagrams are of the branch currents shown in Figure 10–6.

Alternatively, you can create a current vector diagram, as shown in Figure 10–7.

Finally, by using the current triangle and adding vectors, you arrive at the same circuit total current of 6.18 A.

5. With the assumed 24 V power supply applied, the circuit current is 6.18 A. The real impedance of the circuit can now be determined by using Ohm's law:

$$Z_T = \frac{E}{I_T}$$

$$= \frac{24 \text{ V assumed}}{6.18 \text{ A assumed}}$$

$$= 3.88 \ \Omega$$

This method is sometimes easier than the reciprocal method for determining the impedance of a parallel circuit. To see how assuming a different voltage supply affects the circuit, substitute 12 V for the assumed voltage and then assume 48 V. You will conclude that no matter which voltage you "assume" the total $Z$ is the same. Remember that the currents

you solved for are not actual circuit currents:

$$Z_T \text{ at } 12 \text{ V: } Z_T = 3.88 \ \Omega$$

$$Z_T \text{ at } 48 \text{ V: } Z_T = 3.88 \ \Omega$$

## PARALLEL RESONANT CIRCUITS

You know that in a parallel circuit the inductive current and capacitive current are 180° out of phase and subtract from each other. As you can verify from the vector diagrams of the currents, if the capacitive current equals the inductive current (a condition known as resonance), then the net reactive current for the circuit is zero. This produces a minimum line current at the point of resonance. Again, resonance is the frequency point for the circuit where $X_L$ equals $X_C$, which means that $I_L$ equals $I_C$. This minimum line current indicates that there must have been maximum impedance. In theory, when a parallel LC circuit reaches resonance, the total circuit current should reach zero.

## TechTip!

The flywheel effect of a resonant circuit refers to the mechanical flywheel concept. A mechanical flywheel uses the inertia of initial energy to keep a wheel spinning even during periods when the input energy has disappeared. In the electrical "flywheel," the circuit appears to have energy in the system even though the initial energy from an input source has disappeared. Even when the input sine wave is at zero volts, current still flows in the LC "tank" between the capacitor and the inductor. Therefore, the current continues to flow even though the flywheel circuit is at a point with no further input energy.

**Current Sine Waves at Resonance**

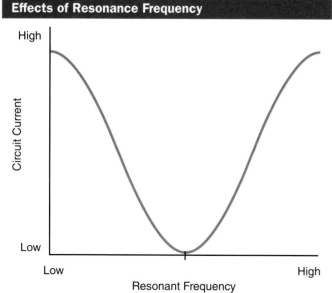

**Figure 10–8** Sine waves of a current occur at resonance.

Figure 10–8 shows the current relationship at resonance. The in-phase current is the result of the resistance of the coil. Figure 10–9 shows a graph of frequency versus line current around resonant frequency ($f_r$). At resonant frequency, the capacitive current and the inductive current are equal and cancel each other out.

Figure 10–10 is an LC resonant circuit called a tank circuit. Note that the current in the inductor or capacitor branch of the circuit is very high at resonance when compared to the total line current. The individual branch currents do not affect the $I_T$ line current because each is 90° out of phase with the in-phase line current and is opposite the other. As the AC supply voltage reverses polarity, the stored energy in the inductor's magnetic field and capacitor's electrostatic field charge and discharge within the tank. This cycling effect generates a sine wave at the resonant frequency of the parallel LC branches. This sine wave generation is the flywheel effect of an LC tank circuit.

As you learned earlier, an increase in frequency decreases capacitive reactance, increases total current, and decreases impedance. An increase in frequency from resonance also decreases the power factor.

**Effects of Resonance Frequency**

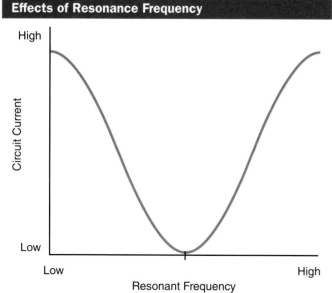

**Figure 10–9** The effects of resonant frequency on a parallel RLC circuit yield the minimum line current.

**Tank Circuit**

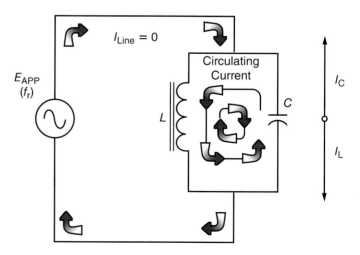

**Figure 10–10** A tank circuit is created by inductance and capacitance in parallel.

Table 10–2 shows the effects of changing variables in a parallel RLC circuit. As you will note, some of the values in Table 10–2 have question marks; those answers depend on the original circuit before increasing or decreasing a variable. The top two rows are based on increasing or decreasing frequency from resonance.

 TechTip!

An internal tank circuit assumes that there are no losses of energy within the tank. As you know, this is not entirely true; if it were, we would have invented perpetual motion. In fact, there is resistance in the coil circuit and some resistance in the capacitor circuit. There is resistance to the connecting circuit wiring as well that produces watt loss as the current moves from capacitor to coil and back, as discussed in line loss in the *DC Theory* text. The tank circuit does need energy from the line, but the concept of a parallel tank circuit is used extensively in the practice of power factor correction. This common practice of using a tank circuit to correct power factor is discussed in detail in some texts, where power factor correction is explained in greater detail.

### Table 10–2

| Variable | XL | IL | XC | IC | IR | IT | ZT | VA | PT | VARs | Angle | % PF |
|---|---|---|---|---|---|---|---|---|---|---|---|---|
| Inc freq from resonance | Inc | Dec | Dec | Inc | Same | Inc | Dec | Inc | Same | Inc | Inc | Dec |
| Dec freq from resonance | Dec | Inc | Inc | Dec | Same | Inc | Dec | Inc | Same | Inc | Inc | Dec |
| Inc inductance from resonance | Inc | Dec | Same | Same | Same | ? | ? | ? | Same | Dec | Dec | Inc |
| Dec inductance from resonance | Dec | Inc | Same | Same | Same | ? | ? | ? | Same | Inc | Inc | Dec |
| Inc capacitance from resonance | Same | Same | Dec | Inc | Same | ? | ? | ? | Same | Inc | Inc | Dec |
| Dec capacitance from resonance | Same | Same | Inc | Dec | Same | ? | ? | ? | Same | Dec | Dec | Inc |
| Inc resistance from resonance | Same | Same | Same | Same | Dec | Dec | Inc | Dec | Dec | Same | Same | Same |
| Dec resistance from resonance | Same | Same | Same | Same | Inc | Inc | Dec | Inc | Inc | Same | Same | Same |
| Inc voltage of supply | Same | Inc | Same | Inc | Inc | Inc | Same | Inc | Inc | Inc | Same | Same |
| Dec voltage of supply | Same | Dec | Same | Dec | Dec | Dec | Same | Dec | Dec | Dec | Same | Same |

*Inc = increase value; Dec = decrease value; Same = no change; ? = depends on other factors*

Trends of Values to Increase, Decrease, or Remain the Same if Changing One Variable at a Time Starting at Resonant Frequency

## SUMMARY

The voltage across all legs of a parallel RLC circuit is the same. The current flow in the resistive leg is in phase with the voltage. The current flow in the inductive leg lags the voltage by 90°, and the current flow in the capacitive branch leads the voltage by 90°.

The total current can be found by using a vector diagram and trigonometry or by using an algebraic formula. Remember to find the currents in a parallel circuit instead of vectoring oppositions as we did in calculating impedance in series circuits. The angle found using the current triangle vector is the phase angle that tells whether the current is leading or lagging the line voltage and by how many degrees. The angle to the horizontal in the current triangle vector is the same angle as calculated for the circuit power triangle.

The impedance ($Z_T$) is equal to the applied voltage divided by the total circuit current ($I_T$). $Z_T$ is maximum at resonance frequency ($f_r$) because the $I_T$ is minimum. You can also find $Z_T$ by using an assumed voltage that is chosen just to make the math easier. With the assumed voltage, you get assumed currents, but the result is that you find the actual circuit impedance, no matter what voltage we assume.

The idea of a resonant tank circuit is used to explain power factor correction. This is called the flywheel effect.

Now you have a fairly good understanding of a parallel RLC circuit. From this understanding, you can change one variable at a time and predict how that would change the circuit results. Because the reactance of the coils and capacitor changes with frequency, you have to know the starting point to determine how increasing or decreasing the frequency would alter the entire circuit characteristics.

## CHAPTER GLOSSARY

**Arccosine** Abbreviated *arccos* and shown on most calculators by the symbol $cos^{-1}$. The inverse function of the cosine of an angle $\left(\frac{1}{\text{cosine}}\right)$. This calculates what arc has a cosine of the referenced decimal number.

## REVIEW QUESTIONS

1. In a parallel RLC circuit, what is the relationship of the following?
   a. Applied voltage and branch voltage
   b. Total current and individual branch current
   c. Component voltage and component current in R, L, or C component branches
2. In Figure RQ10–1, why is the Pythagorean Theorem used to calculate the *total* current?
3. Power factor is the ratio of _____ to _____. Explain.
4. What determines the phase angle between the total current and the applied voltage in a parallel RLC circuit?

5. A tank circuit operates on the so-called flywheel effect. Explain.
6. Explain why assuming a voltage results in calculating the true circuit impedance.
7. If a parallel RLC circuit is at resonance, increasing the frequency makes the circuit appear more _____.
8. What affect does changing the frequency below resonance have on the true power of the circuit?
9. By adding capacitors to the resonant circuit, the total current of the circuit _____.
10. At resonance, the power factor of the circuit is at _____ percent.

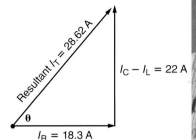

**Figure RQ10–1**

## PRACTICE PROBLEMS

All Practice Problems refer to Figure PP10–1.

1. Find the total reactance in the figure.
2. Find the current in each branch.
3. Find $I_T$.
4. Find $Z_T$.
5. Using $E_T$ and $I_T$, find $Z_T$. Does this answer agree with Problem 4?
6. What is the true power in this circuit?
7. What is the apparent power (volt-amps)?
8. What is the power factor?
9. What is the phase angle?
10. Find $Z_T$ using an assumed voltage other than that given. Does it agree with Problem 4?
11. Calculate the reactive power, and draw the power triangle for the total circuit.

**Figure PP10–1**

# 11

# COMBINATION RLC CIRCUITS

# T O P I C S

COMBINATION RLC CIRCUITS

CIRCUIT ANALYSIS: RESISTANCE,
    INDUCTANCE, AND CAPACITANCE

CIRCUIT TOTAL VECTOR ADDITION

VOLTAGE DROP CALCULATIONS FOR
    COMBINATION CIRCUITS

POWER CALCULATIONS

SERIES CIRCUITS IN PARALLEL

POWER FACTOR CORRECTION

COMPLEX CIRCUIT EVALUATION

FORENSIC EVALUATION

# O V E R V I E W

Most AC circuits have some combination of resistance, capacitance, and inductance. In fact, many electrical systems have series and parallel combinations of these components in the same circuit. These types of circuits are referred to as combination circuits or as complex circuits. Because of the different phase angles involved, vector analysis is the only sure way to analyze a combination circuit of this type.

This chapter teaches you how to use your vector analysis skills in the solution of combination circuits. For easier vector analysis with the number of different components represented in combination circuits, you will see many of the vectors in this chapter drawn in "head-to-tail" fashion, as opposed to the more familiar phasor configuration. Remember that all the information you learned previously still applies. Series circuits rules apply to series circuits and parallel rules apply to parallel circuits at the circuit segment level. Tools such as superposition, Kirchhoff's laws, Thevenin equivalent circuits, and other such methods work in AC combination circuits. However, the calculations must be made using vector analysis. In this chapter, we examine series circuits in parallel with other series circuits and parallel circuits in series with other parallel circuits.

Power factor correction is explained, and the needed calculations for single-phase circuits are explored. We also approach the troubleshooting concept of taking readings and calculating back into the circuit what unknown components must have been involved: a "forensic" analysis.

# O B J E C T I V E S

After completing this chapter, you will be able to:
· Solve for all quantities in a combination RLC circuit
· Draw vectors for current, impedance, and voltage and triangles for impedance and power as dictated by the circuit type
· Determine a lead or lag phase angle at any point in a complex circuit
· Solve for power factor and be able to correct a lagging power factor to a predetermined percentage or to unity
· Find unknown component values from actual readings in a circuit

# COMBINATION RLC CIRCUITS

Using the current for the vector reference in a series circuit simplifies the analysis. Conversely, the voltage reference is the simplest choice for a parallel circuit. The secret for solving for unknowns in any combination RLC circuit is to reduce the complex circuit to a single equivalent load and source for voltage. This method was taught in the *DC Theory* text and is called the Thevenin equivalent circuit. There is one difference; in *DC*, this load is called resistance. In *AC*, it is called impedance and may have a phase angle.

This approach is similar to the approach used in solving for total resistance in series and parallel combinations in *DC Theory*. The difference is that in an AC circuit containing inductance, capacitance, and resistance the vector components of the series equivalent circuit are not in phase with one another. These series vectors must be reduced to their vertical and horizontal components, which can then be vectorially added together. The sum of the vertical components can be added to the sum of the horizontal components using the Pythagorean Theorem.

# CIRCUIT ANALYSIS: RESISTANCE, INDUCTANCE, AND CAPACITANCE

Consider the procedure to solve for the parameters of combination circuits containing inductance, capacitance, and resistance. Take a look at the circuit in Figure 11–1. The circuit is largely a series circuit with two "zones" of parallel circuits. Each component or parallel combination is identified as vector impedance. For example, the 10 $\Omega$ series resistor is $Z_1$, the combination of the 8 $\Omega$ resistor and the 8 $\Omega$ $X_L$ inductor in parallel is $Z_2$, and so forth around the circuit. As with any complex circuit, we need to break the small zone circuits into manageable equivalent components. Because the large circuit can be identified as a series, we start by creating a series component equivalent of each of the parallel sections.

**Combination RLC Circuit**

**Figure 11–1** This combination RLC circuit has both series and parallel components.

## FieldNote!

There is tendency to think that many of the tough circuit evaluations are not used in the electrician's everyday work. Even though you do not often see an electrician with a calculator in his tool pouch, the knowledge is critical in understanding circuits when they do not seem to be working properly or when the values of the circuit measurement do not appear to be correct. An electrician who has a working knowledge of complex circuits and the characteristics that can seem improbable will be better qualified to diagnose circuit problems.

## PARALLEL COMPONENT VECTOR ADDITION

To add vector components together, the magnitude and direction of the parallel combinations ($Z_2$ and $Z_4$) must first be solved. To determine the impedance of each of these vectors, use the assumed voltage method as discussed in Chapter 10.

We do not know the actual voltage across the parallel branch yet, but we can still find the parallel circuit impedance by vectoring the assumed currents from an assumed voltage. For $Z_2$, assume a voltage of 8 V across the parallel components. Applying the assumed voltage of 8 V, an assumed 1 A flows through each component. The current through the resistor is in phase with the voltage, and the current through the inductor lags the voltage by 90°. Using the Pythagorean Theorem, the total current equals the square root of 2 as follows:

$$I_{Z2} = \sqrt{I_R^2 + I_L^2}$$

$$= \sqrt{1 + 1}$$

$$= \sqrt{2}$$

$$= 1.414 \text{ A at } 45° \text{ lag}$$

$$Z_2 = \frac{E_{assumed}}{I_{Z2}}$$

$$= \frac{8 \text{ V}}{1.414 \text{ A}}$$

$$= 5.66 \text{ } \Omega \text{ at } 45° \text{ lag}$$

Therefore, $Z_2$ has an impedance of 5.66 Ω. You can use the arctangent trigonometric function to find that the current and impedance have a lagging factor of 45°.

This same result could be reached quickly with a scientific calculator as follows. For $Z_2$, you know that:

$$\overline{Z}_2 = \frac{\overline{R} \times \overline{X}_L}{\overline{R} + \overline{X}_L}$$

where the bar over the $Z$, $R$, and $X_L$ means that they are vectors. You also know that:

$$\overline{R} = 8 \angle 0° \text{ and } \overline{X}_L = 8 \angle 90°$$

Substituting yields:

$$Z_2 = \frac{8 \angle 0° \times 8 \angle 90°}{8 \angle 0° + 8 \angle 90°}$$

Performing this vector calculation with a scientific calculator yields:

$$\overline{Z}_2 = 5.66 \text{ } \Omega \text{ at } 45° \text{ lag}$$

Repeat the same process for $Z_4$, using the assumed voltage method or a

## TechTip!

The tangent of $\theta_{Z2}$ is equal to:

$$\tan \theta_{Z2} = \frac{I_L}{I_R}$$

$$= \frac{1 \text{ A}}{1 \text{ A}}$$

$$= 1$$

$$\arctan (\tan^{-1}) 1 = 45°$$

scientific calculator to find the $Z_4$ impedance. Using 12 V as the assumed voltage gives a current through $Z_4$ of 1.414 A, the same as for $Z_2$ (you can see how assuming a "workable" voltage can make this portion of problem solving easy).

Using the assumed voltage and newly found current, solve for the impedance of:

$$Z_4 = \frac{E_{assumed}}{I_{assumed}}$$

$$= \frac{12 \text{ V}}{1.414 \text{ A}}$$

$$= 8.49 \text{ } \Omega \text{ at } 45° \text{ lead}$$

Since the values of the current through the resistor and through the capacitor are both 1 A, tan θ is same as tan θ through the $Z_2$ group because the current flow through those components was also equal to 1 A. The tangent of that angle is also equal to 1. Since this is a capacitive circuit, the angle is negative instead of positive; therefore, θ = −45° and $Z_2$ = 8.49 Ω at −45°, or leading effect.

If the capacitor and inductor had different values relative to the resistor in the group, the angle theta (θ) would calculate to a different magnitude. Because the current through each of the components is equal (the resistance and reactance being equal), the current flow through each component is also equal in the example circuit.

**Table 11–1**

|   | $Z_1$ | $Z_2$ | $Z_3$ | $Z_4$ | $Z_5$ |
|---|---|---|---|---|---|
| $I$ | ? | Assumed 1.414 A | ? | Assumed 1.414 A | ? |
| $Z$ | 10 Ω | Actual 5.66 Ω | 4 Ω | Actual 8.49 Ω | 6 Ω |
|   | at 0° | at 45° lag | at 90° lead | at 45° lead | at 90° lag |

Table to Track Each Zone of Impedance for Figure 11–1

For clarity, you can start a chart or table to keep track of the individual circuit "zones," as depicted in Table 11–1.

Here is another method, using the product-over-sum for parallel inductance that was introduced in earlier chapters. Both $Z_2$ and $Z_4$ combinations could be separately solved using the formula but without the vector direction reference:

$$Z = \frac{R \times X}{\sqrt{R^2 + X^2}}$$

For example, using $Z_2$ parameters:

$$Z_2 = \frac{8 \times 8}{\sqrt{8^2 + 8^2}}$$

$$= \frac{64}{11.31} = 5.66 \ \Omega$$

## Arrowhead Method

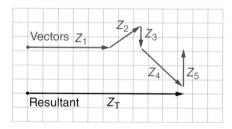

**Figure 11–2** The vector addition "arrowhead method" is used for series circuit impedance.

**Table 11–2**

| Component | $Z_1$ (Ω) | $Z_2$ (Ω) | $Z_3$ (Ω) | $Z_4$ (Ω) | $Z_5$ (Ω) |
|---|---|---|---|---|---|
| Vertical | 0 | $Z_2 \times \sin(45°) = 4$ | −4 | $Z_4 \times \sin(−45°) = −6$ | 6 |
| Horizontal | 10 | $Z_2 \times \cos(45°) = 4$ | 0 | $Z_4 \times \cos(−45°) = 6$ | 0 |

Finding Horizontal and Vertical Components of Vectors for Vector Addition

## CIRCUIT TOTAL VECTOR ADDITION

To find the circuit impedance, we vectorially add the oppositions in series. Figure 11–2 shows the five impedance values of Figure 11–1 added together graphically using the arrowhead-to-end or head-to-tail method. The resultant vector for this circuit is 20 Ω at 0°. Note that $Z_3$ and $Z_5$ have no horizontal component since they are a pure capacitance and pure inductance, respectively. Likewise, $Z_1$ has no vertical component since it is a pure resistance.

This is the solution for this problem. Vectors $Z_2$ and $Z_4$ must be reduced to their vertical and horizontal components. Table 11–2 lists the vertical and horizontal components and their calculation. The information in this table is based on vector addition of horizontal and vertical components found using trigonometry. The vector addition as seen in Figure 11–3 is the result of breaking each vector into its horizontal and vertical components.

Note that the negative values for $Z_3$ and $Z_4$ are due to the capacitive effect of the parallel components.

The net resultant of the total opposition provided by this circuit impedance triangle is 20 Ω of impedance at a 0° phase angle, as shown in Figure 11–3.

## VOLTAGE DROP CALCULATIONS FOR COMBINATION CIRCUITS

Now that we know the circuit impedance of all the components combined into one equivalent component is 20 ohms, we can determine the circuit current when 120 V AC is applied.

**Horizontal and Vertical Components**

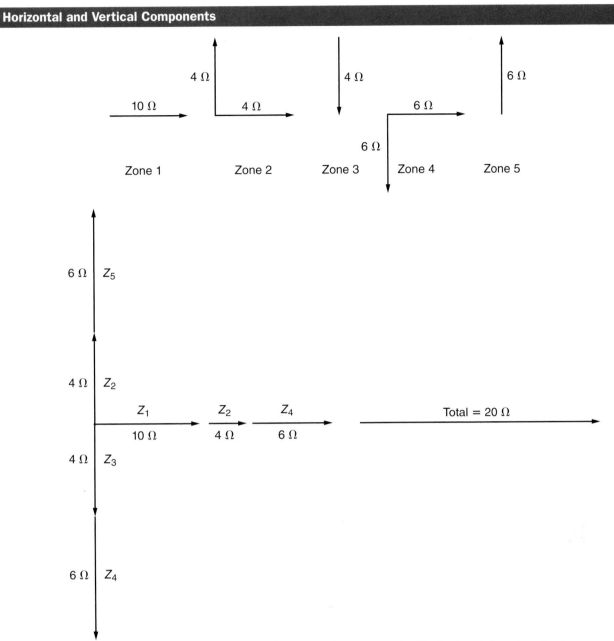

**Figure 11–3** The opposition provided by the components is represented by horizontal and vertical components.

The simple Ohm's law formula of $I = \dfrac{E}{Z}$ tells us that the circuit current is 6 A and the phase angle is 0° between the line current and the line voltage (they are in phase with each other). If we know the current is 6 A, and if the current is the same through the series circuit, we can determine the volt drop on each zone, as described earlier. Table 11–3 summarizes the results.

| Table 11–3 | | | | |
|---|---|---|---|---|
| $Z_1$ | $Z_2$ | $Z_3$ | $Z_4$ | $Z_5$ |
| $E_{Z1} = I_T \times Z_1$ | $E_{Z2} = I_T \times Z_2$ | $E_{Z3} = I_T \times Z_3$ | $E_{Z4} = I_T \times Z_4$ | $E_{Z5} = I_T \times Z_5$ |
| $E_{Z1} =$ 6 A × 10 Ω | $E_{Z2} =$ 6A × 5.66 Ω | $E_{Z3} =$ 6 A × 4 Ω | $E_{Z4} =$ 6 A × 8.49 Ω | $E_{Z5} =$ 6 A × 6 Ω |
| $E_{Z1} = 60$ V | $E_{Z2} = 33.96$ V | $E_{Z3} = 24$ V | $E_{Z4} = 50.94$ V | $E_{Z5} = 36$ V |
| at 0° resis | at 45° ind | at 90° cap | at 45° cap | at 90° ind |

*Resis = resistive component; Ind = inductive component; Cap = capacitive component.*

Calculating the Voltage Drop of Each Zone of Figure 11–1

The method depicted in Figure 11–4 is referred to as "adding vectors head-to-tail," as explained in Appendix A, Section A.10. The vector values with their magnitude and the angle of direction are taken from Table 11–3. Each zone of the circuit has a voltage value and a directional vector associated with it. The vectors are drawn individually as Zone 1 (60 V at 0° angle), Zone 2 (33.96 V at 45° lag), Zone 3 (24 V at 90° lead), Zone 4 (50.94 V at 45° lead), and Zone 5 (36 V at 90° lag). By using any of the vector addition methods explained in Appendix A, the final resultant vector (the circuit voltage) is found to be 120 V.

Figure 11–4 shows the vector addition of the voltages. As you will note, the voltages added arithmetically add up to much more than the original applied voltage of 120 V. Adding these voltage vectors with the known phase angles again produces a vector sum of 120 V AC. These are actual voltages that can be measured across each of the zone components. One of the methods to find the parallel impedance of a zone used an assumed voltage. This is *not* an assumed voltage but the actual voltage of the circuit. From this real voltage, we can now find the real current in each of the parallel component zones.

For $Z_2$, each of the two components has an ohmic value of 8 Ω with 33.96 V across them. Each 8 Ω component of the parallel has a current through it as determined by $I = \dfrac{E}{\text{opposition}}$. Using Ohm's law, we calculate 4.245 A of current through the resistance leg and

4.245 A of current through the inductive leg, lagging by 90°. Remember that for parallel circuits we add currents, not oppositions. We can use the Pythagorean Theorem to add these two currents, which are 90° out of phase with each other, and we again have 6 A as we expected from the line current calculation. We know this 6 A is 45° out of phase with the voltage across the Zone 2 components. Using the 6 A and the 33.96 V, we confirm the real impedance is:

$$Z = \frac{E}{I}$$
$$= \frac{33.96 \text{ V}}{6 \text{ A}} = 5.66 \text{ }\Omega$$

For $Z_4$, each of the two components has an ohm value of 12 Ω with 50.94 V across them. Each 12 Ω leg has 4.245 A. The current through the resistive leg lags the current in the capacitive leg by 90°. Again, by adding these current vectors, or using the Pythagorean Theorem, we return to the line current of 6 A. The actual impedance of this Zone 4 is:

$$Z = \frac{E}{I}$$
$$= \frac{50.94 \text{ V}}{6 \text{ A}} = 8.49 \text{ }\Omega$$

This confirms our original assumed voltage method of finding the $Z$ of the parallel zone.

## POWER CALCULATIONS

The power calculations follow a simple format of using the current through the opposition of each component. The formulas

$$P = I^2 \times R$$
$$P = I^2 \times X_L$$
$$P = I^2 \times X_C$$

allow us to determine the power, whether true or reactive, for each component. Table 11–4 shows the respective calculations for each zone.

Adding all the watts together (all on the horizontal axis in Figure 11–5) yields 721.3 W. Adding the VAR$_C$ to the VAR$_L$ yields 0 VARs total.

**Figure 11–4** This voltage vector addition of series voltage drops is used for the circuit in Figure 11–1.

**Final Power Vectors**

**Figure 11–5** These final power triangles are for power calculations used for Figure 11–1.

Therefore, the final power triangle would look like Figure 11–5 and the final figure would appear as a watt vector of 721.3 W at a phase angle of 0°. This should be the same as the apparent power of 6 A × 120 V or 720 VA. Because of rounding of numbers, these two calculations are not exactly the same. However, they are close enough to confirm the procedure. We can also confirm that the phase angle of the power triangle is 0°, as was the original impedance triangle. The $\frac{W}{VA}$ calculation also yields 1 or the unity power factor known as 100%. Power factor expressed as a percentage of the apparent power that is consumed as true power is also defined as:

$$\% \ PF = \cos \theta \times 100$$

$$= \cos 0° \times 100 = 100\%$$

| Table 11–4 | | | | |
|---|---|---|---|---|
| $Z_1$ | $Z_2$ | $Z_3$ | $Z_4$ | $Z_5$ |
| $6^2 \times 10 \ \Omega$ | $4.25^2 \times 8 \ \Omega$ | $6^2 \times 4 \ \Omega$ | $4.25^2 \times 12 \ \Omega$ | $6^2 \times 6 \ \Omega$ |
| | $4.25^2 \times 8 \ \Omega$ | | $4.25^2 \times 12 \ \Omega$ | |
| 360 W | 144.5 W | $144 \ VAR_C$ | 216.8 W | $216 \ VAR_L$ |
| | $144.5 \ VAR_L$ | | $216.8 \ VAR_C$ | |

Calculating Each Zone Power for Figure 11–1

 FieldNote!

**Unity power factor** is considered to be a power factor of 1. This means the volt-amp rating (VA) of apparent power times a multiplying factor of 1 will yield the true power in watts (W). Unity is also understood to be 100% power factor, meaning that 100% of the apparent power is consumed as true power. A power factor of 1 or 100% means the same thing. There is no such thing as over 100% power factor or over unity.

## SERIES CIRCUITS IN PARALLEL

The other variation of a combination circuit is the series circuits in parallel with each other. Consider Figure 11–6. This circuit is typical in a small commercial application with several different motors on a branch circuit, all operating at one time. Each of the series circuits is typical of a motor that has inductance and resistance in series. We want to correct the power factor created by all the inductive loads of the motors, so we find the value of the last parallel component—a capacitor.

To analyze the circuit, first break the circuit into smaller segments to be treated individually and then assemble them into the circuit equivalent component. Branch 1 (impedance $Z_2$) is a series circuit with 21.21 $\Omega$ of $R$ and 21.21 $\Omega$ of $X_L$. Branch 2 ($Z_2$) is a motor with 34.34 $\Omega$ of $R$ and 20 $\Omega$ of $X_L$. Branch 3 ($Z_3$) is a motor with 30 $\Omega$ of $R$ and 52 $\Omega$ of $X_L$. Branch 4 ($Z_4$) is a capacitor. Build a table as shown in Table 11–5 to help track the branch values. Construct a $Z$ triangle for each series circuit to find the impedance of each branch to fill in the column for impedance. Then, calculate the current in each branch based on the impedance.

Because the branches are all in parallel, the next step is to vector the currents calculated in Table 11–5. The vector diagram in Figure 11–7 represents this vector addition.

You may find the vertical and horizontal components of each branch current vector to add them or use a scientific calculator to find the vector sum. Using the resistive and reactive values and the sine and cosine functions, you can calculate the vertical and horizontal components for each of the branches, as shown for Branch 2 in the example on the next page:

**Series Circuits in Parallel**

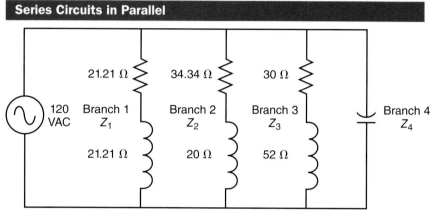

**Figure 11–6** Series circuits are shown in parallel. (**Note:** The capacitor value is to be determined.)

**Table 11–5**

| Branch 1 | Branch 2 | Branch 3 | Branch 4 |
|---|---|---|---|
| $Z_1 = \sqrt{R^2 + X_L^2}$ | $Z_2 = \sqrt{R^2 + X_L^2}$ | $Z_3 = \sqrt{R^2 + X_L^2}$ | $Z_4$ |
| $Z = \sqrt{21.21^2 + 21.21^2}$ | $Z = \sqrt{34.34^2 + 20^2}$ | $Z = \sqrt{30^2 + 52^2}$ | ? |
| $Z = 30\ \Omega$ at 45° lag | $Z = 40\ \Omega$ at 30° lag | $Z = 60\ \Omega$ at 60° lag | |
| $I_1 = \dfrac{120\ V}{30\ \Omega} = 4\ A$ | $I_2 = \dfrac{120\ V}{40\ \Omega} = 3\ A$ | $I_3 = \dfrac{120\ V}{60\ \Omega} = 2\ A$ | |
| at 45° lag | at 30° lag | at 60° lag | |

Tracking the $Z$ and $I$ or Each Branch of Parallel Series Circuits

**Resultant Currents**

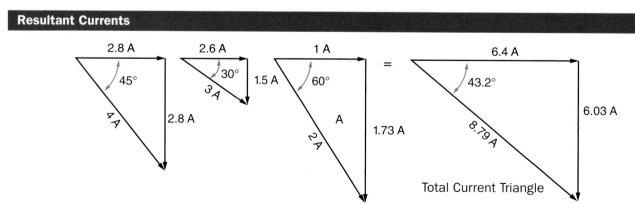

**Figure 11–7** Using the horizontal and vertical components of each branch current vector creates a resultant current for the first three branches of Figure 11–6.

For the vertical or reactive component:

$$\sin \theta = \frac{\text{Opposite side } (O)}{\text{Hypotenuse } (H)}$$

$$\sin 30° = \frac{O}{3 \text{ A}}$$

$$O = \sin 30° \times 3 \text{ A}$$

$$= 0.5 \times 3 \text{ A} = 1.5 \text{ A}$$

For the horizontal or resistive component:

$$\cos \theta = \frac{\text{Adjacent side } (A)}{\text{Hypotenuse } (H)}$$

$$\cos 30° = \frac{A}{3 \text{ A}}$$

$$A = \cos 30° \times 3 \text{ A}$$

$$= 0.866 \times 3 \text{ A} = 2.598 \text{ A}$$

The vertical and horizontal components for the other two branches are found similarly.

As you see in the vector diagram, the horizontal components all add to yield 6.4 A and the vertical components add to yield approximately 6 A for a vector sum of 8.79 A at phase angle to the line voltage of 43.3° lag. This angle tells us that the power factor so far is the cosine of 43.3° × 100, or 72.8%.

The voltage across each branch of the parallel circuit is the line voltage of 120 V. Even though the components are depicted as separate $R$ and $X_L$ components, they are the same motor component containing resistance. They cannot be measured individually as $E_{XL}$ and $E_R$ but can be measured as a total component voltage.

## POWER FACTOR CORRECTION

As you have seen in the previous circuit in Figures 11–6 and 11–7, there is a power factor of 72.8% lag without a capacitor in the circuit. This power factor is a result of the inductive current causing reactive power that is held in the magnetic field of the coils every time the magnetic field expands and collapses.

This effect creates a system inefficiency, which means we must deliver more current to the circuit than is actu-

 TechTip!

A power factor is usually not corrected to 100%. As a rule it is hard to correct to exactly 100% when the load may change, which means the original power factor may change. You do not usually want to over correct, or add more capacitance than is needed, because the power factor would never be over 100% but with too much capacitance could become a leading power factor. This means there would be more line current than at 100% correction, although it would be a leading current. This would again reduce the efficiency of the delivery system in terms of volt drop and watt loss in the line wires. Penalties are usually not assessed by the power supplier if the power factor is corrected to 95% and a rebate is not given if the power factor is higher than 95%. There is little advantage to buying more capacitors and installing them without a reduction in your cost of electricity.

ally needed to support the true power, or real work. If we can reduce the apparent power to the circuit, in this case, 8.79 A × 120 V = 1,054.8 VA, then the line current can be reduced and less current is needed from the source. The solution to drawing additional current from the line is to create a "tank" circuit using a capacitor as one-half of the tank, as discussed in Chapter 10.

If we want to eliminate all excess current from the line, we need to supply all the inductive current from the tank of the capacitive current. In other words, we offset the 6 A of inductive current with 6 A of capacitive current. Working backward from what we need to supply, we can find the amount of needed $X_C$ to create 6 A of $I_C$ at 120 V:

$$X_C = \frac{E}{I_C}$$

$$= \frac{120 \text{ V}}{6 \text{ A}} = 20 \ \Omega$$

From this information, we can now calculate $C$ in farads using the formula:

$$C = \frac{1}{2\pi f X_C}$$

$$= \frac{1}{(377)(20)} = 0.0001326 \text{ farad}$$

$$= 132.6 \ \mu\text{F (when 60 Hz is applied)}$$

Therefore, the needed capacitance to correct the power factor to 100% is 132.6 μF.

Suppose a 43.3° phase shift is too large but we do not want to correct to exactly 100%.

## FieldNote!

When ordering and installing capacitors for power factor correction, capacitors are specified in Capacitive Kilo Volt-Amps Reactive (C-KVAR) and with the rated voltage to be connected. Electricians do not normally use the microfarad rating for ordering.

To do this, we only need to determine how far we do want to correct. Let us correct to a standard figure of 95% power factor. To do this, we need to see what the current triangle would look like if the power factor were 95%. The angle is found by using the arccos (cos $^{-1}$) 0.95 = 18.195°. The angle θ is now established at 18.2°, instead of the original 43.3°. If we know the angle and the horizontal vector of resistive current stays at 6.4 A, then the vertical component can be calculated. Using trigonometry, the vertical side or remaining reactive current after correction is found to be:

$$\tan \theta = \frac{\text{Oppositive side}}{\text{Adjacent side}}$$

Opposite side = tan θ × Adjacent side

$$= \tan 18.2° \times 6.4 \text{ A}$$

$$= 2.1 \text{ A}$$

The opposite side is 2.1 A remaining after correction from the capacitor. The uncorrected current due to inductors was 6 A, and approximately 2 A remains; therefore, we added 4 A of capacitive current to the circuit by adding a capacitor in parallel. Use the formulas that follow to determine the capacitor value:

$$X_C = \frac{E}{I_C}$$

$$= \frac{120 \text{ V}}{4 \text{ A}}$$

$$= 30 \text{ }\Omega$$

THEN

$$C = \frac{1}{2 \pi f X_C}$$   ***Note:*** In this formula *C* is in farads.

$$= \frac{1}{(377)\,30}$$

$$= 0.00008842 \text{ F } (88.4 \text{ }\mu\text{F})$$

As you can see, we needed a smaller microfarad capacitor to correct the power factor to 95% than we needed to add to correct the power factor to 100%.

## COMPLEX CIRCUIT EVALUATION

The last circuit configuration to analyze is a series circuit with two parallel combinations, as in Figure 11–8. We use parts of the previous parallel circuit to simplify the calculation but reconfigure the circuit to make sure we apply the proper rules. We start by combining small series or parallel circuits into equivalent circuits and record values in a table for easy reference, as shown in Table 11–6. Assume a voltage of 120 V across each of the parallel branches.

**Figure 11–8** Two parallel circuits are shown in series.

| **Table 11–6** | | | |
|---|---|---|---|
| **$Z_1$** | **$Z_2$** | **$Z_3$** | **$Z_4$** |
| $Z = \sqrt{21.21^2 + 21.21^2}$ | $Z = \sqrt{34.34^2 + 20^2}$ | $Z = \sqrt{30^2 + 52^2}$ | $Z = 30\ \Omega$ |
| $Z = 30\ \Omega$ at 45° lag | 40 $\Omega$ at 30° lag | 60 $\Omega$ at 60° lag | 30 $\Omega$ at 90° lead |
| $I_1 = \dfrac{120\text{ V}}{30\ \Omega} = 4\text{ A}$ | $I_2 = \dfrac{120\text{ V}}{40\ \Omega} = 3\text{ A}$ | $I_3 = \dfrac{120\text{ V}}{60\ \Omega} = 2\text{ A}$ | $I_4 = \dfrac{120\text{ V}}{30\ \Omega} = 4\text{ A}$ |
| at 45° lag | at 30° lag | at 60° lag | at 90° lead |

Each Zone Impedance Using an Assumed Voltage and Current

## IMPEDANCE CALCULATION

Because Zones 1 and 2 are in parallel, parallel circuit rules apply. Vector the currents, or use algebraic formulas, to determine the actual impedance that would produce this assumed current with the assumed voltage. You saw earlier in this chapter, in the calculations following Figure 11–7, how to use the sine and cosine functions to solve for the vertical and horizontal components of these branches. This calculated value is the actual impedance of $Z_1$ and $Z_2$ in parallel. Do the same for $Z_3$ and $Z_4$ parallel circuits. Figure 11–9a shows the vector addition for $Z_1$ and $Z_2$, and Figure 11–9b shows the vector addition for $Z_3$ and $Z_4$.

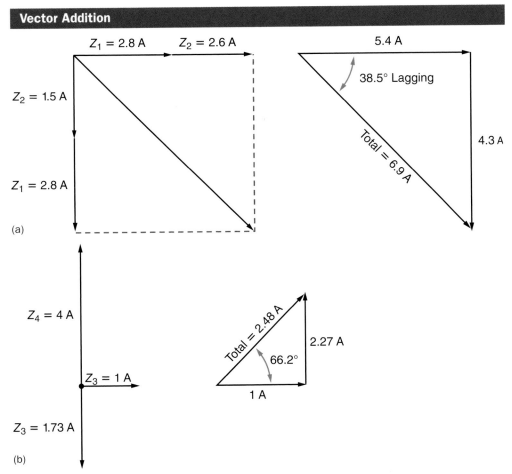

**Vector Addition**

(a)

(b)

**Figure 11–9** (a) Vector addition of assumed currents in parallel is used for branches $Z_1$ and $Z_2$. (b) Vector addition of assumed currents in parallel is used for branches $Z_3$ and $Z_4$.

By referring to both figures we know the assumed current vector sum if 120 V is assumed as the branch voltage.

From this, calculate the actual zone impedance of Zones 1 and 2 as:

$$Z = \frac{120 \text{ V}_{\text{assumed}}}{6.9 \text{ A}_{\text{assumed}}}$$

$$= 17.4 \ \Omega \text{ of } Z$$

(at 38.5° inductive effect)

Calculate the equivalent impedance of combined $Z_3$ and $Z_4$ as:

$$Z = \frac{120 \text{ V}_{\text{assumed}}}{2.5 \text{ A}_{\text{assumed}}}$$

$$= 48 \ \Omega \text{ of } Z$$

(at 66.2° capacitive effect)

## Circuit Impedance Triangle

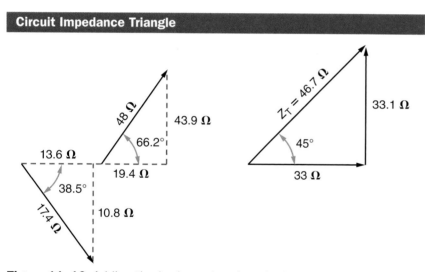

**Figure 11–10** Adding the horizontal and vertical components together yields a circuit impedance triangle.

## Voltage Vector Addition

**Figure 11–11** Voltage vector addition using horizontal and vertical components.

Now the combined equivalent Zone 1 and 2 are in series with the combined Zones 3 and 4 and series circuit rules apply for adding series impedances. Series circuit rules dictate that we add oppositions to find the total $Z$ of the circuit. Figure 11–10 adds these two equivalent impedances to get a total $Z$ for the circuit of 46.7 $\Omega$ at a 45° phase angle. The vertical and horizontal components were found using the sine and cosine functions, as illustrated earlier. With 300 V applied, the line current is approximately 6.42 A.

### VOLTAGE CALCULATION

Now that we have actual circuit impedances and a real line current, we can determine what voltage drop each component has. Use the line current as the constant because it is the same through the series circuit in whole. The formula to find the voltage drop across $Z_1$ and $Z_2$ is:

$$E = I_T \times Z_{\text{equiv}}$$

$$= 6.42 \times 17.4 \ \Omega = 111.7 \text{ V}$$

The voltage dropped across that parallel combination is leading the circuit current by 38.5° (the current is lagging). The second parallel combination uses:

$$E = I_T \times Z_{\text{equiv}}$$

$$= 6.42 \times 48 \ \Omega = 308.16 \text{ V}$$

The voltage in this part of the circuit lags the line current by 66.2° (the current is leading). These two voltages are what we would measure across each of the branches with a voltmeter. We cannot tell with a voltmeter what the phase angle is in reference to the current. We cannot just arithmetically add the voltages because they are at different angles to the line current. By vector addition, we find that the total (resultant) line voltage is approximately 300 V, the same as the applied voltage. Again, because of decimal rounding, the resultant is not exact. See Figure 11–11 for voltage vector addition using horizontal and vertical components.

## Power Calculation Triangle

$Z_1$ & $Z_2$                    $Z_3$ & $Z_4$

**Figure 11–12** This power calculation triangle is for a circuit as in Figure 11–8.

***Note:*** drawing is not to scale to allow for easier reading.

## POWER CALCULATIONS

The simplest way to calculate the true, apparent, and reactive power is to go to the final voltage triangle vector, and multiply each voltage vector times the line current (Figure 11–12).

Zones 1 and 2 have:

111.7 V × 6.42 A = 717.1 VA

Zones 3 and 4 have:

308.16 V × 6.42 A = 1,978.4 VA

Total watts for the circuit are:

211.78 V (at 0°) × 6.42 A = 1,359.6 W

Reactive VARs are:

212.45 V (at 90°) × 6.17 V
= 1,363.9 VARs

The result of all this is apparent power of:

300 V (at 45° leading) × 6.42 A
= 1,926 VA

The percent power factor is:

$$\% \ PF = \frac{1{,}359.6 \text{ W}}{1{,}926 \text{ VA}} \times 100$$

$$= 70.6\%$$

OR

% $PF$ = cos 45° × 100 = 70.7%

The slight difference in power factor calculations is due to decimal rounding.

## FORENSIC EVALUATION

We use a simple parallel circuit to find an unknown value in the circuit based on the reading we can make in the cir-

## RLC Circuit

**Figure 11–13** This RLC circuit has some measurements and an unknown component.

FieldNote!

Forensic evaluation: Many times electrical personnel need to figure out what an actual circuit would look like in schematic form by using circuit values that are collected from the already-operating circuit. This process requires a thorough understanding of how circuit components react with each other and how they would affect actual circuit readings. With knowledge of what could be, the measured values can be used to construct the realistic schematic of the complex circuit and create a working model of an "in use" circuit.

cuit. If we have a simple parallel RLC circuit as in Figure 11–13 with readings from an ammeter, voltmeter, and power factor meter, we can decipher the unknown quantities. We know that Branch 1 is resistive, Branch 2 is unknown, and Branch 3 is capacitive.

The current readings are as shown in Figure 11–13, and the circuit power factor reads 70.7% lagging. We need to find the component of Branch 2. Because we have a parallel circuit, we know that the currents are added vectorially to get a resultant $I_T$.

Figure 11–14 shows the current vectors needed to obtain the circuit meter readings. We know that we must have had 6 A of $I_L$ to end with a resultant of 2.82 at a phase angle of 45° (arccos 0.707 = 45°) and that the line current is lagging, as it would in a more inductive circuit. Now we can calculate the unknown component as an inductor with a current of 6 A $I_L$.

Since:

$$X_L = \frac{E_L}{I_L} = \frac{120 \text{ V}}{6 \text{ A}} = 20 \text{ }\Omega$$

AND

$$L = \frac{X_L}{2\pi f}$$

Then the inductor in Branch 2 is equal to:

$$L = \frac{20 \text{ }\Omega}{2 \times 3.1416 \times 60}$$

$$= 0.053 \text{ H (53 mH)}$$

The resistance of Branch 1 is equal to:

$$R_{\text{Branch 1}} = \frac{120 \text{ V}}{2 \text{ A}} = 60 \text{ }\Omega$$

The impedance of Branch 3 is:

$$X_{\text{C Branch 2}} = \frac{120 \text{ V}}{4 \text{ A}} = 30 \text{ }\Omega$$

and if:

$$C = \frac{1}{2\pi f X_C}$$

Then the capacitor in Branch 3 is equal to:

$$C = \frac{1}{2 \times 3.1416 \times 60 \times 30}$$

$$= 0.0000884 \text{ F (88.4 }\mu\text{F)}$$

**Current Vectors**

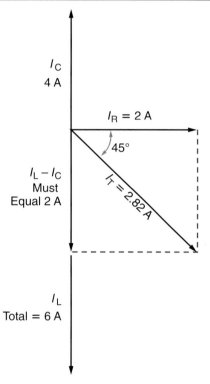

**Figure 11–14** Horizontal and vertical components for current vectors of known meter readings are added together to determine unknown values.

## SUMMARY

The combination of series and parallel rules for solving RLC circuits can be confusing. A basic rule is to add oppositions in series and add currents in parallel. However, you need to track the actual angles involved as you add the vectors representing current or impedance. As you solve for values in the systems, make sure you note the inductive or capacitive effects of the components involved. It is easy to forget the small details as you solve a large complex problem. Power can be calculated by several means as you use $E$ and $I$ for individual components or use $I^2 \times$ opposition. Then make sure you note whether it is true, reactive, or apparent power you are calculating.

Using what you know about circuit characteristics, you should be able to calculate any required values in the circuit and be able to determine what must have been the case as you find readings that indicate how the circuit actually worked. This is a helpful troubleshooting mechanism when you may encounter strange voltages that are only explained by your knowledge of the circuit.

## CHAPTER GLOSSARY

**Unity power factor** Ratio of true power (watts) divided by apparent power (volt-amps) with the dividend as one or the ratio as 1. Unity power factor is also known as 100%, meaning that 100% of the volt-amps are used as watts and the reactive power does not affect the circuit. The power factor cannot be over unity or 100%.

## REVIEW QUESTIONS

1. What is the major distinction of a combination or complex circuit?
2. Explain the rules for finding impedance of a series RLC circuit.
3. Explain the rules for finding impedance of a parallel RLC circuit.
4. Explain how to add vectors with different angles and different magnitude.
5. In what type of circuit is current the constant when vectoring voltage components?
6. To correct a lagging power factor and reduce the line current, you need to add a capacitor in _____.

7. Inductive and capacitive reactance cancel each other in a/an _____ RLC circuit.
8. Unity power factor is also known as _____ percent.
9. If you overcorrect a lagging power factor, the percent power factor goes _____ and the line current goes _____.
10. Explain how to find the microfarad value of a capacitor if you only know the current to the capacitor and its voltage.
11. In Figure RQ11–1, vector $Z_2$ goes up and vector $Z_4$ goes down. Why?

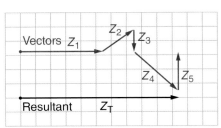

**Figure RQ11–1**

## PRACTICE PROBLEMS

Problems 1 to 10 refer to Figure PP11–1.

1. Find $Z_{R2L1}$ of $R_2 + L_1$ using the assumed voltage method.
2. Find $Z_{R3C1}$ of $R_3 + C_1$ by the same method as Problem 1.
3. Find $Z_{total}$.
4. Diagram the circuit (vectorially).

For Problems 5–10, apply 200 V AC at the source.

5. If 200 V AC is applied, find the line current.
6. The voltage drop across $R_1$ would be _____ with a 200 V AC source voltage.
7. Calculate the phase angle of lead or lag for the total circuit voltage and current.
8. If the source is operating at 60 Hz, find the henry value of $L_2$.
9. How much voltage would be measured across $C_2$?
10. Determine the apparent power of this circuit.

**Figure PP11–1**

# 12

# AC FILTER CIRCUITS

# O V E R V I E W

In previous chapters, you learned about resonance, inductive reactance, and capacitive reactance. At certain frequencies, these characteristics can be used to design circuits that allow current and voltage to pass to the load. At other frequencies, they can be used to design circuits where current and voltage are filtered out, and do not appear at the load. These special circuits are called filters or wave traps.

The frequency filter distinguishes one radio or television station's signal from another by allowing certain frequencies to reach the amplifier circuits while trapping others at the filter. It is also the filter that prevents one radio station from interfering with another. It is not unusual to have unwanted frequencies generated on an AC power line because various types of loads are operating. These generated frequencies may have considerable power. These same frequencies can cause interference with radios, televisions, computers, or other electronic devices that are operating on the same power line. The most common types of interference are static or a low hum. Power line filters can be installed to prevent these types of interference.

DC combined with AC is a common design with many electronic circuits. This concept is used in many systems as a base voltage and a signal voltage. The AC signals are sometimes referred to as AC riding on a DC level. This principle is used in circuits that have both DC levels of voltage; superimposed on that DC voltage is an AC voltage. This is common in amplifier circuits: the DC level is used to operate the amplifier components such as transistors and the AC voltage is the signal to amplify. The DC level is a component that is not to be passed from stage to stage of an amplifier, while the AC component is to be passed on.

In this chapter, you learn about the various types of filters and how they work. This information is used in the design of a variety of filters, ranging from radio and television circuitry to harmonic filters used in a range of power system applications.

# O B J E C T I V E S

After completing this chapter, you will be able to:
· Explain the theory of operation of common types of filters
· Identify low-pass filters
· Explain why half-power point is significant
· Calculate values for high-pass filters
· Draw the pass bands for various filters
· Explain how a band-reject filter functions
· Design simple filter circuits

# FILTER OPERATION AND CLASSIFICATION

### FILTER OPERATION

Figure 12–1 shows the basic concept of filtering. Note that with different frequency components coming into the filter only one frequency com-

ponent is allowed to leave. The low-pass filter blocks the high frequency (100 kHz) and passes the low frequency (1 kHz). The high-pass filter works in an opposite manner in that it passes the high frequency and blocks the low frequency.

### FILTER CLASSIFICATION

Many types of electrical filters are used for different applications:

- DC combined with AC (not an actual filter—AC is superimposed on DC)
- Transformer coupling (to block DC)
- Capacitive coupling (to block DC)
- Low-pass filter (blocks higher frequencies)
- High-pass filter (blocks lower frequencies)
- Band-pass filter (passes only a concentrated area of frequencies)
- Band-reject filter (blocks only a concentrated area of frequencies)
- Other circuit filters (interference and resonant)

Transformer coupling of amplifier stages is often used in audio amplifiers. The concept is that transformers do not operate on DC but do respond to the fluctuating voltage of an AC signal. We know that transformers must have motion of the magnetic field created by the AC waveforms. The transformer does not transform a steady DC level. Therefore, the DC level of one stage is blocked, or ignored, by the transformer and the AC level is transformed to a higher, or possibly lower, level for the next stage or to an output device (see Figure 12–2).

Capacitive coupling or RC filtering is also used when the DC must be "filtered out" or blocked and the AC part of the amplified voltage is allowed to pass. The filter or coupling capacitor is an inexpensive method to block the DC level. See Figure 12–3 for the placement of a DC coupling capacitor. The concept used is based on the idea that a capacitor blocks DC and passes AC.

**Filter Concept**

**Figure 12–1** The filter concept indicates that a filter passes the correct frequency to a load.

**Transformer Coupling**

**Figure 12–2** Transformer coupling joins amplifier stages.

As you saw in earlier chapters, a capacitor can charge to a DC value and then appears as a countervoltage to the applied voltage. If the applied voltage does not change, the capacitor voltage does not change and appears as open because no current flows. This feature allows the capacitor to appear as open to a DC level voltage, but an AC voltage rising above, and falling below, the steady DC level appears as an AC that is oscillating above and below a steady reference point. Therefore, the AC component appears to pass through the capacitor and the DC value is blocked by the capacitor. The coupling of the stages of an amplifier passes the AC signal to the next stage.

## LOW-PASS FILTERS

A simple low-pass filter uses an inductor in series with a load resistor. A low-pass filter is shown in Figure 12–4. At low frequencies, the chosen coil's inductive reactance is low and little voltage is dropped across the inductive reactance. Most of the source voltage is dropped across the resistance of the load ($R_L$). Remember $X_L = 2\pi fL$ and that with an impedance triangle with little reactance almost all of the voltage drop is due to resistance.

As the frequency increases, the inductance does not change but the $X_L$ increases. The result of the increase in $X_L$ is that more voltage is dropped across the inductor and less voltage is dropped across the load. As you can see in the graph in Figure 12–4, the voltage across the load ($R_L$) starts to decrease as the frequency increases and the $X_L$ increases, until little of the source voltage is dropped at the load. A common application for choosing chokes (coils) is if the $X_L$ value (measured in ohms) is 10 times greater than the load resistance (also measured in ohms) there is virtually no signal voltage across the load.

The opposite is also true. If the value of $X_L$ is 10 times less than the value of the resistance, most of the sig-

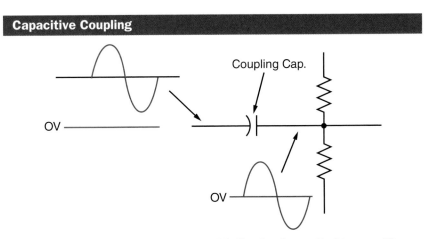

**Figure 12–3** Capacitive coupling or RC filtering is applied to amplifier stages.

**Figure 12–4** This graph represents the output of the RL low-pass filter.

nal reaches the load, as is the case at the low starting frequency. Typically, low-pass filters are designed to deliver most of the signal to the load at lower frequencies. To illustrate this point mathematically, use Figure 12–4 as the schematic and values of 1,000 $\Omega$ for the resistor and 0.16 H for the coil. The circuit has 100 V at 100 Hz applied:

$$X_L = 2\pi fL$$

$$= 2 \times 3.14 \times 100 \times 0.16$$

$$= 100.48 \ \Omega \text{ at } 100 \text{ Hz}$$

If you start with a circuit AC voltage of 100 V at 100 Hz, you develop a voltage divider with two components: a 1,000 $\Omega$ resistor and 100.5 $\Omega$ coil.

**Voltage Vector**

**Figure 12–5** This voltage vector represents values in Figure 12–4 at 100 Hz.

**Voltage Vector**

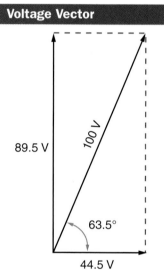

**Figure 12–6** This voltage vector represents voltage values for Figure 12–4 at 2,000 Hz.

An impedance triangle results in a $Z$ of approximately 1,005 $\Omega$ of impedance. The resultant series circuit current is 0.0995 A. This circuit current creates a voltage drop across the resistor of

$$0.0995 \text{ A} \times 1,000 \ \Omega = 99.5 \text{ V}$$

The same current of

$$0.0995 \text{ A} \times 100.5 \ \Omega = 9.99 \text{ V}$$

across the coil is shown in Figure 12–5. Use the same steps to find the circuit current and voltage drops as the frequency increases.

When the frequency increases to 2,000 Hz, the shape of the impedance and the voltage vector change to those shown in Figure 12–6 and explained in the subsequent example:

$$X_L = 2\pi f L$$
$$= 2 \times 3.14 \times 2,000 \times 0.16$$
$$= 2,010 \ \Omega \ \text{at } 2,000 \text{ Hz}$$

Solving for circuit impedance and voltage drops as above, the voltage vector now appears as in Figure 12–6, with an angle of lag of 63.5°. This causes a voltage drop of 89.5 V across the coil and 44.6 V across the resistor, trapping a larger amount of voltage at the coil (choking off the voltage supply) and allowing a smaller amount of voltage to be passed to the load resistor at higher frequencies.

Now, increase the frequency to 10 kHz (10,000 Hz) to view the impedance and voltage triangles, as shown in Figure 12–7. As you can verify by the mathematics that follow, a large portion of the source voltage appears across the "choke" and a small value appears across the load resistor:

$$X_L = 2\pi f L$$
$$= 2 \times 3.14 \times 10,000 \times 0.16$$
$$= 10,048 \ \Omega \ \text{at } 10,000 \text{ Hz}$$
$$Z_T = \sqrt{R^2 + X_L^2}$$
$$= \sqrt{1,000 \ \Omega^2 + 10,048 \ \Omega^2}$$
$$= 10,097.6 \ \Omega$$
$$I_T = \frac{E_T}{Z_T}$$
$$= \frac{100 \text{ V}}{10,097.6 \ \Omega} = 0.0099 \text{ A}$$
$$E_R = I_R \times R$$
$$= 0.0099 \text{ A} \times 1,000 \ \Omega = 9.9 \text{ V}$$
$$E_L = I_L \times X_L$$
$$= 0.0099 \text{ A} \times 10,048 \ \Omega = 99.5 \text{ V}$$

### HALF-POWER POINT

To find the **half-power point** of a filter, we do a quick calculation regarding $X_L$ and $R_L$. From the previous example, it is easy to ascertain that half power is defined as the point at which the load resistance is dissipating half the maximum value. It is easy to assume this is true when $X_L$ equals the value of the resistance, and in fact, this is the case.

**Impedance Triangle and Voltage Vector**

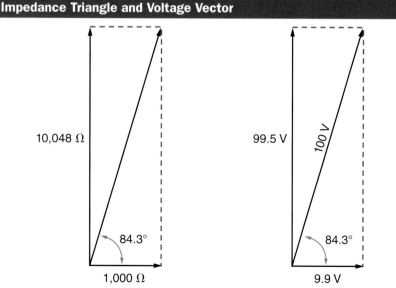

**Figure 12–7** The impedance triangles and the voltage vector represent values for Figure 12–4 at 10,000 Hz.

To prove it, start by considering that the *maximum* power is dissipated by the resistor when the voltage on the load resistor is equal to the supply voltage. This is true because at this point the voltage across the resistor is maximum; therefore, the current flow through the resistor is greatest, and the power dissipation is maximum. This maximum power occurs at the maximum voltage drop across the load resistor, which is represented as $E_{sup}$.

The formula for the maximum power is given by:

$$P_{max} = \frac{E_{sup}^2}{R_L}$$

Solving for $E_{sup}$ gives:

$$E_{sup}^2 = P_{max} \times R_L$$

AND

$$E_{sup} = \sqrt{P_{max} \times R_L}$$

The voltage for half power is given by:

$$E_{1/2} = \sqrt{\left(\frac{P_{max}}{2}\right) \times R_L}$$

Substituting for $P_{max}$ yields:

$$E_{1/2} = \sqrt{\frac{\left(\frac{E_{sup}^2}{R_L}\right)}{2} \times R_L} = \sqrt{\frac{E_{sup}^2}{2}}$$

The voltage drop across the resistor can also be calculated using the voltage divider formula:

$$E_{1/2} = \frac{R_L}{\sqrt{X_L^2 + R_L^2}} \times E_{sup}$$

Substituting for $E_{1/2}$, this means that:

$$\sqrt{\frac{E_{sup}^2}{2}} = \frac{R_L}{\sqrt{X_L^2 + R_L^2}} \times E_{sup}$$

Squaring both sides yields:

$$\frac{E_{sup}^2}{2} = \frac{R_L^2}{\sqrt{X_L^2 + R_L^2}} \times E_{sup}^2$$

Dividing both sides by $E_{sup}^2$ gives:

$$\frac{1}{2} = \frac{R_L^2}{X_L^2 + R_L^2}$$

Cross-multiplying gives:

$$X_L^2 + R_L^2 = 2R_L^2$$

## TechTip!

When a circuit allows half of the power to pass through a filter and appear at the load, the filter is said to be at the half-power point. The object of most filters is to allow half or more of the power to appear at the load and be able to block or stop half of the circuit power at the filter, based on the designed frequency. The desired frequency should allow half or more of the power to pass and should be able to block at least half of the undesired power. This is typically the point where 70.7% of the source voltage appears at the load. If this happens, it is assumed that 70.7% of the current appears at the load. 70.7% of the voltage multiplied by 70.7% of the current equals 50% of the volt-amps or power, or the half-power point.

And subtracting $R_L^2$ from both sides yields:

$$X_L^2 = R_L^2$$

Notice that this is true even if $X_L$ is negative. Of course, inductive reactance cannot be negative; however, capacitive reactance can be, so the same formula holds for a series RC circuit.

At half power, the voltage across the load is the same as the voltage drop across the coil, as can be seen in the impedance triangle and voltage vector. The angle of lag is 45°, and the voltage across the load resistor is 0.707 times the line voltage. The current flowing through the load is 0.707 times the maximum possible value. The product of 70.7% of the voltage at 70.7% of the current is approximately 50% of the power.

All frequencies that lose less than the one-half maximum power at the coil are considered to pass to the load. All frequencies that produce more than half-power dissipation at the coil are rejected and never reach the load.

### INDUCTIVE LOW-PASS FILTER

As an example, design a low-pass filter that passes all frequencies up to 400 Hz to a load of 600 Ω. The half-power point occurs when $X_L = R_{load}$. With these two values equal, half or more of the power is delivered to the load at any frequency up to 400 Hz.

## TechTip!

Low-pass filters are simple to construct with a resistor and a capacitor tuned to allow low frequencies to pass to the load but block the high frequencies. Referring to Figure 12–8, determine which maximum frequency you want to pass and calculate the capacitive value at that frequency that will produce an $X_C$ that will draw enough current to drop half the total voltage on the series resistor ($R_S$). A variable resistor or variable capacitor can be used to fine-tune the circuit values.

To find the henry value of the inductor when $X_L$ equals 600 Ω at 400 Hz, use the following formula:

At the half-power point at 400 Hz:

$$X_L = R_L = 600 \ \Omega$$

$$X_L = 2\pi f L$$

OR

$$L = \frac{X_L}{2\pi f}$$

$$= \frac{600 \ \Omega}{6.28 \times 400 \ \text{Hz}}$$

$$= 0.239 \ \text{H}$$

### Low-Pass Filter

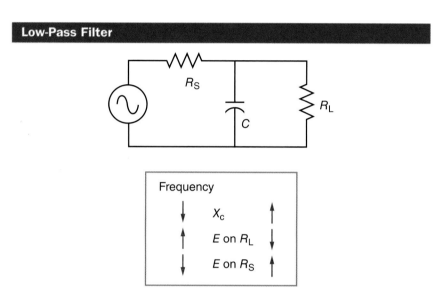

**Figure 12–8** This low-pass filter has a capacitor across the load.

### Load Voltage versus Frequency

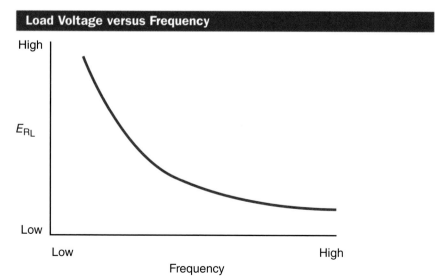

**Figure 12–9** Load voltage versus frequency is shown for the circuit in Figure 12–8.

## CAPACITIVE LOW-PASS FILTER

Another low-pass filter is shown in Figure 12–8. This filter has a capacitor in parallel with the load resistor. The circuit has a series resistor, $R_S$, to drop the voltage that is not delivered to the load. At low frequencies, the capacitor exhibits a high reactance, and most of the circuit current flows through the load resistor rather than the capacitor branch. With $R_L$ larger than $R_S$, a greater percentage of the line voltage drops across $R_L$. If the frequency increases, the capacitor's reactance decreases and more current flows through the capacitor. With this condition, the series resistor drops more voltage and causes the load voltage to decrease. This is depicted in the chart associated with Figure 12–8.

As the frequency is increased, the capacitive branch draws greater current because of the decreasing value of $X_C$. The circuit impedance decreases as the capacitive current increases. The circuit current increases and as a result, greater current flows through the series resistor ($R_S$). This causes the voltage across $R_S$ to increase, with the voltage across the parallel circuit of the filter capacitor and $R_L$ decreasing. See Figure 12–9 for a graphical representation of this filter's effect on load voltage. This type of filtering is often used across the power line to reduce high-frequency interference. It filters out all of the higher frequencies and allows normal 60 Hz frequency power to pass.

## COMBINED LC LOW-PASS FILTER

Another example of a low-pass filter is shown in Figure 12–10. This filter consists of an inductor in series with a capacitor and a load resistor in parallel as the load. As you can surmise, at low frequencies the $X_L$ is low and the $X_C$ is high by comparison. At the lower frequencies, little voltage is dropped across the inductor. Most of the source voltage is across the very high reactance of the capacitor and the load. As the frequency is increased, more of the source voltage is across the inductor, and the voltage across the capacitor and the load decreases. This filter has a sharper slope and is more efficient than the filter in Figure 12–8 because both the inductor and the capacitor reduce the voltage across the load simultaneously as the frequency increases.

When the circuit reaches the resonant frequency ($X_L = X_C$), the output signal peaks. This is followed by a sharp drop in the output signal (voltage) as the frequency continues to rise. A graph of this load voltage versus frequency is shown in Figure 12–10.

## HIGH-PASS FILTERS

A typical high-pass filter circuit schematic is shown in Figure 12–11. A simple high-pass filter consists of a capacitor in series with the load. This configuration is easily recognized as a simple series RC circuit.

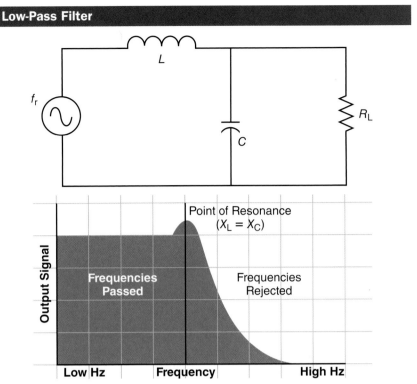

**Low-Pass Filter**

**Figure 12–10** This low-pass filter uses an LC circuit for sharper cutoff. The output voltage versus the frequency is shown for the circuit in the diagram.

TechTip!

Some intercom systems use the power line to carry the signal, and this filter would block these low frequencies of 60 Hz. Other control systems use the power line to carry the signals for energy control, lighting control, etc. The filter is set at the receiver to pass only the desired signal frequency and block the normal 60 Hz line frequency. By using a specific capacitor in series, a simple and cheap filter is achieved.

**High-Pass Filter**

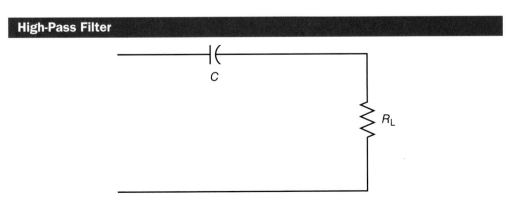

**Figure 12–11** A high-pass filter can be simple.

At low frequencies, the $X_C$ is very high, and the capacitor drops the most voltage. As indicated in the impedance and voltage triangle of Figure 12–12, as the frequency is increased, less voltage is dropped across the capacitor and more voltage is dropped across the load. This type of filter can be used to eliminate interference (at power line frequencies) from entering the load. To design the filter to trap a specific frequency, we need to find the components that produce the half-power point for the circuit. In the first example, we trap any frequencies that are 1,000 Hz and lower. See the graph of voltage versus frequency for this type of filter depicted in Figure 12–12.

As you saw previously, the half-power point for this filter occurs when the capacitance reactance ($X_C$) equals the load resistance at the desired low cutoff of the filter frequency. First, find the capacitor that creates the desired reactance to produce half power at 1,000 Hz.

## FieldNote!

High-pass filters can be used in audio circuits to cut out the low frequencies. Some technicians refer to these types of filters as "rumble filters" or "bass-cut filters." They can be used to cut out background low-frequency noise or reduce sound to the woofer speakers. To find the cutoff frequency at which the one-half power point is reached, use the formula:

$$\text{Frequency (cutoff)} = \frac{1}{2\pi RC}$$

**Figure 12–12** Voltage and impedance triangles lead to a graph of voltage versus frequency for the circuit.

---

### Example

At 1 kHz and a load of 1 k$\Omega$
If $X_C = R_L$
Then $X_C = 1,000\ \Omega$ at 1,000 Hz

Therefore, $X_C = \dfrac{1}{2\pi fC}$, where $C$ is in farads. Solve for $C$, then find the reactance.

**Solution:**

$$C = \frac{1}{2\pi fX_C}$$

$$= \frac{1}{6.28 \times 1,000 \times 1,000}$$

$$= \frac{1}{6,280,000}$$

$$= 0.159\ \mu F$$

Finding the reactance at 60 Hz and the same microfarad capacitor:

$$X_C = \frac{1}{2\pi fC}\ \text{where } C \text{ is in farads}$$

$$= \frac{1}{2\pi \times 60 \times 0.000000159}$$

$$= \frac{1}{6.28 \times 60 \times 0.000000159}$$

$$= 16,691.4\ \Omega$$

---

As previously shown, the voltage triangle for the series RC circuit is different at 1,000 Hz from its appearance at 60 Hz. The opposition offered by the capacitor is more than 16 times the opposition of the load at 60 Hz, and most of the voltage is trapped at the capacitor and does not appear across the load.

### CAPACITIVE HIGH-PASS FILTER

When the $X_C$ value is one-tenth as great as the load resistance, little, essentially no, voltage signal is dropped across the capacitor. As an example, consider a filter that passes all frequencies above 400 Hz to a 600 $\Omega$ load. The first step is to calculate the value of $C$. Again, we assume a half-power point where the load opposition equals the series

drop component opposition. In other words, $X_C$ equals $R$ load at 600 $\Omega$. At this point at 400 Hz, one-half of the power is delivered to the load. At any higher frequencies, more of the circuit power is delivered to the load.

The capacitance value equals:

$$C = \frac{1}{2\pi fX_C}$$

$$= \frac{1}{6.28 \times 400 \times 600}$$

$$= \frac{1}{1,507,200}$$

$$= 0.66\ \mu F$$

As frequencies increase above this value, $X_C$ decreases even further, less voltage is dropped at the capacitor, and more voltage is dropped at the load resistor in series.

## INDUCTIVE HIGH-PASS FILTER

In Figure 12–13, an inductor is in parallel with the load resistor. At low frequencies, the inductive reactance ($X_L$) is low, allowing most of the circuit current

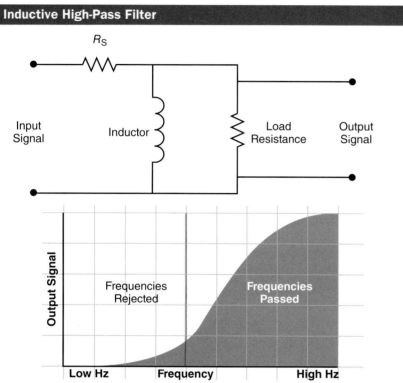

**Inductive High-Pass Filter**

**Figure 12–13** An inductive high-pass filter uses RL, and a graph shows voltage versus frequency curves for the schematic.

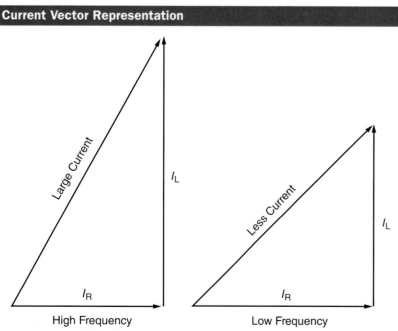

**Current Vector Representation**

**Figure 12–14** Current vector representation is shown for the circuit in Figure 12–13.

to flow through the inductor. Using $E_L = I \times X_L$ would indicate that the parallel voltage drop is low and the load voltage is low. To exaggerate this effect, imagine the frequency is 0 Hz. The $X_L$ of the coil is 0 Ω—in other words, a short circuit with no voltage drop. As the frequency increases and the inductive reactance ($X_L$) increases comparatively, more current flows through the parallel resistive load. Since the resistance did not change, the voltage across the load increases. When the value of the inductive reactance ($X_L$) becomes 10 times the value of the load resistor, essentially all the signal current flow is through the load resistor and the inductor no longer has any effect on the circuit. To take this to an extreme, assume the frequency goes to infinite hertz. The $X_L$ becomes so great that it appears as an open circuit. See Figure 12–13 to see the effects of increasing frequency on the voltage across $R_L$. See Figure 12–14 for a sample of the current triangles of the parallel $R_L$ circuit.

## COMBINED LC HIGH-PASS FILTER

In Figure 12–15, the series resistor ($R_S$) is replaced with a capacitor. Again, at the low frequencies more of the source voltage is across the high $X_C$ of the capacitor (because of its high reactance at low frequency) and less voltage is across the inductor and the load (because of the low reactance of the inductor at low frequency).

As frequency is increased, the capacitive reactance decreases, the inductive reactance increases, and a greater proportion of the source voltage drops across the parallel coil and resistor combination. Therefore, the voltage across the load increases with the increasing frequency. A sharper cutoff of frequencies occurs because of the combined effect of falling capacitive reactance and simultaneously rising inductive reactance (Figure 12–15). remember, you can determine the half-power point where the frequency passes enough power to the load at the low frequency cutoff point by calculating the value of frequency when $X_L$ equals $X_C$.

The value of resonant frequency ($f_r$) is when $X_L$ and $X_C$ are equal, or:

$$f_r = \frac{1}{2\pi\sqrt{LC}}$$

# BAND-PASS FILTERS

Bandwidth refers to the resonant frequency and the frequencies on either side of the resonant frequency that allow the voltage to be delivered to the load rather than being shut out, or blocked. Specifically, bandwidth refers to the usable range of frequencies that allows a signal to pass from input through the filter to the output of a filter circuit, which is designated as the load. The span of frequencies results in the range, or band, of frequencies. The bandwidth of the band-pass filter is considered the range of frequencies that allows output voltage at the load to be at least 70.7% of the maximum output voltage that occurs at exact resonance. As previously explained, this is considered to be the half-power point. A series resonant band-pass filter would appear as in Figure 12–16. This tells us that the lower end of the frequencies that are allowed to pass provides 70.7% of the maximum voltage.

The frequency at the upper end also allows 70.7% of the maximum voltage to pass. These frequencies are referred to as the lower and the upper cutoff frequencies, respectively. The exact middle of the curve is the resonant frequency, which allows maximum voltage to appear at the load. Therefore, this is the band of frequencies that passes at least 70.7% of the source voltage to the load. The formula for bandwidth is as follows: Bandwidth = Upper cutoff frequency − Lower cutoff frequency.

## SERIES RLC BAND-PASS FILTER

A series RLC band-pass filter can be used to create a filter network. The concept of series circuit resonance is used for a series LC circuit as in Figure 12–16.

**High-Pass Filter**

**Figure 12–15** This high-pass filter uses LC components, and the graph shows voltage versus frequency curves for the schematic.

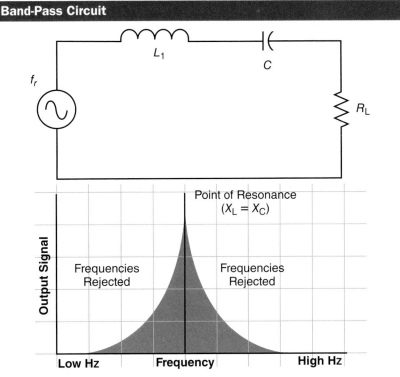

**Band-Pass Circuit**

**Figure 12–16** This band-pass circuit uses high $Q$ components, and its graph shows voltage versus frequency.

With this type of series circuit, the resonant frequency causes the $X_L$ and $X_C$ of the coil and capacitor to cancel each other to create a minimum circuit impedance and, therefore, allow a large circuit current to flow. This large circuit current allows a large voltage drop across the RL at resonant frequency and permits a large percentage of the input voltage, and power, to be delivered to the load. All other frequencies drop voltage at the series components of inductance or capacitance and do not reach the load. This situation is depicted in the graph associated with Figure 12–16.

You can see by the graph in Figure 12–16 that at low frequencies there is a large voltage drop at the series capacitor. This occurs because of the large capacitive reactance in comparison to the inductive reactive component. At resonance, the two reactive components cancel and the $Z$ of the circuit is low. This causes a large current to flow through the load, and a large voltage is dropped at the load. As the frequency increases, the $X_C$ decreases and the $X_L$ increases. As $X_L$ increases, the $Z$ of the series circuit increases, the circuit current decreases, and less current flows through $R_L$, producing a lower load voltage and current. The resonant frequency ($f_r$ or $f_0$) for this circuit is determined by:

$$f_r = \frac{1}{2\pi\sqrt{LC}}$$

The bandwidth of a filter is affected by the $Q$ factor of the circuit. The $Q$ factor is the ratio of the reactive power in the inductor to the true power of the full circuit resistance. The $Q$ of the coil is determined by the $\frac{VAR}{W}$ of the circuit at resonance. This can also be expressed as $\frac{XL}{R}$. A higher value of $Q$ results in a smaller bandwidth. If the $Q$ is higher, the $XL$ is large compared to the resistance of the entire circuit. As the frequency goes above resonance, the voltage drops at the series coil due to $XL$. Likewise, if the frequency drops below resonance, the

effect of the capacitor is more apparent. The ratio of change is higher with a larger $Q$ of the circuit, which creates a smaller bandwidth. The formula is:

$$BW = \frac{f_r}{Q}$$

Where:
$BW$ = bandwidth
$f_r$ = frequency at reasonance
$Q$ = quality

To find the actual lower cutoff frequency, use:

$$f_1 = f_r - \frac{BW}{2}$$

For the upper cutoff frequency, use:

$$f_2 = f_r + \frac{BW}{2}$$

See the example that follows for Figure 12–16.

To determine the bandwidth, the quality of the circuit must first be determined:

$$Q = \frac{X_L}{R}$$

$$BW = \frac{f_r}{Q}$$

$$f_1 = f_r - \frac{BW}{2}$$

$$f_2 = f_r + \frac{BW}{2}$$

### Example

$X_L$ is 1,000 $\Omega$, resistor is 100 $\Omega$, and $X_C$ is equal to 1,000 $\Omega$ at resonant frequency for this example is 500 Hz. Find the cutoff frequencies.

**Solution:**

$$Q = \frac{1,000}{100}$$

$$= 10$$

$$BW = \frac{500 \text{ Hz}}{10}$$

$$= 50 \text{ Hz}$$

$$f_1 = 500 - \left(\frac{50}{2}\right) \text{ or } 475 \text{ Hz for lower limit}$$

$$f_2 = 500 + \left(\frac{50}{2}\right) \text{ or } 525 \text{ Hz for upper limit}$$

Note that $f_1$ (minimum frequency) and $f_2$ (maximum frequency) are the minimum and maximum frequencies for these components.

A general rule of thumb relative to the $Q$ value of the components is that a circuit with high-quality components equals a small, or narrow, bandwidth. A circuit with low-quality components equals a wide bandwidth.

## BAND-PASS FILTER WITH PARALLEL LOAD

Parallel LC band-pass filters use a filter network as in Figure 12–17. The primary use for this type of circuit is to pass a specific frequency so that the load receives a high percentage of the source voltage and power. As you learned in previous chapters, a tank circuit exists when a circuit contains a coil and a capacitor in parallel. In the tank circuit, the inductive current and the capacitive current are 180° out of phase with the same voltage across each component. When the LC circuit is at resonance, the currents cancel each other out and the circuit current from the source goes to a minimum, creating a maximum circuit impedance. This maximum value of circuit impedance occurs only at resonant frequency for the coil and capacitor in the circuit. At this resonant frequency, a small amount of current flows through $R_S$, so only a small voltage drops on $R_S$ and most of the desired voltage drops across the load, as depicted in the associated graph in Figure 12–17.

## FieldNote!

The band-pass filter is designed to pass certain frequencies within its design range and to attenuate (diminish) the frequencies outside its design range. The band-pass filter is really a combination of a low-pass filter design and a high-pass filter design so that only a mid-range frequency is allowed to pass power to the load. There are several variations of the actual design, depending on the precise needs to control the load frequency.

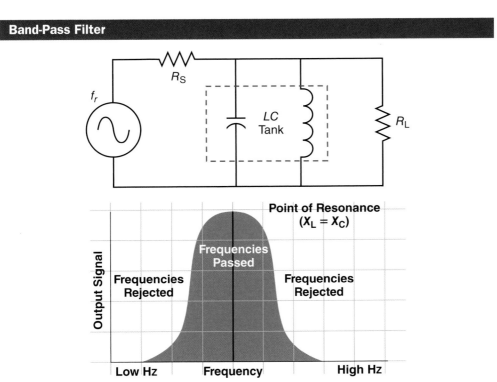

**Figure 12–17** This band-pass filter uses low $Q$ components, and its graph shows voltage versus frequency.

## Band-Pass Filter

**Figure 12–18** This band-pass filter has high resistance ($R_L$).

In Figure 12–18, the components of the LC parallel filter are considered low $Q$. In a parallel RLC circuit, the $Q$ of the circuit is expressed as the ratio of the $R$ to the $X_L$ of the circuit. If the $R$ of the load ($R_L$) is low, the $Q$ of the filter is low. The bandwidth is still expressed as $\dfrac{f_r}{Q}$, so the bandwidth is compara-tively larger with low resistance loads. As before, a higher value of $Q$ results in a smaller bandwidth. This means that with a high current draw of a load, the $Q$ decreases and the frequency band-width becomes greater.

In Figure 12–18, the load resis-tance is high, creating a small current load and the $Q$ of the filter circuit is higher. Again, the bandwidth of the circuit is $\dfrac{f_r}{Q}$, meaning the bandwidth of the filter is smaller, as depicted in the graph of Figure 12–18.

## BAND-REJECT FILTERS

A band-reject filter, or band-stop filter, as illustrated in Figure 12–19, is an ex-ample of a band-reject filter with high $Q$ components. This circuit consists of an inductor and a capacitor con-nected in parallel with each other and in series with the load resistor. (No-tice that to go from band-pass to band-reject filtering the load was moved from the parallel to the series posi-tion with the LC tank portion of the circuit.) At resonance, the impedance of the resonant circuit is at maximum, and a minimum current flows to the load. The high impedance is due to the inductive and capacitive currents canceling each other. At resonance, little current flows to the load; there-fore, little of the source voltage is dropped across the load resistor.

## Band-Reject Filter

**Figure 12–19** This band-reject filter has high $Q$ components. The graph for band-reject filter uses high $Q$ components as shown in the schematic.

At frequencies below or above resonance, the LC parallel trap allows more line current to flow. As a result of this circuit response, more current flows through $R_L$ and more of the source voltage is delivered to the load. In other words, any frequency other than resonance delivers voltage to the load.

## BAND-REJECT FILTER WITH PARALLEL LOAD

Figure 12–20 is an example of a band-reject filter circuit with low $Q$ components. In this case, the load is connected in parallel to the resonant series LC circuit. A resistor ($R_S$) is connected to this configuration in series with the source. At resonance, the inductive reactance and the capacitive reactance cancel each other because their reactances are 180° out of phase. This places the load resistor ($R_L$) in parallel with a very low impedance, and the current through the LC filter is high. The current flow through the series resistor ($R_S$) is at maximum

## TechTip!

Filters are used throughout the electrical industry to reduce or eliminate unwanted frequencies or pass desired frequencies. They are used extensively in electronic equipment to filter DC ripple from power supply outputs or audio circuit tone and sound controls. By making some of the capacitive or inductive components variable, the resonant frequency points can be adjusted to let through specific broadcast frequency signals for radio and TV stations.

at this point, causing a large voltage drop across $R_S$ and thereby producing a minimum voltage across the load resistor. Figure 12–20 shows that the bandwidth rejection increases for low $Q$ components. As the frequency is any value other than resonant, the LC series circuit $Z$ increases and the line current decreases. As the line current decreases, less voltage is dropped on $R_S$ and more on $R_L$, thereby passing the frequencies other than resonant.

**Figure 12–20** This band-reject filter uses low $Q$ components. The graph of voltage versus frequency is for the schematic.

**T-Type Filter**

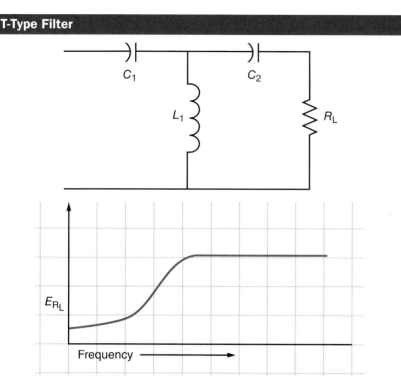

**Figure 12–21** A T-type filter is used to pass high frequencies. The graph of voltage versus frequency is for the schematic.

**Low-Pass T-Type Filter**

**Figure 12–22** This low-pass T-type filter has a related graph of voltage versus frequency.

# COMPLEX FILTERS

### T-TYPE FILTER

More often than not, filters are more complex than the ones described in the previous examples. Figures 12–21 and 12–22 show two T-type filters (resembling the capital letter T in schematic form). The filter in Figure 12–21 is a high-pass filter, and the one in Figure 12–22 is a low-pass filter. Several sections of T-type filters may be joined in some applications. These types of filters improve filtering by increasing sharpness of the cutoff frequencies.

The high frequencies are allowed to develop across the load by the inductor ($L_1$; Figure 12–21). At low frequencies, the inductor essentially acts as a shunt across the load. See the graph in Figure 12–21 to see the effects of a filter that passes only the higher frequencies to the load. The concept is one of trapping the low frequencies at the capacitors that have high reactance at low frequencies, with a larger volt drop across the coil with higher reactance at high frequencies.

In Figure 12–22, the low frequencies are allowed to pass by the inductors ($L_1$ and $L_2$) and the capacitor acts as a high impedance for the load. The graph in Figure 12–22 shows the effects of the filter passing the low frequencies and trapping the higher frequencies.

### π-TYPE FILTER

Figure 12–23 is an illustration of a π (pi)-type filter. This filter is commonly found in power supplies to smooth the rectified AC wave to a smoother DC wave. The representation in Figure 12–23 of an input to the filter shown is the 120 Hz pulses of a full-wave rectifier supplied by a 60 Hz AC source and full-wave rectification. The capacitors usually have very large capacitance (10 to 1,000 μF), and at 120 Hz have low reactance. The low reactance means that the current to the capacitors is comparatively large.

**π-Type Low-Pass Filter**

Figure 12-23 The π-type low-pass filter schematic and graph displays voltage input and output.

**High-Pass π-Type Filter**

Figure 12-24 This high-pass π-type filter has a capacitor between the inductors.

TechTip!

To fully visualize frequency reproduction or passing of high, low, or specific frequencies, the use of an oscilloscope is the desired tool. With a "scope," the frequencies of the input signal voltage can be graphically seen. After the filter at the load, the actual value of effective frequency can be observed to verify the filter's operation and effectiveness.

The inductance, at the same time, has a value in the range of 10 to 100 H. This combination presents a high impedance (opposition) to the changing voltage and current of the rectified input. The capacitors charge to the peak value of the rectified voltage. If the input is 100 $V_{RMS}$ (voltage root mean square), the output is 141.4 VDC. This filter would be classified as a low-pass filter, allowing low frequencies (such as DC with no frequency) and blocking the 120 Hz ripple frequency.

A high-pass π-type filter is shown in Figure 12-24. In this circuit, the inductors form the legs of the π, with the capacitor between them. Low frequencies are blocked by the capacitor and shunted through the inductors around the load. The high-frequency components of the input develop little voltage across the series capacitor ($C_1$), allowing most of the voltage to be produced across the load ($R_L$) at high frequency.

## OTHER COMPLEX FILTERS

Even more complex filters are shown in Figures 12–25 and 12–26. Figure 12–25 is a complex band-pass filter, and Figure 12–26 is a complex band-reject filter.

Notice that the band-pass filter has the resonant circuit components in series with the load ($R_L$) and that the

band-reject filter has the tank circuit in series with the load ($R_L$). These filters can be tuned to pass a given band of frequencies and reject interfering frequencies operating close to the desired band. These combinations may also be combined to form even more complex filters. Engineers specializing in this field are usually the designers of these types of filters.

**Complex Band-Pass Filter**

**Figure 12–25** This complex frequency filtering circuit uses a combination of filters to provide band-pass filtering.

**Complex Band-Reject Filter**

**Figure 12–26** This complex filtering circuit is used to provide band-reject filtering.

## SUMMARY

In general, characteristics for high-pass filters are the following:

- Capacitance is connected in series with the load. The $X_C$ is low for high frequencies to be passed to the load, while low frequencies are blocked by a high $X_C$.
- Inductors are connected in parallel with the load. The shunt $X_L$ has a high reactance to high frequencies, which causes current to flow through $R_L$, while low frequencies are bypassed through the inductor.

Characteristics for low-pass filters are the following:

- Inductors are in series with the load. The high $X_L$ for high frequencies serves as a choke or block, while low frequencies are passed to the load.
- A bypass capacitor is connected in parallel with the load. The high frequencies are bypassed by a small $X_C$, while low frequencies are not affected by the shunt path and flow through $R_L$.

Filters are becoming increasingly important in electrical work. Computers radiating signals or information that escape through their power source allow for anyone with access to a receptacle or breaker box to collect sensitive information. In worst-case scenarios, such "information leaks" can jeopardize government and corporate security.

## CHAPTER GLOSSARY

**Half-power point** The point at which the load resistance is dissipating half the maximum power that could occur at the load.

## REVIEW QUESTIONS

1. Discuss the basic objectives of low-pass, high-pass, band-pass, and band-reject filters.

2. What are the underlying concepts that make it possible to create filters using $R$, $L$, and $C$ components?

3. How is the half-power point related to the voltage drop across the load resistor in a high-pass or a band-pass filter?

4. Discuss the applications for filters using low $Q$ components; discuss those for high $Q$ components.

5. Explain bandwidth in terms of $Q$ and list the upper and lower limit formulas in a series RLC bandpass filter. Give a numeric example of $Q$, $BW$, $f_1$, and $f_2$.

6. Explain the two types of $\pi$ filters and their uses.

7. What is meant by a band-stop filter circuit?

8. Draw a schematic diagram of a typical simple low-pass filter.

9. Name five types of filters for which you can recognize and discuss the output frequency curve.

10. The output of a high-pass LC filter increases as the $X_L$ _____.

# PRACTICE PROBLEMS

Assume a low-pass RL filter for Problems 1–3:

1. The load resistor has a voltage across it when the frequency is _____ the half-power point.

2. The half-power point is defined as the point where $X_L$ is equal to _____.

3. What is the cutoff frequency for a low-pass RL filter having a 3.3 kΩ resistor and a 1 mH coil?

Assume a low-pass RC filter for Problems 4 and 5:

4. Low-pass RC filters have the capacitor connected in _____ with the load resistor.

5. Design a 2 kHz low-pass RC filter with a 1 kΩ series resistor; that is, find $C$.

Assume a low-pass LC filter for Problems 6–8:

6. In a low-pass LC filter, the output signal peaks when $X_L = $_____ (resonant frequency).

7. What is the peak frequency for the speaker in Figure PP12–1?

8. Find the new resonant frequency if the capacitor were changed to a 10 μF capacitor.

9. Using a 0.1 μF capacitor, find the resistance needed to make a high-pass 300 Hz RC filter.

10. Find the cutoff frequency for a high-pass $R_L$ filter with a 22 kΩ resistor and a 500 μH coil.

11. What is the center frequency for a series band-pass filter with a 100 μH coil and an 800 pF capacitor?

12. Find the center frequency for a parallel band-pass filter with a 100 μH coil and a 100 pF capacitor.

13. Find the center frequency for a series band-reject filter with a 42.9 mH coil and a 0.0041 μF capacitance.

14. If the $Q$ of the circuit in Problem 13 is 3, what is the bandwidth?

15. Find $f_1$ and $f_2$ for the circuit in Problem 13.

**Figure PP12–1**

# 13

## GENERATORS

# O V E R V I E W

English physicist Michael Faraday discovered the basic theory of electrical generation in 1831. He discovered that a magnetic field can be used to produce an electrical current. Practically all commercial electrical power is produced using this principle.

Mechanical energy delivered from raw manpower, water, wind, fossil fuels (coal and oil), and nuclear reactors is used to turn the rotor of a generator. Some of these energy sources, such as fossil fuels and nuclear reactors, must first be converted into another form such as steam to turn the rotor of a generator. This chapter acquaints you with both DC and AC generators.

Although AC is available at most sites, DC has applications that AC cannot support. DC has been used for precise speed control of motors and for large DC motors found in many industrial and manufacturing applications. DC motors and generators are also used in locomotives. Where DC is required, electricians often find DC generators.

As variable frequency drives become increasingly common, the use of DC generation and DC motors will become less frequent. However, the understanding of DC equipment is still necessary to a professional electrician. Eventually, DC power distribution will be found only in those places where extremely high torque per horsepower is required (DC motors) or where the nature of the work requires DC, such as in electrolysis applications.

This chapter covers AC generation fundamentals and shows the relationship between magnetism (which you have previously studied) and production of electrical power. It identifies the major parts of a DC or AC generator and explains the fundamental operating principles of each. Remember that DC machines will be with us for many more years, and knowledge of how they operate and how to install and repair them will be a valuable skill. AC generators are used everywhere from small portable generators, to truck mounted diesel engine–driven generators, to permanent standby or emergency generators, to the large commercial power-generating stations. A thorough understanding of AC generators is needed when working in today's technical workforce.

# O B J E C T I V E S

After completing this chapter, you will be able to:

· Identify the major parts of a DC generator
· Describe the principles of operation of the DC generator
· List the advantages of different generator connections
· Explain the parallel connections for DC generators
· Describe the operation of AC generators
· Identify key parts of the AC generators and their functions
· Mathematically determine the relationship of revolutions per minute, frequency, and number of poles
· Explain the voltage, frequency, and power controls on an AC generator
· List the requirements for paralleling AC generators

# INDUCTION BY MAGNETISM

As you studied briefly in Chapter 1 and more in Chapter 2, a voltage is induced into a conductor when it is passed through a magnetic field. The effect is called electromagnetic induction. If the conductor is connected to a complete circuit, current flows. Figure 13–1 shows a conductor being moved downward between the poles of the two magnets. The poles of the magnets create a field that is moving from north to south. The downward motion of the conductor induces a voltage into the conductor, the polarity of which causes the current to flow and the meter to deflect in the direction shown. The electrons move because of the interactions between the magnetic field of the permanent magnets and the electromagnetic fields of the electrons themselves. Note that without movement there is no current flow.

If the motion in Figure 13–1 were reversed, it would change the voltage polarity and reverse the flow of current. This is because the direction of the field interactions is opposite. The same would be true if the poles of the magnets were reversed and the motion was downward; the field interactions would be reversed, and current would flow in the opposite direction.

Remember that relative motion between the magnetic field and the conductor must exist before voltage is generated. This motion can be the motion of the magnetic field instead of the conductor; that is, the magnets can move instead of the conductor. Movement of the magnetic field is an important variation in your study of AC generators.

**Induced Voltage**

Voltmeter

**Figure 13–1** Voltage is induced when moving a conductor through a magnetic field.

**Position A**

Axis of Rotation

Rotation

Magnetic Flux

**Figure 13–2** Position A has no induced voltage.

# GENERATOR CHARACTERISTICS

A generator is a device that converts mechanical energy into electrical energy. Voltage is induced in a conductor when it cuts magnetic lines of flux. This principle, called electromagnetic induction, is the underlying principle of operation for both DC and AC generators.

Figures 13–2 through 13–5 show how this principle works. As the loop is rotated and cuts through the magnetic lines of flux, voltage is induced in the loop. An easy way to remember the relationship of motion, electromagnetic lines of force, and current flow is to use Fleming's left-hand rule for generators, shown in Figure 13–6. This rule is used for electron flow theory explanations.

**Figure 13–3** Position B has maximum induced voltage.

**Figure 13–4** Position C has no induced voltage.

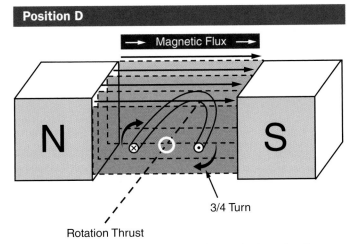

**Figure 13–5** Position D has maximum induced voltage.

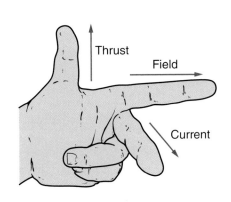

**Figure 13–6** Fleming's left-hand rule for generation.

# SINE WAVE GENERATION AND CONVERSION TO DC

Look at the **armature** loop at position A at the top of Figure 13–7. The position of the wire loop is such that it is moving parallel to the magnetic lines of flux. Now look at the waveform at position A. When the wire loop motion is parallel to the magnetic lines of flux, no voltage is being produced because the wire loop that makes up the armature is not cutting through any of the lines of flux when the loop is parallel to the lines of flux.

Now rotate the armature from position A to position B. As the armature rotates, the motion of the wire loop goes from being parallel to being perpendicular to the lines of flux.

**Figure 13–7** A sine wave is generated by rotating a conductor through a magnetic field.

## FieldNote!

Many people in the electrical professions learn theory based on the conventional current flow theory. When this is the case, they may refer to the "right-hand rule for generators." This reverses the electron current flow idea, and the theory of current flow from positive to negative is intact. To carry this theory further, we use the right-hand rule for coils and that leads to the left-hand rule for motor direction. Both the electron flow practitioner and the conventional current flow practitioner end with the same results. Confusion ensues, however, if you use conventional flow for part of an analysis and electron flow for the other part.

As the armature rotates through this 90° travel, it begins to cut through more lines of flux.

When the armature gets to the 90° point, it is cutting the maximum number of lines of flux per second. Now look at the waveform at position B. Note that when the armature is cutting through the most lines of flux the highest amount of voltage is produced in the positive direction.

Now rotate the armature through another 90°. At this point, position C, the armature is 180° from its original starting point. Note again that the armature is moving parallel to the magnetic lines of flux and that the voltage produced is zero.

As the armature continues to rotate through the next 90°, the armature is again approaching the point, position D, where it will be moving perpendicular to the lines of flux. Take a look at the waveform and notice that the value has gone negative. This change in polarity is due to the motion of the leading edge of the wire loop relative to the direction of the magnetic lines of flux. Notice that the leading edge of the wire loop is indicated by its black color. When the leading edge is moving up, the polarity of the voltage being produced is negative.

As the loop continues to rotate back to its starting point at position A, the voltage again begins to approach zero. The voltage being produced as this wire loop (the armature of the generator) rotates through a complete 360° of travel through the magnetic lines of flux is called alternating voltage because the voltage travels positive for a part of the cycle and then alternates and becomes negative for part of the cycle.

Since the voltage produced by all rotating armatures is alternating voltage, as can be seen in Figure 13–7, the method of removing the voltage from the armature is the key to determining whether the output voltage of the generator is alternating or direct.

## COMMUTATING THE OUTPUT OF AN AC ARMATURE

Since DC generators must produce DC voltage and resultant current, the method of removing the voltage from the armature is different than that used for an AC generator. In the DC generator, the components used to remove the voltage from the armature are brushes and a commutator (Figure 13–8a).

Since the **commutator** is physically connected to the armature loop, the segments have an AC voltage on them. However, in the example generator in Figure 13–8a, the commutator is positioned so that the segment that is shown on top is always the negative side of the circuit. This means that the brush on the top is always the negative brush and the bottom brush is always positive. The output voltage from the brushes is a pulsating DC going from zero voltage to peak voltage but never reversing (Figure 13–8b).

Unlike Figure 13–7, which shows the voltage produced as being AC, Figure 13–8b shows the resulting waveform of the voltage when the voltage is measured at the brushes. Notice how the output is always positive but pulsating DC. It is not smooth like a battery voltage but is DC.

## Producing Pulsating DC Voltage Through Commutation

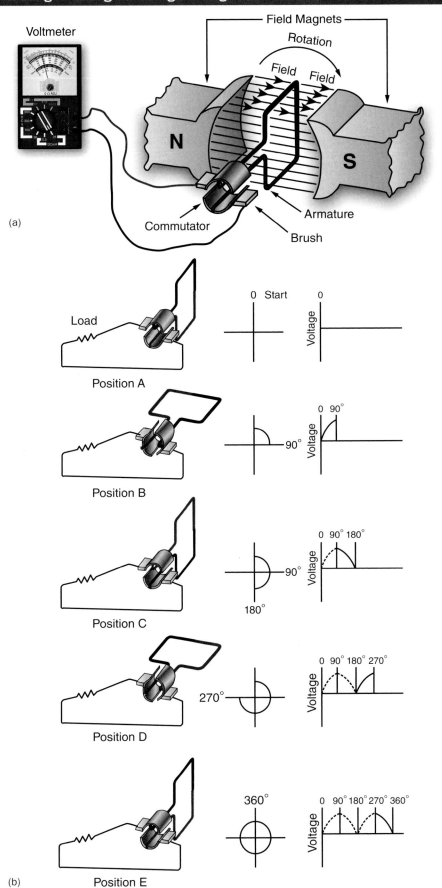

(a)

(b)

**Figure 13–8** (a) A rotating armature has commutator connections to produce DC. (b) The output from a DC commutator is a pulsating DC voltage.

As the armature loop moves from position A to position B in Figure 13–8b, a positive voltage is produced that starts at zero and gradually increases to maximum. As the rotation continues from position B to position C, the loop continues to cut through the lines of flux; however, as the armature position approaches position C, it is producing less positive voltage. When the armature reaches position C, it is moving parallel to the lines of flux; therefore, no voltage is produced.

From position A through position C, the loop produces a positive voltage that has been removed from the armature windings by the **brushes** that have been riding on the same commutator segments throughout this 180° of armature travel. However, as the armature begins its travel from position C to position D, the brushes begin to ride on the opposite commutator segments. The change in commutator segments allows the voltage to remain positive even though the armature is producing an alternating voltage.

As the commutator rotates from position C to position D, the positive lead of the generator is connected to the segment of the commutator that is producing a positive voltage. At position D, the armature loop again produces its maximum voltage and then returns to zero as the armature rotates to position E.

Regardless of which half of the loop is producing a positive voltage and which half is producing a negative voltage, the commutator and brushes always cause the output voltage to remain at the same polarity. This is the basic principle of DC generator operation.

## MAJOR GENERATOR COMPONENTS

The rotating member of the DC generator is the armature. The entire assembly includes the iron core, the commutator, and the windings.

### ARMATURE WINDINGS

The three basic types of windings, depending on the needs of the machine, are lap, wave, and frogleg (Figure 13–9).

Because each loop of the coiled wire in the armature has voltage induced into it, the additional windings on the armature add to the total generated output. If the coils are connected in parallel with one another, the voltage is not additive but the current output is additive. If more voltage is desired, the coils can be connected in series in such a way as to have the voltages added and not the current. A combination of series- and parallel-connected windings creates a higher voltage and higher current. These three conditions can be visualized in the three common connections: the lap winding, where the windings are in parallel; the wave winding, which illustrates the series connection to increase voltage; and the frogleg pattern, which increases voltage and current capabilities. See Figure 13–9 and the following descriptions.

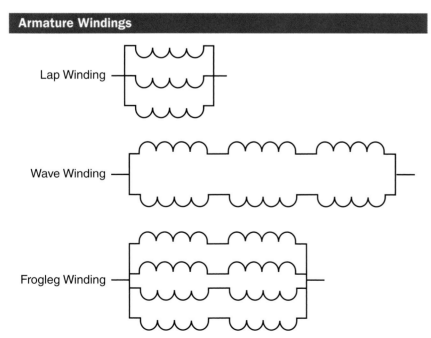

**Armature Windings**

Lap Winding

Wave Winding

Frogleg Winding

**Figure 13–9** There are three types of armature windings.

The connections to the armature and commutator are through brushes. The armature connection points are labeled $A_1$ and $A_2$.

1. Lap-wound armatures are used in machines designed for low voltage and high current. Typically, lap windings are designed with large wire to safely handle large currents. When equipment has lap-wound construction, the windings are connected in parallel. This parallel path construction provides multiple paths for current flow. A common characteristic of lap-wound equipment is that there are as many pairs of brushes as there are pairs of poles. Another characteristic of lap-wound equipment is that there are as many armature current paths as there are pole pieces.

2. Wave-wound armatures are used in machines designed for high voltage and low current. Since the current capacity of wave-wound equipment is relatively low, the winding wire-size is smaller than that of the lap-winding wire and is typically connected in series so that the voltage of each of the windings is additive. Keep in mind that in series circuits the current is the same throughout the circuit. The same is true with wave-wound windings. Even though the windings are connected in series to increase the voltage, the current remains the same throughout all the windings.

3. Frogleg armatures are the middle-of-the-road type of windings. The frogleg configuration, the most common of the winding configurations, is designed for moderate current and moderate voltage. The frogleg armature, commonly found in larger DC equipment, has its winding connected in series and parallel. That is, there are groups of series-connected windings, and these groups are then connected in parallel.

**Carbon Brushes and Commutator**

**Figure 13–10** Carbon brushes ride on a DC commutator.

## BRUSHES

Brushes ride on the commutator to connect the rotating armature to the load (Figure 13–10). The brushes are normally made from a carbon-based material.

Carbon is used for three reasons:

1. Carbon is softer than copper and allows the brushes rather than the commutator to wear (the latter being more difficult to repair).
2. Carbon withstands the high temperatures that may be present because of arcing and friction.
3. Carbon, copper, and moisture form a thin, conductive film on the commutator that lubricates and reduces wear.

## FIELD WINDINGS

The field of the generator produces the magnetic field for the armature. In a spinning armature, the **field windings** are on the stationary piece, or the **stator.** The field is connected to a DC source of power and the magnetic field produced by the coiled wires creates the flux for the magnetic field needed for generation by induction.

## Stator Field Windings

Shunt Field Windings                    Series Field Windings

**Figure 13–11** Stator field windings can be series field and separate shunt field.

The two types of field windings are the series field and the shunt field (Figure 13–11). Series field windings are connected in series with the armature through the brushes. Series windings consist of few turns and large wire. The terminal leads of the series field are labeled $S_1$ and $S_2$.

The shunt field is connected in parallel (shunt) with the armature. Shunt windings are made with many turns of a small wire and therefore have a higher resistance than a series field. The shunt field is also called simply the field and is labeled $F_1$ and $F_2$. The purpose of the field is to produce magnetic flux. The more magnetic flux a particular generator has, the more output voltage it produces. There are controls and limits to the amount of flux available in a magnetic field winding. The amount of current that is allowed to flow in the winding directly affects the flux—the more current, the more flux—until the iron is magnetically saturated and cannot concentrate more flux lines. Generally, the magnetic flux is controlled within the operating range of the magnetic iron, by adjusting the field current to the windings.

### POLE PIECES

Mounted inside the housing of the generator are pieces of metal, usually made of soft, laminated iron or some other easily magnetized metal. These are fixed pieces and do not rotate. The purpose of the pole pieces is to concentrate the magnetic field. The field windings are wound around these pole pieces, forming an electromagnet. The electromagnet sets up the magnetic field necessary for generation. In small generators, the pole pieces are sometimes permanent magnets (Figure 13–12).

## Permanent Pole Magnets

**Figure 13–12** Permanent magnets are used for a field permanently mounted in a stator.

# GENERATOR CONNECTION TYPES

## SERIES GENERATORS

As the name implies, the series generator is connected so that the series field windings are connected in series with load to the armature. As current flows to the connected load, it passes through the series field and the generator voltage increases. The series generator must be **self-excited,** which means that the pole pieces must contain some amount of residual magnetism to start producing a voltage in the armature. In other words, the magnetism left in the iron stator pole pieces must be strong enough to start producing output voltage. As the output load current and the series field current increase, the magnetic field of the generator becomes stronger and further increases the output voltage. The process continues as shown in Figure 13–13 until the controls on the field excitation do not allow the field to become any stronger or until the iron core becomes magnetically saturated. The residual magnetism produces an initial output voltage that permits current to flow through the field if a load is connected to the generator. In a series generator, the output voltage increases as the load current increases.

As additional loads (current paths) are connected to a series generator, the output voltage continues to increase until the magnetic cores saturate (Figure 13–14) or the field control resistance (diverter) prevents any additional current from going through the series field. The amount of voltage generated by a series generator depends on the strength of the magnetic field produced by the pole pieces, the number of turns of wire on the armature, and the speed of rotation of the armature. The more field current, the more voltage; the more speed, the more voltage; the more turns of the coils on the armature, the more voltage. Because of the varying voltage, series generators are best suited for use with a constant load.

**Excitation versus Output Voltage**

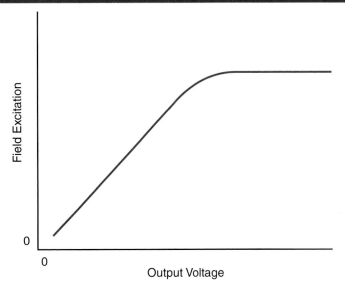

**Figure 13–13** Output voltage rises with increase in excitation until saturation of iron prevents any further increase in induced voltage.

**Series Generator**

Add Load 2 and the generator becomes saturated (cannot produce any more voltage or current required by $L_1$ & $L_2$).

Given Voltage Output

$L_1$     $L_2$

$A_1$  DC  $A_2$   $S_1$        $S_2$

Diverter

**Figure 13–14** A series generator generates higher voltage until field saturation or until the diverter "diverts" current from the series field.

## SHUNT GENERATORS

Shunt generators, the second winding configuration for DC generators, get their name from the field windings being wired in parallel with or shunted across the generator output.

**Regulating Shunt Field**

**Figure 13–15** A regulator can be used to adjust the amount of current through the shunt field, thereby controlling the output voltage.

Self-excited shunt generators use residual magnetism to start the generation process. This is done by applying the residual voltage (generated by the residual magnetic field left over from the last operation) to the shunt field to create an initial current. The shunt generator provides maximum output voltage before the load is applied. As the load increases on a shunt generator, the output voltage decreases.

To attempt to control the output voltage of a shunt generator, an electronic voltage regulator is sometimes installed as part of the generator circuit. The electronic voltage regulator senses the changes in the output voltage and makes adjustments to the shunt field current. The regulator causes less current to flow through the shunt circuit when the voltage is sensed to be too high or more current to flow in the shunt field when the output voltage goes too low. Figure 13–15 shows how the voltage regulator, the shunt field, and the output voltage are all related. A simplified explanation of the voltage regulator box is that it acts like a series variable resistor (or rheostat) and voltage control to the shunt field. This regulates the output voltage available to the load. In reality, the device is more than a series resistor. The circuitry is more complex in that it has a controller (sometimes a microprocessor-based computer).

## COMPOUND GENERATORS

As you have seen, the generator voltage can change from the no-load condition with no current output to the full-load condition with full-rated current output. In most cases, the equipment connected to the generator should have the same voltage output whether at no load, light load, or full load. To provide this feature, some adaptations to the series generator of the shunt generator is required. We can combine the best features of each generator and create a compound generator.

Compound generators contain both series and shunt fields (Figure 13–16). The relationship of the strengths of the two fields in a generator determines the amount of compounding for the machine. Since the voltage regulation of a series generator can be poor and a shunt generator has good voltage regulation, combining the two gives better circuit flexibility and load control.

There are two subdivisions of the compound generator: short shunt and long shunt, compounding. The long-shunt compound variation has the shunt winding into the longer connection point in parallel with the combined armature and series winding circuit.

**Long-Shunt Connection**

Series

Shunt

Field Control

Load

Armature

**Figure 13–16** A "long-shunt" connection can be used for a compound-wound DC generator.

The short-shunt configuration has the shunt field connected in parallel with the armature, or short connected across the armature. The series field is then wired in series with the armature and the load (Figure 13–17).

Depending on the number of turns in the series field versus the shunt field and the controls that determine the current through the two fields, three ways (classifications) of compounding windings in a generator are possible: **flat compounding, overcompounding,** and **undercompounding.** Figure 13–18 shows the typical voltage and current relationships in the different compounds. When the compounding of series fields and the compounding of shunt fields aid each other in producing electromagnetic force (inducing voltage and current), the compound is called cumulative compounding. When the series windings oppose the shunt field windings in producing electromagnetic force, the compound is called differential compounding.

Refer to Figure 13–18. The following are characteristics of the different compound generators:

1. The overcompound generator's full-load voltage is greater than the no-load voltage with cumulative compounding.

2. The undercompound generator's full-load voltage is less than the no-load voltage, but the series component of the compound makes it a better voltage regulator for loads than the shunt. This is still a cumulative compounded generator.

3. The flat-compound generator has a load voltage equal to the no-load voltage and is still a cumulative compounding connection.

4. The differential compound generator output voltage drops as more current is drawn by the load. Differentially compounded generators were used for DC welding purposes.

Most commercial compound DC generators are normally supplied by the manufacturer as overcompound machines.

**Short-Shunt Connection**

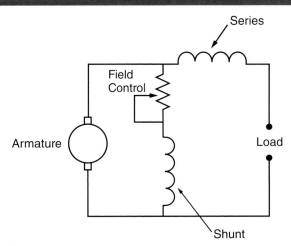

**Figure 13–17** A "short-shunt" connection can be used for a compound-wound DC generator.

**Voltage Output Curves**

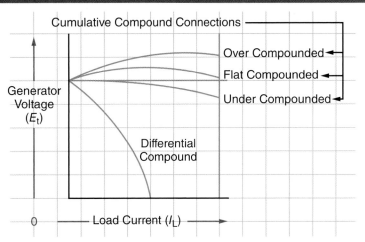

**Figure 13–18** Voltage output curves vary with the different connections of generators under load.

## GENERATOR LOSSES

The power equation for a generator or motor is:

$$P_{\text{in}} = P_{\text{out}} + P_{\text{loss}}$$

This means that the power used to turn or rotate a generator must always be greater than the output power delivered by the generator to perform work. It also means that not all the power a generator receives can be converted into useful mechanical or electrical energy; there is a loss, and this loss is almost entirely heat.

The relationship between power out and power in is called the generator's efficiency and is noted with the lower-case Greek eta (η). The equation for efficiency of a machine is:

$$\eta = \frac{P_{\text{out}}}{P_{\text{in}}}$$

OR

$$\% \text{ Efficiency} = \left(\frac{P_{\text{out}}}{P_{\text{in}}}\right) \times 100$$

For a generator, the equation becomes:

$$\eta = \frac{P_{\text{out}}}{(P_{\text{out}} + P_{\text{loss}})}$$

And for a motor, it is:

$$\eta = \frac{(P_{\text{in}} - P_{\text{loss}})}{P_{\text{in}}}$$

Generator power losses can be broken into two main classes: electrical and mechanical—(friction and windage). Electrical losses are caused by current flow through various parts of the generator and are sometimes referred to as copper losses. The greatest of these losses is due to the resistance of the windings. The watt loss could be calculated as:

$$I^2 \times R = \text{watt loss}$$

The power loss due to induced currents in the iron core material of a generator is called eddy current loss. This is induced as the armature spins through the flux lines of the pole pieces field. Eddy currents are electrical currents that circulate within the metal. As explained in Chapter 1, the currents can circulate within the conductor. The magnetic field that is cutting the conductor and the iron core induces current into the iron. This induced current is small, but the electric currents tend to circulate in the iron as "eddies" of current. Because the electrical resistance of the iron is high, the currents are small, yet the effect is to create a watt loss in the form of $I^2 \times R$ losses. These losses due to eddy currents in the iron are referred to as iron losses. By cutting the iron into thin slices, and putting them back together, or laminating the iron, the resistance of the iron goes up and the eddy currents go down, thereby reducing the iron losses. The iron losses also consist of the hysteresis losses or friction of the molecules in the iron as they tend to align themselves in the magnetic field. Hysteresis is explained in detail in the *DC Theory* text.

As the DC generator rotates, an alternating current is set up in the armature. This causes the molecules of the iron to realign each time the current changes direction from negative to positive, which changes the magnetic field. This molecular friction produces losses due to hysteresis. Hysteresis losses can be varied by using different grades of steel for the rotor core. High hysteresis steel would have higher losses in the magnetizing of the iron, which are characterized by heat. To reduce the heat (energy) loss due to hysteresis, high silicon steel can be used. The iron losses, the copper losses, and the mechanical friction losses of the bearings, along with the windage losses as the fan moves air over the coils, all add up to the generator losses.

**Magnetic Plane Shift**

**Figure 13–19** As the load on an armature increases, the neutral magnetic plane shifts.

## TechTip!

Laminating the iron means that the magnetic core iron is sliced into thin strips, which increases the electrical resistance of the iron but does not change the magnetic effects of the iron. The iron pieces are pressed back together and fastened in place to create the same magnetic effect as solid iron but with far fewer iron losses due to eddy currents.

## ARMATURE REACTION

In a generator, there are two primary magnetic flux fields: the flux field produced by the field windings around the north and south poles and the armature flux field. The current flow in the armature conductors produces its own magnetic field, which reacts with the stator magnetic field.

The larger the armature current (the more current to the load), the more magnetic affect it has on the stator, or main magnetic field. The rotor reacts with the stator field to bend that field. Notice that if the armature's magnetic field (flux) shifts the magnetic neutral, then the magnetic flux field for the field windings becomes distorted. This distortion of the magnetic fields is referred to as **armature reaction.** Refer to Figure 13–19 to see how the neutral plane is distorted. It can cause a heavy circulating current to be produced in the armature that causes arcing between the commutator segments and the brushes. The arcing between the commutator segments is referred to as commutation. This happens because the amount of voltage that is induced in the armature windings is not balanced at a neutral physical location. The neutral point, referred to as the neutral plane, where the brushes are located, normally has a balanced amount of voltage on each side. See Figure 13–20 for an illustration of the neutral plane shift. As the neutral plane shifts because of field distortion, the voltages are no longer balanced. This is explained in more detail in the course of studying motors and generators.

To offset the effect of the field distortion from the armature's shift caused by the armature's own field from the magnetic neutral plane (caused by self-induction), compensating windings are used to produce a counterelectromagnetic force (Figure 13–21). These windings are placed between the main field poles and are called by several names, such as **compensating, interpole,** or **Thomson-Ryan windings.** The current to the load causes a magnetic field in the compensating windings that is proportional to the load. The more current to the load, the more the rotor magnetic field tends to bend the main magnetic field. The compensating windings oppose the bending efforts and, therefore, keep the neutral plane straight even with a variable load.

**Creating an Armature Reaction**

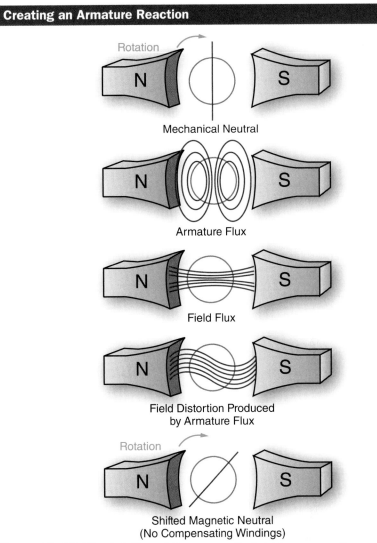

**Figure 13–20** The twisting of the magnetic field because of current in the armature creates an armature reaction.

**Effects of Compensating Windings**

**Figure 13–21** Location and effect of compensating windings are given on the neutral plane of the generator.

## Equalizer Connections

Equalizer Connection

Generator 1

Generator 2
Output
+ −

**Figure 13–22** Paralleling DC compound-wound generators requires the addition of an "equalizer" connection.

## PARALLELING DC GENERATORS

There may be a need for connecting DC generators in parallel to supply enough current for a connected load. An equalizer connection is required to prevent one generator from taking the load and the other from acting as a DC motor. Look at Figure 13–22 to see a schematic of an equalizer connection. The equalizing connection is used to connect the series fields of the two machines in parallel with each other. This parallel connection maintains the same voltage across all series fields and prevents one machine from taking over the other machine as a motor. Notice that the connection must be on the armature side of the series field and connected to the same polarity on each generator. The two generators must be connected in the same pattern, designed for the same voltage output, and have "drooping" speed characteristics. This means that they must act the same way as electrical load is added in that they slow as they do more electrical work. As you study generators and motors in more detail, these characteristics become more apparent.

## AC GENERATOR PRINCIPLES OF OPERATION

The generation of the voltage is the same basic process used in the DC generator (Figures 13–23 and 13–24). The simplest AC generator is constructed of a permanent magnet, **slip rings** (instead of a commutator), brushes, and a single loop (armature). A voltmeter to read generated voltage is the external load.

## AC Voltage Generator

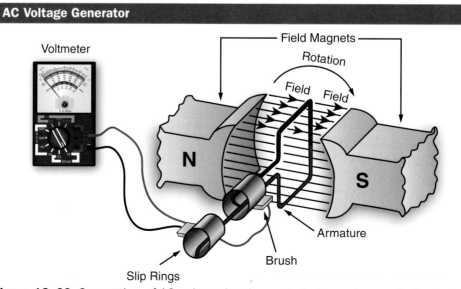

**Figure 13–23** Generation of AC voltage involves rotating armature and slip rings.

## Waveforms of AC Generation

**Figure 13–24** AC generation and output waveform occur as shown.

The armature is the rotating part of the machine in which the voltage is induced exactly the same as the DC description. The AC description of generating AC voltage and resultant current is detailed in Chapter 2. To quickly recap the process use the following summary: The magnets set up the required magnetic field flux. Each end of the wire loop is connected to a separate slip ring. As the loop rotates, each side of the loop cuts lines of flux at the same time. As one side of the loop moves downward, the other side moves upward.

In position A in Figure 13–24, the loop is rotating, but it is cutting few lines of flux. This position is called the 0° position. If the voltage were being measured here, it would be zero (see Figure 13–24, 0 V).

In position B in Figure 13–24, the generator has rotated 90°, and both sides of the loop are cutting through the lines of flux perpendicularly. At this point, the generator is producing the highest voltage. If the voltage were being measured, it would show the output of the generator to be at its highest

"positive" value (+10 V). Notice also that the output increases gradually as the loop rotates from 0° to 90°.

In position C in Figure 13–24, the generator is producing the least amount of voltage again, but this time the loop is in the 180° position, opposite the position shown in position A. The 0 V position is caused by the generator coil traveling parallel to the flux lines (not cutting through them), and this position can be referred to as the zero-crossing point.

Position D in Figure 13–24 shows the loop in the 270° position. It is now cutting the maximum number of flux lines and producing the maximum voltage. The voltage is now "negative" when compared to the voltage being produced in position B. This is because the current is now in the opposite direction through the loop (−10 V).

## CONSTRUCTION OF AC GENERATORS

AC generators, also known as alternators, operate on the same principle of electromagnetic induction as DC generators. Both types of generators pass conductors through a magnetic field to create a voltage and resultant current flow. However, unlike the DC generator, which uses a commutator to rectify the generated voltage, the AC generator uses slip rings to connect the AC output directly to the load. The different outputs of DC and AC generators can be seen in Figure 13–25.

There are two basic types of alternators: revolving armature and revolving field. The revolving armature is used for most basic explanations because it is easier to visualize. However, the revolving armature is used primarily for small-load applications. Both revolving armature and the more prevalent revolving field AC generators produce an alternating sine wave output voltage.

**DC versus AC Generator**

**Figure 13–25** The output voltage from the commutator of a DC generator with multiple poles may look like the top figure. The bottom figure is an alternator output taken from slip rings.

## REVOLVING ARMATURE AC GENERATORS

The **revolving armature** AC generator is not as common as the revolving field AC generator. It is similar in construction to the DC generator in that both types use some form of mechanical moving contacts to connect the external circuit to the armature circuit. The AC generator uses slip rings instead of a commutator. The purpose of the slip rings is to directly connect the armature windings to the load. Since no commutator is used, the output is an alternating voltage instead of a direct voltage.

The slip ring, unlike the segmented DC generator commutator, is constructed as a continuous ring and is not broken into isolated segments. Each end of the rotating loop of the armature is connected to a separate slip ring (Figure 13–26).

A three-phase revolving armature AC generator has three separate sets of slip rings, one for each phase. Each ring would be connected to a windings end. The windings, or loops, are electrically oriented 120° from each other (Figure 13–27). One end of each coil is connected together on the rotor, and the three slip rings are used to bring the three coil ends to an external circuit. In this case, the generator is connected in a wye pattern. This is a typical connection. Wye connections for three-phase systems are explained in detail in Chapters 14 and 15. The output of the three-phase generator would resemble the output wave, as seen in Figure 13–28. As you view Figure 13–28, you should notice that the peak of each phase is 120 electrical degrees away from the next peak. This is true for three-phase AC generators. We can connect the generator to a three-phase power system with three-line wires representing phases A–B–C, as commonly denoted.

Although the revolving armature AC generator can produce an alternating output voltage, the slip rings and brushes limit the size of load it can carry.

**Single-Phase Generation**

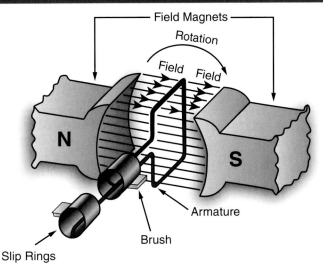

**Figure 13–26** Single-phase generation uses a revolving armature.

**Three-Phase Generation**

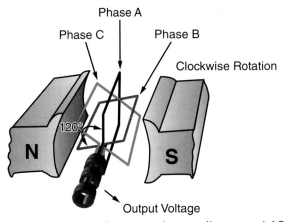

**Figure 13–27** Three-phase generation uses three coils spaced 120° apart connected in wye pattern.

**Voltage versus Time**

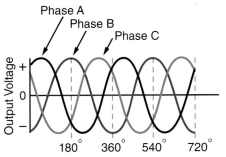

**Note:** One end of each generator (alternator) loop is connected together.

**Figure 13–28** A graphic representation of voltage versus time shows three-phase voltage production.

The higher currents require large slip rings and large brushes and need highly increased maintenance. As the currents and voltages become higher, the sliding contacts are not as efficient, the arcing under the brushes creates heat and wear, and the voltage drops. The high voltages required by some loads mean that much heavier insulation on the armature conductors must be used, which makes the armature larger and heavier to spin. Taken together, these features limit the kilovolt-ampere capacity of the revolving armature generator.

## REVOLVING FIELD AC GENERATORS

The **revolving field** type of generator has the armature windings on the stator and the field windings on the rotor.

**Three-Phase Revolving Field Generator**

Phase A     Phase C     Phase B

3 Phases, 120° Apart

**Figure 13–29** Three phases are mounted on the stator of a rotating field generator.

 TechTip!

The actual voltage generated in the coils may be measured as 120 V RMS from one coil end to the other. When we measure the voltage from one output lead to another, we would read 1.73 times the actual coil voltage; in this example, 120 V RMS × 1.73 = 208 V RMS. This increase in voltage is a result of the phase voltage being out of phase by 120 electrical degrees. Again, we add voltages vectorially to yield the higher voltage. This is an automatic increase in the generated voltage of 120 V per coil to a higher line voltage when the windings are in a wye connection. We use this effect to our advantage as we transmit and use the three-phase power from the generator.

By mounting the windings that provide the output voltage in a stationary position and rotating the magnetic field, the capacity and connection limitations experienced with the revolving armature AC generator are eliminated. Remember that we only need relative motion between the magnetic field and the armature coils. It does not matter whether the conductors move through the magnetic field or the magnetic field cuts through the stationary conductor. Higher voltage and kilovolt-ampere ratings are possible with the revolving field AC generator because the output circuit can be hardwired through stationary, secure connections to the stationary armature instead of being connected through a brush and slip ring arrangement.

The portion of the generator that rotates is the rotor and, in this case, holds the DC magnetic field. The stationary portion is the stator, which is wound with coils to create an armature. Figure 13–29 shows an example of a three-phase revolving field generator. This type of generator stator is constructed by placing the three sets of windings 120° apart. As you can see, a winding belongs to each phase on each side of the stator. Again, they all have a common end tied together in the stator, as you can note in the connection point under the bottom coil.

## ROTOR CONSTRUCTION

Rotating fields are constructed in two ways: the salient pole rotor and the round rotor. The round rotor is also called a turbo rotor.

### SALIENT POLE CONSTRUCTION

Figure 13–30 shows the **salient pole** construction. This particular rotor is used on large hydroelectric generators. As you can see, many individual, or distinct, poles are placed around the periphery of the rotor. This is because the number of poles and the speed of the rotor dictate the output frequency.

With hydroelectric generators, the speed is quite slow, so the number of magnetic poles is high. Much smaller salient pole rotors are used in some transportable generators.

Notice the pole faces arranged around the outside of the rotor. They jut out and are pronounced. This is why they are called salient poles. Each pole face is magnetized by its own set of coils. North and south poles are adjacent to each other so that every north pole is between two south poles, and vice versa.

This type of rotor construction is heavy because of the iron pole faces and the copper windings. Such rotors are subject to high wind resistance (making it harder to spin) and centrifugal forces.

### ROUND ROTOR CONSTRUCTION

As you can see in Figure 13–31, the **round rotor** has windings that are wound longitudinally. Round rotors are generally smaller and lighter and are found in the high-speed, two- or four-pole generators used in large utility generating stations. Although such a rotor usually turns much faster than the salient pole rotor, its longer, narrower construction minimizes wind resistance and centrifugal forces. The outside surface of the rotor is smooth, and the actual field windings are not exposed.

## EXCITATION SYSTEMS

Regardless of whether the field is revolving or stationary, it must create a magnetic field so that the armature windings can cut through it (or be cut through, in the case of the revolving field) and produce the output voltage. Many types of excitation systems are used. A few of the more important ones are discussed here.

### PERMANENT MAGNET FIELDS

Some smaller generators use a permanent magnet to provide the field. This type of construction is usually limited to small auxiliary generators used for

**Salient Pole Rotor**

**Figure 13–30** This rotor of a rotating field generator uses salient pole construction.

**Round Rotor**

Coil of One Pole

**Figure 13–31** A round rotor of a rotating field generator has specific poles that are not visible.

**Permanent Magnet Rotor**

**Figure 13–32** The stator of a PMG has permanent magnets on the stationary portion.

excitation or control purposes. Such a generator is called a **permanent magnet generator** (PMG; Figure 13–32). This generator has no need for a DC source of power to create an exciter magnetic field. The speed is set to produce the desired frequency, and the output voltage is controlled externally to the generator.

## DC ELECTROMAGNETIC FIELD

Most generators create a magnetic field (magnetic field flux) on the rotor or stator by using DC to "excite" the coils of wire, creating a steady magnetic field. Generators use some sort of DC supply to provide the current for their field excitation. The DC source that provides this current is called an exciter, and the current it provides is called **excitation current.** Exciters are made in a variety of ways, including the fixed exciter and the rotating exciter.

**Excitation Voltage**

**Figure 13–33** The excitation voltage for the DC field on the rotor is shown supplied by a battery.

**Fixed Exciter**

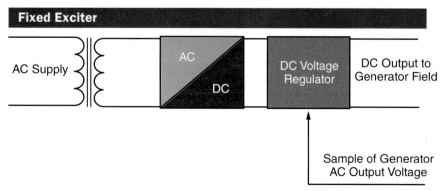

**Figure 13–34** A voltage regulator adjusts the DC excitation voltage to generator field.

An example of a fixed exciter for a revolving field generator is shown in Figure 13–33. Here, a battery is connected to the windings of the field magnets mounted on the rotor. The battery supplies the DC excitation that creates the magnetic revolving field that cuts through the armature windings. The output of the armature is then connected to the load. In this case, the battery is the exciter for the generator, which is not a practical application because there is no control and the battery will discharge.

A block diagram of a fixed exciter is shown in Figure 13–34. In this type of exciter, the battery is replaced with an AC supply, a rectifier, and a DC voltage regulator. The transformer changes the voltage to a level suitable for the exciter input. The regulator controls the generator voltage output by regulating the amount of DC excitation current supplied to the field windings. A sample of the generator output voltage is fed back to the regulator as the reference for voltage control. Some form of this feedback from the actual output voltage is typical of an AC generator with voltage controls. As expected, if the output voltage decreases due to current load increase, the regulator senses this and in turn increases the exciter voltage and exciter current to produce a higher output voltage. The opposite is true for a voltage decrease as the regulator works to keep the output voltage steady.

A rotating exciter is a separate DC generator that supplies the DC current to the field windings of the main generator. This type of exciter can be separate from the main generator or mounted on the same shaft as the main generator. Sometimes this generator is simply a DC generator driven off the same shaft as the AC generator. The output of the DC generator is controlled and fed to the exciter field on the alternator via slip rings and brushes. A brushless exciter is an exciter that is incorporated in the alternator's armature construction.

In a brushless exciter, the armature of the exciter is mounted on the same shaft as the field windings of the main generator. Since the two coils are rotating on the same shaft, there is no need for brushes or slip rings. However, since the output of the exciter armature is AC, it must be changed to DC. This is done by attaching a circular disk to the shaft. The disk has a diode rectifier mounted on it. The output from the exciter is connected to the input of the diode rectifier. The output of the diode rectifier is connected directly to the rotating field windings. The voltage level on the system is controlled by regulating the field current of the exciter.

## GENERATOR COOLING

Generators with small kilovolt-amp outputs are normally air-cooled. Appropriate openings are left in the stator windings, and slots are provided for air to pass through. Air-cooled alternators usually have fan blades attached to one end of the rotor shaft that help circulate the air through the entire unit. Figure 13–35 shows a small generator cooling fan.

Large-capacity alternators are often enclosed and operate in a hydrogen atmosphere. Hydrogen is used as a "cooling" atmosphere for two reasons. One is that the hydrogen is less dense, which

## TechTip!

The brushless exciter uses diode rectifier circuits mounted on the rotating member of the AC generator. The rotating member has an AC voltage induced into its windings as the rotor spins past a stationary DC field. The AC voltage in the rotating armature is then rectified by the rectifier devices and used to supply another coil on the rotor with DC voltage, creating a spinning DC field. This rotating DC field acts as the exciter for the stationary output armature. Therefore, the rotor has both an AC armature and a DC exciter operating on the rotor.

means there is less wind resistance and therefore less mechanical drag on the prime mover. The other is that the hydrogen atmosphere dissipates heat faster than air does; therefore, the heat from the copper losses and the generator's AC losses ($I^2R$, eddy current, and hysteresis) is removed and cooling is more effective.

## FREQUENCY AND OUTPUT VOLTAGE

The frequency output of the voltage is a critical aspect of the AC generator's design. The output frequency is determined by the number of stator poles and the speed of rotation of the rotor.

**Fan Mounting**

**Figure 13–35** A fan is mounted to the shaft under the housing at the left. The fan blows air over the ribbed housing to cool the generator from waste heat.

Because the number of stator poles is not field changeable and is determined by the design of the generator, the only way to vary output frequency is by the speed of the rotor.

The formula for calculating the frequency when the poles and revolutions per minute (rpm) are known is:

$$f = \frac{S \times P}{120}$$

Where:

$f$ = frequency in hertz
$P$ = number of poles
$S$ = speed in revolutions per minute
120 = constant

The number of poles is the total number of north and south poles present in the generator stator. Since they always come in pairs, the poles are always even in number. Two- and four-pole machines are the most common construction types for small generators, but hydroelectric plants and other such generators may have hundreds of poles.

The 120 constant is actually 2 × 60. The 2 changes the number of pole pairs to the number of poles, and the 60 changes revolutions per minute to revolutions per second to match the frequency in cycles per second or hertz. The full explanation of poles, speed,

and frequency can be found in Chapter 2. We use the same formula for single-phase machines and three-phase machines. In three-phase machines, the number of poles is actually the number of poles per phase. For example in Figure 13–29, you see six magnetic poles—or two per phase. In the formula for frequency we would use two poles, so this would be a two-pole, three-phase machine. The frequency at 3,600 rpm is 60 Hz.

Table 13–1 shows the relationship among frequency, speed of rotation, and number of poles for a variety of standard generator types. All the numbers in Table 13–1 were developed using the equation in the following example.

| Example |
|---|
| What is the output frequency of an alternator that contains four poles and is turning at a speed of 1,500 rpm? |

**Solution:**

$$f = \frac{(S \times P)}{120}$$

$$= \frac{1,500 \times 4}{120}$$

$$= 50 \text{ Hz}$$

## OUTPUT VOLTAGE, FREQUENCY, AND POWER

Output voltage is just as important as frequency. Remember that the output voltage is a function of how many lines of flux are being cut each second. With that in mind, you can see that three generator parameters affect the voltage:

1. The length of the armature conductors, determined by the length of each turn and the total number of turns

**Table 13–1**

| Number of Poles | Desired Frequency | | |
|---|---|---|---|
| | 25 Hz | 50 Hz | 60 Hz |
| 2 | 1,500 rpm | 3,000 rpm | 3,600 rpm |
| 4 | 750 | 1,500 | 1,800 |
| 6 | 500 | 1,000 | 1,200 |
| 8 | 375 | 750 | 900 |
| 10 | 300 | 600 | 720 |
| 12 | 250 | 500 | 600 |

Relationship of Speed, Number of Poles, and Frequency

## Synchronized Waveforms

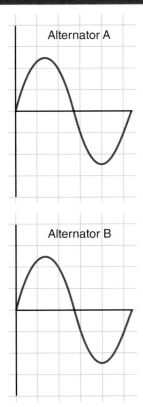

**Figure 13–36** Synchronized waveforms, depicting matched output frequencies and voltages, are needed before paralleling alternators.

2. The speed of rotation of the generator
3. The strength of the magnetic field

The number of turns of the coil is fixed by the generator's design, and the speed of rotation is fixed by the output frequency requirements. Thus, the only option for voltage control is to control the strength of the magnetic field. Since the excitation current controls the magnetic field's strength, it is used for the generator output voltage control. If the generator is acting as a sole source of power, the field control determines the output voltage.

The amount of power (watts) produced depends on the input power. As more electrical current is drawn from the generator, a force slows the generator down or creates more mechanical load. This effect, called motorization

**TechTip!**

As you have most likely observed at a carnival or fair with large, portable, truck-mounted generators, as the rides start and the demand for current increases, the generators have to work harder. This is usually apparent when the diesel engines work harder, creating more noise and more exhaust. As the electrical load or power requirement diminishes, the engines settle back to the idle mode or throttle back. This is a direct indication that as more electrical work is being done more mechanical horsepower is required. Along with the mechanical changes are the voltage regulation controls, which are not as obvious but are constantly adjusting the magnetic field to maintain voltage.

or countertorque of the generator, requires that more mechanical horsepower be delivered to the input of the generator to keep the frequency constant. This automatic control is usually accomplished through a speed-monitoring system or a governor control on the mechanical input.

# PARALLELING AC GENERATORS

Three conditions must be met when paralleling alternators:

1. The phase rotation of the two machines must be the same. This means that the A, B, and C phases must occur in the same sequence on both machines.
2. Each generator must have the same frequency (Figure 13–36).
3. The output voltage of the two machines must be the same.

One of the most common methods of detecting when the phase rotation of one alternator is matched with that of a paralleled alternator is to use a phase rotation indicator as shown in Figure 13–37. This type of indicator tells you whether the sequence of the phases is ABC or CBA. If the directions are not the same, there will be massive short circuits if you try to parallel the generators. Another method to use is the connection to three lamps.

See Figure 13–38 for the lamp connection. Each lamp is powered by the voltage between the phases of each generator. The phase A voltage of generator 1 connects to one side of a light, and the phase A voltage of generator 2

connects to the other side. Likewise, the other two lights are connected between B–B and C–C phases. When the two generators are in phase and the frequency and voltage magnitudes are equal, the lights are off. This indicates synchronism, meaning the two generators are operating to produce a common voltage and frequency. This is the case for all generators on an AC power grid or parallel generators used to power an emergency power source for a hospital.

Another instrument that can be used to parallel two machines is called a **synchroscope** (Figure 13–39). This instrument measures the voltage differences of two alternators being placed in parallel. The base load alternator (the one previously connected to the load) is used as the reference point for measuring the phase voltage relation of the first alternator compared to the second alternator. Because the second generator is normally run slightly faster than the base generator, the synchroscope registers a "fast" reading.

## Phase Rotation Indicator

**Figure 13–37** A phase rotation indicator can be used to check the phase sequence of operating three-phase systems.

## Three-Lamp Method

**Figure 13–38** A three-lamp method can be used to indicate phase rotation and synchronism point.

As the second generator exactly matches the peaks of the same phases, the synchroscope is at the top dead center to indicate synchronism. The two generators are paralleled, and the second generator slows down as it assumes electrical load. Once paralleled, the machines run together to maintain frequency. The power controls are more complicated and can best be studied in detail in specific generator books. The synchroscope meter display indicates whether there is a speed and therefore a frequency mismatch between the two machines being paralleled. The electromechanical synchroscope looks somewhat like a clock with only one hand. The two voltages are connected to the inputs, and if they are in phase, the meter hand points straight up (12 o'clock). The meter can rotate a full 360° in a clockwise direction. When the generators are in parallel, there is no difference between the two generators and the needle stays at the 12 o'clock position.

**Synchroscope**

**Figure 13–39** A synchroscope can verify that the frequencies of two machines are matched.

## SUMMARY

DC current has some applications that make it superior to AC. Many industrial plants use DC generators to produce the power needed to operate large DC motors or for needed DC power supplies.

Still, most generators are AC. AC generators use slip rings to remove the voltage from the armature; DC generators use commutator segments. The commutator and brushes change the AC produced in the armature into DC output voltage. The brushes are used to make contact with the commutator and carry the output current to the outside circuit.

Generator markings include the following:

1. The armature connections are marked $A_1$ and $A_2$
2. The series field windings are marked $S_1$ and $S_2$
3. The shunt field windings are marked $F_1$ and $F_2$

The three factors determining the output of the generator are the following:

1. The number of turns of wire in the armature
2. The strength of the magnetic field
3. The speed of the armature

Two basic types of AC generators (alternators) are used to convert mechanical energy of a drive shaft to electrical energy: the revolving armature and the revolving field. The revolving armature is least used because of the limited power and voltage rating caused by brush and slip ring limitations when connecting the output load to the armature.

The rotor of the revolving field alternator is the rotating magnetic field. Direct current supplied to the field is called excitation current. The number of poles and the speed of the rotor determine the output frequency. The output voltage is controlled by the amount of DC excitation current to the rotating field once the synchronous speed is set to maintain the desired frequency. This increases or decreases the strength of the rotor's magnetic field and results in induction of more or less output voltage and current. The only limit is the amount of current the conductors can carry based on the wire size. When the iron core becomes magnetically saturated, it cannot produce more magnetic effect even if the excitation is increased.

AC and DC generators can be operated in parallel to facilitate the transfer of load and take one generator offline for maintenance or to provide more capacity for an increasing load. Essentially all alternators that supply the nation's power grid are operating in parallel. This means that they need to be added or dropped off as the system's load changes. Proper paralleling of generators is often done automatically through electronic controls but sometimes must be done manually as conditions dictate.

# CHAPTER GLOSSARY

**Armature** The winding in a generator where an induced voltage is created.

**Armature reaction** The bending of the field magnetic flux by a reaction to the armature magnetic field. Armature reaction causes a displacement of the neutral point, with consequent arcing at the commutator and resultant voltage drop.

**Brushes** Sliding contacts usually made of a carbon or graphite alloy. Contacts can be connected to DC commutators or to AC slip rings.

**Commutator** A multi-segment rotating connection that is connected to the armature windings. A commutator is a circular ring that is divided into segments that are electrically insulated from one another.

**Compensating, interpole, or Thomson-Ryan windings** Field windings located physically between the main field poles. Interpoles are used to reduce armature reaction and are connected in series with the armature current.

**Excitation current** The current supplied to the field of an AC generator. The excitation current creates the steady magnetic field that the armature cuts through.

**Field windings** The part of the DC generator that creates the magnetic field that is cut by the armature windings.

**Flat compounding** The effects of compounding in a DC generator so that the no-load output voltage is the same as the full-load voltage. The voltage versus load curve on a graph is essentially flat, or no change in voltage, with change in load.

**Overcompounding** A condition that occurs in a DC generator when the output voltage at no-load is less than the output voltage at full-load. The output voltage increases as electrical load is added.

**Permanent magnet generator** A type of generator in which the field is provided by a strong permanent magnet, sometimes in the stator and sometimes on the rotor.

**Revolving armature generator** A generator that has the field windings on the stator and the armature windings on the rotor.

**Revolving field** A generator that has the field windings on the rotor and the armature windings on the stator.

**Round rotor** A streamlined type of construction where the coils are wound longitudinally on the rotor. This type of construction is generally much lighter than salient pole construction and is used extensively on high-speed generators. Also called a turbo rotor.

**Salient pole** A type of rotating field construction where the field poles are wound individually and mounted along the outside edge of the rotor. *Salient* means projecting outward; projecting or jutting beyond a line or surface; or protruding.

**Self-excited** The method in which the generator receives power to produce the magnetic field for generation. A portion of the output power is fed back to the generator's field as it provides its own excitation current.

**Slip rings** Continuous bands of metal installed around a shaft. Slip rings are connected to the rotating windings and provide a path for the current to reach the brushes (Figure 13–23).

**Stator** The stationary part of the generator.

**Synchroscope** A type of instrument that is used to determine the phase relationship between two separate generator voltages. This instrument is often used for determining synchronization of two generators before connecting the outputs together.

**Undercompounding** The condition that exists when the setup of the generator results in the no-load voltage being greater than the full-load voltage. As the generator supplies more load current, the output voltage decreases.

# REVIEW QUESTIONS

1. Define a generator.
2. What type of voltage is produced in all rotating armatures?
3. In a DC generator, AC is converted to DC by the _____ and _____.
4. Name three types of armature windings connections and discuss how they are used.

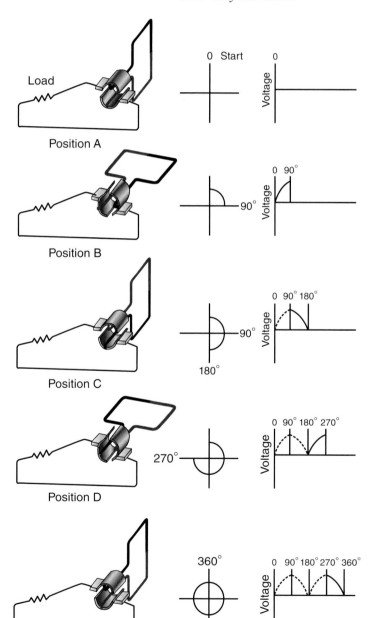

Position A

Position B

Position C

Position D

Position E

**Figure RQ13–1**

5. Discuss the three factors that determine the voltage output of a DC generator.
6. Describe the voltage regulation characteristics of the three DC generator connections.
7. What advantages does a compound-wound field connection generator have over the shunt field connection and the series field connection?
8. What are the effects of armature reaction? What causes it? How can these effects be corrected at manufacture?
9. Explain how electricity is produced through electromagnetic induction.
10. If you have a wire and a magnetic field, how is voltage created in the wire?
11. On a DC generator, how do you reverse the polarity of the voltage to the load?
12. How do you increase or decrease the amplitude of the voltage for an alternator?
13. Using Figure RQ13–1, explain how an AC generator creates a sine wave.
14. What is the physical difference between a DC generator and an AC generator with a revolving armature?
15. What is the difference between an AC generator with a revolving armature and one with a revolving field?
16. What is the difference between a salient pole rotor and round rotor?
17. Explain the relationship between speed of rotation, number of poles, and output frequency.
18. How do you increase or decrease the output power of an AC generator without changing its output frequency?
19. What are the requirements to be met before alternators can be paralleled?

**20.** Explain the use of a synchroscope.
**21.** Why is an AC generator (alternator) that is to be parelleled supposed to run faster than the online alternator?
**22.** Name the various losses within a generator and what can be done to reduce the losses.
**23.** Changing the speed of an alternator changes the output voltage and the _____.

**24.** By increasing the DC excitation to an alternator, the frequency does not change but the _____ of the waveform increases.
**25.** A voltage regulator on an alternator changes _____ _____ to change output voltage.

## PRACTICE PROBLEMS

**1.** What is the actual voltage output of a three-phase generator with each coil producing 120 volts RMS?
**2.** Calculate the efficiency of a generator that has 15,000 W of input energy and 3,000 W of internal power losses.
**3.** If a generator loses 3,000 W of power in the generation process, and 35% is in friction, windage, and iron loss, what is the copper loss in watts?
**4.** What is the output of a generator operating at 82% efficiency if its input is 25 kilowatts?
**5.** What is the power loss for a generator operating at 85% efficiency if its input is 25 kilowatts?

**6.** Find the frequency of a three-phase generator with 12 total poles (four per phase) and a rotational speed of 1,800 rpm.
**7.** Find the needed speed for a single-phase generator with six poles to operate at 40 Hz.
**8.** How many poles per phase are there in a three-phase generator if it operates at 60 Hz and 1,800 rpm?
**9.** What is the expected input for a generator operating at 78% efficiency if it has a 15,600 watt output?
**10.** Find the output frequency of a six-pole, single-phase generator operating at 1,200 rpm.

# 14

## AC MOTORS

# T O P I C S

# O V E R V I E W

In this chapter you are introduced to the AC electric motor and how it uses the power generated by alternators and then converts the delivered electrical energy back into mechanical energy. As you have studied, the generator takes mechanical energy and converts it to electrical energy, which is transmitted to where it is needed; motors then convert the electrical energy back into mechanical energy. This conversion back into mechanical energy is similar to generator conversion in that there are three requirements for conversion: a magnetic field, a conductor, and a supply of current. The result of the interaction of these three elements is motion.

For this chapter, we just explore what makes the motor turn. For detailed motor application, specific controls, and installation, you should refer to a book on motors and controls.

# O B J E C T I V E S

After completing this chapter, you will be able to:
· Explain motor action and the right-hand rule for motors
· Describe the process for creating a rotating magnetic field in a single-phase AC induction motor
· Define the term slip and relate it to induction motors
· Explain how to create a rotating magnetic field in a three-phase motor
· Use connection diagrams to connect three-phase motors in wye or delta patterns
· Calculate the line and phase voltages in a three-phase wye system
· Explain the basics of variable frequency drives and the frequency effects of AC motors

## Magnetically Induced Motion

Original connections give field polarity as shown. Armature current as shown would produce a counterclockwise rotation.

Armature connection changed to give opposite direction of current in armature while maintaining field direction results in clockwise rotation.

Reverse field polarity and armature polarity from middle diagram will result in the same clockwise direction of rotation.

**Figure 14–1** Motion results from a current flow in a conductor in a magnetic field.

## MOTOR ACTION

The basis for an electric motor is that the relation of magnetic properties holds true as we apply current to a conductor, produce a magnetic field, and then bring two magnetic fields into close proximity. We start with the simple motor action of a conductor with electron flow when placed in a magnetic field. The conductor has a magnetic field developed by the current that reacts with the external field, and the conductor tries to move out of the external field as in Figure 14–1. The direction of movement can be explained by the right-hand rule for motors. This right-hand rule uses the same finger denotations as the left-hand rule for generation but changes the orientation, as seen in Figure 14–2. As you note, the first finger on the right hand represents flux direction of the field.

First finger = flux direction
Center finger = electron flow direction in the armature conductor
Thumb = direction of movement or thrust or motion

Remember, the generator uses the thrust of the conductor through a magnetic field to produce current and the motor uses the current and magnetic field to produce thrust. All electric motors work off this same principle.

## SINGLE-PHASE AC MOTORS

All AC motors work because a rotating magnetic field can be produced on a stationary frame, or the stator, of the motor. We will discuss induction motors first as they are the most popular AC motor.

## Right-Hand Rule for Motors

Direction of Flux North To South · Resultant Thrust of Motion · Current Flow in Conductor

**Figure 14–2** The right-hand rule for motor direction is applied when using electron flow theory.

The stator field can be created by having two sets of coils displaced in physical location around the rotor. If you start with a two-pole motor as in Figure 14–3, you notice that two large poles are created by the four coils with the electrical polarities, as indicated at the coil ends. Each set of coils has a separate AC sine wave supplied to it. To do this, the single sine wave needs to be split into two separate waves. Figure 14–4 shows two waveforms split by 90 electrical degrees. Motors that work by splitting a single waveform are single-phase motors. Typically these are **split phase motors** or **capacitor start motors,** although other single-phase motor types use other methods to cause a phase shift. The process of splitting the single phase into two waveforms is as follows: The motor windings (coils wound in the stator) are inductive. Some degree of phase shift occurs because the run winding is generally more inductive than the start winding, which has more turns of smaller conductor and is less inductive or more resistive. (Note that series capacitors are also used in some motors to create a phase shift.) The process of splitting the phase is different for different types of motors. If we apply the waveform marked "start" to the coils marked "start" and the waveform marked "run" to the coils marked "run" in Figure 14–3 we create a two-pole electromagnet that rotates, or revolves, around the stator. If we use the position markings of Figure 14–4 and relate the current at this point to the coils in Figure 14–3, then we can assign the actual pole polarities using the left-hand rule for coils.

- Position 1: Peak current flow in Figure 14–4 in the top and the bottom coils is marked "start," with north on the inside edge of the top coil and south at the inside edge of the bottom coil. There is no motion yet as only the first two poles are established.
- Position 2: Less current flows in the start coils as the sine wave diminishes and current increases in the side or **run windings.**

**Figure 14–3** Magnetic poles and electrical polarities for a two-pole motor.

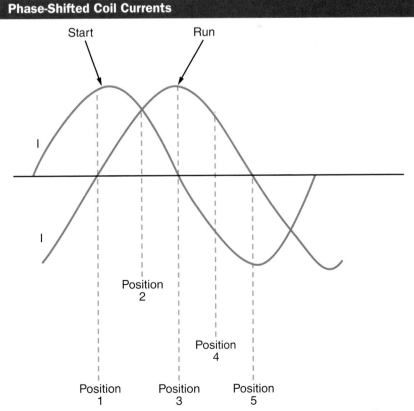

**Figure 14–4** Phase-shifted coil currents are applied to motor coils.

With the electrical polarities at this time as shown, the inside face of the left pole is north and the inside face of the right pole is south. We still have two larger poles with the center of the magnetic pole shifted 45° counterclockwise.

- Position 3: The top and bottom poles receive no current and produce no magnetic field. The side poles' runs have maximum current and are producing maximum flux. The two poles have shifted their center another 45° to 90° counterclockwise from the starting point.

- Position 4: The top and bottom poles now have current again but opposite to the original direction. Using the left-hand rule for coils, you can verify that the magnetic pole faces have reversed from the original and the north pole has moved to the bottom inside edge. As this current is increasing, the side poles are weaker, making the center of the north pole and the center of the south pole move another 45° counterclockwise.

- Position 5: The side poles are again at zero current flow and are demagnetized. The **start windings** are strongest with the north pole at the bottom inside edge, another 45° movement. The two magnetic poles are rotating counterclockwise.

## SYNCHRONOUS SPEED

The speed of the rotating magnetic field depends on the number of poles and the frequency of the waveform applied. For a two-pole motor, the two poles rotate one full rotation around the stator core with each full waveform. With 60 Hz or 60 cycles in 1 second, the poles would have 60 complete revolutions in 1 second. In 1 minute, they would rotate 3,600 times, or 60 × 60. This is the **synchronous speed** of a two-pole motor connected to a 60 Hz supply. You can use the same formula used for generators with just an algebraic

equivalent transposition. The formula for synchronous speed is:

$$S = \frac{120 \times \text{Frequency}}{\text{Number of poles}}$$

where $S$ is synchronous speed measured in revolutions per minute (rpm); 120 is a constant, converting pairs of poles to number of poles and 60 cycles per second to cycles per minute (same equation given in generation equations); and frequency is in hertz.

Number of poles means the total number of magnetic poles—not windings.

> ### Example
> Find the synchronous speed of a two-pole motor when 60 Hz is applied:
>
> $$S = \frac{120 \times 60}{2}$$
>
> $$= 3{,}600 \text{ rpm}$$

## INDUCTION MOTOR

A **squirrel-cage rotor,** as pictured in Figure 14–5, position 1, is made up of conductors that are mounted in the rotor and are short circuited at each end. No electrical connection is made between the rotor conductors and the stator conductors. However, current flow occurs in the rotor conductors (bars) when the motor is operating.

Using Figure 14–5, you can understand how the voltage is induced in the rotor bars; how the current creates a magnetic field on the rotor; and why the rotor follows the rotating field of the stator.

- Position 1: Only a north and a south pole are on the stator; no voltage is induced into the rotor, and no magnetic field is produced by the rotor. The rotor does not move.

- Position 2: As the side stator poles move 45° counterclockwise, the stator's magnetic field begins to cut through the rotor conductors.

## Magnetic Pole Induction

**Figure 14-5** Magnetic poles are induced in a squirrel-cage rotor based on the polarity of the stator poles.

All three requirements for induction are present: magnetic field, conductor, and relative motion. As the stator flux cuts through the rotor conductors, it induces a voltage and resultant current in the circuit created by the conductors that are all electrically connected together at each end. Using the left-hand rule for conductors, you can determine the direction of current flow as the magnetic field wraps around the conductors. The direction is shown on the rotor bars in the diagram. Now you can use the left-hand rule for a coil. As you see, the current comes toward you on the left side of the rotor and flows away from you on the right side of the rotor. This current produces a north pole on the lower left of the rotor. This rotor north is repelled by the stator north, and the rotor begins to move. The rotor north is also attracted by the stator south, increasing the magnetic action. The same actions of repulsion and attraction are occurring with the stator south and the rotor south.

- Positions 3–6: As the stator poles continue to rotate, further cutting action takes place on the rotor conductors, producing rotor poles as indicated by position 3 in Figure 14–5.

## FieldNote!

AC motors were invented by Nikola Tesla—a naturalized American citizen from Croatia who was an inventor, mechanical engineer, and electrical engineer. During the late 1800s and early 1900s, he was a major force in the field of electricity and magnetism. Tesla did theoretical work on the concepts of AC generation and distribution and on AC motors. His inventions enabled Westinghouse Electric and Manufacturing Company to capitalize on AC's advantages, especially an easier-to-maintain AC induction motor. Until his achievements were put into commercial use, motors used DC with its inherent problems; George Westinghouse was a leading promoter of AC, while Thomas Edison had been pushing for DC generation, transmission, and use in motors.

Tesla was involved in many groundbreaking new concepts, including radio. In 1943—long after radio had first been in use—the U.S. Supreme Court declared him the inventor of radio. Many people have heard of a Tesla coil, which is used to produce high-voltage discharges. In 1893—long before they came into everyday use—Tesla was showing people how fluorescent lamps worked. Tesla died in 1943, a forgotten and poor man.

As the stator poles are moving, the rotor conductors are cut, thereby creating an internal current flow in the rotor that continues to create rotor magnetic poles. The only way to induce a voltage into the rotor is if a cutting action is created by the relative motion of the magnetic field. In other words, the rotor *cannot* spin as fast as the synchronous speed of the stator field. If the rotor does spin as fast, there is no cutting action, no induced voltage in the rotor, and no current flow, and no magnetic poles develop on the rotor.

## TechTip!

Under normal circumstances, individual residential housing does not have three phases delivered to the home. There are three wires either "dropped" or run underground "lateral" to the home. However, this does not mean that there are three phases. Typically, the three conductors represent two hot conductors and a neutral from a single-phase source. You study this idea in more detail in Chapter 15. A three-phase system is composed of three "hot" conductors and usually a neutral, which creates a three-phase, four-wire system.

With no magnetic poles, the rotor has no magnetic attraction or repulsion to the stator poles. To induce voltage and resulting current in the rotor, the rotor must **slip** in speed behind the speed of the rotating stator field.

The slip of a motor is usually measured in percent slip. This measures what percent the rotor speed is falling behind the synchronous (sync) speed of the rotating magnetic field. To calculate percent slip of a motor, use the following formula:

$$\% \text{ Slip} = \frac{\text{Sync speed} - \text{Rotor speed}}{\text{Sync speed}} \times 100$$

Sometimes the slip is just expressed as an rpm. For instance, "The slip of the motor is 50 rpm." This statement, however, does not give you an evaluation of how the motor is performing compared with the actual synchronous speed.

### Example

What is the percent slip of a motor that has a synchronous (sync) speed of 1,800 rpm and an actual rotor speed of 1,750 rpm?

**Solution:**

$$\% \text{ Slip} = \left(\frac{\text{Sync speed} - \text{Rotor speed}}{\text{Sync speed}}\right) \times 100$$

$$= \left(\frac{1,800 - 1,750}{1,800}\right) \times 100$$

$$= \left(\frac{50}{1,800}\right) \times 100$$

$$= 2.78\%$$

## MOTOR VARIATIONS

Many methods are used to produce the rotating magnetic field in the stator. Each method has its advantages and disadvantages related to cost, complexity, maintenance requirements, torque, efficiency, and operating characteristics.

Some of the more common varieties of the single-phase induction motor are the split phase, the capacitor start, and the shaded pole. These motors can be connected for different voltages by arranging how the windings are connected to the line. A thorough study of each type of motor and how they are connected can be found in a motors reference book.

As you progressed from a single phase to three phases in the generation of AC, you can use the three phases generated to your advantage when connecting the three-phase motor. This type of motor is extremely popular in commercial or industrial applications, where the phase supply of power is available.

## THREE-PHASE MOTORS

As the name implies, three-phase motors operate using all phases of a three-phase power system. Refer back to the three-phase generator section in Chapter 13 to review generation. The same three phases that are 120 electrical degrees apart are represented in Figure 14–6.

### Three-Phase Two-Pole Motor

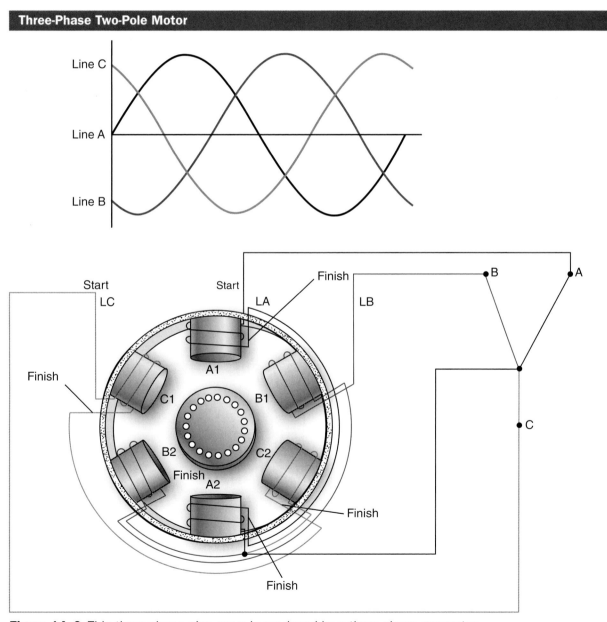

**Figure 14–6** This three-phase sine wave is produced by a three-phase generator.

You use these three phases applied to the motor coil windings of a motor to create a three-phase (3∅) rotating magnetic field. See Figure 14–7 for a rendering of a three-phase, two-pole motor. This drawing represents a wye-connected motor demonstrating that the windings have one common point, just as the wye-connected generator you studied was connected. Motors can also be connected in a different pattern called a delta pattern. First we will discuss the wye pattern, as the transition from the generator to the motor is easier to follow.

## ROTATING MAGNETIC FIELD OF A WYE-CONNECTED MOTOR

Refer to Figure 14–7 to determine how a magnetic field rotates around the stator of a three-phase motor. Figure 14–8 is used to explain how the applied voltage creates the magnetic poles of the stator. As you view the waveform, the waveform above the zero reference indicates current is flowing into the motor windings. When the waveform is below the reference, current is returning from the motor to the power source.

• Position 1 in Figure 14–8: Phase A has zero voltage and zero current. The top and bottom coils are not energized and have no magnetic poles. At the same instant, phase C has approximately 70% of the maximum voltage applied and current is flowing into the coils for phase C. The voltage waveform also indicated that the coil for phase B is energized by 70% voltage, but current is flowing out of the motor toward the source.

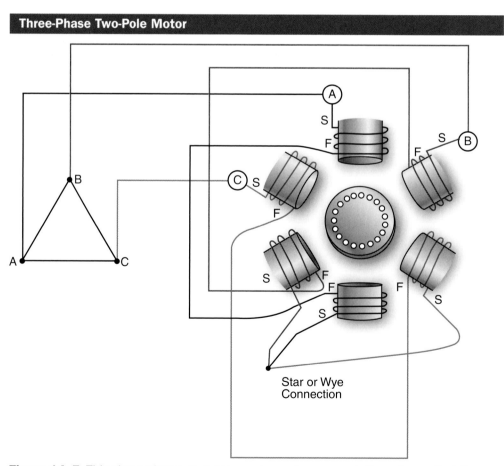

**Three-Phase Two-Pole Motor**

**Figure 14–7** This three-phase, two-pole motor coil representation shows that the windings have a common connection point.

If you use the left-hand rule for coils and note the direction of current flow through the coils, you find that the left coils for phases B and C both produce north poles and the right two coils for phases B and C produce south poles. There are now two poles established—north on the left and south on the right.

- Position 2: At position 2 on the waveform graph, phase A has increased to 50% voltage and current flows into the motor. Phase C has decreased to 50% voltage, but the current is in the same direction. Phase B is stronger, with 100% of the voltage, and the current is flowing to the source. As you can see, phase A has established a north pole at the bottom coil, the phase B left coil has strong north poles, and the phase C left pole is weaker. The centers of the two poles—north and south—have moved counterclockwise.

- Position 3: Phase A has increased to 70% of maximum voltage, phase C is at zero, and phase B has decreased to 70% of maximum. This means that phase C has been demagnetized and produces no magnetic field. The phase B left pole is a little weaker north, and the phase A bottom coil is a little stronger north. The center of the north poles has moved counterclockwise again between phase A and phase B.

- Position 4: Phase A is at 100% voltage, phase B has decreased to 50% of the maximum, and phase C has reversed direction to 50% of the maximum and current is flowing opposite to the original direction. This translates to the magnetic poles for C phase being opposite to what they were in position 1. Now the lower right C coil is at 50% strength and is north, phase A creates the strongest north at the bottom pole, and phase B has become a weaker north at the bottom

**Three-Phase Motor Current**

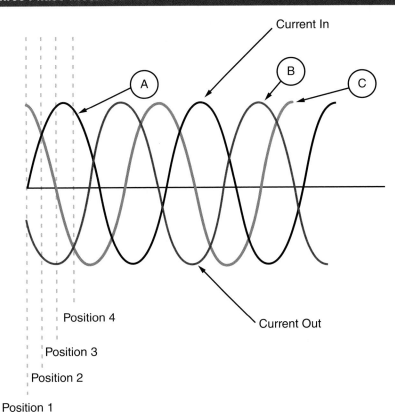

**Figure 14–8** Three phases are applied to motor coils, and each position indicates field motion.

left. The two poles have moved 90° counterclockwise from their original position at time, and are centered over the bottom and top poles.

As you notice, the pole has rotated 90° through the stator positions, and when using phase A as a reference, the waveform has moved 90 electrical degrees. Using this information, you can deduce that the magnetic field rotates through all 360 mechanical degrees as the phase completes the full 360° of electrical sine wave. Therefore, for a three-phase motor, use the same formula for synchronous speed of the rotating magnetic field as was used in single phase:

$$S = \frac{120 \times \text{Frequency}}{\text{Number of poles}}$$

The number of poles is counted as the number of poles per phase.

## TechTip!

When one of the three phases of a three-phase system is disconnected or fails, the system reverts to a single-phase system. The voltages between the phases are normally 120° apart and work in unison. As two conductors supply current to the load, the third conductor provides a path back to the generator. If you add all three currents together with the proper polarity (direction), the total must be zero. The phases are always equal and opposite. If one phase fails, the other two phases become the supply and return and are considered a single-phase sine wave. If this happens to a three-phase motor, the motor is said to be "single phasing" and the rotating magnetic field will not rotate as desired. Often, if the motor is already running under light load, the motor will continue to spin. Under a heavy load, the motor will overheat and may stall. Typically, a three-phase motor with a connected mechanical load will not start under a single-phase condition.

### THREE-PHASE DELTA MOTOR

Another popular three-phase motor connection for an induction motor is the delta connection. The method of connecting the coils wound in the motor stator is determined by the desired operating characteristics, the insulation ratings of the coil windings, and the wire gauge of the coil conductors, as well as the manufacturer's prefer-ence. As shown in Chapter 15, the voltage and current of the delivery system may be different from the voltage and current in the coils of the load. Figure 14–9 helps you determine why the connection of the coils is referred to as the *delta connection*: the coil pattern forms an equilateral triangle that resembles the Greek letter delta (Δ).

By viewing the delta pattern, each corner of the triangle represents one phase connection for the coils. In this example, a phase A coil connected from T1 to T9 and an identical coil is wound with the first coil connected from T6 to T3. In this dual-voltage motor, the coils can be connected in series, as in Figure 14–10, to make them ready for twice the line voltage of the parallel connection shown in Figure 14–11.

## THREE-PHASE INDUCTION MOTOR

Most three-phase motors are **induction motors** as opposed to **conduction motors**. The term induction motor simply means the rotors have voltage induced into them, whereas conduction motors have voltage "conducted" or electrically connected to the rotors. Three-phase induction motors use squirrel-cage windings on the rotor just like single-phase motors. Again, there needs to be relative motion of the magnetic field, meaning the rotor must slip behind synchronous speed of the stator field to have induction in the rotor. As the rotor creates magnetic poles through induction, the number of rotor poles matches the number of stator poles. In this basic theory book, you have only seen examples of two-pole motors, but many more poles can be created. These are explained in further detail in motor books. It does not matter how many poles are on the stator or whether the stator is connected wye or delta; the rotor is the same basic squirrel cage.

**Delta-Connected Motor Coils**

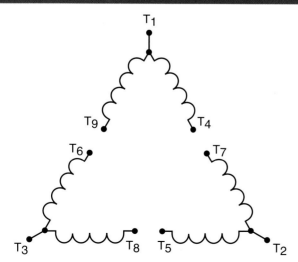

**Figure 14–9** Dual-voltage delta-connected motor coils resemble the Greek letter delta (Δ).

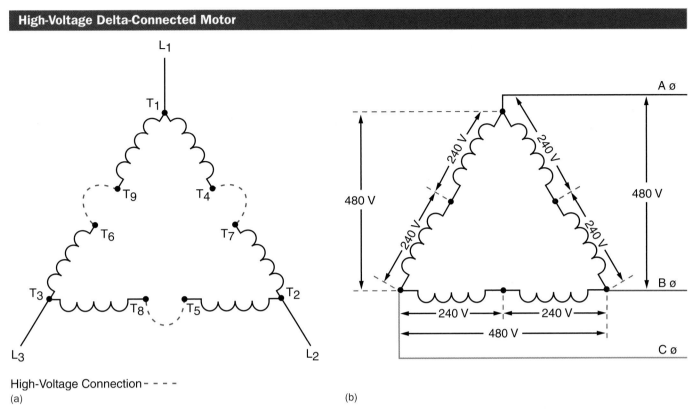

**Figure 14–10** (a) A high-voltage delta-connected motor (b) shows voltage drop across the coils of a dual-delta (series)–connected motor configured for its high-voltage (480 V) operation.

**Figure 14–11** (a) A low-voltage delta-connected motor (b) shows voltage drop across the coils of a dual-delta (parallel)–connected motor configured for its low-voltage (240 V) operation.

## TechTip!

The term conduction motor refers to the method of creating the magnetic field in the rotor. If we use an induction motor, the magnetic field is produced by voltage and current induced into the rotor. In a conduction motor, the voltage and current are connected through conductors (actually carbon brushes and slip rings) and no induction needs to occur. One such conduction motor is known as a wound rotor motor.

## GENERATOR EFFECT IN A MOTOR

As the rotor spins within the stator of a motor, it creates the magnetic poles on the rotor. These created magnetic poles act just like a generator with a rotating field. The rotor is a spinning magnetic field (moving magnetic field), and the magnetic field is cutting the conductors of the stator windings. This generator action in the motor has some interesting effects. The faster the rotor spins, the more generator action occurs. As the motor starts, a large current draw gets the motor running. This is known as "starting" current or inrush current. Actually, the high current at start is the result of the rotor not turning, or turning slowly, and therefore not generating back into the stator. You can determine that the generation is in opposition to the applied electromotive force (EMF) and is therefore considered counter EMF, or counter electromotive force (CEMF). As the motor comes up to speed, the rotor speeds up and the CEMF goes up, which causes the line current to the motor stator to go down—from the higher starting current. The motor still draws current from the line because the motor effect is greater than the generator effect.

Another recognizable result of the generation effect of a motor is that of placing a larger mechanical load on the motor. This causes the motor to slow down, causing more slip, which means more current is induced into the rotor and the generation effect is lessened. A slower generator (spinning rotor) induces less CEMF into the stator, and the current of the stator increases. You can verify that a motor working harder to produce more horsepower draws more current. Thus, you can see that every motor has some generator properties and every generator has some motor properties.

## VARIABLE FREQUENCY DRIVES

Variable frequency drives, known as VFDs, are electronic controls used to control the speed of an AC motor. As was stated earlier, the synchronous speed of a motor is determined by the number of poles per phase and the applied frequency. The actual speed is determined by the amount of slip required to maintain a speed lower than synchronous when using an induction motor. Because the number of poles is normally a design by the manufacturer and not normally adjusted in the field, the only other variable to speed control is to adjust the applied frequency. This is done by electronically altering the frequency to the motor.

The basic block diagram of the VFD is seen in Figure 14–12. The power input can be either single-phase AC or, more likely, three-phase AC and is brought to the controller. A photo of a VFD is seen in Figure 14–13. The VFD has rectifier circuits that convert the AC to DC and then filter it to smooth out the DC and set it to the desired voltage level. This is done in the DC control and power circuits. There are many ways to change the DC back to a desired frequency of AC or "invert" the DC in the block labeled DC-to-AC inverter. The output of the VFD is a frequency and voltage needed to create the desired synchronous speed of the AC motor. Most VFDs are not appropriate for "capacitor start" or "split phase" single-phase motors.

## Electronic Variable Frequency Drive

Three-Phase Input

↓

Diode/Bridge Rectifier

↓

DC Control and Power Circuits

↓

DC to AC Inverter ← Speed Control Signal

↓

Three-Phase AC Motor

**Figure 14–12** These operational components make up the electronic variable frequency drive.

## Typical Variable Frequency Drive

**Figure 14–13** A typical VFD converts AC to DC and then smoothes out the DC.

The reason is that these motors can be slowed to the point where the centrifugal switch can close and create serious operating problems with the motor. A centrifugal switch is found on single-phase motors and is used to disconnect the start windings of a motor after it gets to the right speed. The switch opens the circuit to the start windings and keeps it open while the motor is running near rated speed. If the start windings of a single-phase motor are allowed to stay in the energized circuit, or become reconnected, they overheat and become damaged. More specific details are found in books about motors.

Two of the more common forms of inversion are known as **current source input (CSI)** and **pulse-width modulation (PWM).** The CSI-VFD has an output characterized by the waveforms in Figure 14–14. As you can see, the voltage is not a clean sine wave, and the resultant current is not a clean sine wave either. However, the motor still responds by creating the appropriate magnetic fields and moves the magnetic fields according to the formula for synchronous speed.

## CSI Voltage and Current Wave Forms

Voltage

Current

**Figure 14–14** The CSI voltage and current output waveforms are not smooth.

 FieldNote!

Variable frequency drives (VFDs), also known as adjustable speed drives (ASDs), are constantly being improved and the capability of the electronics upgraded. In a relatively short time frame, the electronic control of large motors and the ability to perform many of the complex functions needed for advanced motor control have been introduced and perfected. Each year more drives are available, and many have new and advanced features used to control a larger segment of the motor control market. Many of the smaller controllers are practically disposable and cannot be repaired, while the large units need advanced troubleshooting skills to keep electrical systems running at peak efficiency. There is always a need to learn more.

The other popular form of inversion to AC is the PWM-VFD, with the waveform as shown in Figure 14–15. By chopping the DC into small pulses and adjusting the width, or time of the pulse, the approximation of voltage appears closer to a sine wave. This is more apparent in the current sine wave, as shown.

The VFDs are used in many control applications, not only to control the running speed of the motor but also to control other operating parameters. The starting speed and **ramp-up** to full speed can be adjusted by controlling the frequency and allowing the frequency and speed to increase with time. The actual speed can be monitored and constant adjustments can be made to maintain exact speed under varying mechanical loads. The time required to stop can be controlled by a **ramp-down** feature that allows the motor to stop quickly, stop immediately, or control the deceleration to a specific time. VFDs are becoming more prevalent, more reliable, more versatile, and less expensive, and they have lower motor maintenance requirements. They have all but replaced the DC speed control systems that have been more accurate and more reliable for years.

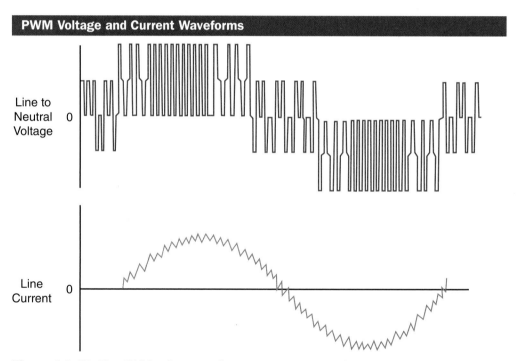

**PWM Voltage and Current Waveforms**

Line to Neutral Voltage

Line Current

**Figure 14–15** The PWM voltage and current output waveforms can be chopped into small pulses to approximate a sine wave.

# SUMMARY

In this chapter, you learned that AC induction motors operate by inducing voltage and therefore current into a squirrel-cage rotor. The method used to induce the rotor voltage is to create a rotating magnetic field at synchronous speed. The field moving through the rotor conductors creates a current, and that current produces magnetic poles on the rotor. The rotor poles then are pushed and pulled by magnetism, and the rotor follows the rotating stator field. Remember that there must be slip in the speed of the rotor as it cannot spin at synchronous speed.

Single-phase motors must create a phase shift in the single phase of the applied voltage. There are several ways to accomplish this, but the two resulting voltages are applied to the start and run windings so that the magnetic stator field rotates. Depending on the particular motor style, the split could be between 30° and 80°. The speed of the rotating magnetic field, or synchronous speed, is computed by a single formula with the frequency and number of poles as the only variables. This formula is the same transposed formula used for generators.

The squirrel-cage rotor was examined to see that there were no electrical connections to the rotor. The coupling to the rotor was only through magnetism, even though there were current and voltage in the rotor. The percent slip was calculated to show that the actual speed of the rotor could vary. The rotor magnetically coupled to the stator reacts to changing load and slows to create more magnetic field strength and more twisting effort known as torque. It was established that the rotor actually acted as a generator and generated a CEMF back into the stator windings.

Three-phase motors were explained to show the effects of applying three-phase voltage to a stator to produce a rotating magnetic field. The result of applying three phases to the motor creates a smoothly rotating magnetic field and allows the squirrel-cage rotor to travel with the stator field. The same formulas for synchronous speed and slip apply equally to single-phase and three-phase motors.

Finally, an introduction to electronic control of motors through the use of VFDs was presented to explain how speed controls can be accomplished. A block diagram of the controller was used to show the sequence of the controller's functions. First, the input waveform is rectified to create DC. Then, the DC is set to the correct levels and inverted to create AC output. Finally, the variable frequency AC is directly connected to the motors to control the synchronous speed of the motor.

# CHAPTER GLOSSARY

**Capacitor start motor** A single-phase motor with main and auxiliary windings designed for direct connection to a single-phase AC source. The auxiliary winding is connected in series with a capacitor and is connected in the circuit for starting purposes only. The capacitor helps shift the phase for the auxiliary (start) winding during starting.

**Conduction motor** A motor that relies on a conductive path that allows current to flow to the rotor during motor operation. This motor typically has carbon brushes that provide an electrical connection to the moving rotor.

**Current source input (CSI)** A method used to electronically control the frequency and the voltage delivered to an AC motor to vary its speed and torque. The AC input is rectified, filtered to DC, then inverted through electronics to provide an AC wave approximation which is adjusted to provide the motor current waveform.

**Induction motor** A motor that relies on the principles of induction to transfer energy to the rotor. Voltage is induced into the rotor as the rotor slips behind the synchronous speed of the rotating field of the stator. There is no direct electrical connection between the AC power source and the rotor.

**Pulse-width modulation (PWM)** A method used to electronically control the frequency and the voltage delivered to a motor for purposes of speed and torque control. The AC input is rectified, filtered to DC, and then inverted back to AC as a pulse where the width of the pulse is modulated to control the AC motor.

**Ramp-down** A process where the motor speed and power is gradually reduced during the stopping process. The motor is provided gradually reduced power during the deceleration time so that the motor and load do not coast to a stop or come to an abrupt stop.

**Ramp-up** A process where the speed of a motor is gradually increased from zero speed to operating speed. The method is used to reduce high torque effects on a stationary load, as the motor tries to accelerate to full speed.

**Run winding** The main winding of magnet wire that produces the magnetic poles of the motor. The run (main) winding is designed to be connected to the power source during the motor-running operation. The run winding is typically larger gauge wire than the start winding and is placed deeper in the slots of the stator core.

**Slip** The difference in speed measured in rotations per minute between the synchronous speed of the rotating magnetic field of the stator, and the slower speed of the induction rotor. Slip is often expressed as a percentage using the formula:

$$\% \text{ Slip} = \frac{\text{Sync speed} - \text{Rotor speed}}{\text{Sync speed}} \times 100$$

**Split phase motor** A single-phase induction motor with main and auxiliary windings. The auxiliary windings are displaced in physical and magnetic position from, and temporarily connected in parallel to, the main windings.

**Squirrel-cage rotor** A rotating member of an induction motor with an iron core and conductors around the periphery. The conductors have induced voltage and resultant current flow as the rotating magnetic field spins on the stator. The stripped down rotor, without iron and with only the conducting bars, resembles a squirrel-cage exercise wheel.

**Start winding** An auxiliary winding in a motor stator that is intended to be connected to the power circuit only during the starting period of the motor. The winding provides the physical and magnetic displacement from the run winding needed to create a rotating magnetic field. The winding is automatically disconnected from the voltage source after a few seconds of starting time. The winding is typically smaller gauge wire than the main (run) winding and is installed nearer the inside of the stator opening.

**Synchronous speed** The speed of the rotating magnetic field around the stator core, measured in revolutions per minute (rpm).

## REVIEW QUESTIONS

1. Explain the right-hand rule for motors.
2. Equate the left-hand rule for generators to the right-hand rule for motors. How do they relate to each other?
3. Why does a single-phase AC waveform need to be split to operate as a single-phase motor?
4. How many actual magnetic pole windings are in a stator of a two-pole, single-phase motor?
5. How is the synchronous speed of an AC motor determined?
6. Explain why a squirrel-cage rotor receives voltage and current without an electrical connection.
7. If a stator has four poles, how many rotor poles are established?
8. Is the rotor pole ahead or behind the stator pole of the same magnetic polarity in the direction of rotation?
9. The formula for percent slip is _____.
10. Three-phase motors use this formula for synchronous speed: _____.
11. Why does a motor draw more line current if its mechanical load increases?
12. Why is the line current much larger for a motor starting than it is for running current?
13. Briefly describe the methods used for electronically controlling the speed of an AC motor.
14. How is PWM achieved in a VFD?

## PRACTICE PROBLEMS

1. Show the two possible connections (low and high voltage) for the dual coils in delta three-phase motors.
2. In Figure PP14–1, which direction will the rotor conductor try to move in the magnetic field shown?
3. If a single-phase motor has a synchronous speed of 1,200 rpm and is operating at 60 Hz, how many poles does it have?
4. A three-phase, four-pole motor is operating at 50 Hz. The actual rotor speed is 1,400 rpm. What is the percent slip?
5. If a three-phase motor is designated as a two-pole motor, how many physical poles are wound on the stator?
6. Using a VFD on a three-phase motor, if the frequency changes from 60 Hz to 40 Hz, what percent does the synchronous speed change?
7. On a dual-voltage, delta-connected motor that is rated for 240/480 V operation, each of the coil windings is rated _____ V.
8. How do you change the direction of rotation of a three-phase motor?
9. What would be the resultant if you were to add all the voltage vectors in a three-phase motor?
10. Why is a motor connection with one common coil connection point referred to as a wye-connected motor?

**Figure PP14–1**

# 15

# TRANSFORMERS

# T O P I C S

PRINCIPLES OF TRANSFORMATION

VOLTAGE, CURRENT, AND POWER
    CHARACTERISTICS

CALCULATIONS FOR PRIMARY AND
    SECONDARY WINDINGS

CHARACTERISTICS OF TRANSFORMER
    OPERATION

TRANSFORMER IMPEDANCE

TRANSFORMER LEAD MARKING

SINGLE-PHASE TRANSFORMER
    CONNECTIONS

MULTI-COIL TRANSFORMERS

THREE-PHASE TRANSFORMER CONNECTIONS

# O V E R V I E W

As you have studied the effects and the characteristics of AC systems, one feature of AC circuits has been consistent: the effects of induction are typically involved when we have a conductor, a magnetic field, and motion. A transformer is an excellent application for the AC waveform that is constantly moving as time progresses. The voltage is continually increasing or decreasing. After studying this chapter, you will easily understand the operation of a transformer that has no moving parts.

This chapter ties the theory of generation you have learned to the operation of motors and other devices that work on AC power. The transformer allows us to increase or decrease the voltage, or increase or decrease the current, as we apply it to various situations, such as distribution systems and power supplies. The transformer allows us to "step up" the voltage and transmit power over long distances and then "step down" the voltage to deliver it to customers at appropriate levels.

This chapter allows you to connect transformers in various circuit configurations to deliver the right voltage and current to a load. The transformer applications allow you to form a basic understanding of an entire AC system from generation, to transmission, to distribution, and finally to utilization.

# O B J E C T I V E S

After completing this chapter, you will be able to:
- Identify parts of a transformer
- Explain how a transformer transfers power
- Calculate voltage, current, and power of a transfer based on formulas
- Describe losses in a transformer
- Identify types of coil and core arrangements
- Identify lead marking and additive or subtractive polarity transformers
- Connect transformer windings in basic circuit configurations

## PRINCIPLES OF TRANSFORMATION

The basic premise of transformers is simple. The concept simply is to create a magnetic field with one conductor—coiled up—and allow that magnetic field to react with another conductor coiled up. The basic isolation transformer is shown in a schematic view in Figure 15–1. The conductor on the left receives voltage and current from a source. This conductor is typically wound around an iron core and is called the primary winding. The primary winding has all the properties of a coil studied so far. Namely, it has resistance, exhibits inductive reactance, and has a magnetic field that surrounds the conductor and creates magnetic polarities. The magnetic polarities of the coil ends can be found at any instantaneous value

**For further reading, perform an Internet search on "vibrators and step-up transformers" or "pulse transformers."**

of the AC wave by using the direction of current flow and the left-hand rule for coils. This magnetic field is constantly changing intensity as the AC current waveform constantly either increases or decreases. As the current changes, the magnetic field expands or contracts and then changes direction. This AC magnetic field gives the needed component for induction—the component of movement.

Figure 15–2a is used to illustrate the action of primary current creating primary flux. Current flows into the negative terminal and out the positive terminal of the primary coil, as with other electrical loads connected to a supply. The primary flux, as verified by the left-hand rule for conductors, expands and is transferred to the secondary coils through the iron core material. As the primary flux moves through the secondary conductors, it induces a voltage with a direction of current flow, as verified by the left-hand rule for conductors. If an electrical load is connected to the secondary, secondary current flows. Notice that the current inside the secondary winding of the transformer flows from the positive terminal toward the negative terminal (Figure 15–2a). The negative terminal of a supply is where current leaves the supply, flowing through the load and back to the positive terminal of the supply. Therefore, the secondary current leaves the negative terminal but flows positive to negative inside the transformer secondary. Refer to Figure 15–2b to see the effects of the secondary current flowing to the load. As secondary current flows, it creates its own magnetic flux. Using the left-hand rule for a coil verifies that the magnetic field created by the secondary current flow has a north pole at the top, compared to the primary coil that has a north pole at the bottom. The magnetic fields are in opposite directions. The effects of this interaction of magnetic fluxes can be determined when reviewing the waveforms in a later section titled "Characteristics of Transformer Operation."

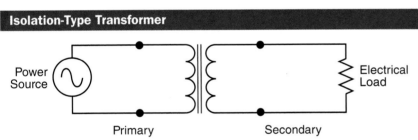

**Isolation-Type Transformer**

Power Source — Primary — Secondary — Electrical Load

**Figure 15–1** An isolation-type transformer has primary and secondary windings.

## FieldNote!

Transformers do not transform DC. The basic premise of a transformer is that it has no moving mechanical parts yet induces voltage and therefore current into an adjacent coil of wire. The generator and a motor are examples of physical movement that allows the induction process to take place. A transformer only has the movement of an expanding and contracting magnetic field, powered by an AC current. DC is considered a steady value, so the element of motion by the magnetic field is not achieved. You may occasionally see a transformer marked as "DC," a misnomer, but it is usually in part of an assembly working with other components that create AC for the transformation or create DC as part of a power supply.

**Creation of Magnetic Fields**

(a)

(b)

**Figure 15–2** (a) The primary current creates a flux that is transferred through the iron core to cut the conductors of the secondary winding. (b) The primary and secondary coil windings both create magnetic fields that are opposite in polarity to each other when current flows.

Referring back to Figure 15–1, you can see that the electrical load is connected to the secondary. A load current then flows in the secondary circuit. The transformer has transferred electrical energy from one circuit (primary) to another circuit (secondary) with no electrical connection. Only magnetic coupling is used to transfer the energy from one conductor to another.

# VOLTAGE, CURRENT, AND POWER CHARACTERISTICS

Transformers are usually used to change the level of the voltage or current but are not designed to use electrical power or create electrical power.

The main purpose of most transformers is to transfer energy while changing the voltage level of the circuit between primary and secondary. Using this concept of transferring energy without creating or using it allows us to understand transformer action.

As the primary winding receives current from the source, it creates a flux based on the applied voltage and the number of turns of wire. The greater the voltage applied, the greater the current flow and, therefore, the greater the created magnetic flux. This flux is distributed equally among the number of conductor turns to give a value of **volts per turn** as a comparative term. This tells us that that there is flux in the primary windings and the more windings, the lower the volts per turn—compared to a primary with few turns. Likewise, a large voltage applied to a fixed number of turns has a larger volts-per-turn ratio compared to the same number of turns and a lower voltage applied.

Volts per turn is an indicator of the amount of magnetic field produced by the primary. If there is good magnetic coupling between the primary and the secondary coils, almost all the primary flux interacts with the secondary winding. In other words, the primary flux cuts through the secondary conductors. The secondary has the same amount of magnetic flux as the primary, and it too has a comparative term of volts per turn. If this is the case, then Volts-per-turn primary = Volts-per-turn secondary. By determining how many turns are used in the secondary and the volts-per-turn ratio, you can determine the secondary voltage.

Another important concept is the reaction of the current. Assume a load is connected to the secondary and current is flowing. The maximum amount of secondary current that can flow without damaging the transformer is based on the design and that current is neither generated nor used in the transformation process. The voltage level between the primary and the secondary relates to the number of windings in the primary and the secondary coils. The number of volts times the maximum amount of current in the primary yields one rating of the transformer measure in volt-amps. As you have studied, this is a measurement of apparent power. The apparent power indicates how much energy enters the primary windings. If essentially no power is deliberately consumed in the transformer, the same amount of apparent power is delivered to the secondary winding and consequently delivered to the load. Using this concept, if the voltage on the primary is higher than the voltage on the secondary, then the current on the primary must be lower than the current on the secondary. The product of primary volts × primary amps must be the same as secondary volts × secondary amps.

The power rating of the transformer is rated in volt-amps because the transformer is designed to transform voltage and current and has no influence on how that power is used. It could be used as watts, volts-amps reactive, or volt-amps. The windings are designed to transform the voltage level based on the number of windings, and the current is based on the circular-mil size of the windings. Larger currents require larger conductors, and smaller currents only need smaller conductors. Therefore, the conductor size and the number of turns dictate the maximum current and voltage the transformer can handle without overheating or being destroyed.

## CALCULATIONS FOR PRIMARY AND SECONDARY WINDINGS

The calculations needed for transformer applications are basic algebra equations.

Power in = power out ($VA_{in} = VA_{out}$),

which is considered the basis for all other calculations. Although the statement is not entirely true, it is the assumption for almost all calculations.

It is not entirely true because there are losses in the transformer in the form of poor magnetic coupling and heat in the core, created by eddy current, hysteresis, and copper losses.

For most transformers, the amount of power lost in the transformer is inconsequential compared to the amount of volt-amps transformed. Unless you are doing transformer efficiency calculations, you should generally ignore the losses as too small to worry about.

The formulas for voltage ratios, current ratios, and turns ratios are as follows:

$$\frac{E_P}{E_S} = \frac{N_P}{N_S} = \frac{I_P}{I_S}$$

Where:

$E_P$ = Voltage applied to the primary

$E_S$ = Voltage developed on the secondary

$N_P$ = Number of turns in the primary winding

$N_S$ = Number of turns on the secondary winding

$I_P$ = Current flowing in the primary winding

$I_S$ = Current that could flow in the secondary winding

## TechTip!

The Energy Policy Act of 2005, also known as the "energy bill," created standards for transformer efficiency in the United States. In October 2005, the Department of Energy put the information as shown in Table 15–1 into effect for dry-type transformers. Specifically, these dry-type transformers use air for cooling and are rated as "low voltage," meaning the input and output voltages are under 600 V. Table 15–1 is a partial listing. Notice the efficiency ratings that indicate that little power is lost in the transformation.

**Table 15–1**

| Single-Phase kVA | Efficiency | Three-Phase kVA | Efficiency |
|---|---|---|---|
| 25 | 98.0% | 30 | 97.5% |
| 50 | 98.3% | 75 | 98.0% |
| 75 | 98.5% | 150 | 98.3% |
| 100 | 98.6% | 300 | 98.6% |
| 25 | 98.8% | 750 | 98.8% |

**Note:** Most distribution-size transformers are rated in kilovolt-amps. Instead of listing a transformer as 75,000 VA, it is listed as 75 kVA.

Efficiency of Single-Phase and Three-Phase Dry-Type Transformers

## Example

If the primary winding has 100 turns and 100 V applied and there are 200 turns on the secondary, what is the secondary voltage?

**Solution:**

(Solve as a ratio problem by cross-multiplying.)

$$\frac{E_P}{E_S} = \frac{N_P}{N_S}$$

$$\frac{100}{E_S} = \frac{100}{200}$$

$$E_S = \frac{100 \times 200}{100}$$

$$= 200 \text{ V}$$

## Example

If the primary voltage is 240 V and the secondary voltage is 120 V, when there is 10 A in the secondary, what is the primary current?

**Solution:**

(Solve as a ratio problem by cross-multiplying.)

$$\frac{E_P}{E_S} = \frac{I_S}{I_P}$$

$$\frac{240}{120} = \frac{10}{I_P}$$

$$I_P = \frac{120 \times 10}{240}$$

$$= 5 \text{ A}$$

## Example

If a 500 VA transformer has a 100 V primary and a 2:1 turns ratio, what is the voltage and current of the secondary?

**Solution:**

$$P = E \times I$$

$$I_P = \frac{P}{E}$$

$$= \frac{500}{100}$$

$$= 5 \text{ A (current of the primary windings)}$$

AND (Solve as a ratio problem by cross-multiplying.)

$$\frac{N_P}{N_S} = \frac{I_S}{I_P}$$

$$\frac{2}{1} = \frac{I_S}{5 \text{ A}}$$

$$I_S = \frac{5 \text{ A} \times 2}{1}$$

$$= 10 \text{ A}$$

AND

$$\frac{E_P}{E_S} = \frac{N_P}{N_S}$$

$$\frac{100 \text{ V}}{E_S} = \frac{2}{1}$$

$$E_S = \frac{100 \text{ V}}{2}$$

$$= 50 \text{ V}$$

Verify:

$$100 \text{ V} \times 5 \text{ A primary} = 50 \text{ V} \times 10 \text{ A secondary}$$

## FieldNote!

There are other methods to change the voltage levels of AC circuits. With the advent of more reliable and higher power electronic components, it becomes possible to alter voltages electronically. Generally speaking, these electronic voltage manipulations are created for particular loads with known operating parameters. These "electronic transformations" do not use the traditional iron cores found in transformers, so they are lighter and cheaper to construct. For higher power applications or nonspecific loads, the iron core transformer is still used extensively.

The ratio of the currents is inversely proportional to the ratios for the voltage and the turns. This maintains the effect of changing voltages and resultant currents yet maintains the volt-amp rating from primary to secondary. The terms **step-up transformer** and **step-down transformer** refer to the transformation of voltage levels and not to current levels. A transformer that isolates the primary and secondary circuits is called an **isolation transformer.** This type of transformer normally has the same primary and secondary voltage and simply separates electrical systems so that no electrical connection exists between the windings.

## CHARACTERISTICS OF TRANSFORMER OPERATION

Transformers come in many configurations. Refer to Figure 15–3 for a core-type transformer where one half of the primary winding and one half of the secondary windings are on each leg of the core. The process of winding first one coil and then the other coil over the first is referred to as concentric winding. The process of using both legs with part of the primary and secondary winding on each leg reduces the transformer losses that result from flux leakage. Generally, the lower voltage winding is placed nearest to the iron core and the higher voltage winding is wound on top of the low voltage winding. Notice in the diagram that it appears as if the core is made of layers of iron sheets. In fact, the iron core is made of many laminations of thin iron pieces. Laminating the iron reduces the losses due to eddy currents. Remember that eddy currents are internal electrical currents that flow through the iron as the magnetic fields are constantly changing and actually inducing current into the core. By laminating the core, the resistance to eddy currents is increased and the losses are reduced compared to a piece of solid iron.

One of the other losses in the iron of the transformer is due to hysteresis. Hysteresis is the opposition to a changing magnetic field within a magnetized material. The molecules must realign each time the magnetic field changes, which is constantly, within the iron core of an energized transformer. The hysteresis losses are in the form of heat, which is another watt loss in the transfer of power from primary to secondary. The use of low hysteresis steel (high-silicon content) reduces the losses due to hysteresis.

One of the most common types of transformer core is the shell type, as shown in Figure 15–4. The lower-voltage winding, either primary or secondary, is wound first on the core. The reason for using a lower-voltage winding first is that the insulation on the **magnet wire** can be a lower rating and still not break down next to the grounded core. The higher voltage winding is wound on top of the other winding, and nearly 100% flux linkage occurs between the primary and the secondary windings. Figure 15–5 shows an H-type core. This core is a little more expensive to make but results in even less flux leakage and improves the efficiency of the transformer.

## FieldNote!

Typically, the conductor windings on a core-type transformer are wound with the lower voltage nearest the core and the higher voltage winding wound on top of the lower voltage coil.

**Core-Type Transformer**

**Figure 15–3** A core-type transformer has half of the primary and half of the secondary windings on each leg.

**Shell-Type Transformer**

**Figure 15–4** A shell-type transformer has center-mounted windings.

**H-Type Transformer**

**Figure 15–5** An H-type core transformer, often called a type-H core transformer, is more efficient than a shell-type transformer.

The basic function of each winding and the general location of the windings have been identified. The actual transfer of power through magnetic coupling can now be examined. Refer to Figure 15–6 to view the waveforms of voltage and current that occur in the primary and secondary windings. We make some assumptions for a perfect transformer even though we know the actual transformer waveforms are a little different. The primary voltage causes a primary current and a primary flux. You can see the effects of the flux in Figure 15–2a. With no electrical load connected to the secondary, the flux also produces a large counterelectromotive force (CEMF) in the primary winding and the current is impeded and, therefore, kept to a low value. This small primary current with no secondary current is the magnetizing current. As electrical load current flows in the secondary, the secondary current produces a magnetic flux opposite to the primary flux because of the direction

*Note:* This illustration displays the *E* and *I* waveform relationships under no load. If an inductive load was added to the secondary, then the *E* and *I* waveforms would not be aligned or in phase.

of the secondary current and the winding direction. The secondary flux is 180° out of phase with the primary flux as seen in Figures 15–2b and 15–6. The effect of the secondary flux is to reduce the effect that the primary flux has on the primary winding. The counterflux of the secondary reduces the CEMF of the primary winding by changing the magnetic effects on the coil. Now, with reduced CEMF on the primary circuit, more current flows in the primary. As we continue to draw more current on the secondary, the primary current also increases until the volt-amp rating of the transformer design is exceeded. The power factor of the load affects the transformer's actual waveform relationships between secondary and primary. The power factor of the load is not transferred identically from the secondary to the primary.

Compare the magnetic field sine wave of the primary to the magnetic field waveform of the secondary. The two fields are 180° out of phase (exactly opposite). When there is current flow in the secondary, the magnetic field of the secondary opposes, or cancels, some of the effect of the primary. With no current in the secondary, or no electrical load connected, the primary acts as a coil with a CEMF produced by the magnetic self-induction, known as inductive reactance ($X_L$).

There is current in the primary, but it is limited by the $X_L$ to a small amount. This small primary current with no secondary current is referred to as **exciting current** or **magnetizing current.** When a load is connected to the secondary, current flows through the secondary coil and the magnetic field produced negates some of the effect of the primary flux. The reduced flux of the primary does not produce as much CEMF in the primary, and the primary line current increases. The result is that as we draw more current from the secondary the primary current increases. This is a result of the interaction between the primary flux and the secondary flux.

## Voltage, Current, and Flux Waveforms

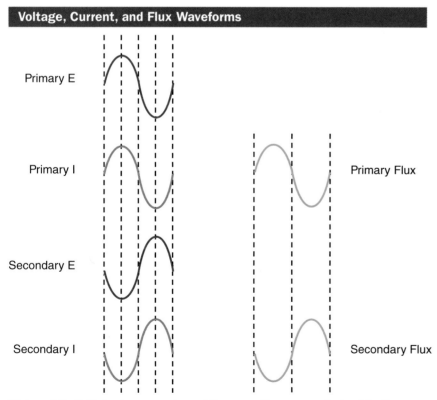

Primary E

Primary I

Primary Flux

Secondary E

Secondary I

Secondary Flux

**Figure 15–6** Voltage, current, and flux waveforms are derived in the primary and secondary circuits of a transformer.

# TRANSFORMER IMPEDANCE

As mentioned, the impedance of the coils (the $X_L$ and the $R$) in the transformer affects how the transformer works. One of the ratings for a transformer is the percent impedance rating. This rating is based on the full load ratings of the transformer and how much impedance is introduced to the power delivery system. The impedance is created in the transformer by these factors:

- Type of core, which affects the percentage of coupling
- Type of iron influencing permeability
- Wire size and type affecting wire resistance
- Number of turns of wire in the windings affecting the inductance

The percent impedance determines how much current can pass through the transformer under the extreme conditions of a short-circuited secondary. If the transformer has a short circuit on the secondary, the impedance of the supply transformer determines the available fault current at the transformer secondary.

To find the percent impedance of a transformer when not available on the nameplate, a test procedure is required. Figure 15–7 shows a single-phase transformer with a variable AC voltage source connected to the primary winding. The transformer secondary winding is shorted with an ammeter connected to measure the secondary current. The primary voltage is increased slowly from zero while watching the secondary amps. We increase the primary voltage until the secondary amperage is the full-rated secondary current. This process of allowing current to flow in the secondary with only a small AC voltage in the primary tells us how much the transformer impedes current flow to the secondary. To calculate percent impedance, use the following formula:

$$\% \text{ Impedance transformer} = \frac{\text{AC voltage reading of primary source voltage}}{\text{Rated primary voltage}} \times 100$$

### Example

A 25 kVA single-phase transformer rated 480 V primary 240 V secondary is tested for percent impedance. The test source voltage reaches 24 VAC when the shorted secondary current reaches 104.17 A. What is the percent impedance?

**Solution:**

$$\% Z = \frac{\text{Test voltage}}{\text{Rated voltage}} \times 100$$

$$= \frac{24 \text{ V}}{480 \text{ V}} \times 100$$

$$= 5\%$$

### Test for Transformer Impedance

**Figure 15–7** To test for transformer impedance, short-circuit the secondary and then measure the full secondary current with a small test voltage on the primary.

The percent impedance is used to determine the compatibility of transformer paralleling and to calculate the secondary fault current if a short occurs in the secondary. This fault current is used for calculations regarding arc flash hazards with power systems. Systems need design criteria for fuses and circuit breakers that can safely interrupt the fault currents available on the system. These ratings are found on circuit protection and other equipment as the interrupting current (IC) rating, or the fault current that the equipment must be able to withstand. The amount of energy available immediately in a short-circuit accident is tremendous.

The formula for finding the short-circuit current, or fault current, when normal full voltage is applied to the primary is:

$$I_{\text{short circuit}} = \frac{I_{\text{full load secondary}} \times 100}{\% \text{ Impedance}}$$

### Example

A 25 kVA single-phase transformer is rated for 480 V primary 240 V secondary and a 5% impedance. How much fault current would the transformer have at the secondary terminals if a short circuit occurred?

**Solution:**

Find the secondary full load current:

$$\text{Secondary full load current} = \frac{\text{Transformer VA}}{\text{Secondary volts}}$$

$$= \frac{25,000 \text{ VA}}{240 \text{ V}} = 104.17 \text{ A}$$

Find the short circuit current at the secondary:

$$\text{Secondary short circuit current} = \frac{\text{Full lead sec current} \times 100}{\% \text{ Transformer impedance}}$$

$$= \frac{104.17 \text{ A} \times 100}{5} = 2,083.4 \text{ A}$$

## Transformer Lead Markings

**Figure 15–8** Single-phase transformer lead markings for single-voltage and dual-voltage windings.

# TRANSFORMER LEAD MARKING

Transformer leads (or bushings) are marked to provide the user with identification as the transformers are connected into different configurations of use. As you view the transformer, the higher voltage winding is marked with "H" designations and numbered H1 to H4, or other H markings. Look at Figure 15–8. The schematic view of the transformer shows the high-voltage connection on the top side and starts with H1 on the top left. This is a consistent marking standard. The other side of the same coil windings is always H2.

## Polarity Lead Markings

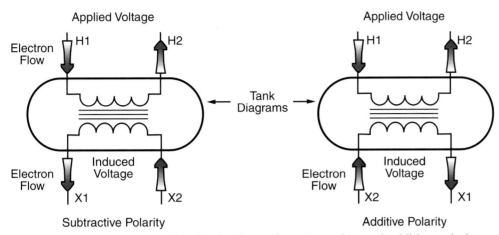

**Figure 15–9** Standard identification is shown for subtractive and additive polarity lead markings.

As you view the schematic, the low voltage winding has "X" designations. The X designation varies as to where X1 starts—on the bottom left or the bottom right. The difference is a part of a marking agreement that categorizes the transformer into **subtractive polarity** or **additive polarity.** The standard identification for the low-voltage side is shown in Figure 15–9. The process has nothing to do with the transformer principles, only with the means of bringing the leads from the internal coils out to the external connection points.

To determine the lead marking of a transformer where the secondary markings are not present or are not clear, use the process shown in Figure 15–10. Use a small applied AC voltage to the high-voltage coil and place a jumper from H1 to the secondary lead that comes out of the transformer on the same side as H1. Now measure voltage from H2 to the other secondary coil lead. If the measured voltage is less than the applied voltage, then the transformer is wound as a subtractive polarity transformer and H1 is adjacent to X1. If the reading is more than the applied voltage, the transformer is wound as an additive polarity and H1 is adjacent to X2. The small battery symbols shown on the transformer winding in Figure 15–10 help explain the instantaneous voltage that is encountered during the measurement.

## Polarity Tests

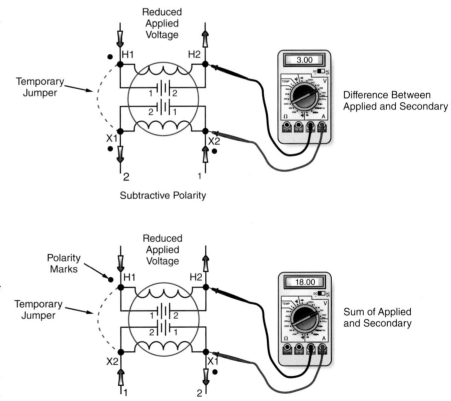

**Figure 15–10** Tests can be made for polarity and proper lead marking for additive or subtractive transformers.

## TechTip!

Figure 15–10 is a representation of the instantaneous voltages that occur in the transformer winding represented by batteries. The battery symbols are indications of the voltage values available at the same instant in time. The polarity marks are additional indications that tell the user where current enters the transformer (the marked H lead) and where current leaves the transformer secondary (the marked secondary lead). The subtractive polarity shows the two battery voltages opposing each other. The additive polarity shows the two battery voltages aiding each other. These permanent marks are helpful on instrument transformers if the lead markings are destroyed.

It is important to note that the primary is a load to the supply and the polarities show electron flow from negative to positive. The secondary is a source of voltage and the internal voltage shows the current flow within the source going from positive to negative. Refer to the secondary electrical polarities and note that current is leaving X1 going to the load and returning to X2 from the load in both test connections. The battery polarity internal to the supply now makes sense, and you can see why the two coil voltages oppose each other in the subtractive polarity and aid each other in the additive polarity.

Once the lead marking is established as correct, transformers can be connected in various patterns and the instantaneous polarities and the output waveforms are synchronized.

## SINGLE-PHASE TRANSFORMER CONNECTIONS

Single-phase transformers transform one sine wave of one voltage source at the input to another single sine wave of a new voltage source at the output. The coils that are wound on the core can be one single primary winding to one single secondary winding, as already discussed. A variation of this process is to wind two separate coils for the primary and two coils for the secondary, as illustrated in Figure 15–11. In this illustration, the transformer is being used as a step-down transformer, with each primary coil rated for 230 V and each secondary coil rated for 115 V. With this pattern, the primary could be connected for up to 460 V by placing the two coils in series. Do this by connecting a jumper from H2 to H3 and applying 460 V to H1 and H4. The coils can be connected in parallel by connecting H1 to H3 (odd-numbered leads), connecting H2 to H4 (even-numbered leads), and applying 230 V across H1 and H2.

**Single-Phase Transformer**

460 V Primary: Connect H2 to H3

230 V Primary: Connect H1 to H3, H2 to H4

230 V Secondary: Connect X2 to X3

115 V Secondary: Connect X1 to X3, X2 to X4

**Figure 15–11** A dual-voltage primary and a dual-voltage secondary as used for a single-phase transformer.

The secondary coils can be connected in series as well, X2 to X3, and the output voltage of 230 V is taken from X1 and X4. Parallel connections of the secondary coils (odd numbers connected together and then even numbers connected together) produce 115 V output. So, for this example, the voltage can be 460/230, 230/230, 230/115, 460/115. The primary is the first voltage, and the secondary voltage is after the backslash. The rating of the transformer is rated with all windings connected to give the maximum kilovolt-amp transformation.

If a single transformer does not have enough kilovolt-amps to power the load, more transformers can be connected in parallel. Figure 15–12 illustrates a transformer with a single-voltage primary and a dual-voltage secondary. It is extremely important that the markings on the leads are correct for this type of connection. If the leads are not providing voltage in phase with each other, short circuits and damage can result. Notice that the H1 leads of both transformers are connected together, as well as both H2 leads, to place the primaries in parallel. Both secondaries are configured for the same secondary voltage, and the X4 leads are connected in parallel, as well as the X1 leads. The current splits at the primary, energizing both primary windings, and both secondaries add to the output current. The total kilovolt-amps of the bank of two transformers is the sum of the two individual kilovolt-amp ratings. The two ratings do not have to be identical, but the voltage input and output must be identical.

# MULTI-COIL TRANSFORMERS

As previously discussed, transformers come in many patterns for specific applications. One such style of transformer is a single-phase transformer used to step down distribution voltages for residential, single-family dwellings.

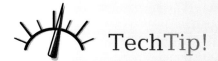

## TechTip!

When electron flow enters H1, representing some point on the sine wave, electron flow leaves X1 at the exact same point in time. This fact is of little consequence when using a single isolation transformer. If the windings need to be connected in parallel or series, or if a three-phase circuit is constructed, the instantaneous current flow direction is critical. If the coils are connected together and expected to aid each other and the currents are flowing in opposite directions, then a short circuit results.

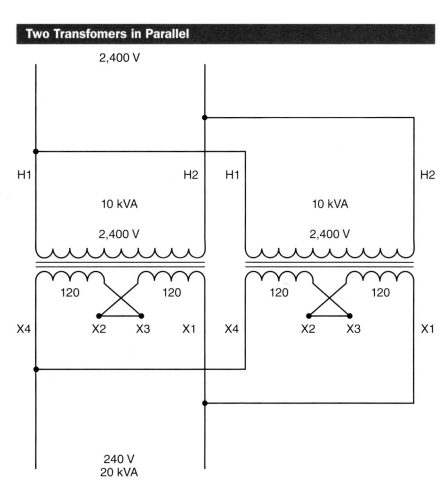

**Figure 15–12** Two 10 kVA transformers in parallel deliver 20 kVA to the load.

*Note:* This transformer has six taps, with three 2½% taps for voltage below nominal and three 2½% taps for voltage above nominal. These terms are used in manufacturers' descriptions of their transformers.

The transformer in Figure 15–13 is an example of this type of transformer, although the primary voltage can be much different from the standard normal rating depending on the distribution feeder. As you see in the illustration, the primary has many tap points so that the volts per turn can be adjusted based on the actual voltage encountered in the field. In this case, the primary voltage could be anywhere between 516 and 444 V and the number of windings on the primary can be adjusted from maximum to minimum. The effect is to create the correct volts per turn on the primary to yield the proper flux and produce 240 V across the two secondary coils.

A standard secondary voltage system is created as 240 V across two coils with a connection point in the middle that is grounded. This establishes a three-wire, single-phase supply rated at 120 or 240 V with a nominal 115 to 230 V. Figure 15–14 shows another transformer with loads connected to the secondary three-wire system. Some loads operate at 120 V, as in L1 to neutral or L2 to neutral, and some loads are connected directly from L1 to L2 for 240 V. If you were to view the 240 V sine wave, it would appear as one large sine wave. The waveforms from L1 or L2 to neutral also appear as a single sine wave at one-half the amplitude of the L1 to L2 waveform.

**Transformer with Multiple Taps**

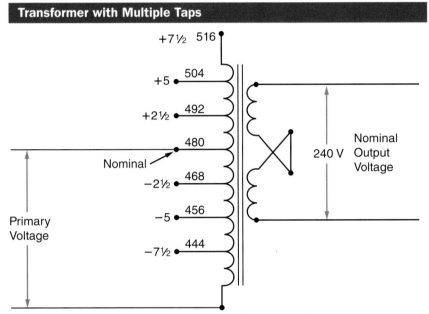

**Figure 15–13** A transformer with multiple taps on the primary can be adjusted for various supply voltages.

**Single-Phase Three-Wire System**

**Figure 15–14** This single-phase three-wire system has loads at 120 V to neutral and 240 V line to line.

## THREE-PHASE TRANSFORMER CONNECTIONS

You now know how single-phase transformers operate using mutual induction and the designed ratio be-tween the primary and the secondary windings. You can perform the same transformer actions with three-phase systems. Figure 15–15 is a pictorial view of three single-phase transformers connected to provide all three phases for a secondary load of a three-phase motor and several single-phase loads.

**Figure 15–15** This wye-wye transformer pattern has three-phase and single-phase loads.

The system depicted in Figure 15–15 is called a wye-wye because the schematic view of the coils appears as in Figure 15–16 and resembles the capital letter Y. As can be noted in the pattern, each transformer transforms one phase. The voltage on each coil is 2,400 V on the primary. The line-to-line voltage is actually 1.732 ($\sqrt{3}$) times the phase voltage of 2,400 V. This is the nominal line voltage of 4,160 V, but only 2,400 V is across each coil from H1 to H2. This factor of 1.732 is a constant used in three-phase systems because adding voltages arithmetically is not possible as the voltages are 120° out of phase.

Figure 15–16 also shows the secondary connected in a wye pattern, with the center point of the wye grounded to create a neutral point reference to ground. This connection forms a three-phase, four-wire wye system. Each transformer steps each phase down from 2,400 to 120 V, or at a 20:1 ratio. The secondary coils are delivering 120 V each, and an individual sine wave is 120° apart from the other sine waves. We can again add the phases that are 120° apart by vector addition. The same factor of $\sqrt{3}$ or the agreed-upon factor

of 1.732 is used to determine the line-to-line voltage: 120 V × 1.732 = 208 V. You can see how 120 V single-phase loads are connected from line to neutral or across the coils of the secondary. In addition, the motor is connected for 208 V, and it uses all three phases to operate as an induction motor.

The other major connection pattern is the delta connection. Refer to Figure 15–17 for a wiring diagram view of the connection as a three-wire delta primary and a four-wire delta secondary. Figure 15–18 depicts schematically how the three individual phases are connected. With this pattern, in the secondary, we have a lot of three-phase power and only one phase supplying the single phase of 120 to 240 V. This pattern, known as the four-wire delta, has another voltage that is peculiar to this arrangement. The voltage from the ground to the top phase connection is 1.732 × the line to neutral voltage. For this example, the "phase with the higher voltage to ground," known as the "high leg" or "wild leg," is 1.732 × 120 V = 208 V. Care must be taken not to get this leg mixed up with the other two when connecting 120 V loads.

## Wye-Wye Schematic

**Figure 15–16** This wye-wye schematic pattern shows example voltages.

## Delta-Delta Wiring Diagram

**Figure 15–17** A delta-delta connection pattern for three single-phase transformers is a three-phase arrangement.

## Delta-Delta Schematic

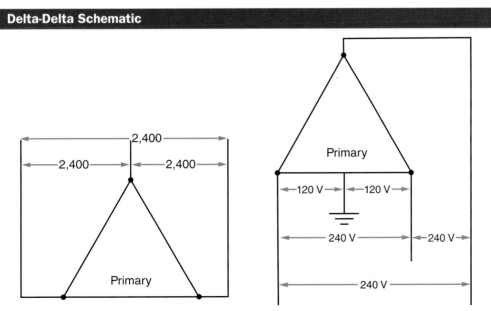

**Figure 15–18** A delta-delta pattern with a three-phase four-wire secondary provides three-phase and single-phase power.

The line-to-line voltage in a delta pattern is the same as the phase voltage, unlike the arrangement in a wye system. The volt-amp rating of these three-phase patterns is three times the single-phase kilovolt-amps if all the single-phase transformers are the same.

Many connections and transformer calculations create the desired voltages, currents, and kilovolt-amps required by the load. These two patterns are examples of how the voltage can be transformed to yield various voltages and supply various loads. Books on transformers can be used to study transformers in more detail as your education continues.

## SUMMARY

This chapter is a primer on transformation of AC voltages and currents. This is by no means the complete coverage of transformer types, styles, or connection patterns. You have studied the basic concepts of transformer action that uses the three conditions for induction, with a moving magnetic field providing the motion. A discussion focused on how voltage, current, and power are transferred through the transformer without an electrical connection. The supporting calculations for basic transformer applications have been provided.

Coil characteristics and transformer lead markings that allow you to connect transformers in standard connections were also discussed. Slightly more complex multi-coil transformers were presented to allow you to see that many variations and applications are used to provide the correct current, voltage, and power to the load being served. Single-phase transformers and popular three-phase connections allow you to see how common voltages you need for electrical loads such as motors can be delivered from AC generation systems. Something important to the installer is the voltage taps designed into the transformer. The transformer is designed to operate at nominal primary voltage, such as 480 V. Because of line resistance and other plant loads, however, the actual primary voltage may be 468 V. Voltage taps allow the installer to accommodate this problem.

## CHAPTER GLOSSARY

**Exciting current or magnetizing current** A relatively small current used to magnetize the core of a transformer but does not provide for the secondary load current. It is the primary current when no electrical load is connected to the transformer secondary.

**Isolation transformer** An electrical transformer usually designed to have the same level of voltage at the secondary terminals that it has on the primary terminals. No electrical connection exists between the primary and the secondary, creating a separate secondary circuit "isolated" from the original source.

**Magnet wire** Wire with a coating of insulating varnish that provides the voltage rating for the wire. The wire is specifically designed to be used in coil winding of motors, generators, or coils. The wire fits into slots for easy winding and is used to produce a magnetic field.

**Step-down transformer** An electrical transformer designed to have a lower voltage at the secondary terminals than it had at the primary terminals.

**Step-up transformer** An electrical transformer designed to have a higher voltage at the secondary output than it has at the primary input.

**Subtractive or additive polarity** Polarity refers to the secondary lead markings when compared to the primary lead markings. With a subtractive polarity transformer, if the leads are brought out so that H1 and X1 are connected together, a voltmeter between H2 and X2 reads the difference between the primary and the secondary. An additive polarity transformer indicates that if H1 and X2 are connected together a voltmeter between H2 and X1 will read the sum of the two coil voltages.

**Volts per turn** Volts per turn is used as a reference point for the amount of magnetic flux produced by a coil. (The more volts per turn, the more flux.) It is not a specific unit of measure but a way to relate the primary turns and voltage to the secondary turns and voltage.

## REVIEW QUESTIONS

1. Describe what is meant by primary and secondary windings of a transformer.
2. Explain what is meant by a step-up transformer.
3. Why would an isolation transformer be used?
4. If the secondary of the transformer has one-half the turns of the primary, what is the relation to the transformer voltages?
5. Explain why transformers are not rated in watts.
6. Explain why the current ratio is inverse to the voltage ratio.
7. Why does the primary circuit of a transformer have current even when there is no load in the secondary?
8. Why is the polarity of the transformer important?
9. Explain what is meant by a "high leg" on a transformer secondary.
10. Why are transformer cores made of laminated steel?

## PRACTICE PROBLEMS

1. A transformer has 10 A in the primary. The turns ratio is 1:4. What is the secondary current under full load?
2. A transformer has 120 V and 10 A on the secondary. What is the transformer primary volt-amp rating?
3. When connecting three-phase transformers in a wye pattern and the coil voltage is 120 V, what is the line-to-line voltage?
4. Using Figure PP15–1, show how to connect a transformer for 460 V primary and 115 V secondary.
5. What is the total kilovolt-amp rating of two 50 kVA transformers connected in parallel with each other?
6. If the voltage changes on a step down transformer from 480 V to 240 V, what is the turns ratio?

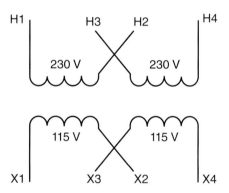

**Figure PP15–1**

7. What is the secondary current on a 4:1 step down transformer if the primary current is 25 A?

8. Find the short circuit current at the secondary of a single-phase transformer with the following information: 25 kVA, 240/120 V, 6% impedance.

9. Using Figure PP15–2, identify the primary and secondary lead markings on the transformer and note whether it is additive or subtractive polarity.

10. Using Figure PP15–3, connect the three single-phase transformers to create a wye-wye, three-phase transformer bank to yield the voltages indicated.

**Figure PP15–2**

**Figure PP15–3**

## OVERVIEW

Calculations and analysis of circuits with only resistors can be easily performed using simple arithmetic, addition, subtraction, multiplication, and division. The only concern is to be certain that you pay attention to the sign of the calculation, that is, negative or positive. This is true whether the circuit being analyzed is AC or DC.

Mixing resistors, inductors, and capacitors into your calculations complicates the issue. Analysis of such circuits requires a more sophisticated approach to the mathematics, namely, the use of vectors.

In this appendix, we review how to solve systems vectors by adding, subtracting, multiplying, and dividing them. A proper understanding of vectors is necessary for you to understand the behavior of the variables in AC circuits that contain resistance, inductance, and capacitance.

Look at Figure A–1. The **reactance** (3 Ω) and **resistance** (4 Ω) in a circuit are at a 90° angle to each other and are acting on a common point. Vector analysis provides the means for calculating the combined or net effect of these two forces. In this example, the resulting combination is equal to a magnitude of 5 Ω and an angle of 36.9° from the horizontal axis.

Vectors are also used to show the phase relationships between voltage and current in AC circuits; therefore, you must rely heavily on vector mathematics to solve circuits with inductive and capacitive components.

This appendix also covers information on solving for the **resultant vector** value for any combination of multiple vectors, using several methods to solve those problems.

## SCALARS, VECTORS, AND PHASORS

### SCALARS

**Scalars** are numbers used to represent magnitude only; they do not take direction into consideration. Assume that you are lost in the woods. As you walk down the path, you come upon a sign like that shown in Figure A–2. Does this sign help? It tells you that it is 3 miles to the highway, but in which direction? This sign would represent a scalar because it contains only a magnitude. If the sign were firmly planted in the ground and had an arrow painted on it pointing toward the highway, it would become a vector because it contains both the magnitude and the direction. Figure A–3 represents a vector with both magnitude (3 miles) and direction (direction of arrow).

### VECTORS

A **vector** is a symbol that indicates both magnitude and direction. A vector tells not only *how much* but also *in what direction.*

**Vectors for Resistance, Reactance, and Impedance**

Net Effect = 5 (Impedance)

36.9°

Reactance

Resistance

Common Point (Origin)

**Figure A–1** The vector result is given for a reactance and a resistance in the same circuit.

**Scalar Value**

**Scalar Value**

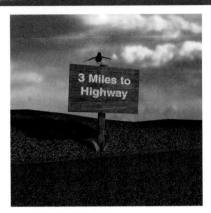

**Figure A–2** A scalar path sign shows only magnitude.

**Vector Value**

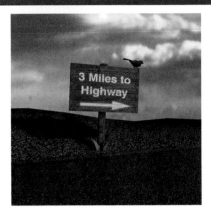

**Figure A–3** A vector path sign shows both magnitude and direction.

A vector is represented graphically by an arrow. The length of the arrow represents the magnitude. The tip of the arrow represents the direction of the vector and is identified by its angle of rotation from 0°. For example, the direction of the vector in Figure A–1 is 36.9° counterclockwise from the horizontal axis.

## PHASORS

A **phasor** is a vector that rotates. A voltage, current, or both in an AC circuit is represented by a phasor that rotates at the frequency of the AC waveform. Although phasors are somewhat more powerful and used differently than vectors, manipulation of them in the circuit analysis that you are working with is identical to manipulating vectors. The remainder of this appendix and text refer to all electrical quantities as vectors even though some of them are, strictly speaking, phasors.

## VECTOR REFERENCING

As stated previously, a vector is drawn as a straight line with an arrow placed at one end. The arrow represents the direction of the vector, and the line length represents the magnitude of the vector. The vector can represent any quantity, such as inches, miles, volts, amps, ohms, or the various units of power.

The zero reference (0°) is a horizontal line to the right. The direction or angle of other vectors is positive when measured in a counterclockwise direction. In Figure A–4, a vector with a magnitude of 4 is at angle 0°. The second vector is drawn with a magnitude of 3 at an angle of 45° from the first vector. The third vector of 4 at an angle of 90° is referenced from the first vector. It is important to note that the third vector is referenced from the 0° line and not to the previous vector at 45°.

Notice that the three vectors could also be referenced in a clockwise direction using the negative values. The first vector would still be 4 at 0°, the second would be 3 at −315°, and the third would be 4 at −270°.

**Vector Rotation**

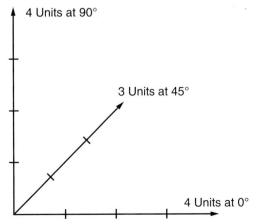

**Figure A–4** Vector counterclockwise rotation shows reference of magnitudes and angles.

## RECTANGULAR AND POLAR REPRESENTATION

So far in this appendix, all the vectors have been represented in what is called **polar form**: a magnitude and an angle. Vectors used in AC circuit analysis can also be referenced by expressing them as the vector sum of two other vectors that are at 90° from each other. This is called **rectangular form**.

## FieldNote!

Later in this section, you will see that it is possible to perform basic arithmetic operations (addition, multiplication, division) with vectors that are expressed in either the polar or the rectangular form. One application of these operations, working directly with vector math, is in solving problems related to circuit impedance. When calculating the total impedance in a parallel circuit comprised of branches that contain both resistance and reactance, you can use the product-over-sum equation, using a vector representing the impedance of each branch of the circuit. Therefore, the equation

$$Z_T = \frac{Z_1 \times Z_2}{Z_1 + Z_2}$$

can be used to find the combined impedance and the associated angle of the parallel branches. To do this, first multiply the two vectors for the numerator, find the sum of the two vectors for the denominator, and then divide the numerator by the denominator. For example, find the total impedance ($Z_T$) of two parallel branches of an AC circuit with one branch represented by an impedance ($Z$) of 6 at $\angle 30°$ and the second branch impedance of 5 at $\angle 60°$.

$$Z_T = \frac{6\angle 30° \times 5\angle 60°}{6\angle 30° + 5\angle 60°} = \frac{30\angle 90°}{10.6\angle 43.5°} = 2.9\angle 46.5°$$

Again, the required vector math is presented at the end of this section. Remember that the product-over-sum method can be used on only two branches at a time.

**Right Triangle with Sides Squared**

**Figure A–5** This right triangle has the sides squared.

For example, the vector shown in Figure A–1 can be expressed in polar form as 5 at an angle of 36.9°. This is usually written as 5∠36.9°. The vector in Figure A–1 can also be represented as the sum of one vector at 0° plus another vector at 90°. In this case, the 0° vector is 4 Ω long, and the 90° vector is 3 Ω long. The entire expression is usually given as 4 + i3 or 4 + j3, where +i or +j means that the second vector goes up vertically or 90°.

# RIGHT TRIANGLES AND TRIGONOMETRY

To manipulate vectors effectively, the electrician must be familiar with the characteristics and behavior of right triangles and the relationships of the sides of a right triangle. The next two sections describe these important concepts and serve as a refresher for your (probably) long-forgotten trigonometry studies.

### RIGHT TRIANGLES

Look at Figure A–5. A right triangle is a triangle that has a 90° angle. The **hypotenuse** is the longest side and is always the side that is opposite the 90° angle. Pythagoras of Samos figured out that the sum of the square areas bordered by each of the two sides of the right triangle would be equal to the square area bordered by the hypotenuse, or longest side. This is stated mathematically as follows:

$$c^2 = a^2 + b^2$$

Where:
$c$ = Length of the hypotenuse
$a$ = Length of one side
$b$ = Length of the other side

The previous equation is called the **Pythagorean Theorem** in honor of its discoverer. Using the Pythagorean Theorem, the hypotenuse in Figure A–5 can be found as follows:

$$c^2 = 8^2 + 6^2$$
$$= 64 + 36 = 100$$
$$c = \sqrt{c^2}$$
$$= 10$$

## Example

Look at Figure A–6. Which side is the hypotenuse? What is the length of the hypotenuse if two of the sides have values of 3 and 6?

**Solution:**

$$c^2 = a^2 + b^2$$
$$= 6^2 + 3^2$$
$$= 36 + 9$$
$$= 45$$
$$c = \sqrt{45} = 6.71$$

## SINES, COSINES, AND TANGENTS

Since the sides of a right triangle have a mathematical relationship to each other (the Pythagorean Theorem), it should come as no surprise that the ratios of the various sides of the right triangle also have specific values.

Figure A–7 is a right triangle with the various sides and angles labeled. Each angle has a side opposite and a side adjacent to it. Table A–1 shows the relationships of each angle to each of the sides. Use Figure A–7 and Table A–1 to understand the definitions given in Table A–2.

**Pythagorean Theorem**

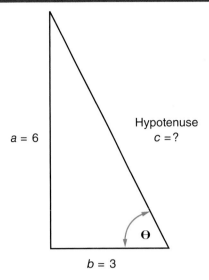

$$c^2 = a^2 + b^2$$

**Figure A–6** The Pythagorean Theorem is illustrated in this example.

**Opposing and Adjacent Sides**

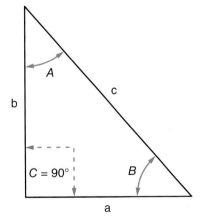

**Figure A–7** A sample triangle for sine, cosine, and tangent shows that each angle has an opposing and an adjacent side.

| Table A–1 | | |
|-----------|-----------------|------------------|
| **Angle** | **Side Opposite** | **Side Adjacent** |
| A | a | b |
| B | b | a |

Angles and Their Related Sides (see Figure A–7)

| Table A–2 | | | |
|-----------|------|--------|---------|
| **Angle** | **Sine** | **Cosine** | **Tangent** |
| A | $\sin(A) = \dfrac{\text{Opposite}}{\text{Hypotenuse}} = \dfrac{a}{c}$ | $\cos(A) = \dfrac{\text{Adjacent}}{\text{Hypotenuse}} = \dfrac{b}{c}$ | $\tan(A) = \dfrac{\text{Opposite}}{\text{Adjacent}} = \dfrac{a}{b}$ |
| B | $\sin(B) = \dfrac{\text{Opposite}}{\text{Hypotenuse}} = \dfrac{b}{c}$ | $\cos(B) = \dfrac{\text{Adjacent}}{\text{Hypotenuse}} = \dfrac{a}{c}$ | $\tan(B) = \dfrac{\text{Opposite}}{\text{Adjacent}} = \dfrac{b}{a}$ |

Note: Sine is abbreviated as *sin*, cosine is *cos*, and tangent is *tan*.

Table of Trigonometric Definitions (see Figure A–7)

Several memory tricks are often used to remember this relationship. **O**scar **H**ad **A** **H**eap **O**f **A**pples or **O**h **H**eck **A**nother **H**our **O**f **A**gony are two of the many. They work as shown in the following equations:

$$\sin = \frac{\text{Opposite (Oscar)}}{\text{Hypotenuse (Had)}}$$

$$\cos = \frac{\text{Adjacent (A)}}{\text{Hypotenuse (Heap)}}$$

$$\tan = \frac{\text{Opposite (Of)}}{\text{Adjacent (apples)}}$$

Some believe that remembering these clever memory devices is more difficult than remembering the original definitions. You should use whatever method is easiest for you.

After the **sine, cosine,** or **tangent** of the angle are known, the angle itself can be found using the trigonometric functions on a scientific calculator or the trigonometric tables.

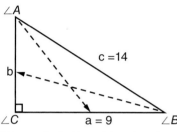

**Figure A–8** Use this triangle for the examples.

---

### Example

Using the same triangle in Figure A–8, find the number of degrees in ∠B.

**Solution:**

$$\cos(B) = \frac{\text{Adjacent}}{\text{Hypotenuse}} = \frac{9}{14} = 0.643$$

The scientific calculator shows that the **arccosine** of 0.643 is 50°. Note in this problem that the opposite side became the adjacent side to the hypotenuse because the reference angle changed. For this problem, side *a* is the base of the triangle. Also note that the decimal (0.643) remained the same because of the ratio (9:14) but the angle changed because of the use of the cos function instead of the sin function.

---

One last point should be noted. All the angles in a right triangle must total 180°. This means that the right angle (∠C = 90°) + ∠A + ∠B = 180°. If you knew from the first problem that ∠A was 40°, then you could calculate the remaining angle by simple addition and subtraction.

Since 90 + 40 = 130, and 180 − 130 = 50, then ∠B = 50°.

## VECTOR ADDITION AND SUBTRACTION

Vectors can be added and subtracted in a variety of arithmetic and geometric ways. The following sections describe those methods and give examples of how each may be employed.

### VECTORS IN THE SAME DIRECTION

Since vectors can be used to represent quantities such as volts, amps, ohms, and the various units of power, they can be added, subtracted, multiplied, and divided. Several methods can be used to perform vector addition.

---

### Example

The hypotenuse of the triangle in Figure A–8 is 14 and side *a* is 9. How many degrees are in ∠A?

**Solution:**

Since the lengths of the hypotenuse and the opposite side are known, the sine function can be used:

$$\sin(A) = \frac{\text{Opposite}}{\text{Hypotenuse}} = \frac{9}{14} = 0.643$$

But 0.643 is not the angle; it is the sine of the angle. You must use a scientific calculator and the inverse sine function (sometimes called the **arcsine**) to determine the angle. The way you determine the inverse sine depends on the type of calculator you are using. Either enter 0.643 and press the arc or inv sine button or enter the arcsine (0.643) and press the equal (=) sign. The answer is arcsine (0.643) = 40°.

The same process is applied when using the cosine function or the tangent function.

Regardless of the method used, they must be added with a combination of geometric and algebraic addition. This is called vector addition. (Note that vector addition is quite easy on most scientific calculators; however, you should understand the fundamentals.)

One method is to connect the starting point, or tail, of one vector to the endpoint, or head, of the other one. This works easiest when the vectors are in the same direction. In Figure A–9, three vectors with the same angle (0°) are being added. The total sum is $7 + 5 + 3 = 15$.

Now look at Figure A–10 and consider having two batteries connected in series the way they are in a flashlight. The bulb in the flashlight is designed to operate on 3 V. Since the standard flashlight cell is only 1.5 V, two batteries must be added together to make 3 V. In vector terms, it would look like one vector of 1.5 V plus another vector of 1.5 V (Figure A–11).

## VECTORS IN OPPOSITE DIRECTIONS

To add vectors that are in opposite directions (180° apart), subtract the magnitude of the smaller from the magnitude of the larger. The result is a vector in the same direction as the vector with the larger magnitude. Assume that the batteries in Figure A–10 are 3 and 5 V, respectively. Somehow, one of the batteries was placed in the flashlight backward. The voltages would oppose each other. This means that 3 V of the 5 V battery would try to overcome the 3 V of the other battery. The result would be a vector with a magnitude of 2 V in the same direction as the 5 V battery (Figure A–12).

In numerical form, this equation would look like adding a positive number to a negative number:

$$+5 + (-3) = +2$$

Since adding a negative is the same as subtracting, the previous equation reduces to:

$$5 - 3 = 2$$

**Simple Vector Addition**

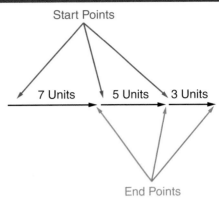

**Figure A–9** Simple vector addition is clear in this example.

**Voltage Addition**

**Figure A–10** A flashlight with two batteries reaches the required volts.

**Voltage Vector Addition**

**Figure A–11** Two 1.5 V vectors added together produce a total of 3 V.

**Vector Addition with Opposite Directions**

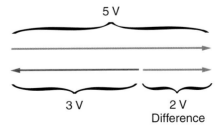

**Figure A–12** Adding vectors with opposite directions (180°) requires subtraction of the smaller magnitude from the larger magnitude.

## VECTORS IN DIFFERENT DIRECTIONS

Vectors with directions other than 0° and 180° from each other can also be added. An example is shown in Figure A–13. A vector with a magnitude of 4 and a direction of 20° and a vector with a magnitude of 3 and a direction of 45° are added together. The addition is made by connecting the starting point (tail) of the second vector to the endpoint (head) of the first vector. The direction of the vector, stated as the number of degrees of the angle, is always referenced to the X-axis, which is always 0°. The resultant is drawn from the starting point of the first vector to the endpoint of the second. This is called the triangular method. It is possible to add more than two vectors in this fashion.

**Vector Addition with Different Directions**

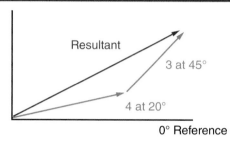

**Figure A–13** Adding vectors with different directions means connecting starting points to endpoints.

## PARALLELOGRAM METHOD

The parallelogram method can be used to find the resultant of two vectors that start at the same point instead of connecting the starting point of the second vector to the endpoint of the first vector. A parallelogram is a four-sided figure whose opposite sides are parallel to each other. A rectangle is a parallelogram with 90° angles.

For example, consider the vectors $10\angle25°$ and $12\angle55°$. Remember that the vectors must begin at the same point and that all angles are referenced off the X-axis (0°). To find the resultant of these two vectors, form a parallelogram using the vectors as two of the sides (Figure A–14). The resultant is drawn from the corner of the parallelogram where the two vectors intersect to the opposite corner.

**Parallelogram Method**

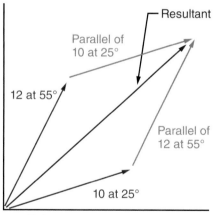

**Figure A–14** The parallelogram method uses vectors as two of the sides.

## USING THE RECTANGULAR COMPONENTS

As was hinted at previously, vectors can be represented as the sum of their two components (called rectangular form or rectangular notation) or as a magnitude at an angle (polar notation). Figure A–15 shows two vectors.

Table A–3 shows the two ways that each vector can be represented. Be aware that the letter $j$ is itself a vector defined as $j = 1\angle90°$.

| Table A–3 | | |
|---|---|---|
| **Vector** | **Polar** | **Rectangular** |
| $V_1$ | $6.4\angle51.3°$ | $4 + j5$ |
| $V_2$ | $3.6\angle33.7°$ | $3 + j2$ |
| Polar and Rectangular Formats for Vectors (see Figure A–15) | | |

## Example

Add the vectors $V_1$ and $V_2$ in Figure A–15.

**Solution:**

The problem is solved by first entering the polar form into a scientific calculator and adding the results. The steps for entering polar vectors vary from calculator to calculator, so you should consult your calculator's instructions for step-by-step instructions.

$$V_1 + V_2 = V_T = 6.4\angle 51.3° + 3.6\angle 33.7° = 9.89\angle 45°$$

Next, add the vectors using their rectangular components. The sum of the two vectors is equal to the sum of their horizontal components added to the sum of their vertical components:

$$V_1 + V_2 = V_T = (4 + j5) + (3 + j2) = (7 + j7)$$

Are the two answers the same? For the answer, refer to Figure A–16. This figure is the vector ($V_T$) as determined by adding the horizontal and vertical parts of the two component vectors. Notice that $V_T$ forms a right triangle with the horizontal and vertical axes. This means that the tangent of the unknown angle (??) is equal to 7/7. In other words, **?? = arctangent(7/7)** = 45°. What about the length? From the Pythagorean Theorem, $V_t = \sqrt{7^2 + 7^2} = \sqrt{98} = 9.89$.

**Vector Notation**

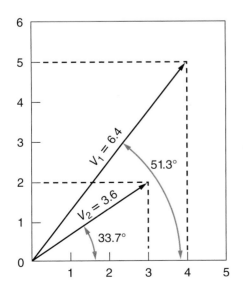

**Figure A–15** Vector notation is shown for the example.

**Sum of Vectors**

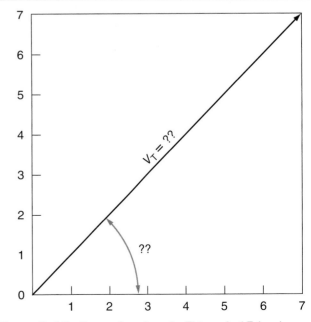

**Figure A–16** Sum of vectors in Figure A–15 is shown.

## MULTIPLYING AND DIVIDING VECTORS

You will be called on to multiply and divide vectors in your work as an electrician. For example, the use of Ohm's law requires vectors for voltage, current, and impedance (AC resistance). To multiply two vectors, you multiply their magnitudes and add their angles. To divide two vectors, you divide their magnitudes and subtract their angles.

---

### Example

Given: $V_1 = 5\angle 20°$ and $V_2 = 4\angle 30°$

Problem 1: What is the product of $V_1$ times $V_2$?

**Solution:**

$$V_1 \times V_2 = 5\angle 20° \times 4\angle 30° = (5 \times 4)\angle(20° + 30°) = 20\angle 50°$$

Problem 2: What is the quotient of $V_1$ divided by $V_2$?

**Solution:**

$$\frac{V_1}{V_2} = \frac{5\angle 20°}{4\angle 30°} = \left(\frac{5}{4}\right)\angle(20° - 30°) = 1.25\angle -10°$$

---

**Vector Multiplication**

Figure A–17

**Vector Division**

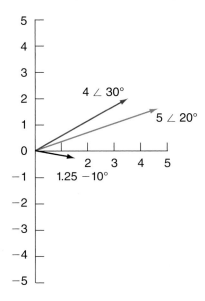

Figure A–18

## SUMMARY

Scalar quantities have only magnitude. Vectors are lines that indicate both magnitude and direction.

Vectors can be added, subtracted, multiplied, or divided. The direction of a vector is indicated by the arrowhead at the end. When a single vector is produced from combining two or more vectors, it is called a resultant. From 0°, vectors rotate in a counterclockwise direction.

The sum of all the angles in a right triangle is 180°. The relationship between the length of the sides of a right triangle and the number of degrees in its angles can be expressed as the sine, cosine, or tangent of a particular angle.

The sine function is the relationship of the opposite side divided by the hypotenuse. The cosine function is the relationship of the adjacent side divided by the hypotenuse. The tangent function is the relationship of the opposite side divided by the adjacent side.

The hypotenuse is always the longest side of a right triangle. The opposite and adjacent sides are determined by which angle is being used as the reference angle.

## APPENDIX GLOSSARY

**Arccosine** Abbreviated *arccos* and shown on most calculators by the symbol $cos^{-1}$. The inverse function of the cosine of an angle $\frac{1}{cosine}$. This calculates what arc has a cosine of the referenced decimal number.

**Arcsine** Abbreviated *arcsin* and shown on most calculators by the symbol $sin^{-1}$. The inverse function of the sine of an angle $\frac{1}{sine}$. This calculates what arc has a sine of the referenced decimal number.

**Arctangent** Abbreviated *arctan* and shown on most calculators by the symbol $tan^{-1}$. The inverse function of the tangent of an angle $\frac{1}{tangent}$. This calculates what arc has a tangent of the referenced decimal number.

**Cosine** Abbreviated *cos*. For a given angle other than the 90-degree angle in a right triangle, the trigonometric function that is the ratio between the leg adjacent to the given angle and the hypotenuse.

**Hypotenuse** In a right triangle, the side that is opposite the right angle. The hypotenuse is the longest side of a right triangle.

**Phasor** A vector that rotates. Phasors are used to describe voltages, currents, and other such quantities in electrical systems.

**Polar form** Representation of a vector as a magnitude and an angle.

**Pythagorean Theorem** A theorem in geometry stating that the square of the length of the hypotenuse of a right triangle equals the sum of the squares of the lengths of the other two sides, or $c^2 = a^2 + b^2$.

**Reactance** The amount of opposition to current flow resultant from a magnetic field in an inductor or an electrostatic field in a capacitor.

**Rectangular form** Representing a vector as the sum of two other vectors that are at right angles to each other.

**Resistance** The physical opposition to electrical current. Resistance (measured in ohms) is caused by the energy loss that occurs when an electron displaces other electrons in a valence ring.

**Resultant vector** The final vector derived when all the component vectors are combined to create a final vector.

**Scalar** A number with magnitude only. For example, 5 miles is a scalar.

**Sine** Abbreviated *sin*. For a given angle other than the 90-degree angle in a right triangle, the trigonometric function that is the ratio between the leg opposite the given angle and the hypotenuse.

**Tangent** Abbreviated *tan*. For a given angle other than the 90-degree angle in a right triangle, the trigonometric function that is the ratio between the leg opposite the given angle and the leg adjacent to the given angle. Also equal to the sine of the given angle divided by the cosine of the given angle.

**Vector** A number with both magnitude and direction. For example, 5 miles going due east is a vector.

**Alternating current** A current that varies, or "alternates," from one polarity to another. The current still flows from negative to positive, but the power source changes polarity in relation to time.

**Ampere** The unit of electrical current flow, often abbreviated as amp or just A. It is a measure of the movement of electrons as 1 coulomb per second past a fixed point.

**Apparent power** The amount of power that is delivered to an AC circuit. It is calculated by multiplying line voltage and line current. It is the amount of power apparently consumed but is not the true power of a circuit with reactive components.

**Arccosine** Abbreviated *arcos* and shown on most calculators by the symbol $cos^{-1}$. The inverse function of the cosine of an angle $\left(\frac{1}{cosine}\right)$. This calculates what arc has a cosine of the referenced decimal number.

**Arcsine** Abbreviated arcsin and shown on most calculators by the symbol $sin^{-1}$. The inverse function of the sine of an angle $\left(\frac{1}{sine}\right)$. This calculates what arc has a sine of the referenced decimal number.

**Arctangent** Abbreviated *arctan* and shown on most calculators by the symbol $tan^{-1}$. The inverse function of the tangent of an angle $\left(\frac{1}{tangent}\right)$. This calculates what arc has a tangent of the referenced decimal number.

**Armature** The winding in a generator where an induced voltage is created.

**Armature reaction** The bending of the field magnetic flux by a reaction to the armature magnetic field. Armature reaction causes a displacement of the neutral point, with consequent arcing at the commutator and resultant voltage drop.

**Brushes** Sliding contacts usually made of a carbon or graphite alloy. Contacts can be connected to DC commutators or to AC slip rings.

**Capacitance** 1. The property of a circuit element that permits it to store charge. The part of the circuit exhibiting capacitance. 2. The unit of measure is the farad and the formula variable is *C*. The ratio of the electric charge transferred from one to the other of a pair of conductors to the resulting potential difference between them. (Excerpted from American Heritage Talking Dictionary. Copyright ©1997 The Learning Company, Inc. All Rights Reserved.)

**Capacitive reactance** The opposition to AC current flow caused by a capacitor. The symbol for capacitive reactance is $X_C$. The formula to calculate capacitive reactance is

$$X_C = \frac{1}{2\pi f C}$$

Where:

$X_C$ = ohms of reactance

$f$ = frequency of the applied voltage measured in hertz

$C$ = capacitance in farads

**Capacitor** An electric circuit element used to store charge temporarily. In general, it consists of two metallic plates separated and insulated from each other by a dielectric. A capacitor may also be referred to as a condenser. (Excerpted from American Heritage Talking Dictionary. Copyright ©1997 The Learning Company, Inc. All Rights Reserved.)

**Capacitor start motor** A single-phase motor with main and auxiliary windings designed for direct connection to a single-phase AC source. The auxiliary winding is connected in series with a capacitor and is connected in the circuit for starting purposes only. The capacitor helps shift the phase for the auxiliary (start) winding during starting.

**CEMF (counter EMF)** The voltage induced in an inductor by the changing magnetic field. The voltage induced is "counter to," or in opposition to, the voltage that produced the original magnetic field.

**Commutator** A multi-segment rotating connection that is connected to the armature windings. A commutator is a circular ring that is divided into segments that are electrically insulated from one another.

**Compensating, interpole, or Thomson-Ryan windings** Field windings located physically between the main field poles. Interpoles are used to reduce armature reaction and are connected in series with the armature current.

**Conduction motor** A motor that relies on a conductive path that allows current to flow to the rotor during motor operation. This motor typically has carbon brushes that provide an electrical connection to the moving rotor.

**Conductor** A material that easily passes electrical current. Examples include silver, copper, and aluminum.

**Cosine** Abbreviated *cos*. For a given angle other than the 90-degree angle in a right triangle, the trigonometric function that is the ratio between the leg adjacent to the given angle and the hypotenuse.

**Current source input (CSI)** A method used to electronically control the frequency and the voltage delivered to an AC motor to vary its speed and torque. The AC input is rectified, filtered to DC, and then inverted through electronics to provide an AC wave approximation which is adjusted to provide the motor current waveform.

**Dielectric** A nonconductor of electricity, especially a substance with electrical conductivity less than a millionth ($10^{-6}$) of a siemens. A dielectric has the ability to insulate against a current flow between conducting surfaces. (Excerpted from American Heritage Talking Dictionary. Copyright ©1997 The Learning Company, Inc. All Rights Reserved.)

**Direct current** A current that flows in one direction only without relationship to time.

**Electromotive force** The electrical pressure generated between two areas with different amounts of electrical charge. The unit of measure is the volt, and in formulas *E* represents electromotive force.

**Electron flow theory** The theory in which current flows from a negative charge to a positive charge.

**Excitation current** The current supplied to the field of an AC generator. The excitation current creates the steady magnetic field that the armature cuts through.

**Exciter DC** Magnetic field for a generator, whether spinning or stationary.

**Exciting current or magnetizing current** A relatively small current used to magnetize the core of a transformer but does not provide for the secondary load current. It is the primary current when no electrical load is connected to the transformer secondary.

**Farad** The unit of capacitance equal to the capacitance of a capacitor having an equal and opposite charge of 1 coulomb on each plate and a potential difference of 1 V between the plates. The larger the farad value, the more charge a capacitor can hold. (Excerpted from American Heritage Talking Dictionary. Copyright ©1997 The Learning Company, Inc. All Rights Reserved.)

**Field windings** The part of the DC generator that creates the magnetic field that is cut by the armature windings.

**Flat compounding** The effects of compounding in a DC generator so that the no-load output voltage is the same as the full-load voltage. The voltage versus load curve on a graph is essentially flat, or no change in voltage, with change in load.

**Frequency** The number of complete waveforms completed in 1 second. Frequency is a measure of how often the waveform is completed in relation to time, expressed in cycles per second. The unit of measure is the hertz (Hz), named after Heinrich Hertz.

**Half-power point** The point at which the load resistance is dissipating half the maximum power that could occur at the load.

**Henry** Unit of measure for inductance. A coil has an inductance of 1 henry when a current change of 1 ampere per second causes an induced voltage of 1 volt. The henry is a value based on the physical characteristics of the inductor (coil). The unit of measure is the henry, abbreviated as H. The symbol used in formulas is L.

**Hypotenuse** In a right triangle, the side that is opposite the right angle. The hypotenuse is the longest side of a right triangle.

**Impedance** The vector sum of the oppositions found in some AC circuits. The vectors may include inductive reactance, capacitive reactance, and resistance. The vector addition of these components results in the total opposition to the AC current flow. Impedance is measured in ohms and is represented by the letter $Z$ in formulas.

**Inductance** The property of an electric circuit displayed when a varying current induces an electromotive force in that circuit or in a neighboring circuit. A circuit has inductance when magnetic induction occurs.

**Induction motor** A motor that relies on the principles of induction to transfer energy to the rotor. Voltage is induced into the rotor as the rotor slips behind the synchronous speed of the rotating field of the stator. There is no direct electrical connection between the AC power source and the rotor.

**Inductor** The name given to an electrical circuit component that exhibits the properties of inductance. If a coil of wire creates self-induction, creating a counterelectromotive force (CEMF), then it is referred to as an inductor.

**Insulator** A material that does not allow electrical current to flow easily. Examples include rubber, plastic, and mica.

**Isolation transformer** An electrical transformer usually designed to have the same level of voltage at the secondary terminals that it has on the primary terminals. No electrical connection exists between the primary and the secondary, creating a separate secondary circuit "isolated" from the original source.

**Lagging power factor** Indicates that the circuit current waveform is behind or "lagging" the circuit voltage waveform. If the current lags the voltage, the power factor will be less than 1 or less than 100%. A lagging power factor indicates that the circuit has a net inductive effect on the current.

**Leading power factor** Indicates that the circuit current waveform is ahead of or "leading" the circuit voltage waveform. If the current leads the voltage, the power factor will be less than 1 or less than 100%. A leading power factor indicates that the circuit has a net capacitive effect on the current.

**Leakage flux** Flux lines that do not link properly in an inductor. Some flux lines are lost to the surrounding space and do not complete the magnetic path. Leakage flux reduces the overall magnetic field and the resulting inductance.

**Magnet wire** Wire with a coating of insulating varnish that provides the voltage rating for the wire. The wire is specifically designed to be used in coil winding of motors, generators, or coils. The wire fits into slots for easy winding and is used to produce a magnetic field.

**Microfarad** $1 \times 10^{-6}$ farads. Abbreviated as μF.

**Micro-microfarad** See picofarad. Abbreviated as μμF.

**Nanofarad** $1 \times 10^{-9}$ farads. Abbreviated as nF.

**Ohm** The unit of electrical resistance, often shown as the Greek letter omega (Ω).

**Overcompounding** A condition that occurs in a DC generator when the output voltage at no-load is less than the output voltage at full-load. The output voltage increases as electrical load is added.

**Peak-to-peak value** The full value of the AC sine wave measured from the positive peak to the negative peak, also referred to as the P-to-P value.

**Periodic table of elements** A tabular arrangement of the elements according to their atomic numbers so that elements with similar properties are in the same column.

**Permanent magnet generator** A type of generator in which the field is provided by a strong permanent magnet, sometimes in the stator and sometimes on the rotor.

**Permeability** The degree to which a material focuses magnetic lines of flux, or the ease with which magnetic lines of force distribute themselves through a material. Permeability is a factor compared to air (permeability factor of 1). There is no unit of measure, just a factor compared to air. The symbol used for magnetic permeability in a formula is the lowercase Greek letter mu (μ).

**Phasor** A vector that rotates. Phasors are used to describe voltages, currents, and other such quantities in electrical systems.

**Picofarad** $1 \times 10^{-12}$ farads. Abbreviated as pF. Also called a micro-microfarad (abbreviated as $\mu\mu$F).

**Piezoelectric** Electricity being created by stress or pressure in a material—especially a crystalline material.

**Polar form** Representation of a vector as a magnitude and an angle.

**Power factor** A factor applied to the apparent power to yield true power. The power factor decimal is expressed as a percentage. It is also the ratio of watts divided by volt-amperes expressed as a percentage of true watts compared to apparent volt-amperes.

**Pulse width modulation (PWM)** A method used to electronically control the frequency and the voltage delivered to a motor for purposes of speed and torque control. The AC input is rectified, filtered to DC, and then inverted back to AC as a pulse where the width of the pulse is modulated to control the AC motor.

**Pythagorean Theorem** A theorem in geometry stating that the square of the length of the hypotenuse of a right triangle equals the sum of the squares of the lengths of the other two sides, or $c^2 = a^2 + b^2$.

**Ramp-down** A process where the motor speed and power is gradually reduced during the stopping process. The motor is provided gradually reduced power during the deceleration time so that the motor and load do not coast to a stop or come to an abrupt stop.

**Ramp-up** A process where the speed of a motor is gradually increased from zero speed to operating speed. The method is used to reduce high torque effects on a stationary load, as the motor tries to accelerate to full speed.

**Reactance** The amount of opposition to current flow resultant from a magnetic field in an inductor or an electrostatic field in a capacitor.

**Reactive power** The form of power that is produced by the reactive components of a circuit, such as the inductive or capacitive reactance. It is energy stored in a magnetic field or an electrostatic field and is returned to the circuit as the fields diminish. Even though this is a form of energy for the circuit, it is not consumed. It is measured in volts-amperes reactive (VARs) because it is caused by the reactive current, 90° out of phase with the voltage.

**Rectangular form** Representing a vector as the sum of two other vectors that are at right angles to each other.

**Reluctance** The opposition that materials present to the flow of magnetic lines of flux (similar to electrical resistance). Permanent magnets have a high reluctance and temporary magnets have a low reluctance. The symbol is the Greek letter rel ($R$) and the force is measured in ampere-turns per weber.

**Resonance** The value in hertz at which inductive reactance and capacitive reactance are equal (in resonance) in a circuit. At series *resonant frequency,* the circuit impedance is at a minimum and the circuit current is at a maximum.

**Resultant vector** The final vector derived when all the component vectors are combined to create a final vector.

**Revolving armature generator** A generator that has the field windings on the stator and the armature windings on the rotor.

**Revolving field generator** A generator that has the field windings on the rotor and the armature windings on the stator.

**Root mean square** The root mean square (RMS) of an AC waveform is the square root of the mean, or average, of all the instantaneous values squared. The RMS gives the effective value of the AC. This RMS value has the same heating effect as DC of the same value.

**Round rotor** A streamlined type of construction where the coils are wound longitudinally on the rotor. This type of construction is generally much lighter than salient pole construction and is used extensively on high-speed generators. Also called a turbo rotor.

**Run winding** The main winding of magnet wire that produces the magnetic poles of the motor. The run (main) winding is designed to be connected to the power source during the motor-running operation. The run winding is typically larger gauge wire than the start winding and is placed deeper in the slots of the stator core.

**Salient pole** A type of rotating field construction where the field poles are wound individually and mounted along the outside edge of the rotor. *Salient* means projecting outward; projecting or jutting beyond a line or surface; or protruding.

**Scalar** A number with magnitude only. For example, 5 miles is a scalar.

**Self-excited** The method in which the generator receives power to produce the magnetic field for generation. A portion of the output power is fed back to the generator's field as it provides its own excitation current.

**Self-inductance** The property of an electrical component (such as a coil of wire) to induce a voltage into itself as the current through the component changes.

**Semiconductor** A material that falls between conductors and insulators in terms of electrical conductivity.

**Sine** Abbreviated *sin.* For a given angle other than the 90-degree angle in a right triangle, the trigonometric function that is the ratio between the leg opposite the given angle and the hypotenuse.

**Slip** The difference in speed measured in rotations per minute between the synchronous speed of the rotating magnetic field of the stator, and the slower speed of the induction rotor. Slip is often expressed as a percentage using the formula:

$$\% \text{ Slip} = \frac{\text{Synch speed} - \text{Rotor speed}}{\text{Synch speed}} \times 100$$

**Slip rings** Continuous bands of metal installed around a shaft. Slip rings are connected to the rotating windings and provide a path for the current to reach the brushes.

**Split phase motor** A single-phase induction motor with main and auxiliary windings. The auxiliary windings are displaced in physical and magnetic position from, and temporarily connected in parallel to, the main windings.

**Squirrel-cage rotor** A rotating member of an induction motor with an iron core and conductors around the periphery. The conductors have induced voltage and resultant current flow as the rotating magnetic field spins on the stator. The stripped down rotor, without iron and with only the conducting bars, resembles a squirrel-cage exercise wheel.

**Start winding** An auxiliary winding in a motor stator that is intended to be connected to the power circuit only during the starting period of the motor. The winding provides the physical and magnetic displacement from the run winding needed to create a rotating magnetic field. The winding is automatically disconnected from the voltage source after a few seconds of starting time. The winding is typically smaller gauge wire than the main (run) winding and is installed nearer the inside of the stator opening.

**Stator** The stationary part of the generator.

**Step-down transformer** An electrical transformer designed to have a lower voltage at the secondary terminals than it had at the primary terminals.

**Step-up transformer** An electrical transformer designed to have a higher voltage at the secondary output than it has at the primary input.

**Subtractive or additive polarity** Polarity refers to the secondary lead markings when compared to the primary lead markings. With a subtractive polarity transformer, if the leads are brought out so that H1 and X1 are connected together, a voltmeter between H2 and X2 reads the difference between the primary and the secondary. An additive polarity transformer indicates that if H1 and X2 are connected together a voltmeter between H2 and X1 will read the sum of the two coil voltages.

**Synchronous speed** The exact speed of a rotating member to produce a desired frequency for a generator. This same term is used to describe the speed that is produced by a specific frequency to make an induction motor run.

**Synchroscope** A type of instrument that is used to determine the phase relationship between two separate generator voltages. This instrument is often used for determining synchronization of two generators before connecting the outputs together.

**Tangent** Abbreviated *tan*. For a given angle other than the 90-degree angle in a right triangle, the trigonometric function that is the ratio between the leg opposite the given angle and the leg adjacent to the given angle. Also equal to the sine of the given angle divided by the cosine of the given angle.

**True power** The actual dissipated watts of a circuit. This is the form of energy expended by the conversion of electric energy into other forms of energy. It is the power measured in watts.

**Undercompounding** The condition that exists when the setup of the generator results in the no-load voltage being greater than the full-load voltage. As the generator supplies more load current, the output voltage decreases.

**Unity power factor** Ratio of true power (watts) divided by apparent power (volt-amps) with the dividend as one or the ratio as 1. Unity power factor is also known as 100%, meaning that 100% of the volt-amps are used as watts and the reactive power does not affect the circuit. The power factor cannot be over unity or 100%.

**Valence ring or shell** The outermost shell of electrons in an atom.

**Vector** A number with both magnitude and direction. For example, 5 miles going due east is a vector.

**Vector sum** The binary vector operation that yields a vector of which the length and direction are represented by the diagonal of a parallelogram of which the sides represent the given vectors being added.

**Volt** The electromotive force that pushes electrons through the conductors, wires, or components of a circuit. It is similar to the pressure exerted on a system of fluid using pipes. The higher the pressure, the more flow. Specifically, the volt is the amount of work done per coulomb of charge (volts = joules per coulomb) and is represented by the letter *V*. In calculations, voltage is represented by the letter *E*. Remember that voltage is the force required in creating flow but that volts do not flow through the circuit.

**Volts per turn** Volts per turn is used as a reference point for the amount of magnetic flux produced by a coil. (The more volts per turn, the more flux.) It is not a specific unit of measure but a way to relate the primary turns and voltage to the secondary turns and voltage.